ONE WORLD, BIG SCREEN

ONE WORLD,
BIG SCREEN

HOLLYWOOD,

THE ALLIES, AND

WORLD WAR II

M. TODD BENNETT

THE

UNIVERSITY OF

NORTH CAROLINA

PRESS *Chapel Hill*

© 2012 The University of North Carolina Press
All rights reserved
Designed by Richard Hendel
Set in Utopia and Aller types
by Tseng Information Systems, Inc.
Manufactured in the United States of America

The paper in this book meets the guidelines for permanence
and durability of the Committee on Production Guidelines for
Book Longevity of the Council on Library Resources.

The University of North Carolina Press has been a member of
the Green Press Initiative since 2003.

Library of Congress Cataloging-in-Publication Data
Bennett, M. Todd.
One world, big screen : Hollywood, the Allies, and World War II /
M. Todd Bennett.
p. cm.
Includes bibliographical references and index.
ISBN 978-0-8078-3574-6 (cloth : alk. paper) 1. World War, 1939–
1945—Motion pictures and the war. 2. Motion pictures—United
States—History—20th century. 3. Motion pictures—Political
aspects—United States—History—20th century. I. Title.
D743.23.B46 2012
791.43′6584053—dc23
2012011965

Portions of this work have appeared previously, in somewhat
different form, as "Culture, Power, and *Mission to Moscow*: Film
and Soviet-American Relations during World War II," *Journal
of American History* 88 (September 2001): 489–518, and "The
Celluloid War: State and Studio in Anglo-American Propaganda
Film-Making, 1939–1941," *International History Review* 24
(March 2002): 64–102, and are reprinted here with permission.

Filmstrip on title page and chapter openers courtesy of
iStockphoto/Thinkstock.

16 15 14 13 12   5 4 3 2 1

CONTENTS

Acknowledgments, *ix*

Abbreviations, *xiii*

Introduction, *1*

1 The "Magic Bullet": Hollywood, Washington, and the Moviegoing Public, *24*

2 "Pro-British-American War Preachers": Internationalism at the Movies, 1939–1941, *53*

3 One World, Big Screen: The United Nations and American Horizons, *89*

4 Kissing Cousins: How Anglo-American Relations Became "Special," *136*

5 Courting Uncle Joe: The Theatrics of Soviet-American Matrimony, *169*

6 Negotiating the Color Divide: Race and U.S. Paternalism toward China, *217*

Conclusion, *256*

Notes, *275*

Selected Bibliography, *321*

Index, *343*

ILLUSTRATIONS

A moment made for the media: the Big Three first meet at 1943's Tehran Conference to solidify the United Nations, *2*

Franklin Roosevelt illustrates Allied strategy during a 1942 Fireside Chat as Americans follow along at home, *97*

Humphrey Bogart stars in *Sahara* (1943), Columbia's dramatization of Allied inclusivity, *110*

Office of Facts and Figures poster portraying China as America's friend in the fight for freedom, 1942, *114*

Office of War Information poster championing the United Nations, 1943, *115*

Britons cheer American soldiers parading through London's Trafalgar Square on United Nations Day, 1943, *120*

United Nations Information Organization poster upholding collective security, *131*

The Allied family is besieged in *Mrs. Miniver* (1942), winner of the Best Picture Oscar, *138*

The reunion of an American GI and his British war bride in New York City, 1945, *151*

U.S. Army staff sergeant Samuel Rochester and his "adopted" mother, Mrs. Norman Rawlence, of Bremerton, England, join hands at the American Red Cross Club's Mother's Day Tea Dance, London, 1943, *152*

Peter (David Niven) and June (Kim Hunter) Carter are an Anglo-American couple happily reunited in *A Matter of Life and Death* (1946), *156*

"Uncle Joe" Stalin (Manart Kippen) explains Soviet foreign policy to U.S.
   ambassador Joseph Davies (Walter Huston) in *Mission to Moscow*
   (1943), *179*

Aspiring Soviet musician Nadya Stepanova (Susan Peters) meets
   American conductor John Meredith (Robert Taylor), beginning an
   international romance in *Song of Russia* (1943), *201*

Detective Charlie Chan (Sidney Toler) does his bit for the Allies in
   Charlie Chan in the Secret Service (1944), *218*

Acting as a surrogate father, an American soldier stationed in China
   wipes a local child's face, *225*

Gene Tierney in yellowface as Haoli Young, the Eurasian object of the
   affection of Johnny Williams (George Montgomery) in *China Girl*
   (1942), *242*

Father Francis Chisholm (Gregory Peck) heals a Chinese boy with
   modern Western medicine in *The Keys of the Kingdom* (1944), *254*

Allied cameramen and photographers cover the Soviet-American linkup
   at the Elbe River, 1945, *258*

Victorious American and Soviet soldiers locked in fraternal embrace,
   1945, *259*

A jubilant GI and a matronly Briton celebrating V-E day in London,
   1945, *260*

Newsreel cameras roll as China's delegation signs the United Nations
   Charter at the San Francisco Conference, 1945, *262*

ACKNOWLEDGMENTS

In various forms, this manuscript has been my almost constant companion for more than fifteen years. Together, we have traveled far on a circuitous route leading from Lubbock, Texas, to Washington, D.C., with stops in such places as Moscow, London, and Athens (Georgia, that is). On our geographical and intellectual journey, the book and I have encountered many people who enriched us, and it is my great pleasure to acknowledge them.

The ideas behind this work took shape during my graduate student years. Texas Tech University's Jim Harper first encouraged my interest in culture and foreign relations (baseball, too, but that is another story). Professors Joe King and George Flynn nourished the study, as did my fellow graduate students, particularly Joe Brown and Les Cullen. Few deserve more credit than William W. Stueck Jr., my dissertation adviser at the University of Georgia. Bill gave me an opportunity and pushed me to make the most of it, and I can always count on him to be in my corner. More could not be expected of an adviser. Committee members Lester Langley, Laura Mason, David Roberts, and especially Bryant Simon, who broadened my understanding of the world beyond the dissertation, offered invaluable suggestions. I was fortunate to find an outstanding community of scholars among the graduate students in Athens, including Brad Coleman, Brian Etheridge, Tao Peng, Jonathan Sarris, Evan Ward, and Karin Zipf.

I have had the good fortune of holding several postgraduate appointments, and colleagues at each institution have nurtured both me and this project. Richard Davies took a visiting junior scholar under his wing at the University of Nevada–Reno. Tyler Anbinder and Dorothea Dietrich extended opportunities to teach at The George Washington University and The Corcoran College of Art and Design, respectively. The U.S. Department of State's Office of the Historian serves as a leading center for the study of the history of American foreign relations, and I thank my former coworkers there for seven years of intellectual stimulation. Evan Dawley, the late Peter Kraemer, David Nickles, Joe Wicentowski, and Alex Wieland directly contributed to this book. Edward C. Keefer and Louis Smith receive special recognition for mentoring so many of us so well. I am grateful for the ongoing support of my colleagues in East Carolina University's Department of History, chaired by Gerry Prokopowicz.

Research funding came thanks to the generosity of the Franklin and Eleanor Roosevelt Institute. The history departments at East Carolina, Georgia, and Texas Tech also granted financial support that underwrote my research and other expenses. Fellowships awarded by Georgia's graduate school and the university's Center for the Humanities and Arts provided me with crucial time to conceptualize and write.

Thanks go to Chuck Grench of the University of North Carolina Press, who steadily guided the manuscript as it matured into a book. Others at the press, including Dino Battista, Sara Cohen, Beth Lassiter, Ron Maner, and Stephanie Wenzel, helped as well. Copyeditor Ellen Goldlust-Gingrich sharpened the text. I am indebted to the press' readers—Thomas Doherty, Clayton Koppes, and Frank Ninkovich—for reviewing the manuscript so carefully and offering such good advice. The finished product was improved by their constructive feedback, as well as that of other scholars who read drafts over the years: Laura Belmonte, Robert Buzzanco, Nick Cull, Seth Fein, Walter Hixson, Warren Kimball, John Moser, and Richard Pells.

Archivists and librarians facilitated access to the records on which this book is based: Noelle Carter of the University of Southern California's Warner Bros. Archives; Barbara Hall and Kristine Krueger of the Academy of Motion Picture Arts and Sciences; Galina Kuznetzova of the State Archives of the Russian Federation; David Langbart and his coworkers at the U.S. National Archives and Records Administration; Shelley Lightburn of the United Nations Archives and Records Management Section; Madeline Matz and her colleagues at the Library of Congress's Motion Picture, Broadcasting, and Recorded Sound Division; Roger Smither, keeper of the Imperial War Museum's Film and Photograph Archives; and the helpful staffs of the Franklin D. Roosevelt Presidential Library and Museum and of the United Kingdom's National Archives.

Friends and family who suffered through this lengthy project with me deserve medals or something. Mere words of gratitude will have to suffice for the time being. Dear friends Chris and Shawna Fisher, Steve Galpern and Patti Simon, Amy Garrett and Rob Weland, Adam Howard, Jason Parker, and Jim Siekmeier gave advice and encouragement. I received love and support from members of my family, foremost among them my grandparents, the late Basil and Robbie Webb; my father, the late Bonner Bennett; Ginger Bennett, who sacrificed a great deal for my work; the Bob Webb family; and Darlyne Rasmussen, whose enthusiasm is infectious.

Most of all, I thank my mother, Cheryl Bennett, who always gave me the space to explore and the permission to go wherever that led me, and my partner in life, Kathleen Rasmussen, who gives me a home. Together, Dr. Rasmussen and I make a Burns and Allen–like team. Kathy is the lovely and talented one, and I anticipate our next act with great excitement.

ABBREVIATIONS

BBC	British Broadcasting Corporation
BMP	Bureau of Motion Pictures
CBS	Columbia Broadcasting System
CPI	Committee on Public Information
CPUSA	Communist Party of the United States of America
FBI	Federal Bureau of Investigation
FDR	Franklin D. Roosevelt
HUAC	House Un-American Activities Committee
KDK	Komitet po Delam Kinematografii (Committee on Cinematography Affairs)
MGM	Metro-Goldwyn-Mayer
MOI	Ministry of Information (U.K.)
MPPDA	Motion Picture Producers and Distributors of America
NBC	National Broadcasting Company
OFF	Office of Facts and Figures
OGR	Office of Government Reports
OWI	Office of War Information
PCA	Production Code Administration
RAF	Royal Air Force
RKO	Radio-Keith-Orpheum
ROC	Republic of China
UN	United Nations
UNIO	United Nations Information Office; United Nations Information Organization (after 1944)
UNO	United Nations Organization
VOKS	Vsesoiuznoe Obshchestvo Kul'turnykh Sviazei s Zagranitsei (All-Union Society for Cultural Relations with Foreign Countries)

ONE WORLD,
BIG SCREEN

INTRODUCTION

Take another look. Newspapers the world over published a photograph midway through World War II that fixed the United Nations (UN)—the wartime alliance spearheaded by the United States, United Kingdom, Union of Soviet Socialist Republics, and Republic of China (ROC)—in the public imagination. Taken in November 1943, the photo focused narrowly on three Allied leaders—Franklin D. Roosevelt, Winston S. Churchill, and Joseph Stalin—sitting under the portico of the Soviet embassy in Tehran, site of the first Allied summit. By association, the image illustrates the political, military, and economic issues that the larger-than-life figures discussed, and these issues together comprise the dominant narrative of both the war and the alliance to this day.[1] Through its studied air of leisurely fraternity, the famous picture—a single frame that combined with other snapshots (of 1943's Cairo summit with Jiang Jieshi, say, or of 1945's victory parades) to create a visual history of the UN that plays like a movie in the mind's eye—also conveyed, and intentionally so, senses of Allied unity, strength, and determination to worldwide audiences skeptical about the coalition's staying power.

Another unpublished shot of the same scene effectively pulls back the curtain to expose the puppeteer's strings, revealing that the standard representation of the UN conceals as much as it reveals. The second photo, taken at a greater distance by an unknown photojournalist, incorporated not just Roosevelt, Churchill, and Stalin but also newsreel cameramen, photographers, and reporters dutifully recording the made-for-

Stalin, Roosevelt, and Churchill pose for the cameras, conveying an air
of unity, at the Tehran Conference, 29 November 1943. U.S. Army Air Force
photograph, 61–158(5), Franklin D. Roosevelt Presidential Library and
Museum, Hyde Park, N.Y.

media moment. Whereas the close focus on the high politics symbolized
by the three figureheads—arranged at the top of the embassy's stairway
for a hero's shot, to use the lingo of Hollywood filmmakers—once seemed
natural, the lesser-known photo's greater perspective shows the setup to
be a contrivance. Attention turns from the iconic subjects to the active
participation of the filmmakers, photographers, and journalists in creating an illusion of partnership. More broadly speaking, the second photo
provides a window through which one can see a perception—of global
unity, a family of nations—being formulated.[2]

One World, Big Screen, like that unpublished photo, takes a fresh approach that reveals a transnational cultural dimension to the histories of the United Nations,[3] World War II,[4] and foreign relations more

broadly.[5] Despite the impression conveyed at Tehran, the UN's greatest powers entered the fray with little in common beyond mutual enemies. Contemporaries recognized that the alliance was a shotgun marriage, consummated only because Axis aggressions—Germany's June 1941 invasion of the USSR, Japan's attack on Pearl Harbor the following December—unceremoniously thrust its members together. The Declaration of the United Nations, a January 1942 statement of loyalty and war aims, hardly obscured the obvious fact that the Allies made strange bedfellows. Their divergent geostrategic objectives detracted from the war effort by dividing Allied strength and complicating military planning. The vast distances and many languages separating the Allies slowed the transportation of supplies and transmittal of information. Their ideological, social, and even physical differences caused distrust, dampened popular enthusiasm for sacrifice, and limited the political support on which diplomatic flexibility depended. Moreover, mutual suspicion hindered the development of an internationalist spirit considered necessary for an effective postwar peacekeeping organization to become reality.

Many Americans had reservations about the United Nations not because they were antiwar but because the idea of a multilateral alliance departed from established U.S. tradition. The UN, which grew to include forty-seven member states and involve U.S. soldiers in theaters of battle across the world, was the most extensive overseas entanglement in the history of the United States, a country that, by custom, steered clear of such snares. (The United States had fought in Europe for nineteen months only as an independent "associate" of the Triple Entente during World War I, the closest analogue.) That tradition only deepened during the interwar years, the heyday of U.S. isolationism, when Americans opted to go it more (but not completely) alone in a world that appeared hostile. Disillusioned, they remembered the Great War as a costly failure: fighting it had not made the world safe for democracy despite the tens of thousands of doughboys sacrificed in democracy's name. Interwar critics retroactively blamed the Western allies for not only dragging the United States into that conflagration but also scuttling a fairer, more sustainable settlement at the Paris Peace Conference. A lesson of World War I, then, was to avoid any foreign affair that could ensnare the nation in another unwanted, ruinous war, and noninterventionists rose to assume leadership of interwar U.S. diplomacy on the strength of their resolve to do just that. Membership in multilateral organizations, starting with the League of Nations, was rejected because such institutions limited U.S. freedom of action. Bilateral alliances that entailed open-ended obligations were shunned; instead, neutrality laws designed to limit American congress with belligerents were passed.[6]

After the United States became embroiled in World War II and party to the UN, however, Americans were suddenly forced to rub elbows with a veritable Babel of foreign allies who spoke, looked, and behaved strangely. No great Allied power generated more anxiety than the Soviet Union, with which the United States had established diplomatic relations only eight years earlier. Communist, authoritarian, Stalinist Russia and its capitalist, democratic cobelligerents made awkward allies. Westerners were uneasy if confused about what little news trickled out of the USSR about Stalin's purges. The August 1939 Nazi-Soviet Pact cast a long shadow of distrust over the alliance, giving rise to fears that Stalin, in another moment of doubt, would again reach a separate deal with Hitler, thereby leaving Anglo-Americans holding the bag in Europe. The pact, Stalin, and his purges combined to sustain speculation that all totalitarian states, whether led by "brown Bolsheviks" or "red fascists," shared the same basic traits and represented equally grave threats to Western democratic interests.[7] Such hostility explained why the Western Allies delayed opening a second front, the Kremlin suspected, a contretemps that opened fresh wounds within the coalition. Later, as victory neared, divergent postwar goals—Washington's quest for the open door, Moscow's desire for a security buffer in Eastern Europe—further alienated the anti-Axis partners from each other.

Whereas ideology and interests set apart the USSR, race marginalized the ROC. China was terra incognita to the majority of Americans despite the historic U.S. involvement in East Asia, Jiang's ongoing civil war against Mao Zedong's communists, and the ROC's decadelong war against Japan. Two-fifths of those surveyed could not place the vast country on a world map, according to a 1942 poll. Moreover, Chinese people were held in low esteem. As Edward Said and his scholastic successors have shown, U.S. knowledge, whether gleaned from diplomatic reportage, Hollywood movies, or expert observations, understood the Orient as the Other—that is, a racially distinct, culturally exotic, politically chaotic, economically backward, and therefore generally inferior land relative to the Occident. Within that frame of reference, China was stereotyped as harmless but insignificant. And preconceptions of Oriental racial inferiority sustained domestic intolerance that manifested in not just Jim Crow segregation and Japanese internment but Chinese exclusion as well: the notorious Chinese Exclusion Act of 1882 that generally barred Chinese either from immigrating to or becoming citizens of the United States remained in force at the outset of the war. Thus, white Americans struggled to fit the erstwhile Asiatic strangers into the UN's body politic.[8]

Although the majority of Americans were far more comfortable with Britons, who appeared, thought, and spoke much as Americans did, disquiet nonetheless remained about partnering with the United Kingdom. Anglophobia enjoyed a rich tradition in the United States, particularly among Irish and German Americans and nationalists, the latter of whom still clung to the "ancient grudge" against John Bull, shorthand for the plethora of grievances that had sparked the American Revolution. To be sure, the turn-of-the-century Anglo-American diplomatic rapprochement had brought the two nations closer together.[9] But the memory of World War I reversed whatever progress had been made, as interwar critics charged that British propagandists had hoodwinked impressionable Americans into sending their sons to die for a meaningless cause while His Majesty's Government made off with the spoils. More alarming still, isolationists alleged starting in 1939, the British were yet again trying to dupe the American public into joining another European war and pulling London's chestnuts out of the fire. Opponents did not fall silent even after the United States intervened and Anglo-American partnership became a fact. Britain's subpar battlefield performance in 1942 fueled the Pacific-first movement, which lobbied for decoupling from Britain in Europe and redirecting U.S. energies toward the Pacific to confront Japan independently. At the same time, liberals continued to question whether it was appropriate for the United States, with its democratic aspirations, to align itself with imperialistic, aristocratic Britain. African American anticolonialists objected to the British Empire for suppressing people of color, including Mohandas Gandhi's Indian independence movement, with which protoblack nationalists identified.[10]

Wartime diplomats, propagandists, and media moguls mobilized popular culture, especially cinema, to heal those rifts and create from scratch an imagined international community. If the united nation is an imagined concept, as Benedict Anderson argues, then the United Nations was a cultural construct, and a fragile one at that. Masking the Allies' many differences behind an illusion of solidarity served to win the war. An Allied victory was not a foregone conclusion, especially from the vantage point of 1941–42, when the Axis held a decided advantage over the dispirited, disunited United Nations. Propaganda helped to raise morale, unite the Allies, and give them the moral high ground. Pro-UN publicity won the peace as well. And here the memory of the Great War left a more constructive legacy, for FDR and his top foreign policy advisers well recalled how Woodrow Wilson, in 1918–19, contributed to the U.S. Senate's rejection of the Treaty of Versailles by speaking too late and failing to craft a bipartisan consensus on behalf of U.S. global responsibility. Determined to repeat neither Wilson's missteps nor the country's fateful decision not to join the League of Nations, a mistake blamed for giving rise to yet another catastrophic war insofar as it rendered the League impotent to deal with subsequent global aggressors, contemporary Wilsonians (FDR foremost among them) strove to instill the habit of international cooperation from the outset with an eye toward building an effective peacekeeping organization this time around.[11]

The UN campaign, carefully stage-managed by the state in the name of national security, also shaped the everyday experience of the world at war. Drawing on the latest mass communications techniques and best public relations practices, cultural authorities marketed the alliance to consumers as a community or family of nations, packaged with such universal values as security and progress, freedom and peace. The invention of multilateral communion effectively mediated foreign affairs for domestic audiences, constructing subjective, inauthentic versions of actual events that nevertheless seemed more genuine than the real thing in some respects. Nowhere did mass communications do more to fill the void between fact and fiction than in the United States. For most Americans, far less likely than their overseas companions to experience firsthand the horrors of battle, what was later remembered as the "good war" was literally "over there"—unseen, imagined, and thus susceptible to manipulation.[12]

Since civilians fought the war partly on imagination, the mass media was doubly important insofar as it gave them an emotional investment in the United Nations and made salient what lay beyond U.S. borders. By portraying faraway friends, enemies, and events, movies and other means of communication opened windows onto the world, providing vicarious experiences that reduced the vast psychic and geographic distances separating domestic consumers from their overseas comrades. In short, the media brought foreign affairs home, merging international relations with domestic life, wedding the public with the private, and erasing the boundaries, already blurred during wartime, between civilian spectatorship and martial participation. Daily newspapers carried news from Chongqing to London to Moscow and beyond. Family members received letters from GIs stationed overseas, many of them away from home for the first time. Americans endured a virtual Blitz by listening to Edward R. Murrow's radio dispatches and by watching newsreels and documentaries such as *London Can Take It* (1940), all of which translated Britain's suffering into a shared albeit vicarious transatlantic experience. Moviegoers explored China and developed sentimental attachments to "Chinese" figures via the silver screen. And audiences toured the Soviet Union from the comfort of their theater seats, a meaningful service given the rarity of glimpses inside that police state. In documentary-style features or those shot "on location"—from a 1944 adaptation by Metro-Goldwyn-Mayer (MGM) of Pearl S. Buck's book *Dragon Seed* to *Mission to Moscow*, a 1943 Warner Bros. picture based on the memoir of a former U.S. ambassador—the "truth" made Jiang's China appear less alien and Stalin's Russia more "normal."[13]

Cinema was ideally suited to bring Allied unity to life. Hollywood, then in its golden age, served as pop culture's centerpiece, and a remarkable 85 million Americans (more than three-fifths of the overall U.S. population, which totaled 131 million in 1940) visited movie theaters each week. Polls taken at the time, when the standard theater bill included a newsreel, a short documentary, a cartoon, and a feature or two, revealed that audiences regarded films as leading sources of not only entertainment but also information about current events. Unlike radio, photography, or the printed word, Hollywood movies combined sight and sound—breathtaking settings, glamorous stars, stylish costumes, snappy dialogue, stirring musical scores, and realistic acoustic effects. Seasoned entertainers artfully interwove these elements into a sensuous, emotive, and popular idiom projected onto the big screens of darkened theaters before what were considered to be spellbound audiences.[14]

That concoction was thought so mesmerizing as to be capable of psychically transporting audiences across space and time, forging worldviews even as it imaginatively connected spectators with foreign peoples, faraway places, and distant eras. Designed to resemble European castles, Egyptian temples, and Oriental fantasylands, the great movie palaces of the day served as magic carpets for viewers' imaginative travels. In those theatrical middle grounds—located somewhere between here and there, we and they, and now and then—fans the world over witnessed styles, mannerisms, and decors and then mimicked them in real life, a phenomenon taken as further proof of cinema's ability to transcend the divide between fantasy and reality. Social scientific research and anecdotal evidence indicating that movies modeled behavior within that immersive theatrical environment—men's undershirt sales famously plummeted after Clark Gable appeared bare-chested in Frank Capra's *It Happened*

One Night (1934)—gave ammunition to opponents who blamed Hollywood for causing everything from juvenile delinquency to criminal activity to sexual promiscuity. During wartime, the industry's list of critics grew to include isolationists, who alleged that the many on-screen conversions performed by larger-than-life stars such as *Sergeant York*'s (1941) Gary Cooper, Tyrone Power in *A Yank in the RAF* (1941), and *Casablanca*'s (1942) Humphrey Bogart seduced fans into becoming internationalists, thereby manipulating the ongoing discussion about the country's proper role in the world.[15]

The production, distribution, and exhibition of pro-UN cinema involved Americans in a transnational cultural exchange orchestrated by allied states in conjunction with nonstate (nominally, in the USSR's case) motion picture industries.[16] To be sure, Washington and Hollywood hijacked that exchange to some extent and turned it so that influence mostly flowed outward from the United States. If the U.S. cultural colossus performed as anticipated in that regard, then the American home front received an unexpected amount of foreign stimuli. The Ministry of Information (MOI), Britain's top propaganda agency, produced *London Can Take It* for the U.S. market, and *Mission to Moscow* contained footage taken by Soviet cameramen. China's consulate in Los Angeles vetted *Dragon Seed* before it reached the screen. Allied pictures played in American theaters, and British, Chinese, and Soviet propagandists targeted the United States.

Allied interaction was so incestuous as to make distinctions between domestic and foreign expression difficult at times. Anglo-American officials prepared and coordinated joint propaganda. Hollywood dominated the United Kingdom market to the point that U.S. firms owned nominally "British" studios whose output defies easy national categorization. The epicenter of a vast industry that earned at least 35 percent of its gross revenue overseas, Hollywood absorbed much of the best talent from abroad—Alfred Hitchcock leaps to mind—and foreign-born artists, some refugees from Nazism, were destined to play roles in cinema's depiction of inter-Allied brotherhood. Replicating cosmopolitanism on-screen thus came rather naturally to Hollywood, a multinational business enterprise with worldwide interests led by executives who were often first- or second-generation immigrants.

Official and commercial practices finely filtered that conversation, producing distorted versions of external events that played at local theaters. Wartime censorship shielded citizens from imported data—photos of dead or severely wounded GIs, for example—that contradicted the official propaganda line. That is said not necessarily to take issue with the Roosevelt administration's establishment of the U.S. Office of Censorship or Office of War Information (OWI). Rather, the point is to state the obvious: however essential it may have been in motivating the country to fight a just war, propaganda (the deliberate attempt to influence attitudes and behavior by manipulating information) met its job description.[17] The OWI resolved to follow a "strategy of truth," and it refrained from telling the Big Lie associated with its Nazi counterpart. But the OWI did not tell the whole truth and nothing but the truth. Instead, the agency, which advised Hollywood and vetted the industry's wartime production, selected facts that fit its predetermined agenda, ignored inconvenient truths that did not, and spread biased narratives meant to inspire loyalty to the cause. Complete honesty took a backseat to boosting internationalism. Liberties were taken with the truth to predispose Americans toward the Allies. Positives were accentuated; negatives buried. Consequently, theatergoers were presented with an on-screen utopia where there were no disputes among the peoples of the United Nations, who sought only to serve humanity and live in harmony when the Axis was defeated. *Variety* observed the propaganda machine at work, transforming even Stalinist Russia into a beacon of freedom. Pro-Soviet Hollywood movies, approved by the OWI, effectively put the Soviets "through the wringer, and they have come out shaved, washed, sober, good to their families, Rotarians, brother Elks, and 33rd Degree Masons," the entertainment trade daily commented in 1942.[18] Such fairy tales may have contributed to Allied unity, but they misled viewers about the realities of international politics, inflating expectations that goodwill would extend indefinitely.

As interpreted by the major Hollywood studios—Twentieth Century–Fox, Warner Bros., Paramount, MGM, Radio-Keith-Orpheum (RKO), Columbia, Universal, and United Artists—diplomacy became just another form of entertainment, more romantic, dramatic, and heroic than the real thing. Hollywood's editorial line was set less by actors or directors—who, though important in shaping how a particular film communicated, were relegated to the political sidelines in the studio system—than by the high-ranking executives (financiers, studio heads, and producers) who ran the business. The industry remained relatively apolitical until 1939 because as a rule, taking sides in real-time international disputes jeopardized ticket sales, especially overseas. Commercial developments caused Hollywood's subsequent politicization, as did the personal politics of movie moguls. Most—with the major exception of Louis B. Mayer, a Republican who backed Herbert Hoover—subscribed to the New Deal consensus. Jews (the Warner brothers and independent producer Walter Wanger) and non-Jews (Daryl F. Zanuck, Fox's production head) alike participated in anti-Nazi politics and endorsed President Roosevelt's pro-Allied, internationalist foreign policy. Such activists wanted to help the White House raise public awareness about the international situation. Even the most politically engaged filmmakers were in the movie business to turn a profit, however. Their creditors and investors demanded as much. And experience told that boring, didactic, geopolitical lessons of the type recommended by well-meaning but clueless OWI bureaucrats spelled box office poison. Sentimental international romances, exciting Allied combat dramas, and global morality tales, conversely, could sugar-coat the otherwise bitter propaganda pill and instruct the masses without sacrificing earnings.[19]

Hollywood's dream factory, never a stickler for accuracy, developed cinematic methods for teaching lessons about the spirit if not the letter of international politics without alienating paying customers. The United Nations was contrasted with its mirror image, acquiring a clearer identity in the process. Allied cultural guardians engaged in a war of words with their Japanese and German counterparts, especially Nazi propaganda minister Joseph Goebbels, by demarcating the UN from and pitting it in a Manichaean struggle against what lay beyond its pale: the Axis Other. Director Frank Capra's *Prelude to War* (1942), the first in his seven-part *Why We Fight* orientation film series sponsored by the U.S. War Department, was among the war's seminal texts insofar as it powerfully established a widely copied interpretative template. *Prelude to War* adapted enemy footage to seize the moral high ground for the Allies by labeling World War II an all-out fight between good and evil, freedom and slavery. Whereas the aggressive enemy, routinely represented elsewhere as a German war zombie or Japanese subhuman beast, strove to dominate the world and enslave its population, the peace-loving Allies fought a just war for self-defense, liberty, and a brighter, safer tomorrow.[20] The bad guys nailed their scripted parts even if the Allies did not always act in accordance with their white hat image.

The big screen's global taxonomy contained a common thread running throughout contemporary American political talk. According to FDR's oratory, Henry R. Luce's publishing empire, and former Republican presidential hopeful Wendell Willkie's 1943 best seller, *One World*, among other sources, Americans, Britons, Chinese, and Soviets were converging in the war's melting pot, becoming one and forging a single identity as they shed their erstwhile isolationist, imperial, "backward," or communist ways. Films translated such thinking onto the silver screen through various metaphors for interdependence—teamwork, reciprocal Lend-Lease aid, and later the United Nations Organization (UNO)—that highlighted the cooperation required to achieve wartime victory and postwar security.

Likening the UN to a family of nations was the most common analogy used to make multinational alliance legible to popular audiences. People have for centuries invoked the word "family" to describe nongenealogical human relationships, from nations to transnational spiritual communities to world organizations. Collective security arrangements lend themselves to the comparison because their parties, like family members, comprise a community more or less committed to one another's well-being. Within that context, familial phraseology naturalizes associations among dissimilar people. Affective terms personalize otherwise dispassionate affairs of state. Friendly references signal a desire for good relations in the here and now; moreover, to address one's allies as kin invites permanence, as families share a bond unbreakable by the whims of the moment.[21]

For all of those reasons, Americans employed terms of endearment during World War II. Britons were upheld as Americans' cousins, a special relationship evinced by Roosevelt and Churchill's celebrated personal rapport. U.S. statesmen, FDR included, courted the USSR, and Stalin's image underwent an extreme makeover that transformed him into kindly Uncle Joe. Viewing the ROC through the lens of Orientalism, white Americans saw Sino-American relations as a paternal mission to uplift their childlike Chinese wards. Features and documentaries, from *Sahara* (1943) to *The True Glory* (1945), affirmed the band of brothers formed by Allied soldiers in the heat of battle. And posters portrayed British, Chinese, and Soviets as Americans' anti-Axis friends in the fight for the Four Freedoms.

Domestic and foreign events conspired to make the traditional nuclear family a gendered symbol of international belonging. Females comprised the vast majority of home front moviegoers—70 to 80 percent, according to Hollywood's overestimate—and the discourse of UN kinship by design spoke to them and the upturned gender order in wartime America, where women moved into the workforce and military auxiliaries and assumed additional domestic responsibilities in the absence of men. At first, pop culture encouraged women to emulate Rosie the Riveter. Yet expanding feminine independence sparked anxieties that the status quo was being permanently revolutionized, a fear fueled by latent misgivings about the alliance with the Soviet Union, where females were seen to exercise greater economic freedoms. Such fears manifested in exaggerated concerns about masculine women, lesbianism, and sexual promiscuity run amok among juveniles and "victory girls." Ultimately, that fear would lead the culture to reverse course and reinforce gender norms by celebrating domesticity with rhetorical commendations given to mothers, wives, and homemakers and with punishments meted out to those who challenged the established order.[22]

Representing the Allies as a nuclear family of nations simultaneously contained feminine autonomy at home and incorporated America's disparate overseas partners within the U.S. field of vision. Hollywood romances commonly welcomed the major powers into the alliance by characterizing those nations as females. Heterosexual love transcended international differences, according to these sentimental narratives, which invited fictional British, Chinese, or Soviet women to enter the normative family of nations through courtship with or marriage to American men—but only if the women abandoned their autonomy, racial identity, or national loyalty, as the case may have been. Incorporating fictional Soviet women proved difficult, however, because in the United States they were widely assumed to have been somehow unsexed by communism, leaving them unnaturally masculine and divorced from the trappings associated with femininity: beauty and fashion, consumption, and heterosexual romance. MGM's *Song of Russia* (1944) drew on and reversed that stereotype in the name of Allied unity, portraying an impressionable young ideologue who, after evincing disinterest in bourgeois sexuality, eventually weds an American expatriate. In the process, she trades her socialist politics and independence for U.S.-style consumer capitalism and assumes her customary "place" as his helpmate.

Whereas love trumps doctrine in *Song of Russia*, gendered romance negotiated the Sino-American racial divide. Hollywood's internal censorship rulebook, the Production Code, included an antimiscegenation clause that strictly prohibited on-screen interracial romance. Yellowface, the then common but now disreputable theatrical practice whereby whites enacted Asian characters on stage, skirted the code's ban, however, allowing Gene Tierney and Sylvia Sidney, under yellow makeup and chinoiserie fashion, to rehearse "Chinese" females romantically involved with U.S. males in Zanuck's *China Girl* (1942) and United Artists' *Blood on the Sun* (1945), respectively. Such films set aside contemporary fears about miscegenation's threat to white racial purity and domesticated Chinese. Their characters stole American hearts, as did Madame Jiang (née Mayling Soong) during her 1943 U.S. tour.

Metaphorical matrimony came most easily to Jane Bull, famously characterized as a middle-class homemaker familiar to Americans in 1942's *Mrs. Miniver* by MGM. Pictures from Wanger's *Eagle Squadron* (1942) to *I Live in Grosvenor Square* (1945) framed the budding Anglo-American "special relationship" as a bilateral romance. The boy usually got the girl. An international love triangle was often the biggest obstacle standing in their way, and it was resolved amicably when the third party—either a Yank or a Brit, depending on the scenario—voluntarily withdrew from competition. Not that transatlantic romance needed much encouragement—American men married at least forty thousand British war brides, a figure that vastly underestimates the number of assignations that occurred while 3 million U.S. soldiers were stationed in the United Kingdom from 1942 to 1945. Not all of those couples stayed together, and transatlantic unions did not always advance bilateral goodwill. But those relationships and the more than fourteen thousand children they yielded personified Anglo-American intimacy.[23]

All such kinship discourses—international romances, fraternal combat epics, or paternal fantasies—facilitated the big screen's one-world sensibility by emotionalizing inter-Allied relations, culturally deconstructing the barriers between Us and Them, and reducing real-world complexities to a lower common denominator. Insofar as family served as a big tent that accommodated the Big Four's differences, the analogy normalized the UN's internal inconsistencies, which otherwise would have argued against internationalism, for everyone knew from personal experience that familial relations involved some degree of difference and conflict. "We all know that, in a family, brothers and sisters and parents differ," British author Basil Mathews noted in his 1943 book about the Allies. "The family in which all members held the same views would, indeed, be very dull. So it is with nations."[24]

Internationalist discourse, produced and distributed transnationally, framed lived experience to facilitate nothing less than a new way of seeing that redrew world geography as Americans understood it. Nationalism typically surges in the heat of war, historicized as a crucible that reduces sociopolitical pluralism and forges a common civic identity against external foes.[25] World War II was no different: Americans fought and sacrificed primarily for country—or home, as misty-eyed Hollywood movie stars so often characterized it. But wars do not always hold form. By any measure, the U.S. misadventure in Vietnam, for example, called into question the core values that had previously held the imaginative nation together. Although the "good war" stands in marked contrast to Vietnam in many respects, it, too, stretched the American imagination precisely because it was a *world* war, the broadest in human history. Success for the United States and its forty-six Allies depended on connecting theaters of battle spread across the globe; shipping personnel and supplies over vast distances by air, land, and sea; and communicating, coordinating, and cooperating to an unprecedented degree, all while struggling to maintain a sense of common purpose. World War II, then, should be remembered not only as America's finest hour but also as a global moment when American, British, Chinese, and even Soviet interconnectivity grew and the notion of a human community reasserted itself. That is not to say that the Allies always saw eye-to-eye: they did not, of course. Neither is it to deny that globalism existed before the war or argue that American isolationism and nationalism would never rise again. Rather, it is to say that foreign places became better known and peoples more closely acquainted amid the war's circumstances, leading to a watershed in the accepted worldview. Having accustomed themselves to the give-and-take of alliance politics, Americans crossed an intellectual threshold beyond which isolationism and parochialism gave way to internationalism and cosmopolitanism. Feeling themselves by war's end to be citizens of a world interconnected as never before, Americans did what they refused to do when the last shots of World War I had been fired. They shouldered the burdens of global leadership by joining the UNO, the postwar peacekeeping body modeled, both nominally and practically, on the wartime multinational United Nations alliance, which was widely regarded as the nucleus or core of future international cooperation. Indeed, the fiction of Allied solidarity became fact under the guise of the United Nations Information Office (UNIO), an intergovernmental planning board headquartered in London and New York starting in 1942. The first agency to feature "United Nations" as part of its title, the UNIO produced an avalanche of pro-UN publicity before being folded into the UNO when that body was founded in 1945.[26]

The big screen framed one-world philosophy primarily by and for American eyes. Movies upheld international familiarity, to be sure, but also presumed that the Allied household would conform to the American nuclear family norm and be husbanded by the United States. Historian David Engerman's observation that U.S. Cold War universities, working hand in glove with the state, "produced knowledge *of* the world so that the United States could best fulfill its national mission *in* the world" applies to wartime cinema as well. If gendered language signifies unequal power relationships, then it is noteworthy that *Mrs. Miniver*, *China Girl*, *Song of Russia*, and other Hollywood romances feminized Britain, China, and the USSR relative to the United States. (By contrast, Churchill's characterization, at 1945's Potsdam Conference, of the bilateral relationship as a union between an American "young lady" and British gentleman left his interlocutor, President Harry S Truman, cold.) Furthermore, on-screen convergence theories—from Capra's orientation films to *Mission to Moscow* to Fox's pro-China epic, *The Keys of the Kingdom* (1944)—held that the Allies were becoming more alike in the war's crucible, but only to the extent that others were adopting the American Way. Any foreign movements toward liberal democratic capitalism signified teleological progress pointing to a U.S. ideal. Jiang received support partly because he represented an Americanized "new China"; Stalin garnered U.S. backing because he appeared to be a postrevolutionary returning the USSR to the "normal" international community. In short, They were made to resemble Us, not the other way around. And while the screen's one-world aesthetic cultivated a more inclusive, equitable American worldview of the type advanced by Vice President Henry Wallace, who insisted in vain that the "century of the common man" was dawning, it also prepared the way for what Luce so famously termed the "American Century" in his influential 1941 *Life* magazine editorial. That is to say that an ideological foundation was laid for the expansion of U.S. power to render the postwar world even more conducive to the realization of American aims.[27]

Nationalism endured, and the ongoing quest to achieve national interests coincided with and would soon eclipse all the utopian talk of universalism. A behind-the-scenes dynamic between Washington and Hollywood drove the UN project. By the outbreak of World War II, Hollywood had risen above its immigrant, working-class roots to enter the mainstream as a respectable middle-class entertainer. Its best movies even acquired status among intellectuals as works of art worthy of preservation and study. Nevertheless, Hollywood still had critics, and questions remained as to its fitness for public service. Aside from some crude propaganda ordered by George Creel's Committee on Public Information during World War I, film had never participated in U.S. public diplomacy initiatives. Granted, the United States went without such a program from 1919 until 1938, when the State Department established the Division of Cultural Relations. But the United States had been among the slowest developed countries to adapt, in part because the American foreign policy establishment was averse to such innovations. State Department efforts, when they did begin, catered solely to foreign elites with high culture: academic exchanges, fine art exhibitions, and so on. Even cultural diplomats, who in theory should have been most receptive, initially excluded cinema on the grounds that it did not appeal to the highbrow target audience. To be sure, some officials—including Nelson Rockefeller, who drew heavily on film while serving as coordinator of inter-American affairs— were ahead of the curve in terms of appreciating that Hollywood movies could build international goodwill or promote U.S. interests. But there were just as many, if not more—including Joseph P. Kennedy, whose prior experience as a film financier did not prevent him from criticizing movies he found harmful when he was U.S. ambassador to London from 1938 to 1940—who doubted that Hollywood, renowned for its violent gangster pictures and light romantic comedies, could shoulder the heavy responsibilities of educating the public about world affairs or properly representing the nation abroad. And skeptics could cite chapter and verse regarding occasions when commercial pictures had done the exact opposite and, for one reason or another, caused diplomatic dustups or given the United States a black eye.[28]

Widely associated today with the United States, Hollywood became fully American by virtue of its extensive patriotic service during World War II, when the industry's commercial objectives complemented Washington's geopolitical agenda and established the foundation for a cozy corporatist partnership. Corporatism, a form of socioeconomic organization common in the United States during the New Deal and the war, involved formal collaboration by public and private interests to achieve prosperity by promoting domestic business growth and overseas commercial expansion as well as by other means. It operated at certain nodes of contact between the public and private spheres, including the major studios' trade association, the Motion Picture Producers and Distributors of America (MPPDA), and the association's Foreign Department, known as the "little State Department." It also involved a revolving door through which elites—such as Kennedy; MPPDA president Will H. Hays, a onetime member of President Warren G. Harding's administration; and Robert Riskin, Capra's screenwriter, who became an OWI official—moved easily between government and industry.[29]

Authorities invested significant financial and human resources in cinema as the conviction grew that, if managed properly, it could advance the nation's political and economic interests. Armed with a Progressive approach to popular education holding that an enlightened public would respond appropriately to the world's challenges, officials believed, correctly or not, that culture was tied to the exercise of U.S. power, both at home and abroad, an important intellectual development traced in chapter 1. That belief, which underlay the corporatist arrangement, rested on three assumptions. First, a consensus developed that propaganda, commonly likened to a "magic bullet" or a "hypodermic needle," was almost invariably able to inculcate ideas into the body politic, thereby altering people's thoughts and determining their actions. That theory rested, in turn, on the day's dominant school of social psychology, behaviorism, which was guided by the principle that behavior is environmentally determined and can be conditioned. Such notions must be taken seriously, albeit with a grain of salt, as scholars have since established that film, literature, and art do not convey universal, immanent meaning since audiences enjoy wide interpretive latitude. Even students of reception concede that cinema stands in a class apart, however. Film's sensuous experience is so overwhelming that it imposes an intellectual straitjacket on spectators, forcing them at a minimum to play on its discursive terrain.[30] In any event, wartime social scientists, publicists, and lawmakers thought that movies could move the masses, a supposition well backed by contemporary anecdotal evidence and scholarly research.

Cinema involved important commercial considerations as well, a second corporatist shibboleth. A major component of the U.S. economy, the motion picture industry ranked eleventh and fourteenth among all American industries in terms of assets and volume, respectively, in 1937. Hollywood executives earned the second-highest corporate salaries that year, and in 1945, the majors generated more than $1.4 billion in gross sales from their monopolization of the production, distribution, and exhibition of motion pictures. Moviemaking stimulated such subsidiary industries as photography, cosmetics, and advertising, and the studios employed almost a quarter of a million people across the country as box office attendants and theater ushers, carpenters and camera operators, and makeup artists and hairdressers, among other occupations. Moreover, it was axiomatic that Hollywood movies generated foreign trade revenues and fueled U.S. economic growth by acting as "salesmen" for American-made products placed on screen. The *Saturday Evening Post*, noting the concomitant increase in both U.S. and Hollywood exports, had first speculated in 1925 that trade followed film, which displayed household appliances, automobiles, and other consumer goods in such a "handsome environment" as to stimulate foreign "demand for American wares." The MPPDA's president, Hays, seized on that notion when he lobbied U.S. trade and diplomatic officials to support Hollywood exports, regularly claiming that each foot of exported film generated one dollar of American industrial revenue.[31]

Finally, it became accepted that Hollywood advertised not just American products but also the United States and its people, institutions, and foreign policies. New mass communications technologies, especially motion pictures and radio, had combined with accelerating democratization to revolutionize statecraft. Pushed by their totalitarian counterparts, U.S. foreign policy makers—including Roosevelt, who used the media to legendary effect—perceived, albeit belatedly, the changed landscape. For the first time, they validated and expanded public diplomacy, once relegated to the backwaters of the Department of State, to succeed in the increasingly competitive international marketplace of ideas by promoting national values and explaining foreign policy before the world court of public opinion. Luce popularized that novel idea in his "American Century" editorial, which argued in part that the United States could best achieve its global objectives by relying less on brute force than what would later be called "soft power": the authority exerted by a nation when its material culture, ideology, and institutions attract foreigners and assist its drive to secure vital interests. Hollywood movies, estimated at the time to occupy some 80 percent of the world's screen time, served as potent weapons in that regard, for they spread ideas in entertaining ways. Combined, these three premises led members of the foreign policy establishment to put aside their skepticism and welcome Hollywood as a partner in their Dale Carnegie–like mission to win friends and influence people across the globe.[32]

Hollywood benefited as well. Carrying Washington's water enabled déclassé movie moguls, relative newcomers to U.S. halls of power, to earn bona fides as true, patriotic Americans, a hedge against censorship drives of the type mounted by lay moral reformers, Protestant and Catholic clergy, and political conservatives since the century's first decade. More tangible rewards also accrued. The American industry had dominated the global marketplace since World War I. But foreign governments from London to Tokyo had since raised defenses—tariffs, quotas, taxes, and outright bans—against the American cinematic onslaught, blamed for ruining local customs, upsetting trade balances, and draining monetary reserves.[33] At the same time, the Department of Justice brought a 1938 antitrust suit that hung over the moguls, who risked losing their extensive theater chains. Only Washington could protect Hollywood's interests, and executives asked the White House to temper federal prosecutors and the State Department to roll back foreign protectionism. Officials agreed to help on the condition, evidence suggests, that Hollywood produce wholesome, patriotic films that supported U.S. foreign policy and reflected well on American society.

The American motion picture industry came to play a lead role in pro-UN propaganda. Subsequent chapters, 2–4 especially, investigate the wonders movies worked in disseminating knowledge about the wider world that placed the United States at the center of the global community. Americans were ignorant about foreign affairs and suspicious of the Allies, concluded official studies. Enlisted by the OWI to counteract that state of affairs, Hollywood taught theatergoers how to be citizens of the world. Capra's *Prelude to War* served as a primer on international politics that explained why, with whom, and against what Americans were fighting. Humphrey Bogart, the star of *Casablanca*, arguably the war's most memorable film, demonstrated the acceptability of sticking one's neck out for someone else. In *Sahara*, he shared the spotlight with a tank, which became a model UN as it collected a ragtag band of stray Allied soldiers—white and black, American and not—who learned that tolerance and teamwork could defeat Nazism in North Africa. Distributed by the industry's War Activities Committee, such official documentaries as *The Price of Victory* (1942), *Oswego* (1943), and *Watchtower over Tomorrow* (1945) schooled viewers in good international behavior, lessons reinforced by *Wilson*, Zanuck's 1944 biopic focusing on the ex-president's failed but farsighted attempt to secure U.S. membership in the League of Nations. These efforts, combined with FDR's oratory, UN-themed public festivals, Willkie's *One World*, and more, conveyed two main messages: first, that Americans lived among (mostly) friendly neighbors on a planet interconnected as never before; and, second, that the United States would have a responsibility as a victorious Great Power to be active internationally to protect that community from future outlaws.

The U.S. stance vis-à-vis Great Britain proved central to the sea change in the American worldview. The empirical record—letters written by audience members, film reviews, opinion polls, and more—indicates that six years of exposure to a steady stream of internationalist, pro-British expression helped tip the perceptual balance. Whereas Anglophobia and isolationism once had been fashionable, by war's end an enduring sense prevailed that the United States and Great Britain shared a "special relationship," an image that obscured actual transatlantic political, economic, and cultural disputes, including those regarding cinema.[34] Perhaps the best evidence of publicity's efficacy was the concerted autumn 1941 effort to nip it in the bud by opponents who staked the anti-interventionist movement on a sensational congressional investigation of movie propaganda. Isolationists blamed Hollywood for turning popular opinion against them, citing a wave of films—director Michael Curtiz's *The Sea Hawk* (1940) starring Errol Flynn; Hitchcock's *Foreign Correspondent* (1940); and Alexander Korda's *That Hamilton Woman* (1941), with Vivien Leigh and Laurence Olivier, to name a few—with "drugging" and misleading the American people into yet another foreign war. The probe came to an abrupt end when its anti-Semitic overtones deservedly drew public censure, but not before it identified those responsible: British propagandists, the Roosevelt administration, and Hollywood entertainers conspiring behind the scenes to awaken American moviegoers to the world's dangers.

Atlanticism only intensified after the United States declared war. *Mrs. Miniver* charmed audiences, winning an Academy Award as 1942's Best Picture. It was one of the first wartime pictures made by American and British movie legends (others included Zanuck's *Thunder Birds* [1942], Michael Powell and Emeric Pressburger's *A Matter of Life and Death* [1946]) to romanticize transatlantic ties. Churchill, whose way with words and stubborn tenacity made him a celebrity in the United States, also enthralled. The media interpreted his rapport with FDR—they exchanged almost two thousand messages and met thirteen times; the prime minister stayed with the Roosevelts when he visited the United States—as evidence of Anglo-American brotherhood, an impression reinforced by the joint combat documentaries *Tunisian Victory* (1944) and *The True Glory*, directed by Capra and Carol Reed, respectively. All told, it seemed clear to most that Britons and Americans—"cousins" linked by history, culture, and interests—were as kindred as two peoples could be. To paraphrase George Bernard Shaw, however, the United Kingdom and the United States were separated by a common movie language as well. Hollywood pictures continued to pour into the United Kingdom during the war, generating handsome earnings, in sterling, that in ordinary times were converted into dollars and remitted to the studios' New York financial offices. Expenditures on foreign movies became an urgent and controversial matter because they drained London's currency reserves, depleted by the purchase of wartime supplies from the United States. A simmering Anglo-American film trade war boiled over when the British Treasury and Board of Trade imposed additional restrictions, including a profit freeze, on Hollywood. Crying foul, the MPPDA requested assistance from its corporatist partners; Roosevelt, Secretary of State Cordell Hull, and lesser officials came to the industry's defense time and again over the years, using Washington's growing leverage to extract concessions from London. But the issue never went away—additional taxes and protective trade measures worsened the situation, in fact—and it remained an irritant just below and sometimes above the surface of the imagined special relationship.

Conflict emerges even more clearly in chapters 5 and 6, which show that pro-UN expression met with less success when it came to the Soviet Union and China, however. Hollywood, the OWI, and American moviegoers all failed to see Chinese as full and equal partners. Granted, negative Asian stereotypes were transferred to the Japanese enemy, who solely embodied the "yellow peril" traditionally said to threaten Western superiority. And a wave of movies—from Charlie Chan mysteries to Sino-American romances—valorized American congress with like-minded Chinese allies who fought for the Four Freedoms. The problem, however, was that every picture meant to uphold China somehow perpetuated the dominant racist thinking of the day. While Sidney Toler (Charlie Chan, America's favorite "Chinese" character), Katharine Hepburn (*Dragon Seed*), and the many other Caucasian actors who masqueraded under yellow masks onstage promoted inclusion to the extent that such performances deracinated Chinese and destabilized fixed racial identities, yellowface was primarily a form of racial parody that, like its close relative, blackface, sustained the status quo and its inherent power differential: whites could pass as typecast "Chinese," but Asians could not pass as whites. Hollywood's standard operating practices literally marginalized Chinese American actors, including Marianne Quon, Keye Luke, Victor Sen Yung, and Benson Fong (all best known for their roles as Charlie Chan's children), to the sidelines, where they performed model minorities in supporting parts: Westernized Chinese, loyal U.S. helpmates, noble peasants, and so forth. Hollywood thus conveyed the general and unfortunate impression that Sino-American community rested less on mutual understanding than on paternalism, a motif that reduced China to a subordinate position in the globe's pecking order. If one were to take what appeared on-screen as a guide—and many people did—then it seemed that Americans, be they John Wayne in *Flying Tigers* (1942), Alan Ladd in Paramount's *China* (1943), or Gregory Peck, who played Father Francis Chisholm, a Catholic missionary, in Fox's *The Keys of the Kingdom*, had a paternal, civilizing duty to shepherd feminized, infantilized Chinese dependents toward a modernized, Christianized, Americanized destiny.

Despite their best efforts to position popular thinking, gatekeepers lost control after propaganda left their hands and entered the marketplace, where pro-Soviet teachings, for example, encountered deep-seated anti-communist beliefs. American wartime culture, according to historian John Morton Blum, promoted change in some areas (civil rights, for example) but resisted elsewhere: historical memory, old habits, and tradition argued against departures such as condominium with the Soviet Union.[35] Contrary to the expectations of cultural custodians, moreover, audiences did not sit in darkened theaters too gullible or captivated by what appeared on screen to engage it critically. Rather, diverse consumers negotiated with cinema, accepting, adapting, or reinterpreting it as historical circumstance and individual viewpoint demanded. As a result, a gap typically opened between the transmission and reception of meaning, whatever the intended message. On-screen idealizations of Stalin's USSR, including *Mission to Moscow*, *Song of Russia*, and MGM's *North Star* (1943), unintentionally widened the gulf. Finding the disparity between fiction and fact too wide, numerous observers—from philosopher John Dewey, a liberal, to the anticommunist members of the Motion Picture Alliance for the Preservation of American Ideals, an industry pressure group—regarded them as communist propaganda. Such rosy portraits of the Soviet Union even caused authorities, Federal Bureau of Investigation director J. Edgar Hoover included, to suspect that subversives had infiltrated Hollywood, charges that would lead the House Committee on Un-American Activities to investigate in 1947.

Miscommunication only increased when films crossed international borders, on the other side of which lay different cultural, historical, and political contexts that opened intellectual space for alternative meanings.[36] Among the United Nations campaign's great ironies is that its attendant transnational exchange, despite all the familial rhetoric, often exacerbated the type of diplomatic, commercial, and ideological tensions it was supposed to quell. Just as Soviet pictures contributed to an anticommunist backlash in the United States, Hollywood exports provoked concern about American cultural expansion in the USSR. Exploiting loosened Soviet domestic restrictions that, among other things, had prohibited Hollywood imports since the 1920s, the State Department and OWI instituted an official U.S. information program to the USSR. An integral part of FDR's overall strategy to court Stalin, the program was originally designed as a confidence-building measure. However, popular audiences starved of foreign culture for almost a generation tended to read even pro-Soviet American imports not in the way intended, as expressions of goodwill, but as evidence of the superior quality of life available in the West. As

Germany's defeat neared and the postwar era came into view, the U.S. diplomats on the ground in Moscow—future Cold War hard-liners Ambassador W. Averell Harriman and his deputy, George F. Kennan, containment's architect—drew a lesson from that experience: material culture could work to long-term U.S. advantage by ideologically corroding communism from within. None of this was lost on the Communist Party's chief ideologue, Andrei A. Zhdanov, who would go on to engineer a postwar cultural purge that cleansed not only the USSR itself but also the entire Eastern Bloc of contaminating Western influence, American film included. Taken together, Zhdanov's purge, the beginnings of which were already apparent to U.S. observers by late 1944, and the American cultural penetration that helped precipitate it provide a cultural dimension to our understanding of both the UN's disintegration and the Cold War's origins, supporting the historiographic view that ideological competition lay at the heart of the Soviet-American rivalry.[37]

At the beginning of World War II, however, Allied authorities anticipated few of these developments when they embarked on a project to invent international unity. To them, movies offered a superior means to join together the disparate, fractious United Nations confederation in the public mind. While that theory did not always prove correct, managed public discourse at least momentarily imagined a broader, more inclusive cognitive geography in which the Allies seemed to comprise a single family of nations.

THE "MAGIC BULLET"

HOLLYWOOD, WASHINGTON, AND
THE MOVIEGOING PUBLIC

In the 1940 Warner Bros. film *Dr. Ehrlich's Magic Bullet*, actor Edward G. Robinson plays Dr. Paul Ehrlich, the real-life Nobel Prize–winning German physician who discovered a cure for syphilis. A founder of what became known as chemotherapy, the doctor's remedy involved a pharmacological "magic bullet," a chemical toxin that selectively targeted and killed disease-causing organisms. Neither he nor his biopic addressed propaganda's effectiveness. But another "magic bullet" theory, so prominent as to be conventional social scientific wisdom at the time of the picture's release, did. Also called the "hypodermic needle" model, it boldly asserted that propaganda exerted tremendous power over people by subcutaneously injecting data into the body politic that, like a chemical toxin, eradicated countervailing beliefs, implanted new ideas, and thereby manufactured thoughts and actions.

In short, there was widespread agreement that propaganda worked, that it could condition human behavior. No mass communication technology appeared to carry greater influence, for good or ill, than cinema. No other medium, not even radio, matched film's sensory appeal, its audibility *and* visibility, in the pretelevision age. Movies were consumed in darkened theaters, immersive environments where viewers were said to be transfixed by what appeared before them on the big screen. Hollywood, maker of the planet's most popular movies, only multiplied the effect. Hundreds of millions of people worldwide attended theaters each week, and observers documented, sometimes disapprovingly, the apparent ease with which Hollywood pictures made strong and lasting impressions on suggestible viewers. Hollywood served as a leading tastemaker, and it became clichéd to note the fans who mimicked the fashions, mannerisms, and mores modeled on-screen by their favorite larger-than-life stars.

Hollywood's capabilities led policymakers to turn to film propaganda when the need arose to inspire Americans to join forces with the Allies against the Axis powers, an objective that turned moviemaking into a sort of defense industry worthy of official patronage. Enlisting the American motion picture industry, however, required negotiations among studio executives and U.S. government officials, who had divergent priorities. Commercial filmmakers initially failed to see how propaganda could be profitable; civil servants, diplomats especially, did not immediately appreciate how movies could be made to serve the public interest. And propaganda of any kind at first seemed downright dangerous to the republic. During the war years, however, those competing views were reconciled as Hollywood and Washington developed a corporatist framework for the projection of internationalism.

Practiced for centuries, propaganda acquired disreputable and even sinister connotations thanks in large part to World War I and the Third Reich. In hindsight, Americans felt manipulated by the Great War's crude sloganeering. British operatives were held responsible for misleading the United States into joining that meaningless fight with unsubstantiated rumors of German atrocities in Belgium. Such tales left interwar isolationists opposed to propaganda on the grounds that it promoted belligerence.[1] The historical reputation of the Committee on Public Information (CPI), the first U.S. propaganda agency, created in 1917 and led by newspaperman George Creel, plummeted along with that of Woodrow Wilson and his war. To disillusioned Americans, the CPI's repeated assurances that the Great War would make the world safe for democracy rang hollow in the wake of the Great Depression, the rise of fascism, and the collapse of the Versailles peace. Moreover, early accounts charged the Creel Committee with hypocritically undermining liberty through jingoistic output that encouraged nativist vigilantism against radicals, immigrants, and members of ethnic groups. By 1939, these developments led journalist I. F. Stone to warn Americans against repeating the CPI's "organized mass idiocy" if they were drawn into another overseas war.[2]

As soon as it became associated with totalitarianism, propaganda was thoroughly discredited in the Western democracies. Despite their differences, the USSR, Fascist Italy, and Nazi Germany were lumped together as totalitarian states by informed observers in part because all three used propaganda to unprecedented degrees and in similar ways. Germany's Adolf Hitler and Reich Minister for Popular Enlightenment and Propaganda Joseph Goebbels leapt to mind as the most noxious and enthusiastic propagandists. But all totalitarians, regardless of ideology, were said to be adept at crushing the independent media, subordinating every aspect of public culture to the party-state, and then using propaganda to brainwash and control their minions. Nazis and Soviets alike ruled by virtue of their "complete control . . . of [the] press, schools, theater, broadcasting, and every other agency of propaganda," wrote *Christian Science Monitor* foreign correspondent William Henry Chamberlin.[3]

Antifascists defined propaganda as positively un-American, outlining a nightmare scenario in which it helped spread the contagion of dictatorship to the United States. After a pro-Nazi rally attracted twenty-two thousand swastika-carrying followers to New York City's Madison Square Garden in February 1939, the Committee for Cultural Freedom issued a manifesto alerting Americans to the fact that in Nazi Germany, "intellectual and creative independence is suppressed and punished as a form of treason. Art, science, and education have been forcibly turned into lackeys for a supreme state." The committee, a group of noncommunist intellectuals organized by Marxist philosopher Sidney Hook, warned that the "tide of totalitarianism is rising throughout the world. It is washing away cultural and creative freedom along with all other expressions of independent human reason." France's fall to Germany in June 1940, the speed of which was partly attributed to the activities of Nazi fifth columnists, provocateurs among them, operating within the Third Republic, touched off a brown scare in the United States. *Dictator Isms and Our Democracy*, a tract that envisioned the chilling aftereffects of authoritarian takeovers of American cities, including the institution of official propaganda and censorship ministries, exemplified the widespread fear of expanding fascism reaching U.S. shores.[4]

Conservatives alleged that the country already had a dictator in its midst: President Franklin D. Roosevelt, who sought an unprecedented third term in 1940 after attempting to pack the Supreme Court in 1937. His administration's opponents claimed that each federal agency included a publicity arm for the sole purpose of promoting the New Deal, the Democratic Party, and FDR himself, paving the way for a homegrown autocracy. The president's extensive state-run apparatus rivaled those found in Hitler's Germany, Joseph Stalin's Russia, or Benito Mussolini's Italy, or so argued the *American Mercury*'s managing editor, Gordon Carroll. Roosevelt, whom Carroll called the "Fuhrer," supposedly "set out to show the world how a real propaganda machine, geared to soaring political ambition and the modern collectivist tempo, should regulate the lives and votes of [millions of] gullible persons." The New Deal's public relations network could well evolve into a propaganda ministry of the kind overseen by Goebbels, added *New York Herald Tribune* syndicated columnist and Committee for Cultural Freedom member Dorothy Thompson. John T. Flynn, chair of the New York City chapter of the isolationist America First Committee, similarly cautioned in 1940 that the administration's informational activities made it "possible to do here what has been done in Germany and Italy."[5]

Propaganda's equation with dictatorship gave ammunition to civil libertarians, who deemed it undemocratic. Elitist, mass persuasion revealed what little confidence authorities had in the general public's ability independently to reach wise conclusions or develop moral clarity. Promotional work distorted the facts, inflamed passions, and manipulated citizens, interfering with free, reasoned public discourse. Ideally, democracy depended on well-informed, objective discussion of issues in the public square, philosopher John Dewey declared in 1939, and propagandists, who had "developed an extraordinary facility" for spreading lies and arousing emotions, endangered that process.[6]

Liberals continued to register objections after U.S. entry into the war in December 1941, the point at which most other antipropagandists muted their opposition. When rumors spread in early 1942 that the Roosevelt administration was considering establishing a central war information office, the proposal struck some civil libertarians as an ominous drift toward authoritarianism. The *Journal American* predicted in March that Washington's "bureaucratic propaganda centers of 'enlightenment'" would rival Berlin's if left unchecked. The next month, Chamberlin railed in *Christian Century* against the "powerful build-up for the creation in America of an organization comparable" to Goebbels's propaganda ministry. Once founded, Chamberlin explained, such a ministry would "terrorize Americans into abandoning their normal faculties of criticism and common sense and closely imitate the method of government by unlimited propaganda which is so characteristic of the totalitarian state." Moreover, the journalist reminded readers that the war was being fought in the name of freedom from fascist slavery, and he called attention to just how much the establishment of a U.S. propaganda ministry contradicted that mission: "It would be a ghastly irony if, in the name of a crusade against totalitarianism, an essentially totalitarian technique of propaganda and thought control should be set up in this country. We do not want a Gobbels [*sic*] in America, not even a Gobbels who might write an ode to the Statue of Liberty."[7]

All opponents could agree on the need to treat propaganda as a controlled substance since it was so potent as to be injurious to public psychological health. Toxicity and disease recurred as descriptors of publicity's disabling effect on rationality. Rockefeller Foundation official John Marshall, who channeled funding to scholarly studies of mass persuasion throughout the 1930s, spoke of propaganda as "pathology." It turned "people into automatons," robots "incapable of thought," according to Donald Slesinger, the onetime dean of social sciences at the University of Chicago who directed the foundation-sponsored American Film Center. Representative Emanuel Celler spoke in favor of prophylactic legislation, similar to "our National Food and Drug Act," designed to protect the public's moral health by requiring the labeling of information. The New York Democrat got his wish in 1938, when Congress passed the Foreign Agents Registration Act, which criminalized foreign propaganda by subjecting its distributors to fines or prison sentences if they failed to register with the Department of Justice and/or follow U.S. regulations.[8]

Behavioral psychology informed the "magic bullet" theory. Critical of the intuitive, subjective, and hence unscientific nature of Freudian psychoanalysis, the field's foundational orthodoxy, behaviorists prioritized what was observable and measurable: human behavior, taken to be the product not of internal consciousness but of external stimuli. If environment determined behavior, then it also stood to reason that human action could be manipulated by altering the causal conditions. Scientifically speaking, the concept of conditioning connected environment with behavior. Over the next several decades, experimental psychologists would subject conditioning to further analysis, only to discover that the learning process was in fact a good deal more complicated than had been anticipated. Still, the studies that established conditioning's operability— the same texts that elevated behaviorism to its preeminent position in the psychological profession—had a direct and influential bearing on the emerging theory and practice of mass communications. To be sure, *Propaganda and Promotional Activities* (1935), an authoritative bibliography of pertinent research coedited by University of Chicago political scientist Harold D. Lasswell, referenced cutting-edge neobehaviorist literature that questioned linear conditioning. But it also cited the classic work of Ivan Pavlov, the Russian physiologist who conditioned canine reflexology, and of John B. Watson, named vice president of the J. Walter Thompson advertising agency after his seminal if notorious "Little Albert" experiment of 1920 established him as behaviorism's founding father.[9]

Academic research and anecdotal evidence alike supported the conclusion that mass persuasion conditioned humans. Princeton University's Office of Radio Research, underwritten by the Rockefeller Foundation, released a pioneering 1937 study showing that listeners were strongly influenced by on-air programming. Another foundation beneficiary, the Communications Group (a collection of scholars dedicated to understanding the mass media's effects that included Lasswell, public opinion expert Hadley Cantril, and sociologist Robert S. Lynd) reported in 1940 that groupthink occurred "when millions of people, through the press, the radio, or the motion pictures, are all told the same thing, or approximately the same thing, at the same time."[10]

Many more such examples could be cited. But the single event that most solidified the media's reputation occurred on 30 October 1938, when the broadcast of Orson Welles's radio play of the H. G. Wells novel *War of the Worlds* caused a mass panic among an estimated 1 million listeners who believed that the Earth was under attack by creatures from Mars. Frightened, some listeners jumped in their cars and fled cities on the Eastern Seaboard. Fearful New Yorkers rushed to police stations to receive evacuation orders. A Newark, New Jersey, hospital sedated several hysterical patients. The entire event drew the interest of Cantril, a Princeton psychologist who advised Roosevelt. Two years later, Cantril published a study based on listener interviews that found the whole bizarre episode to be a conclusive demonstration of the mass media's ability, under certain conditions, to manipulate human behavior. If the incredible tale spun by *War of the Worlds* could move people, Cantril's work implied, something more plausible could perform wonders.[11]

That power—the same power that unnerved some liberals—attracted other democrats when circumstances warranted. The change began with France's fall. Nazism was on the march, and liberalism's future seemed to hang in the balance. U.S. national security, moreover, was at much greater risk now that only one major European ally, Great Britain, stood between Hitler and America. Desperate times called for desperate measures, and the balance of opinion started to swing in favor of fighting fire with fire to save democracy in its darkest hour. To survive, the thinking went, republicanism needed to adapt and utilize modern mass communications to match its vocal fascist competitor word for word, decibel for decibel. Doing so meant engaging, both at home and abroad, in what was paradoxically called "democratic propaganda." Defenders were quick to point out that democratic propaganda, unlike its dictatorial counterpart, appealed to reason and aspired to accuracy. In that regard, democratic propaganda was said to be consistent with liberalism insofar as its main objective was not to mislead but to inform the average citizen. John Q. Public needed to be educated about the serious challenge fascism posed to his way of life, and informational activities could do just that. Such an intellectual regimen would awaken Americans from their isolationist slumber and cause them to spring into antifascist action, producing a quick political response that transcended the numerous roadblocks that ordinarily stood in the way of efficient U.S. policymaking. The overall message of Lasswell, who coined the phrase "democratic propaganda," was that Americans should stop worrying and learn to love mass persuasion as nothing more than a technique of modern governance that could serve a benevolent purpose.[12]

Propaganda's propagandists glossed over its antidemocratic implications and muddied the waters in making their case. They defined the term so broadly (to encompass almost any kind of public argumentation) as to make it virtually indistinguishable from other kinds of human communication. Ohio State University education professor Edgar Dale likened persuasion to teaching, a simile that obfuscated the bright line between advocacy and pedagogy. Echoing Lasswell, Dale urged Americans to see propaganda as merely "a valuable means of promoting desirable institutions," including "democracy itself." Pollster George Gallup argued in *The Pulse of Democracy* (1940) that opinion surveys provided policymakers with the necessary "machinery" to hear, answer, and even alter what the people had to say about foreign and domestic affairs. Advertising pioneer Edward L. Bernays emerged as a forceful advocate. For almost two decades, Bernays, who had the added credential of being Sigmund Freud's nephew, had favorably characterized the best propagandists as "invisible governors" for their uncanny ability to grasp "the mental processes . . . of the masses" and pull "the wires which control the public mind." Promoters had a responsibility to use their special talents to defend liberty from Hitler, Bernays wrote in *Speak Up for Democracy*. Published in November 1940, the book outlined a campaign to promote the American way of life. Under his plan, all Americans, from hairdressers to cab drivers to ministers, would serve as amateur propagandists, seizing every opportunity to tout the blessings of democracy by following a strategy, helpfully scripted in the book, comprising speeches, community festivities, local newspaper editorials, and so on. Bernays pushed his plan throughout the war. During a 1943 address at Western Reserve University in Cleveland, he identified 788,257 potential opinion leaders in professional organizations, labor unions, and civic groups who had "access to the minds and wills of their followers." They were urged to "assume their responsibilities and mobilize the psychological front" in democracy's ideological struggle against fascism.[13]

The U.S. declaration of war following Japan's attack on Pearl Harbor foreclosed debate. Now, during the wartime emergency, the unwritten rules were revised so that stoking popular morale fell within the proper scope of federal responsibility. Western civilization appeared to be at stake, and in that atmosphere of crisis, propaganda provided a powerful weapon to help the United States and its allies win the ideological battle. As a total war fought in the mass media age, World War II demanded mobilization of all the nation's resources, including the country's psychological stores. Sloganeering was necessary to raise spirits, justify sacrifice, and explain why and how the United States was fighting a just war. International communication unified the Allies, ennobled their war effort, and appealed to neutrals, while psychological warfare demoralized and fanned the flames of rage against the enemy. And cultural diplomacy advertised the United States to the world. From that perspective, the Roosevelt administration would have been derelict not to institute a strategic communications program, especially given Nazi Germany's head start in the field. Or so argued Peter Odegard, an Amherst College political science professor who became director of the U.S. Treasury Department's war bond sales campaign. Speaking at Princeton in May 1942 in favor of official propaganda, which he likened to a shaman's hex, or "ouanga," Odegard observed that enemy "witch doctors" in Berlin, Rome, and Tokyo were busy trying "to put the great ouanga on us." Washington needed to respond in kind, for U.S. security depended on a counterinformation program robust enough to meet the enemy's ideological challenge, define the country's wartime objectives, and fortify the public's fighting spirit. Maintaining "democratic unity" required as much, he concluded.[14]

Although Odegard's tale seemed fabulous, as if Johnny Weissmuller's Tarzan had discovered enemy witch doctors secreted away somewhere in the jungle, the Roosevelt administration was preparing to put the "great ouanga" on the Axis even as Odegard spoke. The White House had previously authorized only a loose network of agencies to give war news to domestic audiences (including the Office of Government Reports [OGR] and the Office of Facts and Figures [OFF]) and foreigners (Nelson Rockefeller's

Office of the Coordinator of Inter-American Affairs and the Foreign Information Service, the Voice of America's forerunner as the country's international radio broadcaster). To raise morale, which fell below expectations after a post–Pearl Harbor bump, Pulitzer Prize–winning author and presidential speechwriter Robert Sherwood recommended in December 1941 that the administration create a "general information set-up" to serve as "the real voice of the U.S.A." In April 1942, the same month that Chamberlin highlighted the dangers of appointing an American Goebbels, attorney general Francis Biddle sent FDR an organizational plan for a consolidated federal publicity agency. Poet Archibald MacLeish, who doubled as OFF director, endorsed the plan in May and advised Roosevelt to go on the "ideological offensive."[15]

Declaring that the American people ought to be "truthfully informed" about the war effort, President Roosevelt issued a June 1942 executive order establishing the Office of War Information (OWI), split into domestic and overseas branches. Charged with forging "intelligent understanding, at home and abroad, of the status and progress of the war effort and of the war policies, activities, and aims" of the U.S. government, the OWI was empowered to monitor and strengthen public opinion. Despite its euphemistic moniker, the office was unmistakably a propaganda ministry whose raison d'être was to persuade audiences to support the U.S. war effort. That objective often meant not informing the people, only partially informing them, or embellishing the truth. Yet the Roosevelt administration maintained some respect for democratic processes. The OWI, the bureaucratic embodiment of "democratic propaganda," followed a "strategy of truth," an editorial policy designed to enhance the office's credibility vis-à-vis the Nazi propaganda machine. Whereas Goebbels's outfit was reputed to tell outright lies, the OWI did not as a rule deliberately misinform the American public. The private media remained nominally free to speak as they pleased, short of endangering national security: the OWI had no statutory authority to compel information outlets to toe the official line. To be sure, the office's functional bureaus issued official press releases, posters, films (documentary shorts, mostly), and such. But, on paper at least, they could otherwise only offer advice and depend on cooperative movie studios, radio networks, or newspaper and magazine editors to take it.[16]

The main task ahead of the OWI's Bureau of Motion Pictures (BMP), especially its Los Angeles field office, was to get the studios on board. The OWI needed the industry: far more moviegoers would hear the office's spiel if Hollywood intermediated. Movies were popular and persuasive.

The studio system's talented assemblage of writers, actors, and directors churned out entertaining stories augmented by snappy dialogue, emotive performances, quick action, lavish settings, realistic sound effects, and stirring musical scores. Most experts agreed that cinema's sensuous experience was so rich that it not only entertained and informed but also emotionally moved and even overwhelmed audiences. The fact that "ruling classes" seized control of film whenever their interests were threatened proved the medium's importance to Lasswell. Slesinger, the American Film Center's director, upheld cinema as "the most powerful medium of communication" because of its obvious influence over social mores.[17]

The Payne Fund studies helped establish the enduring truism that Hollywood exerted tremendous, even irresistible, influence over the moviegoing public, if not always in constructive ways. More than a decade earlier, in 1928, William H. Short, director of the National Committee for the Study of Social Values in Motion Pictures, a procensorship group, obtained a grant from the fund to underwrite scholarly investigations of movies' effect (negative, the committee presumed) on audiences, especially children. A team of nineteen psychologists, sociologists, and educators spent five years on the studies, a baker's dozen of which were published beginning in 1933. Sophisticated pieces of scholarship, the Payne Fund studies reached a variety of nuanced and even contradictory conclusions. Nevertheless, the studies sustained the procensorship movement (the same drive that led to the formation of the Production Code Administration [PCA] in 1934) as reformers pointed to select findings as definitive proof that Hollywood movies—cinematic magic bullets, the strongest propaganda of all—contributed to antisocial behavior, causing juvenile delinquency, sexual promiscuity, and violence. Five years after the first volume's publication, the editors of *Christian Century*, a regular critic of the silver screen's baneful effects, opined that Hollywood was "a social and educational force of tremendous importance" insofar as it altered the average "movie patron's attitudes, his behavior patterns and his character values." The publication, which called on studio heads to be more "responsible" educators of America's youth, drew particular attention to "the propaganda that so often creeps into such films—propaganda for war, or for liquor, or for the acquisitive life."[18]

A Payne Fund volume by a team of Ohio State researchers found that movies, particularly "impressive" ones featuring heavy doses of action, violence, or sex, so exercised children as to disturb their sleep. University of Chicago sociologist Herbert Blumer's exit interviews with moviegoers convinced him that films played "very vividly upon a given emotion of the individual; his impulses may be so aroused and his imagery so fixed that for a period of time he is transported out of his normal conduct and is completely subjugated by his impulses." One adolescent boy reported that he had learned to kiss by watching the stars do so on-screen; a sixteen-year-old girl confessed that the movies had made her "more receptive to love-making."[19]

Other Payne Fund studies found that movies spoke not just to the heart but also to the mind, suggesting that cinema influenced public opinion. Frank K. Shuttleworth and Mark A. May of Yale University discovered significant attitudinal differences between adolescents who did and did not regularly attend the movies. Research performed by University of Chicago behavioral psychologists Ruth C. Peterson and L. L. Thurstone revealed that "motion pictures have definite, lasting effects on the social attitudes of children." *Son of the Gods* (1930), director Frank Lloyd's sympathetic account of a frustrated interracial romance, left youthful spectators more tolerant. The prison films *Big House* (1930), *Numbered Men* (1930), and *The Criminal Code* (1931) raised awareness of the criminal justice system's faults. Young people exited screenings of *All Quiet on the Western Front* and *Journey's End*, two 1930 critiques of the Great War, less bellicose.[20]

At the same time, Hollywood could be a benevolent force. Rather than cataloging film's sins, journalist Margaret Thorp provided a favorable account of its intimate relationship with fans in *America at the Movies*, a book first published in 1939 and reissued seven years later. Thorp, a former English professor at Smith College, was interested in the manifold ways in which Hollywood served as a positive role model for fans, who patterned their manners, appearance, and decor after what they saw on screen, negotiating the fine line between the real and the imaginary in the process. As a case in point, impressionable young viewers took to heart Hollywood's on-screen instruction on cool social behavior. According to Thorp, "A favorite star can show even more authoritatively than an older sister, and much more explicitly, how to decline an invitation from a bore, how to accept a present, how to avoid and when to permit a kiss. There are minor social skills, too, taught more expertly by the movies than by the books of etiquette and studied carefully by young people of both sexes: how to light your friend's cigarette, how to walk with a girl, how to tip a waiter, how to deliver a wisecrack or a gallant speech."[21]

Hollywood's publicity machine made movie stars seem larger than life, and fashion-conscious fans styled their hair, clothes, and homes after those of their favorite performers. When actor Jean Harlow appeared in director Howard Hughes's *Hell's Angels* in 1930, the term "platinum blonde" entered the lexicon to describe her signature hair color, which many American women copied. Thousands of Greta Garbo's female admirers emerged from beauty parlors with new hairstyles six years later, after the actor, known for her long, wavy tresses, appeared with her blonde hair straight and short, bobbed just above the shoulders. Men were not immune to glamour's allure, as illustrated by the downward effect on undershirt sales of Clark Gable's appearance in *It Happened One Night*, winner of the 1934 Academy Award for Best Picture. Male and female viewers alike decorated their homes to resemble the palaces of their Hollywood heroes featured in fan magazines. Just as fans could "dress in the manner of Claudette Colbert," Thorp wrote, so too could they "furnish a walk-up flat or a two-family house to suggest William Powell's playroom or even the Pickfair [the Beverly Hills mansion of Mary Pickford and Douglas Fairbanks] banquet hall."[22]

Reality and fantasy met on the big screen, a window through which audiences became better acquainted with the wider world. Moviegoing inspired the imagination, a knack handy for building international brotherhood. Theaters provided middle grounds between the genuine and the make-believe, vicariously transporting even the most parochial audiences to distant locales and eras. Designed according to a cosmopolitan aesthetic considered chic well into the 1930s, Hollywood's great movie palaces—Grauman's Chinese Theatre in Los Angeles; the mosque-like Fox Theatre in Atlanta; and Chicago's aptly named Paradise Theater—mimicked stereotypical Oriental and European styles, creating spaces conducive to imaginary flight. According to Thorp, even more modest local theaters made "the small-town boy in Vermont or Arkansas who has never in his life been fifty miles from the farm . . . quite at home on the Place de la Concorde, Broadway at midnight, the Himalayas, or any one of a dozen South Sea islands."[23]

Such mediated glimpses of other places and peoples provided a universal imaginary, some said, a virtual Esperanto that promoted human understanding. Ordinary viewers glimpsed rarefied spaces through the camera's eye, author and critic Lewis Mumford wrote, thereby gaining better appreciation of the subtleties of diplomatic negotiation, for example. Film, like radio, gave consumers "an imaginative sense of participation in a common activity" that made them feel as if they were part of some "vast social unity," according to Cantril and psychologist Gordon Allport. News, art, and entertainment connected the man in the street with major events in faraway places during the global crisis, MacLeish argued in *Atlantic Monthly*: "The single individual, whether he so wishes or not, has become a part of a world which contains also Austria and Czechoslovakia and China and Spain. The victories of tyrants and the resistance of peoples halfway 'round the world are as near to him as the ticking of the clock on the mantel. What happens in his morning paper happens in his blood all day, and Madrid, Nanking, and Prague are names as close to him as the names by which he counts his dearest losses."[24]

Perhaps most important, Hollywood movies sugarcoated the otherwise bitter propaganda pill, easing its ingestion. The best propaganda was the least identifiable as such, and commercial film educated the fans it entertained. Bernays once said as much, characterizing the feature film as "the greatest unconscious carrier of propaganda in the world today." That idea, more than anything else, recommended cinema to the OWI. Although he had spent his career in radio, OWI director Elmer Davis, like Bernays, regarded film as the "most powerful instrument of propaganda in the world, whether it tries to be or not." The former Columbia Broadcasting System (CBS) newscaster explained, "The easiest way to inject a propaganda idea into most people's minds is to let it go in through the medium of an entertainment picture when they do not realize that they are being propagandized." The OWI codified that view in the *Government Information Manual for the Motion Picture Industry*, distributed to studios soon after the agency's creation. The manual, which spelled out the official propaganda line and cinema's role in projecting it, declared that Hollywood had "vital war work to do in helping every individual understand the issues for which we are fighting" and "in keeping every participant informed as to the progress of the war." In fact, the industry had a special part to play, since "through the motion picture, and in many instances through this medium alone, . . . the basic issues and underlying principles of the war effort can be presented to the American people. Motion picture makers reach the common denominator of American public opinion. Their product reaches all classes and creeds and groups. Therefore, upon the motion picture makers rests in large measure the privilege and responsibility of helping America win the war and win the peace."[25]

The manual enumerated themes that explained why and how America was fighting. Getting government-approved content on the big screen proved difficult for an agency without compulsory power or practical leverage, however. Nelson Poynter, a Florida newspaper publisher who headed the BMP's Los Angeles outpost, spent the better part of 1942 conferring with producers, directors, and writers, to little avail. The bureau found that reviewing scripts prior to shooting marginally improved Hollywood's output, but still far too few pictures portrayed the war in the prescribed way: as a worldwide struggle for freedom from fascist slavery. To OWI staffers—well-meaning New Dealers with hardly any experience in the movie business—Hollywood's war was all unreflective guts and glory. Frustrated, Poynter asserted himself, issuing detailed scenario and dialogue suggestions to Paramount, the most uncooperative major studio, in the fall of 1942, after reading the script for *So Proudly We Hail* (1943), a particularly troublesome project about nurses serving in Bataan. Soon thereafter, Poynter's boss, Lowell Mellett, the former OGR chief who now directed the BMP's domestic branch, asked studios to submit all screenplays to the OWI for preapproval.[26]

Variety accused the OWI of censorship as studio brass staged a minor revolt. Poynter and Mellett's coordinated moves bespoke of government encroachment, and executives were not about to surrender significant control. Producers generally resisted input from outsiders—officials, censors, anyone—regarding cinematic content unless it somehow worked to their advantage. As successful businesspeople, moguls' overriding purpose was to turn a profit, not to teach lessons (at least not overtly), which long experience had taught made for poor ticket sales. "If you want to send a message, use Western Union," independent producer Samuel Goldwyn is said to have quipped. That adage neatly summarized Hollywood's aversion to on-screen didacticism, including the recommended teachings of OWI bureaucrats, interloping representatives of a temporary agency with no clue about how to make movies, let alone good ones. To commercial filmmakers, the bromides suggested by OWI propagandists—wordy soliloquies about freedom, boring discussions of the war's meaning, mawkish dramatizations of unity—seemed destined to be box office poison.

Negotiations reached an impasse not because the studios were unsympathetic to the Roosevelt administration's political agenda. Quite the opposite, in fact. Prior to 1939, Hollywood movies were generally apolitical when it came to foreign affairs. The PCA, the industry's internal censor formed in 1934 to forestall calls for greater public oversight of immoral films, is best known for enforcing the Production Code's prohibitions on foul language and graphic depictions of sex and violence. However, it also muzzled politically conscious filmmakers. Citing "industry policy," the PCA, led by Joseph Breen, a lay conservative Catholic, routinely excised foreign politics, social commentary, and other such potentially controversial content from films before they reached the public. Breen's office

worked with the Foreign Department, an arm of the Motion Picture Producers and Distributors of America (MPPDA) known as the "little State
Department," to delete all but the vaguest hints of positions about global
affairs from exported movies and thus maximize international receipts.
Whereas "propaganda" filled the screen elsewhere, MPPDA president
Will H. Hays crowed in 1938 that Hollywood's movies remained sources
of "pure entertainment."[27]

That policy had an unfortunate by-product, however: Hollywood, arguably the world's most influential entertainer, remained largely silent
as Hitler rose. Some observers bristled at the industry's timid editorial
line, arguing that Hollywood had a moral obligation to educate viewers
about the evils of Nazism. The studios needed to produce more films that
engaged the real world and fewer that provided means of escape from
it. Frank Nugent opined in 1938 that Hollywood was wasting its vast collective talent on diversionary entertainment while the shadow of war
haunted the globe. The chief *New York Times* film critic called on filmmakers to achieve a higher "purpose" by redirecting their attention away
from "gangsters, shysters, cattle-rustlers and opium-smugglers" and
toward "some mature aspect of the world in which we live." Similarly, in
January 1939, MacLeish ascribed a recent box office downturn to Hollywood's disconnect with its fan base: the movie capital remained mired
in the habit of supplying mindless schlock while demand increased for
sober fare appropriate for serious times.[28]

Progressive filmmakers took aim at industry policy. Its close ties with
FDR's administration and release of socially conscious movies—including
Little Caesar (1930), a gangster picture starring Edward G. Robinson, and
I Am a Fugitive from a Chain Gang (1932) and *Black Fury* (1935), exposés
of southern prisons and coal mining, respectively—had earned Warner
Bros. a reputation as "the Roosevelt studio." On-screen endorsement of
liberal causes and of the New Deal in particular translated rather easily
into support for the president's increasingly internationalist foreign political agenda. In 1939, the same year that the surviving brothers Warner—
Albert, Harry, and Jack—joined the Hollywood Anti-Nazi League, a
Popular Front organization formed three years earlier to raise political
consciousness and inject antifascist messages into mainstream movies,
Harry published an article in the *Christian Science Monitor* that challenged the conventional thinking in Hollywood. While conceding that
producers had an overriding fiduciary responsibility "to make enjoy-
able, box-office entertainment," he argued that the gathering "dangers to
our institutions and our principles of government" gave rise to an addi-

tional obligation—that is, "to educate, to stimulate and demonstrate [on-screen] the fundamentals of free government." For filmmakers, whose new mission was doubly important since they controlled "the most universally understood medium ever devised," the choice was stark: "The motion picture can be a great power for peace and good will or, if we shirk our obvious duty, it can stand idly by and let the world go to pot."[29]

Independent producer Walter Wanger targeted the "creed that the motion picture industry must offend no one" in the October 1939 issue of *Foreign Affairs*, the journal of record of the American foreign policy establishment. Starting from the premise that movies acted as "America's most direct ambassadors to the masses of the world," Wanger, whose controversial film *Blockade* (1938, United Artists) starring Henry Fonda tested PCA limits by siding with the Republicans in the ongoing Spanish Civil War, insisted that Hollywood ought to work alongside Washington to advance U.S. interests. Filmmakers could do so by reminding foreign audiences threatened by the wave of authoritarianism then inundating the globe "that there still exists a way of life in which the individual" counted and freedom reigned. The typical American screenplay, Wanger wrote, "presents a perpetual epic of the ordinary unregimented individual. This individual chooses a profession, travels at will, loves whom he pleases, outguesses the boss and wisecracks the government. At evening he returns to his home without terror; when he is abed no knock at the door freezes his heart. Surely it is not flag-waving to believe that this simple miracle, the routine of freedom . . . may bring cheer and thought to peoples less fortunate. In no other way can they receive the message."[30]

Wanger would go on to repeat this theme in the *American Journal of Sociology*, the November 1941 edition of which was devoted entirely to the issue of wartime morale. The filmmaker boasted that movies were primed to serve "as instruments of democratic communication" insofar as they could "dramatize anything," international politics included. As such, cinema could provide a vehicle "for inspiring the citizens of a democracy with loyalty, conviction, and courage." If a picture was worth ten thousand words, then "one moving picture which talks and sings and laughs, which re-creates reality with a verisimilitude accomplished by no other medium, is worth ten million words." To unleash film's power, Wanger concluded, movie producers only awaited marching orders from the country's foreign policy experts and their help in keeping open worldwide channels of "free speech."[31]

Hays was more cautious, but even he came around. In his March 1939 report to MPPDA members, he noted that the industry had revised its editorial policy to meet the maturing tastes of its customers, who now demanded pictures that entertained yet also engaged the real world. Accordingly, the association's president endorsed films that "dramatized present-day social conditions," including those that "dealt with issues of war and peace" or "discussed the values of our present-day democracy."[32]

Hollywood's politicization—manifested on the silver screen not only in anti-Nazi movies starting with Warner Bros.' *Confessions of a Nazi Spy* in 1939 but also in internationalist, pro-Allied productions to come—had several causes. Germany's invasion of Poland and the outbreak of war in Europe in September 1939 empowered those who favored taking off the gloves. The personal politics of movie moguls, who called the shots in Hollywood's studio system, determining what did and did not appear in the nation's theaters, cannot be discounted. A select list of the most powerful Jews in the film business reads like a Hollywood who's who: the Warner brothers; Louis B. Mayer, head of MGM; Carl Laemmle, builder of Universal Pictures; William Fox, creator of what evolved into Twentieth Century–Fox; and Nicholas Schenck, president of Loew's, MGM's parent company. Troubled, to say the least, by the Nazis' extreme anti-Semitism, these men enlisted the industry in the fight against Hitler. Non-Jews, including Daryl F. Zanuck, Fox's powerful vice president in charge of production, took up the cause as well.[33]

As fortune would have it, commercial developments made on-screen politicking profitable, nullifying the PCA's rule. Beginning in 1933, the German Nazi Party restricted Hollywood imports on the grounds that American movies were Jewish-made and thus unfit for public consumption. Seven years later, that ban was extended to cover all areas under Berlin's control, which included Austria, Czechoslovakia, Belgium, France, and Norway. Although loosely enforced, that prohibition, mimicked by Rome, removed any concern that antifascist productions would offend viewers in those areas, since from Hollywood's perspective, that market no longer existed. Not incidentally, the ban also provided an incentive for Hollywood to create pro-Allied movies, as the British market grew to become by far the industry's largest source of overseas revenue.[34]

Hollywood's development of a political conscience also owed something to an improved relationship with the government. A cornerstone of the Hollywood-Washington corporatist alliance was laid when a legal matter was disposed in the industry's favor. In 1938, the U.S. Department of Justice, responding to complaints from independent producers and theater owners, sued the major studios for violating the Sherman Antitrust Act. Faced with the real and financially devastating possibility of losing their theater chains, studio representatives, led by the Warner brothers and Hays, turned to the White House for relief. Harry Warner asked President Roosevelt's closest confidante, Secretary of Commerce Harry Hopkins, to intervene on Hollywood's behalf on the grounds that its products advanced the national interest. Movies fostered patriotism at home and generated goodwill for the United States abroad, the studio head argued. Furthermore, pictures bolstered the nation's economy by hawking American-made goods to foreign consumers. Hopkins heard about "the untold benefit derived by the many American industries whose products and wares are shown in our pictures. Electric refrigerators, gas stoves, automobiles, radios, furniture, bathroom-fixtures and a hundred and one other items are daily being sold all over the world by America's greatest salesman—the American film. Our films," Warner added, "shriek 'Buy American.'" The commerce secretary evidently bought the argument. In July 1940, he persuaded federal prosecutors to issue a consent decree allowing the studios to retain their theaters in exchange for discontinuing some unfair distribution practices, such as blind and block booking.[35]

In all likelihood, Hopkins assisted executives in exchange for cinematic support of Roosevelt's defense policies. A similar quid pro quo already had been struck with radio networks. Mellett, the White House's main point of contact with the motion picture industry, informed Roosevelt in December 1940 that an "effective plan" for collaboration with Hollywood was "being developed." Early in 1941, Mellett notified FDR that "the motion picture industry is pretty well living up to its offers of cooperation. Practically everything being shown on the screen, from newsreel to fiction[,] that touches on our national purpose is of the right sort. And there is a lot of it, perhaps almost as much as the picture patrons can take." Moreover, the grateful Warners also promised the president "to do all in our power . . . to show the American people the worthiness of the cause for which the free peoples of Europe are making such tremendous sacrifices." Roosevelt himself sent a cryptic note read before that year's Academy Awards ceremony thanking the industry for its support.[36] That the White House aided filmmakers and ran the risk of having that help exposed by political opponents speaks to officials' confidence in cinema's ability to channel mass opinion.

Hollywood had stood at loggerheads with the OWI at the end of 1942 because Poynter had nothing to offer moviemakers aside from the thanks of a grateful nation. Wartime propaganda did not yet benefit Hollywood financially. The situation changed in early 1943, in part because of the foreign market. The U.S. Office of Censorship, responsible for vetting all incoming and outgoing mail, films, radio broadcasts, and other communications, possessed the authority to determine which productions received export licenses. Most movies did, as censors denied licenses only to a small minority deemed security risks. Overseas BMP chief Ulric Bell, however, arranged to have censors begin to withhold licenses from a broader category of movies that OWI analysts determined did not conform to the government's propaganda guidelines and were thus inappropriate for overseas viewers.[37]

Without licenses, studios could not access the foreign market, a major source of revenue. So the OWI gained considerable leverage by virtue of controlling the issuance of tickets to that market. The maneuver paid immediate dividends, improving publicists' ability to manage cinematic content. Bell reported that executives now took the agency's opinion "a great deal more seriously," and he ascribed the "high efficacy" of the BMP's oversight "to the weight we have been putting upon the overseas angle." An internal OWI study bore out his opinion: the office subsequently eliminated 71 percent of the "negative propaganda values" discovered in the scripts and rough cuts of more than four hundred Hollywood movies.[38]

Bell's strategy, though bold, added the OWI to Hollywood's list of federal partners. Propagandists needed a healthy industry, and Bell resorted to export control neither to crush Hollywood's independence nor ruin its commerce. Rather, his strategy established ground rules by which both parties were expected to play: filmmakers produced wholesome, patriotic entertainment, and in exchange, officials opened foreign markets. As the BMP's Robert Riskin, a screenwriter with Frank Capra's *Mr. Deeds Goes to Town* (1936) and *Meet John Doe* (1941) among his credits, wrote, the agency sought to "safeguard" the industry's "economic progress" as long as Hollywood, a potent weapon in the global war of ideas, produced the "right kind" of movies—that is, those reflecting well on the United States.[39]

Developing a mutually beneficial relationship with the Department of State, the industry's third and final corporatist ally, took longer, primarily because diplomats were slow to realize how movies could further U.S. designs in the world. U.S. cultural diplomacy was an innovation of World War II; never before had the State Department practiced it in any systematic way. The Division of Cultural Relations was created in 1938, when the need to counter Nazi propaganda, which had won converts across the globe since 1933, finally overcame internal resistance to instituting such a nontraditional diplomatic practice. Even then, U.S. efforts were limited. The division targeted only the Western Hemisphere, and it sought neither to enhance U.S. national security nor to evangelize American values. Rather, its idealistic mission was to build goodwill, to evince good neighborliness, in America's backyard. More to the point, public diplomats neglected pop culture, deemed too vulgar and thus entirely unsuitable for cultivating foreign elites, the program's exclusive target audience. Instead, the division's first director, Ben M. Cherrington, a former University of Denver international relations professor, tapped what he and his staff knew best: high culture, officially defined as the nation's premier "intellectual and cultural works," including academic exchanges, fine art exhibitions, and classical music performances.[40]

Some films met that subjective standard, offering insight into how cultural diplomats perceived Hollywood. The Division of Cultural Relations launched a nontheatrical film program in mid-1939 that sent documentaries (but not commercial pictures) produced by state and federal agencies, educational institutions, and nongovernmental organizations to U.S. missions for display to select foreign audiences. The program's purpose was to counterbalance the harm done to both diplomatic relations and America's international reputation by some Hollywood movies.[41]

Diplomats believed that Hollywood unnecessarily complicated U.S. foreign relations. Envoys, the butts of the Marx Brothers' antiestablishment jokes in *Duck Soup*, a 1933 satire of statecraft, could catalog the pictures that caused minor diplomatic incidents even after PCA oversight began in 1934. Chinese consulate officials raised objections to *West of Shanghai*, a 1937 Warner Bros. drama about a group of Westerners held hostage by an evil Chinese warlord. *Devil's Island* (1939) implicitly critiqued the French justice system—the plotline followed the pitiable fate of a good man wrongfully sent to and mistreated at the infamous penal colony—and consequently angered the French consulate. Italy protested *Idiot's Delight*, a 1939 MGM adaptation of Sherwood's hit 1936 Broadway play, which saw Gable and his fellow travelers caught in the crossfire of a European war started by the aggression of an unidentified country (Italy, perhaps?).[42]

Other commercial productions, although wildly popular, left foreign viewers with poor impressions of the United States, its society, and its institutions. The PCA had cleaned up the movies, but the Production Code did not outlaw Hollywood's stock-in-trade. Portrayals of crime or adultery were not banned. Rather, such on-screen acts were merely to be balanced with a "compensating moral value," meaning that the offender received just punishment for his or her transgression. That loophole legitimized gangster movies, a hit Hollywood genre of the 1930s that exasperated public diplomats by perpetuating America's image as a country riddled with crime and violence. Nor did the code spell the end of another cinematic mainstay—the little guy struggling against the powers that be. That David versus Goliath motif resonated during the Great Depression, when the portion of movies portraying the rich and powerful as misanthropic spiked from 5 to 60 percent, according to one estimate. Granted, Charlie Chaplin's plucky Little Tramp character, caught in the wheels of industry in *Modern Times* (1936), Will Rogers's populism, and the Marx Brothers' anarchic assaults on the establishment all celebrated the ordinary person's triumph over adversity. But such fare could also be read as indictments of the corruption, poverty, and disenfranchisement that wracked depression-era America. A State Department official heard complaints to that effect in 1941, when a British counterpart noted that Hollywood's stock characters—the vamp, the gangster, the greedy businessman—created "false and harmful impressions" of the United States abroad.[43]

Perhaps no movie jaundiced diplomats more than Capra's *Mr. Smith Goes to Washington* (1939). The second installment in the director's populist trilogy, which also included *Mr. Deeds Goes to Town* and *Meet John Doe, Mr. Smith* tells the story of Jefferson Smith (played by James Stewart), an idealistic young everyman and surprise appointee to the U.S. Senate. Naive, patriotic, and brimming with faith in the American experiment, Smith goes to Washington, only to be disillusioned when his pet bill to create a boys camp on unused land is foiled by Jim Taylor (Edward Arnold), his state's corrupt political boss, and Senator Joseph Harrison Payne (Claude Rains), Taylor's compromised stooge. Taylor and Payne secretly own the land in question. Their scheme is to introduce legislation authorizing the construction of an unneeded public works project on the land, which they then plan to sell to the government at an inflated price. When Smith threatens to expose their plot, Taylor and Payne instigate a baseless congressional investigation of the junior senator, alleging that he engineered the fraud. But before his fellow senators can reach a verdict, a desperate Smith launches a marathon filibuster, which succeeds when the conflicted, guilt-ridden Payne confesses and exonerates Smith, who is carried, exhausted but triumphant, from the Senate floor.

Mr. Smith is remembered as a populist celebration of democracy, redeemed by the title character's stubborn idealism. And many contemporaries praised Capra for endorsing the American political system after his film's premiere at Washington's Constitution Hall in October 1939, just one month after the outbreak of war in Europe. Other viewers were left with an entirely different impression, however. Senator James F. Byrnes, a future secretary of state, told the *Christian Science Monitor* that the movie misled the American people into believing "that 95 out of 96 Senators are corrupt." The South Carolina Democrat called the film "outrageous, exactly the kind of picture that dictators of totalitarian governments would like to have their subjects believe exists in a democracy." Punitive actions were threatened against Columbia Studios, the picture's distributor, and the *Washington Star* labeled *Mr. Smith* an "affront . . . to our representative form of government" that "ought to go over big in Berlin, Rome, and Moscow because it shows up the democratic system and our vaunted free press in exactly the colors Hitler, Mussolini, and Stalin are fond of painting them." Pete Harrison, publisher of *Harrison's Reports*, a movie trade periodical, protested Capra's attack on U.S. prestige, asking, "How will the people of other countries feel toward this country when they are made to believe that the United States Senate, the entire Congress for that matter, is controlled by crooked politicians?"[44]

The U.S. ambassador to London, Joseph P. Kennedy, a former movie entrepreneur on good terms with Hollywood, lobbied Columbia not to release *Mr. Smith Goes to Washington* in Europe, predicting that Capra's tale would be harmful if exhibited overseas. Columbia nevertheless released the picture, and some foreign audiences did interpret it as an indictment of the American political system. When *Mr. Smith* met with a mixed reception in London, Kennedy fired off a cable to his friend Hays, with a copy going to President Roosevelt: "I consider this one of the most disgraceful things I have ever seen done to our country. To permit this film to be shown in foreign countries and to give people the impression that anything like this could happen in the United States Senate is to me nothing short of criminal." Paris newspapers compared speeches made by the film's compromised senior senator to an address given by Nevada's isolationist senator, Key Pittman. The U.S. embassy in Montevideo sent a telegram to Secretary of State Cordell Hull complaining that the picture smeared the nation's reputation, already at a nadir because of its aloofness from the war. When these reports reached Washington in March 1940, Assistant Secretary of State Breckinridge Long convened a meeting to discuss what future action the State Department "might take to discourage the showing abroad of Hollywood pictures which give an unfavorable idea of the United States."[45]

Such antipathy would soon be eclipsed by a competing viewpoint that saw film as an untapped resource in liberalism's ideological struggle for survival against fascism. The drumbeat of support began in earnest in 1941, as the war (already defined as a crusade for the "Four Freedoms" by FDR in a January speech) gave the nation a spiritual purpose, ended the depression, and reinvigorated confidence in the American way of life. In February, Henry R. Luce, the influential head of the Time-Life media empire, published a *Life* magazine editorial advocating an expansive, nationalistic U.S. foreign policy. In "The American Century," which quickly became famous, Luce, born in China to Presbyterian missionaries, urged his fellow Americans "to accept wholeheartedly our duty and our opportunity as the most powerful and vital nation in the world" by exerting "the full impact of our influence." The country already possessed the tools necessary to spread its influence and preach the blessings of liberal democratic capitalism: "American jazz, Hollywood movies, American slang, American machines and patented products, are in fact the only things that every community in the world, from Zanzibar to Hamburg, recognizes in common," he wrote. Luce thus encouraged everyone from "movie men" to educators to engineers to proselytize, using their "technical and artistic skills" to broadcast an attractive "picture" of America and its ideals, institutions, and prosperity. Foreigners would eagerly welcome such optimistic visions, Luce assured his readers, "if only we have the imagination to see [them]." Public relations expert C. P. Holway made a similar argument in a less noted article that appeared in the *Nation*: Washington should launch an aggressive public diplomacy initiative, or as Holway put it, "an overpowering American advertising campaign with just one thing to sell—the American way." By showcasing the "things," "freedoms," and "opportunities" Americans enjoyed, the "message" of his proposed offensive would be that "these are the things *you* can have, in your own country, in your own home, in your own time—if you want them. Compare all these things to what you have. Then choose."[46]

Appreciation for what is now called soft power was growing. The realization that Hollywood could exert such power only grew in Washington as victory came into sight, encouraged by studio heads who needed diplomatic assistance to maximize peacetime profits. The American motion picture industry had dominated the global film market since World War I, making approximately four-fifths of all movies exhibited around the world. The major studios reaped at least 35 percent of their earnings abroad, mostly in Europe, though some estimates went as high as 50 percent. However, foreign protectionism (most egregiously in Nazi Germany and Fascist Italy, but also elsewhere) squeezed the film capital's profits. Representatives of both the State Department and the Commerce Department's Bureau of Foreign and Domestic Commerce had worked to lower such barriers throughout the interwar years, and the OWI did its bit to avoid further inhibiting cinema's free trade during the war. Yet businesspeople foresaw both opportunities and limits as they looked beyond the armistice. The postwar period promised commercial expansion insofar as Allied forces liberated areas from Axis control and international trade returned to normal. In addition, some of Hollywood's likeliest competitors—the German, Italian, French, and even Soviet film industries—would require some time to recover from fighting-induced damage, which Hollywood was fortunate enough to have avoided. Although poised on the brink of great growth, film industrialists worried that nationalist postwar governments would move to reassert their political and cultural independence, instituting distribution and exhibition set-asides, import quotas, and confiscatory taxes. Subsidized foreign competition was a concern, as was piracy. Moreover, severe trade imbalances and currency shortages vis-à-vis the United States appeared likely to result in toughened exchange restrictions on the firms' foreign profits.[47]

Executives responded to that uncertainty by strengthening ties with the Department of State, the institution best positioned to protect their global commercial interests. State, unlike the OWI, was permanent, and a core mission of its network of overseas posts was to promote American business by erasing international trade barriers. Hays spearheaded the lobbying campaign to enlist diplomats on behalf of the industry's desiderata. The MPPDA chief repeatedly reminded Secretary of State Hull and lesser officials that the studios earned a significant share of their receipts abroad, making them highly dependent on overseas markets. If foreign governments imposed artificial barriers, Hays warned, the American motion picture industry would suffer a serious downturn that would act as a drag on the entire U.S. economy, an argument that must have resonated with Washington's concerns about a postwar recession. Furthermore, he repeated the mantra that Hollywood movies acted as foreign salesmen for other American-made goods. In an October 1943 memorandum to Hull, Hays dusted off the oft-cited axiom that every foot of film shown abroad generated one dollar in U.S. export revenues: "Motion pictures carry to the world *the story of United States products*. It is inescapable that every entertainment picture is . . . an alluring and dramatic demonstration of how Americans live *and what they live with*. It is not necessary to make deliberate presentation of these products for they appear inevitably on the screen. The newest styles, the latest customs, the most recent appliances are to be seen *in use*. The hundreds of millions of desires crystallized by motion pictures make hundreds of millions of customers at home and abroad for United States manufacturers and purveyors."[48]

Hays added another appeal designed to resound in wartime Washington: Hollywood contributed to U.S. national security no less than the U.S. economy. Both popular and effective in projecting ideal versions of the American way of life, movies seemed to be perfect vehicles for conveying U.S. cultural influence, for generating soft power. Reflecting his and his fellow Americans' newfound confidence in U.S. customs, Hays boldly proclaimed that pictures could advertise "the American way of life and our democratic ideals" in the same way that they peddled American-made goods. The MPPDA president elaborated on this theme to the secretary of state, advising Hull that the film capital's products, whose global popularity was undeniable, presented "effortlessly and entertainingly the United States' message to an *interested* world." Movies sugarcoated propaganda for foreign no less than domestic audiences. Hays cautioned, however, that the industry could deliver its "message" only if diplomats intervened on its behalf and helped eliminate "crippling" foreign trade barriers.[49]

Studio executives joined the chorus in praise of Hollywood's contribution to U.S. national interests, with arguments predicated on the assumption that movies influenced non-American as well as American viewers. Fox president Spyres P. Skouras assured a State Department official in February 1944 that his firm's pictures disseminated "American ideas and ideals . . . throughout the world," thereby inculcating "the minds of the people . . . with what is kind, honest, and free." Zanuck told the *Los Angeles Times* that films exerted an unusually heavy impact on international opinion because they provided foreigners with many if not most of their impressions of the United States, adding, "If we do not succeed in showing to the world the advantages of the American way of life, then somebody else will probably come forth with another way of life that may impress the peoples of all countries more, and then all that we have fought for in this war will have been lost." Even Goldwyn conceded that "one of the most important functions of the motion picture industry" was "to present the United States in a proper light to the other nations of the world." He, like Zanuck, therefore urged his colleagues to put the best possible filmic spin on American society to avoid a "distorted viewpoint" that overemphasized "unsavory segments of our national life," including crime, scandal, and socioeconomic inequality.[50]

Such arguments received a sympathetic hearing in Washington. The idea of ensuring that the world could enjoy American films acquired greater currency during World War II, as U.S. diplomats calculated the value of the United States, on the cusp of superpowerdom, having a positive brand. Envoys came around to the view that selected films could advertise America as the country jockeyed for advantage, now and in the future. An early convert, Wallace Murray, chief of the State Department's Division of Near Eastern Affairs, advised Undersecretary Sumner Welles and Assistant Secretaries Adolf A. Berle Jr. and Breckinridge Long in February 1941 to extend the department's educational movie program. Following Margaret Thorp's lead, Murray highlighted cinema's transcendental qualities: "The power of the motion picture to reach unlettered and untraveled audiences is greater than that of any other medium. On the visual plane, a message meets with universal recognition; language is no barrier, the ability to read or even to listen is unnecessary." Cinema combined pictures, words, and music to "display" the United States in the best possible light, he wrote, making movies the ideal "method of conveying to other countries what the United States has achieved." Assistant Secretary G. Howland Shaw informed overseas posts in November 1943 of the department's arrival at the position that "the motion picture is, without question, one of the most powerful means of presenting either a true or distorted picture of life in any given country." For the first time, commercial pictures were approved for use as part of the educational film program, and missions were instructed to expand exhibitions to improve "understanding" of the United States.[51]

Film showings at embassies and consulates constituted mere drops in the bucket. Only Hollywood movies could reach the mass theatrical market, and diplomats shouldered the burden of reducing the international barriers impeding films' dissemination. Doing so was consistent with Washington's broader objective of maintaining open doors through which American products—agricultural, industrial, or cultural—could flow to reach overseas markets and foreigners' hearts and minds. Safe in the belief that American goods could win any open competition, U.S. free traders sought to liberalize the international media market. Confident that overseas audiences would be attracted to America's high standard of living, its entertaining pop culture, and its reliable press, the Roosevelt administration considered proposing the creation of so-called free zones of information in the postwar world. A presidential statement, drafted by Berle in September 1944, called for the recognition of a fifth freedom, the "freedom of information," and urged all nations to permit the unrestricted collection, transmission, and reception of news in "territories under [their] control." The White House never explicitly called on the international community to respect the free movement of information, a formula clearly aimed at the Soviet Union, a wartime ally that some policymakers considered a likely postwar adversary. Rather, it was left to Hull to offer a general endorsement during his 18 September press conference. Still, the secretary's words were meant to signal, however weakly, the administration's determination to promote U.S. influence in places such as Central and Eastern Europe, where the United States exercised little clout vis-à-vis the USSR. Berle acknowledged as much in a report to the State Department's Policy Committee prior to Hull's statement. Washington, Berle argued, should strongly condemn cultural autarky and instead promote "open spheres" in those areas where the United States otherwise would exert only nominal influence. Edward R. Stettinius Jr., named to replace Hull as secretary of state in November, similarly advised the president that in a Soviet-dominated Eastern Europe, the United States could "make its presence felt only if some degree of equal opportunity in trade, investment, and access to sources of information is preserved."[52]

In early 1944, Berle issued a memorandum announcing the department's postwar movie policy. In both content and tone, the document marked just how far envoys had come in their appreciation of popular cinema. A January draft promised official aid for the studios in gaining unfettered access to foreign markets, a policy designed to safeguard the health of a leading domestic industry whose products stimulated subsidiary businesses. Cinema's soft power was not lost on the assistant secretary, who labeled Hollywood movies America's "most potent medium of constructive propaganda in the field of international relations." Movies were such effective advertisers, he wrote, because they were entertainments "not specifically designed to reflect the American way of life or to portray democracy in action." So enthusiastic was his draft memorandum that some of Berle's colleagues worried that it pledged too much support to Hollywood. Leroy Stinebower, chief of the Division of Economic Studies, complained that the draft's rationale, if applied across the board, would result in a postwar Europe inundated with imported American goods, thereby exacerbating the continent's expected trade and currency woes and slowing its recovery.[53]

Berle dispatched a revised memorandum to most U.S. overseas posts the following month. Titled "American Motion Pictures in the Postwar World," the memo began with a sympathetic review of Hollywood's international troubles followed by an expression of Washington's desire to remove any and all obstacles "to the distribution of American films." The State Department, he wrote, had opted to back the motion picture industry because it produced one of "our principal export commodities" and was highly dependent on foreign revenue sources. Moreover, its products acted "as salesmen for American products, salesmen that are readily welcomed by their public." Most important, movies had "important intellectual value. The right kind of film can present a picture of this nation, its culture, its institutions, its method of dealing with social problems, and its people, which may be invaluable from the political, cultural and commercial point of view." Conversely, Berle warned, "the wrong kind of picture may have the opposite effect." The time had come, he stressed, for foreign service officers to internalize "the value of the American motion picture to the national welfare and the importance that the government attaches to [its] unrestricted distribution." However, he added, official assistance came with a price. Private enterprise also had an obligation to fulfill if the corporatist bargain were to be operative: "The Department desires to cooperate fully in the protection of the American motion picture industry abroad. It expects in return that the industry will cooperate wholeheartedly with this Government with a view to insuring that the pictures distributed abroad will reflect credit on the good name and reputation of this country and its institutions." Arthur L. Loew of Loew's understood Berle's implication, promising officials that the industry would pursue internal censorship with vigor, stiffening its peacetime oversight to eliminate any "evils which hitherto have been overlooked."[54]

• • •

"Everything is organized the way we want it," the MPPDA Foreign Department assured Hays after a major reorganization of the State Department in 1944 put Berle's words into administrative action, raising cinema's bureaucratic profile in the process. And so it was. Assumptions and institutions were rearranged in the crucible of war, engendering a corporatist marriage of power and culture that made possible the projection of international brotherhood. Formerly equated in the United States with totalitarianism, propaganda now seemed to accord with liberalism. Previously considered irrelevant, even harmful, to the national interest, Hollywood movies now served the country in war and peace. Journalists recorded the changes. *Variety* reported that the war had "brought home" the "full value of the motion picture as perhaps the most powerful of all communications media" in the international arena. According to *Harper's*, the United States enjoyed a "gigantic reservoir of goodwill" abroad, in no small part as a result of "Hollywood's movies which—in spite of their gangsters and incredibly swank offices and voluptuous females in satin-quilted boudoirs—have been among the most appealing representatives of our civilization because of the very fact that they were so blatantly uninterested in putting our best foot forward." Whereas diplomats of the past would have responded with a "blank stare" if asked about cinema's relevance to foreign politics, they now had a clear answer, wrote Herman Lowe, the *Philadelphia Inquirer*'s Washington correspondent. Hollywood's contribution to the war effort had made Uncle Sam "thoroughly alive to the potentialities" of movies. Foreign policy makers had discovered, albeit belatedly, "that there is ready-made in Hollywood a subtle and powerful weapon to spread the story of democracy and make friends for this country," as "millions around the world obtain most of their ideas about the United States" from Hollywood.[55]

To be sure, enthusiasts such as Lowe downplayed the paradox of propagandizing people to support a war ostensibly fought for freedom; Poynter did not make the same mistake. Disgruntled, he charged in an internal 1943 memorandum that Bell's heavy-handed approach aped "fascist methods."[56] Be that as it may, Hollywood became enmeshed in international politics during the extraordinary days of World War II. Relished by hundreds of millions of fans across the globe, the industry's product emerged as the preferred technology for engineering consent, for conditioning ordinary people to love their country, hate its enemies, and embrace its friends. No other medium—not even radio, cinema's nearest competitor—had as much ability to forge international community, combining sight and sound in an immersive, dramatic, and spellbinding experience that psychically transported theatergoers across time and space, virtually connecting them with distant peoples and worlds, including the members of the United Nations wartime coalition. Whether movies were truly magic bullets that educated even as they entertained remained to be seen, however.

2

"PRO-BRITISH-AMERICAN WAR PREACHERS" INTERNATIONALISM AT THE MOVIES, 1939–1941

Senator Gerald P. Nye had no doubt that Hollywood could move the masses. In fact, Nye and his fellow isolationists insisted that movies wielded disproportionate influence over U.S. foreign policy. The North Dakota Republican outlined the anti-interventionist case against the U.S. motion picture industry during a 1 August 1941 radio address. Speaking from St. Louis, Nye charged that films had "ceased to be instruments of entertainment" and had instead "become the most gigantic engines of propaganda in existence to rouse the war fever in America." The onetime chair of the "Merchants of Death" probe, a mid-1930s congressional investigation that accused profiteering financiers and arms manufacturers with dragging the United States into World War I, detected another international conspiracy to involve the country in an unnecessary foreign conflagration. Produced by businesspeople with a financial stake in a British victory, influenced by foreign agents operating within the United States, and made with the encouragement of an interventionist president, Hollywood's movies "tricked and lied" to millions of theatergoers, leaving them with the impressions that Nazi Germany was their worst foe, Great Britain their best friend, and war their only recourse. Evoking the predominant "magic bullet" theory, Nye likened film to a "drug" designed to cloud "the reason of the American people, set aflame their emotions, turn their hatred into a blaze, fill them with fear that Hitler will come over here and capture them, that he will steal their trade, that America must go into this war—to rouse them to a war hysteria."[1]

Hollywood's product, which Nye considered "the most powerful" propaganda instrument ever, was particularly insidious because entertainment disguised its political message. Commercial pictures were not readily identifiable as propaganda, so unsuspecting ticket buyers were receptive to whatever the films had to say. Whereas one's guard was up at, say, a political rally, the senator explained, "when you go to the movies, you go there to be entertained. You are not figuring on listening to a debate about the war. You settle yourself in your seat with your mind wide open. And then the picture starts—goes to work on you, all done by trained actors, full of drama, cunningly devised, and soft passionate music underscoring it. Before you know where you are you have actually listened to a speech designed to make you believe that Hitler is going to get you if you don't watch out. And, of course, it's a very much better speech than just an ordinary speech at a mass meeting."[2]

Nye's address served as an opening salvo in a counterattack against what one isolationist called "Pro-British-American War Preachers," shorthand for Hollywood's offending output. In September 1941, Nye and his fellow senator Burton K. Wheeler, a Montana Democrat, led a sensational congressional inquiry into Hollywood's alleged warmongering. Isolationist inquisitors were wrong about most things: anti-Semitism lurked just below (and often above) the surface of their conspiracy theory; the threat posed by Nazism to American interests (to say nothing of humanity itself) was real, not a figment of Hollywood's fertile imagination; and U.S. belligerence was necessary and just. Yet anti-interventionists were correct in identifying the remarkable tide of anti-Nazi, pro-British, interventionist movies that flooded American theaters from 1939 to 1941—punctuated by Warner Bros.' *Confessions of a Nazi Spy* (1939) and Alexander Korda's *That Hamilton Woman* (1941)—as being partly responsible for tipping the balance in the national debate about war or peace. Regardless of the extent to which movies triggered what would become a sea change in the American worldview, opponents believed that film was instrumental in causing the shift from isolationism toward internationalism. However misguided isolationists might have been, their words and actions attest to the screen's presumed influence over the public and bearing on matters of state.

So, too, do the endeavors of those identified by anti-interventionists as being responsible for what appeared in theaters. Prominent American and British figures—from President Franklin D. Roosevelt and Prime

Minister Winston S. Churchill to producer Daryl F. Zanuck and director Alfred Hitchcock—cooperated to educate Americans, on the receiving end of a transnational publicity campaign about the world situation.[3] Although driven by different motives, policymakers and filmmakers combined forces toward a single goal: to replace isolationism and Anglophobia, symbiotic cultural trends that thwarted U.S. global activism, with an internationalist, pro-British ethic supportive of greater American involvement in World War II.[4] Proponents of American involvement were unquestionably devious and manipulative, precisely as isolationists charged.[5] Yet such actions sprang from a belief that the Western democracies were in grave danger and that all the stops should be pulled out to oppose Nazism.

Commercial movies were integral to reinventing the American mindset, for they reached a vast audience and, as Nye charged, taught lessons without appearing to do so. Hollywood effectively laundered British propaganda, cleansing it of the foreignness that otherwise would have alienated American viewers. Furthermore, the silver screen made its best case for intervention by appealing to both heart and mind. An untold number of newsreels, documentaries, and features presented moviegoers with an overarching narrative coincident with that heard over the airwaves and read on the printed page: despite superficial differences, Americans shared much in common with Britons, victimized by Nazi aggression but resolute in their historic struggle for freedom from dictatorship; Britain's fight was America's as well, and Americans had a moral obligation to defend liberty, the United Kingdom, and U.S. interests from the fascist menace. If nuance got lost, the translation of European events to the studio stage nonetheless spoke to larger truths and captivated the popular imagination, as evidenced by box office receipts, letters, and reviews. As a result, the big screen—a gigantic engine of propaganda that dwarfed whatever forces the isolationists could muster—crossed the Atlantic to bring the world home, making Britain and its travails seem so palpable and personal as to provide sympathetic American audiences with a vicarious experience that psychologically reunited them with their British relatives. Even before Pearl Harbor, Americans took crucial first steps toward internationalism.

• • •

Insulated by two oceans, preoccupied with the Great Depression, and disillusioned by their mission abroad during World War I, Americans had largely withdrawn from international affairs when European war erupted again in September 1939. The political culture of the 1930s articulated the widespread view that U.S. involvement in the Great War had been a great mistake. Senator Nye's investigation of arms dealers coincided with the publication of *Merchants of Death*, a 1934 Book of the Month Club selection. The antiwar *All Quiet on the Western Front* (1930), Universal's adaption of Erich Maria Remarque's hit novel, won an Oscar for Best Picture. To avoid such costly missteps in the future, Congress passed a series of Neutrality Acts starting in 1935 that restricted American trade with or loans to belligerents, Great Britain included.[6]

Anglophobia and isolationism went hand in hand, for opposition to Britain registered a vote against U.S. involvement in foreign affairs. To be sure, the United States and the United Kingdom shared a great deal—heritage, language, culture, and increasingly geopolitical interests—all of which had produced a rapprochement between the two countries at the dawn of the twentieth century. Not surprisingly, popular culture reflected those ties. Hollywood released a number of pictures in the 1930s that admired Britain, Britons, and British customs. Literature and folklore inspired *A Midsummer Night's Dream* (1935), *The Adventures of Robin Hood* (1938), and *Wuthering Heights* (1938), to name a few. History provided the backdrop for *The Private Life of Henry VIII*, winner of the Academy Award as 1933's Best Picture; *The Charge of the Light Brigade* (1936), a Crimean War drama starring Errol Flynn; and *The Private Lives of Elizabeth and Essex* (1939), a romantic biopic of Queen Elizabeth I with Bette Davis in the title role. Even the British Empire made good theater: Hollywood's imperial epics—among them *The Lives of a Bengal Lancer* (1935), *Wee Willie Winkie* (1937), and *Gunga Din* (1939)—performed well at the box office despite American anticolonialism.[7]

Even so, Anglo-American relations deteriorated in the interwar period, as Anglophobia spiked along with isolationism, and antipathy more than counterbalanced whatever amity existed. From the vantage point of the twenty-first century, when Anglo-American unity is taken for granted, it is easy to forget that there was a time when Anglophobia was as American as apple pie. Anti-British attitudes enjoyed a long tradition in the United States, stretching back to the "ancient grudge," shorthand for the events leading to the American Revolution. American nationalists routinely suspected Britain's motives, believing that its worldly statesmen sought to hoodwink their untutored U.S. counterparts. Irish and German Americans were traditionally hostile to England. London provided a convenient scapegoat for depression-era inhabitants of the rural West, Midwest, and South, the heartlands of isolationism and populism, who regarded the city as the center of moneyed "interests," a vaguely defined group including bankers, industrialists, and the powerful who exploited ordinary folk. Moreover, liberals and many African Americans, including Walter White of the National Association for the Advancement of Colored People, criticized Britain's domestic class system and its empire. Polls showed that most Americans believed that the British oppressed their colonies, and William E. Borah, a progressive Republican senator from Idaho, declared that Britons had not "the slightest conception of real democracy. Has England ever hinted that she would give up India or any of her imperialistic rights?"[8]

Isolationism and Anglophobia dovetailed in recollections of World War I. Britain was blamed for duping the United States into joining what in retrospect seemed to be a pointless fight in which doughboys had died not to make the world safe for democracy but to settle age-old European political scores. Subsequent congressional and academic investigations, the lifeblood of the anti-interventionist movement, charged that British propagandists had manipulated American public opinion, inflaming it to create an artificial basis of support for U.S. involvement. It became widely known, for instance, that the Royal Navy had severed the cable linking Germany to the United States, meaning that all wartime news that emanated from Europe was filtered through British censors. James M. Read's *Atrocity Propaganda* (1941) revisited the sensational *Report of the Committee on Alleged German Outrages*, better known as the Bryce Report after the committee's chair, Lord James Bryce, London's former ambassador to the United States. Released in 1915, the Bryce Report had convinced a large segment of the American public that during the invasion of Belgium, German soldiers had slaughtered infants and raped and butchered women. Read found the Bryce Report's claims to be false, and such scholarly treatises as James Duane Squires's *British Propaganda at Home and in the United States* (1935), Horace C. Peterson's *Propaganda for War* (1939), and Harold Lavine and James Wechsler's *War Propaganda and the United States* (1940) similarly exposed British propaganda. During the Great War, Peterson wrote, John Bull had deviously crafted "a campaign to create a pro-British attitude of mind among Americans, to get American sympathies and interests so deeply involved . . . that it would be impossible for this country to remain neutral." Even more alarming, Lavine and Wechsler, whose volume went to press in May 1940, detailed London's publicity efforts in the United States during both world wars, implying that Britain was at it again.[9]

The American mind-set did become of paramount importance to British foreign policy makers following Germany's offensive in the spring of 1940 and Churchill's subsequent replacement of Neville Chamberlain as prime minister. France's swift fall suddenly left Britain facing Nazi Germany alone, without a reliable European ally. The chiefs of staff concluded in late May that the British government, short of financial, industrial, and military resources, could not hope to succeed without extensive assistance from the United States. As one British Foreign Office diplomat put it, "The position quite simply is that America has it in her power to enable us to win the war, or to prevent us from winning. We should therefore recognize that we want all the help Americans will give us."[10]

Appealing to the American people appeared key to tapping the U.S. supply line. As a consequence of regular elections, partisan politics, and the separation of powers, "public opinion [is] the decisive factor on all the more controversial questions of public policy," including aid to Britain, explained Lord Lothian, ambassador to Washington from August 1939 until his death in December 1940. If clever publicity could somehow touch off an internationalist, pro-British groundswell, the reasoning went, favorable pressure could be brought to bear on Congress and FDR, a political animal who scanned at least five daily newspapers and monitored opinion surveys.[11]

Lothian gained company in calling for an aggressive propaganda campaign aimed at Americans. In July 1940, the American Division of the British Ministry of Information (MOI), the official propaganda agency, stated, "The war has reached a stage where American opinion is of crucial importance." With a nod toward the Roosevelt administration, the MOI added, "There are at last real opportunities of influencing that opinion in a direction favorable to us." And the Foreign Office's Stephen Childs returned to London that month from a fact-finding tour of the United States with the recommendation that Britain launch a propaganda offensive, which he termed "an instrument of war second to none." The overriding objective of a concerted campaign featuring films, the press, and radio, he argued, should be "to bring about as rapidly as possible an American determination to go to extreme limits in the matter of extending assistance to Great Britain so as to ensure victory over the allied dictatorships."[12]

Given Americans' sensitivity to outside manipulation, however, opinion makers had to be very careful not to be caught red-handed. "Anything which looks like propaganda rouses in the Americans a kind of cold fury," Lothian observed. British leaders consequently instituted a "no propaganda" policy that prohibited the direct distribution of materials to or in the United States, materials that were sure to provoke a backlash and set back London's cause if exposed. The rare occasions when Britons were caught meddling with U.S. opinion only reinforced the need to keep a low profile. During the winter of 1939–40, for example, *The Lion Has Wings*, a feature produced by Alexander Korda, premiered in American theaters. Starring Merle Oberon and Ralph Richardson, the docudrama was originally intended only for domestic purposes—that is, to buck up British morale with a heroic portrait of the Royal Air Force (RAF) and patriotic statements about the country's war aims (which amounted to the reestablishment of "truth and beauty and fair play and kindliness," according to Oberon's melodramatic speech). Still, *The Lion Has Wings* crossed the Atlantic when an overenthusiastic Korda, who would go on to produce Graham Greene's *The Third Man* (1949), decided that the film would make a favorable impression on American moviegoers. The MOI agreed and not only split the film's proceeds with Korda but also underwrote his promotional tour of the United States. When the Foreign Office got wind of the plan, it bemoaned the MOI's "deplorable lack of good sense" and foresight. The Foreign Office's F. R. Cowell worried that the episode would heap "unfortunate results upon us from a policy angle since, by staking a claim on the proceeds, the film becomes to a large extent the child of His Majesty's Government, the very thing, of course, which we want to avoid."[13]

Cowell's concerns proved well founded. Although a success in the United Kingdom, *The Lion Has Wings* proved an unmitigated disaster in the United States, where audiences easily spotted its pedigree. *Time* identified it as "Britain's first propaganda film of World War II." Worse, the magazine alerted readers that the British had "forgotten none of their talent for first-rate propaganda . . . developed during World War I" and had evidently again determined to manipulate American moviegoers. *Commonweal*, a Catholic periodical, called the movie "undisguised propaganda." *Variety* questioned the picture's honesty, reporting that its overoptimistic depiction of British air power struck viewers as incongruous with the Phony War's inactivity. As scenes of the RAF's actual September 1939 raid on the Kiel Canal played on-screen, one spectator remarked, "If it's as easy as that, the war'd already be over."[14]

Overt official involvement doomed another feature, *49th Parallel*, based on a screenplay written by the legendary filmmaking team of Michael Powell and Emeric Pressburger. In August 1940, Minister of Information Sir Alfred Duff Cooper opted to fund the project based on director Powell's promise that it would "scare the pants off the Americans and bring them into the war sooner." However, production delays prevented the movie, about a German U-boat crew's vain attempt to cross the U.S.-Canadian border, from reaching U.S. theaters until early 1942, well after the Japanese attack on Pearl Harbor had rendered its original purpose moot. Moreover, the MOI's involvement again raised the specter of foreign manipulation among attendees at an advance screening of the film.[15]

Such missteps lent the MOI a reputation for incompetence—domestic critics dubbed it the "Ministry of Muddle"—and proved the wisdom of the "no propaganda" rule. Although the policy proscribed untruthful, totalitarian-style propaganda that could be traced back to official British sources, it did not outlaw other types of persuasion. Ostensibly accurate "information" was permitted, a semantic loophole that enabled the British Broadcasting Corporation (BBC) to beam programming directly to American radio listeners and the British Library of Information and the British Press Service to establish outposts in the United States. The policy also permitted indirect distribution of British propaganda. Under a publicity-by-proxy arrangement, officials could and did establish working relationships with the American media—trusted journalists, radio correspondents, and filmmakers, who then disseminated the information (laundered and by all appearances homegrown) to consumers. To have maximum effect, in other words, British propaganda required cover and the accompanying credibility and plausible deniability provided by friendly U.S. media.[16]

The American motion picture industry provided some of that necessary cover. British propagandists could not have gotten across their messages without Hollywood's help, for the major studios' oligopoly over production, distribution, and exhibition determined what appeared in theaters. It was fortunate for Britain, then, that Hollywood's politicization had rendered the movie colony's elite quite sympathetic. The same liberal (Zanuck, for example) and/or Jewish (including Walter Wanger and Harry M. and Jack L. Warner) executives who opposed the Nazis supported Great Britain, Germany's prime Western European adversary. These men joined not only the Hollywood Anti-Nazi League but also the pro-British and interventionist Fight for Freedom Committee, effectively throwing their political weight behind Hitler's last remaining opponent. Wanger and the Warner brothers became top West Coast contributors to Fight for Freedom and its predecessor, the Century Group, which counted among its causes support for greater U.S. aid to the United Kingdom. Those activists prevailed on the Motion Picture Producers and

Distributors of America (MPPDA), the industry's trade association and governing body, and its constituent internal censor, the Production Code Administration (PCA), to permit productions that commented on contemporary geopolitics. Moreover, industry leaders established a quid pro quo with the White House by which the Roosevelt administration insulated the major studios from antitrust litigation in exchange for pictures supportive of the president's ever more internationalist and specifically pro-British foreign policy. All such steps toward political engagement led to films that explicitly took sides against Nazi Germany (the first of which was *Confessions of a Nazi Spy*) and for Great Britain.[17]

Not surprisingly, then, when two British filmmakers with official ties traveled to Los Angeles in 1940 for exploratory talks with studio executives on improving Anglo-American cinematic coordination, they received a warm hearing. Sidney Bernstein, owner of the Granada theater chain and an adviser to the MOI's Films Division, and A. W. Jarratt, a General Films Distributors executive then serving in the Royal Naval Reserve, went on separate missions to California in July and October, respectively. During the meetings, Zanuck, independent producer Samuel Goldwyn, Louis B. Mayer of Metro-Goldwyn-Mayer (MGM), and Harry and Jack Warner, among others, expressed interest in distributing select British-made pictures in the United States and incorporating pro-British, internationalist themes in Hollywood productions. Bernstein informed London that he detected "definitely pro-British sentiments" among Hollywood's elite. Yet both he and Jarratt also reported that their interlocutors, though receptive, needed more cultivation and inducements before they could be considered fully on board.[18]

Even friendly moguls needed a financial incentive to proselytize, and foreign commerce combined with the Roosevelt administration's patronage to provide that incentive. Moreover, as discussed in chapter 1, Nazi Germany unwittingly provided American movie moguls with an inducement to produce pro-British films by banning Hollywood pictures in August 1940.

Another situation threatened to prevent the industry from reaping its financial windfall, but the matter's resolution by high-level Anglo-American diplomats ultimately kept the propaganda machine operating. Hollywood movies had dominated the British domestic market since World War I, ruining local producers and distributors in the process. Parliament tried to keep American films at bay with the Cinematograph Film Acts of 1927 and 1938, which set quotas on the number of foreign films that could be shown in the United Kingdom. The American studios nevertheless held their ground, and in 1939, they expected to earn $35 million there.[19]

Hollywood earnings acquired heightened importance in wartime Britain. In the eyes of British Treasury and Board of Trade officials, $35 million represented an extravagant drain on the United Kingdom's extremely limited dollar reserves, which had been set aside to purchase war materials from the United States. Hollywood pictures' essential contribution to home front morale prevented the board from taking the simplest remedial action, further import curtailment. Instead, in October 1939, Oliver H. Stanley, the board's president, proposed restricting the proportion of receipts that the U.S. firms could exchange into dollars from sterling and remit home. Stanley's proposal would have allowed the studios to realize only 50 percent of their 1939 profits and just $5 million annually thereafter.[20]

Alarmed, MPPDA president Will H. Hays turned for help to an old acquaintance, U.S. ambassador to London Joseph P. Kennedy. Kennedy had a good feel for the movie business, in which he had been involved prior to becoming ambassador. Over a decade ending in 1936, he had made a fortune by investing in Radio-Keith-Orpheum, reorganizing Paramount, and independently producing films. Kennedy agreed with Hays's analysis that Stanley's proposal would virtually eliminate Hollywood's leading overseas revenue source, thereby bankrupting the industry and perhaps even precipitating a wider crisis in the U.S. economy, which was still recovering from the Great Depression. The ambassador negotiated with the Board of Trade and the Treasury on the MPPDA's behalf, even going so far as to grant the association special access to the State Department's code for encrypting its transatlantic communications, an unusual liberty designed to avoid the prying eyes of British intelligence. A noted Anglophobe, Kennedy drove a hard bargain in his talks with Stanley. November 1939 saw the conclusion of the Films Exchange Agreement, whereby the studios could remit all of their accumulated profits and half of their 1940 receipts, a significant improvement. Delighted, the head of the MPPDA's Foreign Department, Frederick L. Herron, thanked Kennedy for obtaining "such magnificent terms."[21]

Transatlantic movie finance and propaganda again intersected in the autumn of 1940, when the Films Exchange Agreement came up for annual renewal. Treasury and Board of Trade negotiators repeated their push to reduce Hollywood's remittances. This time, however, the British ambassador, Lothian, who was spearheading the effort to get the American media behind Britain's cause, came to the industry's defense. During renewal talks, Lothian encountered Hays at a Century Group meeting, and Hays took the opportunity to press for the liberalization of U.K. exchange controls. Perhaps sensing a chance to get Hollywood more firmly on London's side, Lothian promised "to find a solution agreeable to all." Thereafter, the ambassador indeed urged his government to meet the industry's needs. And U.S. diplomats credited him with convincing Permanent Undersecretary of the Treasury Sir Horace Wilson to increase to $12.9 million from $5 million the allowable 1941 transfers. From London, the U.S. embassy's films officer, Alan N. Steyne, reported, "Lothian backed up [Hollywood's position] one hundred percent."[22]

If the deal reduced annual remittances as a bone of contention, it left unresolved the issue of the industry's accumulated blocked profits. By the end of 1940, the studios had accrued $18 million in blocked earnings, a figure expected to reach $35 million by the end of 1941. The 1939 Films Exchange Agreement had stipulated that terms would be renegotiated if Britain's foreign exchange situation improved. The studios reckoned that the March 1941 passage of the Lend-Lease Act, which allowed Britain cash-free access to American goods, met that test. Hays toured Washington the same day that Roosevelt signed the act, meeting first with Undersecretary of State Sumner Welles and Secretary of State Cordell Hull. The MPPDA head asked the two officials to see to it that the studios received their accumulated funds, citing "the special contribution which [the industry] is making to the cause of the democracies in the way of cultivating friendship for them." To Welles, Hays "stressed the absolute need of the industry to obtain these funds to carry on the services so essential at present to both governments."[23]

A veteran campaigner for free trade, Hull declared himself "completely in sympathy" and instructed his department to work the issue. Assistant Secretary of State Breckinridge Long recorded in his diary that Hull wanted "to do all he can for the Movie people" because "their pictures are a valuable—and, in our way of life, a necessary and almost indispensable link between Government action and popular psychology." Hull also arranged for Hays to meet with Roosevelt. The president expressed "considerable interest in this matter" and set up a talk with Lord Halifax, who had recently become the British ambassador to the United States following Lothian's death.[24]

Ever the lobbyist, Hays began by briefing Halifax on Hollywood's record of support. Filmmakers "were on [Halifax's] side of the table" and wished for that spirit of cooperation to continue. For it do so, however, the association's members needed London to compromise. Hull and Long subsequently made the same pitch to British officials. The secretary of state urged Ambassador Halifax to take up the matter with the Foreign Office. Long raised the issue with Sir Gerald Campbell, the newly appointed head of British Information Services, the embassy's public affairs arm, adding the thinly veiled warning "that the motion picture industry is a very potent factor in the formation of public opinion in the United States."[25]

Embassy officials sensed that opportunities for influencing American opinion would grow if they aided Hollywood. During his talk with Hays, Halifax wondered aloud whether his government's refusal to compromise would not lead to a campaign in the American press against the apparent British seizure of private assets and pledged to "find a solution." So earnest was the ambassador that U.S. officials assumed that he intended to "drastically alter policy in some way." Indeed, Halifax thereafter urged the British Treasury to release all of Hollywood's blocked assets, stressing the president's and the secretary of state's personal interest in the matter. His pressure apparently carried some weight, as Chancellor of the Exchequer Sir Kingsley Wood announced in November yet another settlement favorable to Hollywood: despite Britain's chronic currency shortage, the studios would be permitted to remit half of their accrued blocked profits up to a maximum of $20 million.[26]

Although there is no direct proof of a propaganda-for-profits quid pro quo, it seems likely that such a deal was at least implicit. There is no better explanation as to why Ambassadors Lothian and Halifax defended Hollywood before their own government; they had no other reason to do so. Surviving British records provide circumstantial evidence, revealing that lower-level officials discussed the merits of loosening the purse strings to give Hollywood an incentive to produce and distribute pro-British movies. In July 1940, John Balfour, who headed the Foreign Office's American Department, advised Sir Frederick Whyte, director of the MOI's American Division, to encourage the relaxation of "dollar remittance regulation for propaganda purposes."[27]

Furthermore, the potential payoffs were sufficient to involve high-ranking principals despite the very real possibility that the negotiations would be exposed, ruining everything. The Roosevelt administration sought to keep the talks out of the public eye for fear that isolationists would accuse the White House and the studios of conspiring with the British to manipulate the American people. In August 1941, only days after the introduction of a congressional resolution calling for the investigation of prowar movie propaganda, Hull advised Hays against traveling to London to oversee negotiations lest "demagogues" get wind of the effort. The next month, as the bilateral talks reached a denouement despite the unfolding congressional probe, Hays reminded the MPPDA's representative in London that it was "vitally important there be no publicity there and no discussion of negotiations by British representatives."[28]

In any event, behind-the-scenes Anglo-American cooperation paid on-screen dividends. Almost overnight, the MOI went from losing to winning the newsreel battle against the Third Reich's Ministry of Popular Enlightenment and Propaganda. A customary part of the era's cinema program, which also typically included a cartoon, a short, and a feature or two, newsreels served as influential news sources whose moving images gave viewers seemingly accurate (and visually arresting) portraits of world events. Control of the flow of newsreels to the United States went a long way toward determining how American moviegoers visualized the European war. Whereas in 1939–40, Joseph Goebbels's productions gained respect by quickly reaching U.S. shores packed with impressive footage of Blitzkrieg battlefield victories, MOI footage, crippled by persistent shipping delays, heavy censorship, and the dearth of comparably awe-inspiring news, cast a lethargic pall.[29]

The MOI soon turned the tables, however, accelerating deliveries to the United States, persuading British censors to ease up, and cultivating the American newsreel firms, including Fox's *Movietone News*, Warner Bros.' *Pathé News*, *Universal News*, and *Paramount News*, all of which maintained staffs in London to cover European events. The U.S. newsreels adopted a pro-British tone (and stopped incorporating German footage) in 1940, when the MOI began to arrange shoots at British military installations and photo sessions with London's newsmakers, leading the ministry's Whyte to boast that the serials were "presenting our war effort in a favorable light."[30]

One series, *March of Time*, was especially receptive to the ministry's overtures. Part of Henry R. Luce's media empire, which also included *Time* and *Life* magazines, the on-screen news journal's political stance mirrored that of its owner, a member of the Century Group and the Council for Democracy, another interventionist and pro-British advocacy organization. During the mid-1930s, the serial's internationalist and antifascist producer, Louis de Rochemont, had opened a London bureau staffed by John Grierson, Edgar Anstey, and Harry Watt, leading British documentary filmmakers who later did work on behalf of the MOI. In addition, the firm's American editors regularly sought advice from British officials before releasing installments that included material about the United Kingdom. As a result, some 22 million Americans who watched *March of Time* each month saw a wealth of sympathetic news reports. *March of Time* released its first pro-British wartime issue, *Battle Fleets of England*, in September 1939, followed in October 1940 by *Britain's RAF* and *Uncle Sam—The Non-Belligerent* three months later. The latter, an exposé of Nazi Germany and the threat it posed to the world, was released amid fierce congressional debate over the Lend-Lease bill, and the report concluded by questioning why the United States was not doing more to help Britain. After seeing the piece, Anstey wrote, "*March of Time* itself is so pro-British that its editors make no attempt to conceal their support." Senator Wheeler, who appeared in a segment that portrayed him as an obstructionist, demanded that the series' editors expunge the scene from what he called a "warmongering picture" that had "for its purpose the arousing of the sympathies and the passions of the American people."[31]

Anglo-American coordination had an even more direct bearing on the MOI documentary *London Can Take It* (1940), which Bernstein, during his July 1940 visit, convinced Warner Bros. to distribute throughout the United States. *London Can Take It* spun the Blitz into an asset for the nation's reputation by claiming that the Luftwaffe's nightly bombing of London and other southern English towns beginning in the summer of 1940 had the twin effects of leveling British society and steeling Britons' will rather than breaking it, as Berlin intended. The film's imagery of people from all walks of life, from the working class on up, seeking safety in the Underground or air-raid shelters without regard to social standing went a long way toward establishing the myth that for Britain, World War II was a "people's war." That theme would become a staple of British wartime propaganda, infusing such homegrown pictures as the MOI short *Britain on Guard* (1940) and Noel Coward's *In Which We Serve* (1942). Historians have since questioned the extent to which the Blitz in particular and the war in general actually leveled society. At the time, however, *London Can Take It* provided made-to-order propaganda for American viewers. Its portrait of egalitarianism countered U.S. criticism of Britain's class hierarchy. Its visual evidence of the physical destruction, human hardship, and death wrought by Germany's bombs established Britons as the war's victims, laying claim to the moral high ground. Perhaps most important, however, was the film's titular thesis that Londoners, despite being rocked by the bombing, could "take it," meaning that they—and by extension all Britons—would live to fight another day with the help of material assistance from the United States.[32]

The MOI handpicked Quentin Reynolds, an American correspondent for *Collier's Weekly* magazine, to narrate the picture so that it would have the widest possible appeal. It was a brilliant move. Delivered with a familiar accent, Reynolds's voice-over narration left American audiences with the comforting if misleading impression that they were privy to an objective report from a fellow countryman when, in fact, they were being subjected to foreign propaganda. (At one point in the film, Reynolds assures viewers that he is a "neutral reporter.")

London Can Take It served as a screen version of Edward R. Murrow's famous radio reports from the city, and Reynolds's matter-of-fact, even world-weary, tone mimicked that of the Columbia Broadcasting System (CBS) correspondent. U.S. radio newscasters generally endorsed internationalism over the airwaves, and Murrow was no exception. His London broadcasts—arranged, not incidentally, by the MOI and the BBC—brought the Blitz home to American listeners, making it seem so palpable as to shrink their physical and cognitive distance from Britons, with whom they developed an emotional attachment. As Archibald MacLeish said at the time, Murrow's word pictures almost enabled audiences to feel the heat of the flames in faraway London, thereby "destroy[ing] the superstition of distance and time." The newscaster's rooftop reports, which began in September 1940, resonated in part because they combined the Blitz's thrilling sounds—droning German planes, wailing air-raid sirens, and exploding bombs—with his tender, heartfelt descriptions of the effects that the attacks had on ordinary Londoners. During a 25 September broadcast, for example, Murrow described a neighborhood where, amid the rubble, he encountered those left homeless by the Blitz picking through what remained of their belongings. One woman clutched only "a blanket, another carried a small baby in her arms, and another carried an aluminum cooking pot." Nevertheless, the will of the British people remained unbroken. The city's storefronts were reported to feature signs that read, "Shattered—but Not Shuttered" or "Knocked but Not Locked."[33]

London Can Take It made a big impression when it premiered in October 1940, giving an estimated 60 million American viewers a human-interest story of the Blitz. Addressing viewers in the second person, Reynolds encouraged them to become active participants in the near real-time narrative unfolding on-screen. Theatergoers saw and heard the nighttime approach of the predatory Luftwaffe bombers and the fire of Britain's air defenses. They watched and listened as besieged Londoners—children, women, and men, rich and poor alike—sought shelter from the battle overhead. Spectators bore witness to the city's destruction via the camera's eye, which surveyed the damage: fires started, a double-decker bus upended, transportation interrupted, businesses ruined, churches and hospitals leveled, homes turned to rubble, families displaced. Viewers no doubt also marveled at London's fighting spirit, for, like a great boxer, according to Reynolds, the city got up each morning after being knocked down, ready for another round. Visual evidence confirmed his analysis: a determined-looking woman peering out of a broken upper-floor window; Londoners going about their daily routines undeterred. The message was clear: the Blitz had united the common people and fortified their will. Although destructive and even lethal, bombs had their "limitations," the narrator concluded, for they could not "kill the unconquerable spirit and courage of the people of London. London can take it."

To its credit, *London Can Take It* did not have the feel of propaganda. Its tone was neither shrill nor bombastic, restraint that helps explain its persuasiveness. Told from Britons' perspective, the documentary naturally made Americans feel as if they were in common cause with their beleaguered cousins across the pond. Reynolds encouraged this nascent sense of transatlantic solidarity by adopting Londoners' point of view as his own. Despite his stated objectivity, Reynolds took Britain's side, liberally peppering his narrative with the first- or third-person as appropriate. ("We haven't had a quiet night now for more than five weeks." "Everyone is anxious to arrive home before . . . our nightly visitors arrive." "They'll [the Germans] be over tonight.") *New York Times* senior film critic Bosley Crowther got the point, writing that the film "unquestionably ennobles the people of London." No one who saw it could "doubt for one moment the magnificent courage and determination of the Londoners as their homes come crashing down around them and they carry on with confidence."[34]

Foreign Correspondent (1940), a feature produced by internationalist firebrand Wanger and directed by Alfred Hitchcock, similarly drew inspiration from the events of the day, including Murrow's Blitz broadcasts. Already world renowned, Hitchcock relocated to the United States in 1939, in part for professional reasons, as producer David O. Selznick had contracted Hitchcock to direct *Rebecca* (1940), his first Hollywood thriller. Semiofficial forces were also at work, however. Prior to his departure from London, two Conservative Party activists appealed to Hitchcock to work for "the better representation of British characters in Hollywood produced films." And after the director's arrival in Los Angeles, he briefed the British consulate there on his mission to make films that would help "correct American misconceptions regarding British people."[35]

Hitchcock redrafted the screenplay, crafting a timeless thriller that skillfully mixed politics and entertainment. Joel McCrea plays John Jones, a fictional New York newspaper reporter assigned to cover Europe's brewing war crisis. The paper's editor sends McCrea's character overseas because only he can provide a fresh perspective: Jones, normally on the local crime beat, has never been abroad; he speaks no foreign languages and is by his own admission ignorant about global affairs. Hitchcock thus deftly enabled ordinary Americans, observing from the comfort of their theater seats, to experience overseas events through the eyes of someone (a reporter, no less) much like themselves—an untraveled, untutored, but commonsensical everyman. From the moment he steps foot on foreign soil, the naive protagonist finds himself in far over his head, as he witnesses the apparent assassination (but actual disappearance) of a Dutch diplomat. (The ordinary, innocent bystander being drawn into sinister events beyond his control was a stock character in Hitchcock's films, most notably *The Man Who Knew Too Much* [1934, 1956], *The 39 Steps* [1935], and *North by Northwest* [1959].) Smelling a front-page story, Jones does some detective work with help from his English sidekick (George Sanders) and fiancée (Laraine Day), tertiary relationships that introduced Anglo-American kinship, an on-screen motif that would become conventional after the United States entered the war. What happens next is convoluted, but the mystery is solved and the villains are exposed: German fifth columnists posing as British peacemakers kidnapped the Dutch diplomat to extract from him secret information useful to Berlin in the event of war.

To this point, the narrative provided a diversion from the day's news. Art and life collide in the last reel, however. With the on-screen world now at war—newspaper headlines flash, quickly taking viewers from the recent past to the present, from Germany's invasion of Poland in September 1939 to its Norwegian campaign in the spring of 1940—events rapidly unfold. Now well acquainted with Nazi perfidy, Jones, once a mere passive observer of the outside world, goes on the offensive. He jettisons his erstwhile journalistic objectivity and political neutrality, sticking his neck out for Britain. In a memorable climax—a re-creation of Murrow's on-air Blitz dispatches, ongoing even as *Foreign Correspondent* played in theaters throughout the fall of 1940—Jones broadcasts from London. With German bombs falling nearby, the studio shuddering, and the lights dimming, he tells his listeners that the sounds they hear are those of "death" coming to the city. To the accompaniment of "The Star-Spangled Banner," Jones, his English fiancée at his side, informs audiences—including not only imaginary radio listeners but also real Americans in theaters—why the bombardment affects them as well as Londoners. As a consequence of Nazi aggression, London and other parts "of the world as nice as Vermont, Ohio, Virginia, California, and Illinois" lay "ripped up and bleeding." Although the dramatic moment was ripe for fiery interventionist rhetoric, Wanger and Hitchcock pulled their punches, perhaps sensing that too blatant politicking would put off some paying customers. Instead, Jones closes by saying merely that the "lights" of democracy have gone "out everywhere except in America" and by exhorting Americans to "keep those lights burning, cover them with guns, build a canopy of battleships and bombing planes around them."

Foreign Correspondent mostly consisted of a nonsensical whodunit, and its ambiguous ending diluted its message somewhat. Contrary readings of the movie's intent speak to the wide interpretive latitude enjoyed by audience members. Writing in the *New York Times*, Crowther, for example, opined that Hitchcock's penchant for "melodramatic hullabaloo" and the plot's "improbable shenanigans" impaired the film's claim to verisimilitude. To the *Motion Picture Herald*, the movie's climax advocated not internationalism but isolationism in its purest, unilateralist form: the United States should oppose the Axis menace by arming itself rather than Britain. Similarly, the *Motion Picture Daily* identified the closing not as a plea for aid to Britain but as "a warning to America to ring itself with steel."[36]

By the same token, the movie's protagonist did not have to make a direct plea for U.S. action, since audiences accompanied him every step of the way along his personal interventionist journey. As such, *Foreign Correspondent*'s intent was readily apparent to most. *Life* lavished attention on the film with a richly illustrated essay, and *Variety* praised the picture's engagement with global affairs as "the kind of thing that must be foremost in the mind of every person who reads today's papers or listens to the radio." Eugene Lyons wrote that Wanger and Hitchcock had spiced their "superthriller with a dash of political moral," adding that art—film, in this case—was even better positioned than the press to convey fundamental truths about Nazism as a result of the severe restrictions placed on journalists operating within the Third Reich. Perhaps the highest compliment came from an unexpected source, Goebbels, who reportedly called *Foreign Correspondent* "a masterpiece of propaganda, a first class production which no doubt will make a certain impression upon the broad masses of the people in enemy countries."[37]

Anti-interventionists reacted strongly to *Foreign Correspondent*. *Christian Century*, a Protestant periodical headquartered in Chicago, the home of the isolationist movement, had long criticized not only FDR's foreign policies but also Hollywood's allegedly immoral influence. The journal's campaigns continued in September 1940, when it condemned Wanger and Hitchcock for teaching Americans the wrong lessons about foreign politics. What most angered isolationists was the movie's equation of peace activism with pro-Nazism, a comparison that struck a blow at their movement's credibility. In a letter to *Christian Century*'s editors, Devere Allen of Wilton, Connecticut, complained about the "sinister" intent of *Foreign Correspondent*, which taught "millions of persons . . . the lesson that the real fifth columnists are the heads of peace organizations, who are secretly agents of the Nazis." The moral of the on-screen story was simple, according to Allen: "Look out for the fellows who are trying to prevent war, because they are the Nazis who start them."[38]

Warner Bros. released *The Sea Hawk* in August 1940, just days prior to *Foreign Correspondent*'s premiere and the announcement of a deal in which the United States traded fifty overage destroyers for leases to British bases throughout the Western Hemisphere. When studio executives launched the *Sea Hawk* project, a remake of an eponymous 1924 silent movie based on Rafael Sabatini's 1915 novel, they did not foresee making a timely political statement. Rather, they merely conceived of the sea epic as a marketable follow-up to *Captain Blood* (1935), a blockbuster that propelled its star, Errol Flynn, to fame. *Captain Blood* and *The Sea Hawk* marked the first and last of the firm's "Merrie England" films—others included *The Prince and the Pauper* (1936), *The Adventures of Robin Hood*, and *The Private Lives of Elizabeth and Essex*—nostalgic costume dramas starring the Australian-born Flynn, among the best-known performers native to the British Commonwealth working in Hollywood. As the international situation worsened, however, the screenwriters assigned to the project—first Seton I. Miller and later Howard Koch, who had coauthored the radio play for Orson Welles's *The War of the Worlds* and would go on to cowrite the screenplays for *Casablanca* (1942) and *Mission to Moscow* (1943)—reworked the script again and again, each time making it more and more pertinent to the day's headlines. As a result, when filming began under the direction of Michael Curtiz in January 1940—the same month that Warner Bros. executives conveyed to MOI officials their "readiness to produce further anti-Nazi and pro-British films"—what had been an apolitical take on sixteenth-century English pirates had become an opinionated commentary on modern foreign affairs.[39]

The Sea Hawk used historical analogies to draw comparisons between

Elizabethan England imperiled by Spanish aggression in the late six-teenth century and Churchillian Britain threatened by Nazi Germany in the twentieth. In each case, it seemed, only freedom-loving England stood in the way of tyrannical designs to enslave the world. The film's opening sequence establishes the connection between past and present. Backed by composer Erich Wolfgang Korngold's foreboding score, the shadow of King Philip II, a metaphorical Hitler, engulfs an enormous map as he speaks of Spain, a metaphorical Germany, and its predestined global dominance. Spain will quickly realize its territorial ambitions, Philip pre-dicts, ticking off the conquests to come, which ultimately encompass the New World and beyond. "One day before my death, we shall sit here and gaze at this map upon the wall," the king assures his advisers. "It will have ceased to be a map of the world. It will be Spain."

Only one country, Elizabethan England, can disrupt the plan. So Philip dispatches his ambassador, Don Alvarez (Claude Rains), to London, where he is to open talks with Queen Elizabeth, played by Flora Robson in a reprisal of her acclaimed role in *Fire over England* (1937), a British-made costume drama coproduced by Alexander Korda. Reaching an accord with Elizabeth is not really the king's goal. Rather, Don Alvarez's mission is a ploy—as was Hitler's at Munich—designed to buy time for the com-pletion of the Spanish Armada, with which Philip plans to eventually beat England into submission. Furthermore, Spain has a highly placed spy in England, Lord Wolfingham, an Elizabethan minister who lends his aid in exchange for the promise of ruling England after the queen is toppled. With that, *The Sea Hawk* commented on contemporary diplomacy, sug-gesting by analogy that accommodation with dictators was chimerical and that those who sought it, be they British appeasers or American iso-lationists, were either knaves or traitors.

Errol Flynn's swashbuckling lead character, Sir Geoffrey Thorpe, and his band of merry men foil the villains' plan. Thorpe, loosely based on Sir Francis Drake, commands the *Albatross*, a pirate ship whose garrulous crew harries Spanish galleons, plundering their arms and treasure not for personal enrichment but for country and queen. Unlike their continen-tal adversaries, Thorpe's privateers—salt-of-the-earth types reminiscent of the ordinary Davids in Britain's modern-day "people's war" against the Nazi Goliath, in the perspective of MOI propaganda—crack wise and play fair. Freedom fighters, the men of the *Albatross* liberate the English galley slaves who power Spanish vessels. (A central theme of the story, Miller wrote in an internal studio memorandum, was that "the gods favor those that sail by the wind against those propelled by the galley-oar.")

Hale and hearty, the sea hawks escape temporary imprisonment and torture aboard a Spanish galleon to save the day for England. Having made his way to London, Thorpe kills the turncoat Wolfingham in a thrilling swordfight and in the nick of time delivers to Queen Elizabeth proof that King Philip is secretly readying the Armada for an assault. Coming to her senses, the queen quickly abandons appeasement and orders that defenses be readied for the Spanish fleet's attack.[40]

The Sea Hawk could well have ended with an even stronger statement. It was supposed to have concluded with a rousing speech in which Robson's Queen Elizabeth made unmistakable references to the contemporary situation:

> And now, my loyal subjects, a grave duty confronts us all, to prepare our nation for a war that none of us wants—least of all your queen. We have tried by all means in our power to avert this war. We have no quarrel with the people of Spain, nor of any other country. But when the ruthless ambitions of a man threaten to engulf the world, it becomes the solemn obligation of all free men to affirm that the earth belongs not to any one man but to all men and that freedom is the deed and title to the soil on which we exist. Firm in this faith, we shall now make ready to meet the great Armada that Philip sends against us. To this end I pledge you ships—ships worthy of our seamen, a mighty fleet hewn out of the forests of England, a navy foremost in the world, not only in our time but for generations to come.

Although the scene made its way into the version of the film exported to the United Kingdom, where *The Sea Hawk* became 1940's second-largest earner, U.S. audiences did not see it. Studio executives apparently lost their nerve at the last moment and cut the speech from prints destined for the domestic market, perhaps unwilling to risk ticket sales for a project that was already a bit of a gamble. With its $1.7 million price tag, the costume drama was among the most expensive movies ever made at Warner Bros. to that point. Instead, American moviegoers saw a more equivocal ending in which the English fleet sails off to face the Armada without the queen's encouraging words.[41]

Even so, Warner Bros. advertisers capitalized on *The Sea Hawk*'s thinly veiled references to the war in Europe. Prior to the film's premiere in August 1940, the studio's researchers drew comparisons between the sixteenth-century Spanish and English fleets and the contemporary German and British navies, estimates that were included among the publicity materials distributed to exhibitors. Just as the Spanish Armada was once poised at England's coast, so, too, did German armed forces seem set to cross the English Channel in mid-1940. Linking past and present when hawking a historical film made good business sense. Plus, establishing the movie's credentials as an accurate historical document insulated the studio from charges that it was proselytizing on Britain's behalf. Still, Warner's promotional campaign took sides in the war. The studio claimed that in addition to action, adventure, and intrigue, *The Sea Hawk* depicted "all the tyranny that shackles men to the tortures of bondage! In a way it all parallels current events with the 16th century—England as the foe of the aggressor, then as now."[42]

The Sea Hawk's anodyne ending, complicated analogies, and historical lessons combined to cause some viewers to overlook its political subtext. Neither *Commonweal* nor *Time*, for example, detected anything in the film relevant to contemporary international politics. The picture's subtleties did not escape most critics, though. "History repeats—in England and in Hollywood," wrote Kenneth McCaleb in the *New York Mirror*. "The picture reminds us that back in the days of Good Queen Bess, the British island Kingdom withstood a Spanish blitzkrieg just as it is standing off the Nazis in this day of George VI." Crowther commended the Warners for injecting a characteristic "note of contemporary significance." Similarly, *Newsweek* announced that screenwriters Koch and Miller had drawn a clear "parallel between Good Queen Bess' glorious days and Winston Churchill's," both times when the country faced "blitzkrieg." The picture proved to be Warner's top box office draw of 1940. During a visit to Hollywood the following summer, the director of the MOI Films Division, Jack Beddington, thanked Harry Warner for "all that he is doing for us."[43]

Korda also drew historical parallels with Britain's current predicament when he returned to the fray with *That Hamilton Woman* (1941). Korda had left Britain for the United States the previous summer, remaining there throughout the war. The producer-director later claimed that Churchill had asked him to relocate to curry U.S. favor by making movies in Hollywood that "would not emanate from official sources." Although no other evidence corroborates the filmmaker's recollection regarding the prime minister's involvement, British playwright R. C. Sherriff, author of *Journey's End*, who moved to Hollywood at the same time, did remember Korda consulting with unnamed British officials. In any event, Korda, who was knighted in 1942 for his service, enjoyed remarkably close official connections. A patriot, he produced a number of pictures—*Sanders of the River* (1935), *Drums* (1938), and *The Four Feathers* (1939)—celebrating the British Empire even before his work on the MOI-sponsored *The Lion Has*

Wings. A leading publicist on behalf of the Conservative Party's Film Association, Korda employed Churchill and the Foreign Office's Sir Robert Vansittart as writers. It has even been claimed that the filmmaker became involved in the private intelligence network that was organized by Churchill, Vansittart, and other Tories during the 1930s, when Korda's London Films offices were supposed to have served as undercover listening posts on Hitler's Germany. While claims that Korda was a spy cannot be proven, his move to the United States coincided with that of William Stephenson, who, under the code name Intrepid, covertly neutralized enemy activities and assisted American interventionists. Manhattan's Rockefeller Center served as headquarters for both Korda and Stephenson's British Security Co-Ordination.[44]

There is no doubt about Korda's purpose in making *That Hamilton Woman.* Not long after his arrival in New York, he set to work on the historical drama, a chronicle of the events leading to Lord Admiral Nelson's victory over a combined Franco-Spanish fleet in the Battle of Trafalgar, the decisive naval engagement of the Napoleonic Wars, in 1805. The movie made that glorious chapter in Britain's past analogous to the present. As Korda wrote in the *New York Herald Tribune* in September 1940, "It is a haunting thing how much the times of Lord Nelson so closely parallel those of today. All of Europe was ruled by a mighty dictator. England was being blockaded mercilessly." The dramatization of Nelson's legendary triumph, which announced the Royal Navy's historic dominance of the seas, reminded American viewers of Britain's exemplary military record, implying that any aid the United States provided would be put to good use, with Britain acquitting itself as ably as before. Furthermore, *That Hamilton Woman* echoed *The Sea Hawk* in making the case that Britain, in the past and 1941 alike, struggled against a "dictator" who meant to be "master of the world."[45]

Furthermore, the picture took aim at American isolationism, equated with weakness and appeasement, a thoroughly discredited policy from the standpoint of 1941. The film's general message was that "those who don't fight for England are lazy or a coward or blind," critic Otis Ferguson pointed out. Nelson, played by Laurence Olivier and Churchillian in his dogged opposition to the dictatorial menace, struggles to amass an anti-Napoleon coalition among states sympathetic with England but reluctant to fight. Weak-willed foreign powers are exhorted to bestir themselves in the name of freedom. The admiral's second in command resents foreigners who are "so scared of Bonaparte that they daren't lift a finger to help the people who still fight him." Softness pervades even London's halls of power, where Nelson overturns the prevailing wisdom that peace can be made with dictators. Such thinking is illusive, he tells the Admiralty, in that the tyrant du jour wants peace only "to gain a little time to rearm . . . and make new alliances." Rather, he concludes, true peace can come only through strength: "Napoleon can never be master of the world until he has smashed us up. And believe me, gentlemen, he means to be master of the world. You cannot make peace with dictators. You have to destroy them—wipe them out." Lord Nelson puts his words into action at Cape Trafalgar, and the movie concludes with a thrilling re-creation of his epic naval victory set to the strains of "Rule Britannia."[46]

The best propaganda was least recognizable as such. Perhaps having learned a lesson from the poor reception Americans accorded *The Lion Has Wings*, Korda tempered *That Hamilton Woman*'s heavy dose of propaganda with entertainment. As if the movie's action-packed battle scenes were not enough, British actors Olivier and Vivien Leigh—he an international star of stage and screen, she fresh off her Academy Award–winning turn as Scarlett O'Hara in Selznick's blockbuster *Gone with the Wind* (1939)—played the featured roles. Korda explained his rationale for asking Olivier to star: "Propaganda can be a bitter medicine. It needs sugarcoating—and *Lady Hamilton* [the movie's original and U.K. title] is a very thick sugarcoating indeed." Olivier and Leigh's participation was even more titillating because they had just married after beginning a love affair on the set of *Fire over England* and divorcing their spouses. They seemed to be reenacting their private lives on-screen in portraying Lord Nelson and Emma, Lady Hamilton, two historical figures who had also had a scandalous affair. The illicit on-screen romance may have caused palpitations at the PCA, which required the title change and the introduction of "compensating moral values" (typically, the female character was made to suffer the worst punishment, as Emma Hamilton became a destitute alcoholic as penance for her sins) before issuing a certificate of approval. Yet the film certainly captured moviegoers' attention. *That Hamilton Woman* turned a solid profit, and no critic failed to note its romantic angle. Several even wondered why the PCA ultimately permitted the affair to be depicted. Ferguson speculated that internationalist Hollywood executives had somehow pushed it through, as the movie was "openly a Bundle for Britain."[47]

Distributed by United Artists—Korda's co-ownership of the firm guaranteed that his film would find an American outlet—*That Hamilton Woman* premiered in April 1941, just weeks after Congress approved the Lend-Lease Act, giving Britain virtually unlimited access to U.S. aid. Trade journals and the mainstream press hailed the picture's commentary on foreign affairs. *Motion Picture Daily* assured exhibitors that customers would flock to the amusing movie even as it drew a clear "parallel between the circumstances then and now." Roscoe Williams, the *Daily*'s film critic, did not object to the fact that the film "refers to Napoleon as 'dictator' and contains dialogue lines which are, of course, pertinent to the present world situation." *Life* happily reported that Korda had made "of Napoleon an earlier Hitler" and sent "an 18th Century warning to America." The *New York Times* noted the "especially timely opinions about dictators who would desire to invade England."[48]

With Lend-Lease in hand, propagandists on both sides of the Atlantic trained their sights on a new, even more ambitious goal, that of advancing U.S. intervention. On 19 May 1941, the War Cabinet's Defence Committee, chaired by Churchill, directed the Foreign Office and MOI to launch "a propaganda campaign with the object of influencing American opinion towards early participation in the war." Toward that end, British-made documentaries framed Lend-Lease as an illustration of both Anglo-American partnership and U.S. internationalism. Ignoring the bitter behind-the-scenes disputes between U.K. and U.S. officials over the program's terms, British publicity contextualized Lend-Lease as physical evidence "of Allied cooperation." Newsreel correspondents were encouraged to photograph materials being made in the United States, shipped across the Atlantic, and unloaded in the United Kingdom. The MOI short *We Won't Forget* (1941) offered "thanks to the United States for all the aid being sent to relieve suffering amongst [Britain's] civilian population." Distributed throughout the United States in June, it shows London air-raid victims eating food, wearing clothes, and using medical supplies sent from the United States. At the end, a firefighter, worker, elderly woman, and young mother face the camera and express their gratitude.[49] Narrated by CBS radio newsman Bob Trout, *America Moves Up* (1941) highlighted the ways in which U.S. supplies relieved human suffering and increased transatlantic affection. As the film shows American medical personnel treating British war casualties, British children drinking milk from U.S. farms, and U.S. industrial goods arriving in British seaports, Trout speaks fondly of Anglo-American humanitarian bonds as evidence of a broadened U.S. worldview. For its part, *Target for Tonight* (1941), director Harry Watt's glorified account of an RAF bombing raid over Germany, updated the United Kingdom's reputation for stoic endurance, recasting it as a country that could mete out punishment as well as take it. Distributed by Warner Bros., the documentary played in more than nine thousand U.S. theaters to an estimated cumulative audience of 50 million.[50]

American moviegoers vicariously entered the war even before the United States did via a string of features about their countrymen serving in Allied armed forces. Fiction reflected fact on this score, as hundreds of U.S. pilots voluntarily served in Eagle Squadrons, RAF units that became operational in 1941. Eagle Squadrons offered ideal subjects for dramatizing not only U.S. intervention but also Anglo-American accord. Numerous such dramas were in production by 1941, as the studios raced to be the first to get their versions before the public. Paramount, Fox, and Warner Bros. were the quickest to wrap up production, and their entries— *One Night in Lisbon*, *A Yank in the RAF*, and *International Squadron*, respectively—reached the screen that autumn. Several others would arrive in theaters after Pearl Harbor. Each followed a narrative formula set by MGM's smash 1938 hit, *A Yank at Oxford*, about a cocksure American who reconciles with his fellow Oxford students after an initial period of estrangement. Politicized variations on that theme, the subgenre's films featured a stereotypically brash and selfishly independent American who arrives in Britain ambivalent toward Britons and the war alike. A provincial man apart, he is annoyed by the foreign habits of his fellow pilots. A cynic, he disbelieves the war's avowed moral principles and stakes. A soldier of fortune, he disobeys orders, causing harm to his comrades in arms. Over time, however, the protagonist develops into an Anglophile and interventionist, a coming-of-age story that implicitly associates his erstwhile Anglophobia and isolationism with immaturity. Firsthand combat experience as an RAF pilot reveals Nazi Germany's genuine threat to Anglo-American security and values. Intimate contact with Britons at war leaves him with newfound respect for their valiant if lonely struggle and the sense that Britons and Americans, despite some superficial differences, are really members of the same family. The final reel shows a cosmopolitan who feels part of a team, a transformation that American viewers were supposed to undergo as well. *One Night in Lisbon*'s stock Yank (played by Fred MacMurray) made one of the infrequent references to transatlantic kinship in pre–December 1941 films when he observed, "It's sort of like being related in a way. You know the way you feel about relatives? They do a lot of things that irritate you, but when it comes right down to it, you are related. You have the same ideas, speak the same language, and have the same plans for the future."[51]

Zanuck made another such allusion in *A Yank in the RAF*, which he produced and cowrote (under the nom de plume Melville Crossman). He outlined the scenario's central drama for his fellow writers: the transformation of an American who arrives in Britain thinking that "all this talk about England, *esprit de corps*, the cause, the team play, etc., is just so much baloney" but eventually learns that Britons "are fighting for freedom, for liberty, for a cause they believe in. He realizes it and it is proven to him. He becomes a part of the *esprit de corps*." At Zanuck's request, the script was cleared by the MOI and British Air Ministry, whose approval was necessary for on-location shooting in the United Kingdom, which lent the movie real-time drama and box office punch. What really made *A Yank in the RAF* marketable, however, was its on-screen romance between two of the studio's brightest stars, Tyrone Power and Betty Grable, on the verge of becoming *the* pinup girl of the war. The romantic adventure traces the personal and political journey of Power's character, Tim Baker, from passive skeptic to interventionist Anglophile. A rakish Texan, Baker joins the RAF not to save the world from fascism but for the adventure—and cash—involved. And he takes his duties far less seriously than his pursuit of Grable's Carol, his estranged girlfriend volunteering in London. Baker's Anglophobia only grows when his British squadron leader, Morley, enters the competition for Carol's heart. (In this case, unlike in the international love stories to come, the romance is between two Americans and is frustrated by a Briton.) The protagonist's attitude changes after several of his RAF chums die in the Battle of Britain, an experience that leaves him with a keener appreciation of the high stakes involved in the struggle against Nazism. Newly enthused, the American aviator downs several German planes in an aerial dogfight, thereby avenging his fallen comrades. Now a war hero, Baker gets the girl by virtue of his newfound maturity. (The story's love triangle, the final barrier to Anglo-American harmony, is amicably resolved as Morley voluntarily steps aside and exits the last scene arm in arm with the Yanks.)[52]

Ronald Reagan's character, Jimmy Grant, underwent a similar transition in Warner Bros.' *International Squadron*, the only difference being his development of a worldview even broader than Atlanticism. Whereas Power's Baker flew on-screen as part of an Eagle Squadron, Reagan's Grant did so in one of the RAF's Foreign Legions, units that in real life were composed of exiled aviators from occupied Belgium, Czechoslovakia, France, and Poland. Having crossed the Atlantic to escape trouble back home and, like Baker, to earn an easy paycheck, Grant initially feels little sense of common purpose with his European colleagues, whose diversity strikes him as odd. His behavior works against the common cause, as he horns in on a French comrade's girlfriend, Jeanette, and evidences poor discipline that leads to the deaths of two members of his squadron. The second fatality causes the guilt-ridden American to have an epiphany, and he takes the place of another man (Jeanette's boyfriend) on a dangerous mission. The determined Grant performs heroically, shooting down several German planes before his craft is felled. Thus redeemed, the American pilot achieves apotheosis, becoming a martyr for the Allied cause, his memory toasted among the surviving members of the international squadron at curtain's close.[53]

By all accounts, audiences embraced the screen's anticipation of U.S. intervention. *International Squadron* did "big" business even in Omaha, the buckle of the isolationist belt, despite a blizzard. The picture was the top moneymaker in Los Angeles in early November. *A Yank in the RAF* earned the second-highest gross revenue of all movies playing in the District of Columbia during that time, trailing only *The Maltese Falcon* (1941), the classic mystery starring Humphrey Bogart as private detective Sam Spade. Zanuck's production was Hollywood's fourth-most-popular for the year, earning an estimated $2.5 million in North America alone. The pictures received a mixed critical reception, as no one could confuse them with great filmmaking. Yet critics acknowledged that the films' creators had skillfully leavened political argumentation with amusement. The *New York Times* applauded the Warner brothers and Zanuck, who spurned no opportunity to feature Grable (and her famous legs) in song-and-dance numbers, for wisely avoiding "fine and fancy speeches" about foreign policy in favor of gripping action, romance, and theatricality. Whereas some "isolationist Senators might well call [*A Yank in the RAF*] pro-British propaganda," *Time* concluded that it was more accurately "pro-box-office propaganda." *Newsweek* likewise foresaw that the public would flock to the "showmanlike and timely variation on the aviation epic" even though it was clearly "supercharged with propaganda."[54]

The warm popular reception speaks to the sea change that had occurred in public attitudes toward Britain, the war, and the wider world by the autumn of 1941. Sixty percent of those asked in 1939 had responded that America's participation in World War I had been a mistake; only 20 percent still subscribed to that position two years later. Whereas suspicion of Britain had once resonated among Americans, by 1941 liberals (and also the Far Left following the surprise German invasion of the Soviet Union in June) had bolted the isolationist movement, leaving it in the sole hands of the Right. Seeing Britain as the last, best hope for preserving liberalism and U.S. security, Americans expressed ever more support for aid. Two-thirds approved September 1940's destroyers-for-bases deal even though Roosevelt had bypassed Congress and flouted the Constitution in reaching it. Congress passed the country's first peacetime draft later in the month, and Americans reelected FDR to an unprecedented third term in November. While Congress debated Lend-Lease in early 1941, polls showed that as many as 68 percent of Americans endorsed the measure. When German tanks rolled into Poland, only one-third of Americans had felt that the United States should supply Britain if doing so risked war; just prior to Pearl Harbor, that figure had doubled.[55]

Movies exerted immeasurable influence on the country's temper. Neither cinema in general nor any particular film was solely responsible for changing American opinions, of course, though the warm receptions of *London Can Take It*, *Foreign Correspondent*, *The Sea Hawk*, *That Hamilton Woman*, and *A Yank in the RAF* indicated that spectators found the on-screen messages unobjectionable if not persuasive. Rather, movies exerted a cumulative effect. Each week from 1939 to 1941, tens of millions of moviegoers consumed a steady diet of newsreels, shorts, and features that articulated pro-British and interventionist themes and rarely if ever expressed opposing points of view. When asked by pollsters, Americans ranked cinema, the press, radio, literature, and word of mouth as the strongest forces shaping their perceptions of the wider world. Even more to the point, a Gallup Poll published in early 1942 found that 86.7 percent of Bostonians and New Yorkers who had viewed pro-British productions came away favorably inclined toward Britain. Moreover, these films were only the most conscious modelers of transatlantic solidarity, a starting point for a more outward-looking, cosmopolitan American sensibility. Other movies offered apolitical takes on Britain, including MGM's *Goodbye Mr. Chips* (1939), *Pride and Prejudice* (1940), and *Waterloo Bridge* (1940). Still others followed 1939's *Confessions of a Nazi Spy* in presenting anti-Nazi points of view—Charlie Chaplin's satire *The Great Dictator* (1940), MGM's *Mortal Storm* (1940), and director Fritz Lang's *Man Hunt* (1941), among others. In addition, the era also saw the release of *Sergeant York* (1941), the Warner Bros. biopic of America's World War I hero, Alvin York, and defense-related pictures such as *Flight Command* (1940), the musical *Navy Blues* (1941), the Bob Hope comedy *Caught in the Draft* (1941), and Bud Abbott and Lou Costello's *Buck Privates* (1941), all of which put benign spins on the nation's mobilization for war. Taken together, these distinct yet related genres composed an internationalist discourse that framed actual events and filmgoers' understanding of global politics.[56]

Regardless of film's actual effect, isolationists believed that movies weighed heavily in tilting the ongoing debate about war or peace. As a result, they waged a concerted and very public counterattack that ultimately led to a congressional inquiry. Anti-interventionists alleged that anti-Nazi, pro-British, prowar movies—the manifestation of a behind-the-scenes conspiracy involving British propagandists, Hollywood executives, and Roosevelt administration officials—were so biased as to interfere with the American people's ability to determine what was in the country's best interest. The alarm first sounded as Congress debated the Lend-Lease bill, the popularity of which put anti-interventionists on the defensive. Frustrated by his inability to get equal airtime, Senator Wheeler asked Hays, "When, if at all, you intend to carry my answer to the President's most recent Fireside Chat? And what, if anything, you are going to do about carrying both sides of the controversy on pending legislation which directly involves the question of war and peace?" The Montana Democrat added that he had received "many complaints" from constituents concerned "that the motion picture industry is carrying on a violent propaganda campaign intending to incite the American people to the point where they will become involved in this war." He closed with a shot across the bow, warning Hays that lawmakers might consider federal regulation of the movies in light of Hollywood's evident partisanship.[57]

Isolationists followed with written and verbal assaults on specific pictures. *Commonweal* launched a broadside against *That Hamilton Woman*, cautioning readers that the sea epic's scruples and politics were equally objectionable in light of its "Britannia-rules-the-waves theme, the Hitler-Napoleon analogy and the fantastic explanation for the necessity of the British Commonwealth." John T. Flynn of the America First Committee called the movie "a pure piece of propaganda." The former editor of the *New Republic* took particular exception to Nelson's on-screen pitch to the British Admiralty, which Flynn took to be "a regular 1941 war speech" in that the lead character was "actually addressing it to the times." What made the speech (and by extension the film) even more dangerous from Flynn's perspective was that the words were uttered by Olivier, a skilled actor backed "by the dramatization of the screen," to an enraptured audience. Echoing comments made by Senator Nye in his St. Louis radio address, Flynn worried that ordinary spectators, "subdued and softened" by the thought that they were merely enjoying harmless amusement, were left wide "open for the reception, without any kind of intellectual resistance," of internationalist dogma. Noting that Korda was a British subject, Flynn added that the weighty "American problem" of war or peace ought to be addressed solely by "the American people." Foreigners, "whose point of view cannot possibly be the American point of view," should not be allowed to wield "an instrument of propaganda of such tremendous power."[58]

Writing in *Christian Century*, journalist Margaret Frakes labeled *A Yank in the RAF*, whose opening coincided with that of the congressional probe, a "decidedly, but subtle, interventionist feature." *Scribner's Commentator*, which ordinarily took an anti-interventionist stance (the previous month it had featured a commentary by the famous aviator cum isolationist Charles Lindbergh), declared that *Yank*'s screenplay "might well have been written by the British Ministry of Propaganda, so efficient is it as an argument for sending our boys over there." The journal sardonically recommended the film to "movie shoppers who don't mind an obvious dose of pro-English propaganda for their money."[59]

On 1 August, the same day that Nye delivered his radio address, he and Joel Bennett "Champ" Clark introduced Senate Resolution 152 calling for a formal "investigation of any propaganda disseminated by motion pictures . . . to influence public sentiment in the direction of participation by the United States in the present European war." The proposed probe fell under the jurisdiction of the Interstate Commerce Committee, conveniently chaired by Wheeler. As the investigation required approval by the full Senate, where isolationists were in the minority, the Montana Democrat instead appointed a subcommittee stacked with critics of the administration's foreign policy to conduct "preliminary hearings," ostensibly to determine whether a full inquiry was warranted. Chaired by Idaho Democrat D. Worth Clark, the subcommittee also included Democrat Homer T. Bone of Washington and Republicans C. Wayland Brooks of Illinois and Charles W. Tobey of New Hampshire. Its token internationalist member was Ernest McFarland, a freshman Democrat from Arizona thought to be a political lightweight.[60]

The hearings began on 9 September amid great fanfare. Drawn by the spectacle of movie magnates being grilled on Capitol Hill, reporters, photographers, and curious onlookers crowded the Senate Caucus Room. During his testimony, Nye reiterated the points he had made over the airwaves. The senator accused Hollywood executives, British propagandists, and White House officials of conspiring to push "our country on the way to war" and to put audiences into a "frame of mind which will make certain that America will not let Britain fail." Industrialists, who comprised a "dangerous fifth column," were said to be guilty of concocting "the most vicious propaganda that has ever been unloosed upon a civilized people," in part because of their extensive financial interests in the United Kingdom. The North Dakotan admitted to being awestruck by the screen's potency, describing it as an "entirely different kind of propaganda." Anyone who went to the theater for mere amusement naturally let his "guard down," Nye said, thus becoming vulnerable to political argumentation "in a way that is pretty hard to get rid of." As prime offenders, he named an odd assortment of pictures that glorified war (*Flight Command* and *Sergeant York*), demonized the Nazis (*Confessions of a Nazi Spy* and *The Great Dictator*), or befriended the British (*That Hamilton Woman* and *Convoy*, a 1940 British import). Movies that fell into the third category, Nye had told his radio listeners, falsely upheld "the grandeur and the heavenly justice of the British Empire" and misleadingly depicted "the courage, the passion for democracy, the love of humanity, the tender solicitude for other people, by the generals and trade agents and the proconsuls of Great Britain."[61]

Subsequent witnesses reiterated Nye's charges. When it was suggested that the subcommittee screen the offending pictures, Tobey protested that the members "would become punch drunk" if they did so. Champ Clark declared that the Hollywood studios tried "to infect the minds of their audiences with hatred, to inflame them, to arouse their emotions, and make them clamor for war. And not one word on the side of the argument against war is heard." The final isolationist witness, Flynn, testified "that the moving-picture industry is using the screen in a concerted effort to make propaganda for the involvement of the United States in this war." Calling film's influence "insidious," he stated his belief that when a patron

goes to a moving-picture show he is not going to a mass meeting. At least he does not think he is going to a mass meeting. He thinks he is going out to enjoy himself, and he takes his wife and his kids to a moving-picture show, and they get their seats, and the lights go down and the darkness envelops them. Then a great orchestra, a great symphony orchestra, begins to pour out its music, which is adapted to underscore the idea which is about to be presented. And then able actors come on the screen . . . whom the people in the audience like very much, and a very interesting story unfolds. The man's mind is completely open, all his defenses are down, and when this story unfolds, after a while, when he is well softened up, they go to work on him with the propaganda. Very often he does not know he is being propagandized.[62]

The hearings attracted some support, if only among anti-interventionists. A manufactured grassroots letter-writing campaign targeted the movie studios and the White House. Charles Kupper of Dallas, Oregon, wrote to ask Universal if it received "money or trade advantages from the allies" in exchange "for spreading propaganda favorable to them." One Baltimore resident and America First Committee member notified Roosevelt that "Wheeler, Nye, Lindbergh and their 20 million Family Followers [are] all true Americans, who love their Beloved USA, [and] will save our great USA independence against the attempt of the handful of 1941 Pro-British-American War Preachers to make us a British colony." Alice C. Reyhner of Paterson, New Jersey, urged FDR to support the "long overdue" inquiry. At least one major metropolitan newspaper, the steadfastly isolationist *Chicago Tribune*, endorsed the investigation. Frakes did so as well, lamenting in the *Christian Century* that "unless you are an interventionist who wants this country to plunge into a shooting war without longer delay, you are probably finding it difficult to enjoy a program in any motion picture theater these days."[63]

The White House, Fight for Freedom, and leading Hollywood interventionists quietly organized the industry's defense. Industrialists at first were unsure about how best to respond. Cowed by Wheeler's allusion to possible federal regulation, Hays publicly denied that filmmakers manipulated audiences and advised others to follow his lead. Zanuck and Wanger refused to buckle, however. After the introduction of the Senate resolution, Zanuck sought advice from Ulric Bell, Fight for Freedom's well-connected executive director. Bell, a 1942 White House appointee to the Office of War Information's Bureau of Motion Pictures, correctly surmised that public opinion now sided firmly with the interventionists. He thus encouraged the studio heads to be aggressive in their rebuttal by claiming that they were simply fulfilling their patriotic duty in alerting Americans to the dangerous world scene.[64]

The White House concurred. Hays attempted to arrange a meeting with Roosevelt prior to the hearings, with an eye toward obtaining FDR's imprimatur for a softer line of defense. Zanuck and Wanger got wind of Hays's plan, however, and worked through Bell to set up their own 27 August conference with Lowell Mellett, a presidential aide who served as FDR's prime emissary to the motion picture industry. Mellett subsequently advised Roosevelt not to see the MPPDA head since all of the industry's other leaders were united in their readiness "to go into these hearings fighting." The president agreed, no doubt cognizant of the extreme political risk that would come with meeting anyone from

Hollywood at the time.[65] Moreover, Bell and White House Press Secretary Stephen T. Early recommended that Wendell L. Willkie spearhead the industry's defense. A Republican who had returned to private law practice after his unsuccessful 1940 bid for the presidency, Willkie was an internationalist who could not possibly be accused of being Roosevelt's accomplice.[66]

Willkie led a spirited defense. On the eve of the proceedings, he sent a statement, later released to the press, to D. Worth Clark questioning the subcommittee's legality on the grounds that the Senate had yet to pass Resolution 152. Declaring that filmmakers were merely informing the public about current events, he also charged the panel with curbing freedom of speech and hence fostering "dictatorship." When Willkie learned to his surprise that the subcommittee's rules prohibited him from cross-examining Nye, Champ Clark, and Flynn, he called three allies of the administration—Harry Warner, Zanuck, and Nicholas Schenck, president of Loew's, MGM's parent company—to testify on the industry's behalf. Warner proudly declared his opposition to the "evil force" of Nazism and added that he was "unequivocally in favor of giving England and her allies all the supplies which our country can spare." Zanuck then took the stand and in no uncertain terms upheld Hollywood as the most American of institutions. The producer recalled the innumerable pictures that "sold the American way of life not only to America but to the entire world. They sold it so strongly that when dictators took over Italy and Germany, what did Hitler and his flunky, Mussolini, do? The first thing they did was ban our pictures, throw us out. They wanted no part of the American way of life." Wild cheers erupted from the Senate gallery.[67]

Whereas filmmakers effectively made their case, investigators undid themselves. Isolationists had found an issue that briefly captured the public's attention. Handled well, the sensational (and generally accurate) revelation of movie propaganda caused by Hollywood's ties to the White House and British agents might have undermined the administration's credibility and weakened the case for U.S. global activism. Instead, the panelists appeared foolish and ill-informed when McFarland, the subcommittee's seemingly innocuous rookie senator, pressed them to describe exactly what they found so objectionable about specific films. Before a room full of reporters, Nye became confused, had difficultly recalling details, and eventually confessed that he had not seen many of the pictures in question. Worse, both D. Worth Clark and Champ Clark not only admitted that they had watched none of the movies but also took pride in their ignorance.[68]

What really doomed the investigation was the appearance that anti-Semitism motivated it. Nye first raised eyebrows during his St. Louis radio address when he named Hollywood's leading Jewish executives, among them the Warner brothers, Goldwyn, and Schenck. At least one listener claimed that Nye had deliberately overpronounced the names to accentuate their ethnicity and seeming foreignness. Implying that a Jewish conspiracy was afoot, he went on to explain that these men, "naturally susceptible" to "racial emotions," "cunningly" used their control of Hollywood's "mighty engine of propaganda" to inoculate unsuspecting moviegoers "with the virus of war." Only bona fide Americans should address the issue of war or peace, he added. The senator was even more outspoken in his testimony before the subcommittee. After denying that he was engaging in "Jew-baiting" and announcing that he had many "splendid Jewish friends," Nye claimed that the charges that anti-Semitism lay behind the probe had been "raised by those of the Jewish faith" to divert the public's attention from the main issue of propaganda. Despite D. Worth Clark's attempts to stop him, Nye referred to Jewish media executives as foreign-born "agitators" who harbored "natural" but "violent animosities" that were dragging "our country and its sons" into an unnecessary foreign war.[69]

Lindbergh's comments were even more damning. During a 15 September America First Committee rally in Des Moines, he accused Jews, in league with British provocateurs and the Roosevelt administration, of "pressing the country toward war." Allegedly driven by their "natural passions and prejudices," Jewish media executives were said to be leading "our country to destruction." As such, they represented a grave "danger," he claimed. Although Lindbergh, a Hitler admirer, was not affiliated with the ongoing movie investigation, his speech tarnished both it and the isolationist movement. Willkie called Lindbergh's speech "the most un-American talk made in my time by any person of national reputation." Even the *Chicago Tribune* ran an editorial distancing itself from the aviator's remarks.[70]

The press turned against the subcommittee. Michael Straight of the *New Republic* demanded an immediate end to the investigation on the grounds that it was "anti-Semitic" and "pro-Nazi." The *Nation* accused the hearings of abetting Hitler by misleading Americans to believe that Jews, not Nazis, were their greatest enemy: "The American people are expected to believe that the Nazi menace is a figment of the Jewish imagination." According to *Life*, the panel, a "kangaroo court," had become "Washington's funniest political circus of the year." The *Washington Post* referred to the probe as the "Witch Hunt on Capitol Hill." Running low on support, the subcommittee recessed on 26 September, never to reconvene. D. Worth Clark quietly disbanded it in December after the attack on Pearl Harbor and the subsequent U.S. declaration of war.[71]

• • •

By causing U.S. entry into World War II, Japan's strike accomplished what film propaganda could not. Even so, isolationists blamed Hollywood for the marked turn in public opinion against them, and they staked the future of the anti-interventionist movement on an ill-conceived investigation of pro-British, prowar movie propaganda. However wrongheaded their motives, isolationists' actions and words spoke to the big screen's presumed bearing on domestic opinion and foreign policy alike. So, too, did the actions and words of the Roosevelt administration officials, Hollywood executives, and British publicists who risked exposure as parties to the transnational mobilization of cinema against Nazism.

To the extent that they framed actual events and left the tens of millions of fans who watched them each week with the impression that Atlanticism was in vogue, movies thus helped broaden the U.S. worldview. But this was just one step in a much longer collective journey. By the end of 1941, if Americans had come to appreciate why their country had to intervene and fight the Axis, they were just beginning to see themselves in league with friendly peoples overseas, as members of a larger international enterprise, or family of nations. When used to describe foreign affairs, familial rhetoric is typically reserved to express feelings of unusual closeness and hopes that good relations will endure. It is therefore instructive to observe how seldom Hollywood invoked bilateral kinship as a thematic selling point prior to 1942, when Americans were just getting reacquainted with the wider world. True, Hitchcock's *Foreign Correspondent* included an Anglo-American romance, but only as a tertiary angle, and Paramount tacked on a clunky speech about transatlantic familiarity to *One Night in Lisbon*. If anything, such film language highlighted Anglo-American differences, as in Zanuck's trendsetting *A Yank in the RAF*, where an unwanted Briton intruded on an exclusive American love affair. The situation would change after Allied leaders formed the United Nations coalition, propagandists established an official line in support of that multinational alliance, and filmmakers developed a cinematic formula for (profitably) teaching prescribed geopolitical lessons to fans.

ONE WORLD, BIG SCREEN THE UNITED NATIONS AND AMERICAN HORIZONS

During a White House ceremony on 1 January 1942, U.S. president Franklin D. Roosevelt, British prime minister Winston S. Churchill, Chinese foreign minister T. V. Soong, and Soviet ambassador to the United States Maxim Litvinov signed the Joint Declaration of the United Nations (UN). Also endorsed by the representatives of twenty-two other countries that day, the declaration formally incorporated the United Nations, the multinational anti-Axis coalition whose disparate members hailed from six continents, spoke a cacophony of languages, and subscribed to a range of beliefs. As such, the document was also an exercise in public diplomacy that gave the appearance of solidarity by portraying the Allies as a collection of diverse nations united against a common foe and bound by a "common program of purposes and principles." Specifically, it averred that the confederacy's members uniformly aspired toward a better, freer, more progressive, and more prosperous world order, a joint mission evidenced by their commitment to defend "life, liberty, independence, and religious freedom" and to preserve "human rights and justice."[1]

Americans took some time to get used to the United Nations, which would grow to include forty-seven member states. The United States was home to a comparatively insular people accustomed to going it alone in and unfamiliar with the ways of the world, and the declaration marked the dawn of a new era, a caesura that would prove as transformative as that caused by Japan's attack

89

on Pearl Harbor the preceding month. One exuberant commentator compared the statement to the American Declaration of Independence in that it internationalized the cause for liberty. U.S. secretary of state Cordell Hull hailed the UN's foundation as "living proof that law-abiding and peace-loving nations can unite in using the sword when necessary to preserve liberty and justice and the fundamental values of mankind." A drawing by *London Evening Standard* cartoonist David Low depicted the Big Four (Churchill, Jiang Jieshi, Roosevelt, and Joseph Stalin, labeled "Uncle Joe") as the fathers of the newborn UN and likened the alliance's birth to the beginning of an internationalist age that presaged peace on Earth.[2]

An opening salvo in a battle of ideas between Allied and enemy propagandists that helped to determine World War II's outcome, the declaration upheld the UN as a community of progressive peoples—a family of nations—determined to win the war, of course, as well as ostensibly dedicated to a peacetime global improvement project founded on the Four Freedoms. To be sure, significant gaps remained between the United Nations as inspirational fiction and reality. Even so, the lived experience of working alongside an unprecedented array of foreign allies, an experience mediated by officially prescribed culture, contributed to a fundamental transformation in America's identity and worldview. Something happened during World War II—a switch in the national psyche was flipped, a dial in the mood turned—so that a people once content to remain relatively isolated from world affairs rather suddenly (and thus far permanently) became convinced that U.S. international activism was not only appropriate but also necessary. The break was not clean, and as scholars have noted, it was caused in part by the arc of historical events, Pearl Harbor and the complicated legacy of World War I foremost among them.[3]

Yet it also owed a debt to plentiful pro–United Nations discourse—on the big screen, mainly, but also in print, over the airwaves, and in the public square—that framed and contextualized day-to-day experience and taught Americans to see the planet anew. Because such talk was transnational—it emanated from private, semiofficial, and official sources both within and without U.S. borders, including the UN's multinational publicity arm—it fostered inter-Allied communication that better integrated Americans into the global network and rendered them less parochial and more cosmopolitan. In short, heavy multimedia coverage of World War II, undoubtedly the most documented event in human history to that time, effectively brought foreign affairs home, leaving ordinary folk with a more palpable albeit virtual feel for the wider world. And the globe suddenly seemed smaller and more interconnected, as well as more dangerous, than ever before as a consequence of the development of mass communication and aeronautics. In that milieu of broadened horizons and shrunken space, Americans—worldlier, more accustomed to outsiders and to the give-and-take associated with international politics—became convinced that the United Nations could be not only the vehicle for winning the war but also the nucleus of a permanent peacekeeping body. It seemed that *One World* had arisen, according to Wendell Willkie's 1943 best seller.

Americans traveled a vast cognitive distance in only four years. In his 1796 farewell address, George Washington had warned his fellow citizens to "steer clear of permanent alliances with any portion of the world." Subsequent generations heeded his advice, generally avoiding foreign entanglements until World War I. Even then, U.S. involvement was tardy, brief, and halfhearted: the country joined the fray only in April 1917, some two and a half years after the first shots were fired, and fought until the armistice in November 1918 not as a full-fledged member of the Triple Entente but as an independent "associated power." Rubbing shoulders with foreigners was considered a necessary evil, something to be done once and quickly before returning to the safety of one's protective barriers, the Atlantic and Pacific Oceans. Few common, enduring bonds developed. Quite the opposite, in fact: the experience left many Americans embittered, feeling as if they had been hornswoggled by their more worldly co-belligerents, especially the British.

Looking back on World War II, an event now enshrouded in decades of gauzy nostalgia, Americans seem to have lent complete, unwavering support to what has come to be remembered as the "good war." And why would they not? A justifiable response to a foreign attack, it ended the Great Depression, defeated fascism, and elevated the United States to superpower status. However, just as the pleasant, enduring memory of the good war ignores some unattractive realities—the internment of Japanese Americans, racially segregated U.S. armed forces, and atrocities committed by Allied forces, to name a few—so, too, does it obscure the disharmony that existed in wartime America.[4]

Discord resonated most strongly at the war's outset, before ultimate success bathed the era in dulcet tones. To be sure, Pearl Harbor temporarily united Americans in sorrow, anger, and wishful revenge. Yet the initial fervor that followed Congress's declaration of war on 8 December 1941 soon wilted against a stream of setbacks in the Pacific, where even Roosevelt conceded, "the news has been all bad." During the first half of 1942, the Japanese took a series of Allied outposts: Guam, Wake Island, the Gilbert Islands, Hong Kong, and finally the Philippines. Those reversals—combined with the April 1942 imposition of anti-inflation austerity measures (higher taxes, wage and price controls, and rationing)—caused grumbling at home. The Office of Facts and Figures (OFF), the chief U.S. propaganda agency at the time, reported as early as February that the "superficial unity which succeeded Pearl Harbor now seems to be ended." Few opposed the war outright. Still, Americans felt "frustrated" and uncertain, as newspaper editorials expressed "dissatisfaction with the progress of the war" and its prosecution by the Roosevelt administration, which appeared "exceedingly confused as to what it is trying to do." Morale worsened the following month, leading the OFF to reach a shocking conclusion: "The superficial unity following Pearl Harbor is not only gone but the sentiment favoring acceptance or consideration of a peace offer from Germany . . . is by no means insignificant."[5]

OFF prepared a special study of the nation's bruised psyche in June. Based on 1,454 interviews conducted in the rural Midwest and South and in the cities of Atlanta, Boston, Chicago, Detroit, and Los Angeles, pollsters found that several "established grievance patterns" continued unabated: domestic politics raged on; rural folk resented urban dwellers, who returned the favor; and whites and blacks distrusted one another. Researchers also discovered "opposition to labor, government, England, Russia, and the Jews; fear that some of our allies may back out and sign a separate peace; misgivings about sending expeditionary forces; skepticism about war aims; and objections to the government's conduct of the war." The Roosevelt administration received blame for the conflict's poor start as a consequence of officials' perceived mismanagement of the country's conversion from peace to war. One-third of respondents felt that Washington, generally speaking, was "doing a poor job of running the war." Many people believed that the government, mired in red tape, was conducting business as usual at a time when extraordinary measures were required.[6]

Interviewees also registered their disappointment with the Allies, whose halting performance on the battlefield contributed to what amounted to a serious crisis in public confidence in both the alliance and Roosevelt's wartime leadership. Americans enumerated a long list of specific grievances against China (seen as inconsequential), Great Britain (too passive), and the Soviet Union (untrustworthy). As for the UN in general, respondents remained confident that it would ultimately triumph. But many—more than a quarter of midwesterners, among whom officials noted a healthy "dislike of Britain"—thought that the new alliance had stumbled badly out of the blocks. A lawyer in Chicago lamented the "reverses" that the Allies had suffered at the hands of the Axis powers, saying, "They've set us back considerably." Another Chicagoan had resorted to turning off her radio to avoid hearing the torrent of bad news. Skeptics even refused to take at face value the UN's stated claim of fighting for higher moral purposes, global freedom, and justice. "We're fighting for the almighty dollar and for trade," a laborer in Detroit complained.[7]

Returns from the 1942 elections provided the clearest indication yet that the tide of opinion was running strongly against Roosevelt, perhaps more so than at any time since his tenure in office began a decade earlier. Republicans made large gains, picking up forty-four seats in the House of Representatives, where they pulled almost even with Democrats. The GOP also gained seven seats in the Senate and turned out of office Democratic governors in several states, including New York, Michigan, and California. Liberal losses throughout the country strengthened the hand of conservative southern Democrats, further reducing the White House's political maneuverability. Moreover, some of the most vociferous incumbent critics of FDR's foreign policies from both sides of the aisle, including isolationist Senator Burton K. Wheeler, a Democrat, and Representative Hamilton Fish, a Republican whose New York district included Roosevelt's own Dutchess County, won reelection.[8]

So keenly attuned to the public mood as to be accused of irresolution by his critics, FDR closely watched opinion polls and daily scoured newspaper editorials. From his perspective, any indication that American voters had soured on their brief overseas experience carried grave potential consequences. Roosevelt regarded domestic unity as a key ingredient of wartime success. Patriotic enthusiasm inspired citizens to fight (and perhaps die) for the country, to purchase war bonds, to perform essential defense work, and so forth. Bickering about foreign policy or home front conditions dampened that enthusiasm and diverted energy from the war effort. Furthermore, disunity could fracture the popular consensus behind intervention, a consensus that had taken years of painstaking effort to construct. On still another level, any displeasure with the war's progress or the country's allies narrowed FDR's options as a military strategist and diplomat. Criticism of Britain and its lackluster wartime performance to date put pressure on the White House to rethink its Europe-first strategy, for example. U.S. officials feared that Stalin would sign a separate peace with Adolf Hitler, and distrust of the Soviets limited FDR's political ability to make any concessions to the Soviet dictator deemed necessary to stave off that catastrophe. Add to that the fact that Roosevelt coalition constituents harbored anti-UN views—Irish Americans opposed Britain, African Americans criticized the British Empire, and Polish Americans were deeply suspicious of the White House's coddling of the Kremlin—and the administration felt as if it had a genuine morale problem on its hands. Voter disaffection with the United Nations as it pertained to the president's political fortunes was best summarized on air in 1942 by Elmer Davis, then a CBS radio newsman: "There are some patriotic citizens who sincerely hope that America will win the war—but they also hope that Russia will lose it; and there are some who hope that America will win the war, but that England will lose it; and there are some who hope that America will win the war, but that Roosevelt will lose it."[9]

White House and State Department officials also worried that the electorate would fall back into its isolationist habit, thereby ruining whatever chance the victorious powers had of crafting a sustainable peace. Several administration officials had ties to Woodrow Wilson, including Roosevelt himself, who had served as Wilson's assistant secretary of the navy and inherited Wilson's internationalist outlook. Modern Wilsonians were haunted by the ex-president's failure to secure U.S. membership in the League of Nations, an absence seen in retrospect as a cause of the global instability that had led to yet another world war. FDR and his key foreign policy advisers were determined not to make the same mistake twice, feeling that the best way to prevent future wars was the creation of some kind of international peacekeeping system. Although exact plans were still being formulated, it was generally agreed that whatever structure emerged would be viable only if each of the UN's four Great Powers played active parts. The American people would have to be in an internationalist frame of mind to support U.S. participation in such a permanent peacekeeping body, a significant departure from tradition. The public had not been in such a mood during Wilson's day, and in retrospect, Wilson was blamed for failing to build a bipartisan coalition in support of the League prior to its rejection by the Senate in 1920. All told, then, these manifold considerations led OFF director Archibald MacLeish to declare in March 1942, "The principal battle ground of this war is not the South Pacific. It is not the Middle East. It is not England or Norway, or the Russian steppes. It is American opinion."[10]

Roosevelt took to the airwaves to counteract the political winds. His first wartime Fireside Chat, given on 9 December 1941, acknowledged that

Japan's attack on the U.S. naval base in Hawaii had punctured the nation's accustomed security and left Americans feeling vulnerable in a world that had grown much, much smaller overnight. Pearl Harbor had taught Americans "a terrible lesson," one that required "abandoning once and for all the illusion that we can ever again isolate ourselves from the rest of humanity." The misperception that national security could be obtained only by retreating behind fortified borders was a thing of the past, as military technology from Japanese bombers to German submarines had developed to the point where "aggressors" could "sneak up in the dark and strike without warning." With the globe having shrunk, Roosevelt encouraged his listeners to reconceptualize world geography and their place in it. What happened in far-flung locales could no longer be considered in isolation from one another: events in Asia, North Africa, and the Caucasus bore on Europe, the Panama Canal, and the Rockies. The rapidly shifting tectonics of the global landscape demanded the development of a sense of world citizenship, of international brotherhood. Americans must come to understand that their security depended on others, Roosevelt said, so "that a successful Russian offensive against the Germans helps us; and that British successes on land or sea in any part of the world strengthen our hands." In short, U.S. and Allied interests were indivisible, and collective security offered the only viable alternative, both now and in the future.[11]

FDR devoted another Fireside Chat, this one delivered on the February 1942 anniversary of George Washington's birth, to buoying the nation's spirit and broadening its outlook. The president, his voice carried by radio into homes across the nation, comforted his audience with the thought that the war's difficult first months were reminiscent of the darkest days of the American Revolutionary War: December 1776, when a small army commanded by General Washington, facing "formidable odds and recurring defeats," beat a hasty retreat across the Delaware River. Then, as in 1942, according to Roosevelt, there was talk that America's "cause was hopeless, and that [it] should ask for a negotiated peace." Yet the young nation had persevered and won its independence. Having taught his history lesson, Roosevelt did something extraordinary: he asked citizens to unfold maps, published beforehand in *Fortune* magazine, the *New York Times*, and other outlets, and follow along at home as he explained UN strategy in response to critics who wrongly "believed that we could live under the illusion of isolationism." In so doing, FDR instructed those still uncomfortable about sending troops so far away to do battle alongside foreigners: "We must fight at these vast distances to protect our supply lines and our lines of communication with our Allies—protect these lines from the enemies who are bending every ounce of their strength, striving against time, to cut them. The object of the Nazis and the Japanese is, of course, to separate the United States, Britain, China, and Russia, to isolate them one from another." The UN's superior industrial capacity and military firepower were sure eventually to overwhelm the Axis powers. Until then, FDR reminded his civilian listeners that they were active participants in the UN's cause and could best contribute to an Allied victory by maintaining a spirit of "unity" not only among themselves but also with their overseas comrades.[12]

Even FDR's considerable oratorical gifts proved insufficient to reverse the trend on their own, however. In June, OFF's Bureau of Intelligence released a nationwide survey of U.S. opinion regarding the UN and geopolitical affairs generally speaking. It found some encouraging signs that citizens were developing a "sense of kinship" with people overseas, including growing recognition that the United States could not win the war without help from foreign powers and anticipation that the Allies would someday cooperate to solve the world's postwar problems. Yet the study discovered a countervailing current as well. The populace possessed only "meager knowledge" about the world beyond U.S. borders, a fundamental "ignorance" that, in OFF's estimation, fostered "marked distrust" of America's foreign partners. Only a minority could name the Allied countries or explain why the United Nations existed. And those who could do so often voiced complaints against the UN's big powers. In sum, Americans did not yet feel as if they "belong[ed] to a union of nations" because they "retained a considerable measure of insularity and a distrust of alien peoples and alien ideas." And that feeling of separateness, of being a country apart, sustained a Fortress America attitude predicated on the idea that U.S. interests were best defended "by retreating behind our ocean barriers" and going it alone in the world. For that reason, the report identified anti-Allied views as "a serious threat to the effective prosecution of the war, as well as to the attainment of future security."[13]

Concerns about popular resistance to the United Nations reached the highest levels of the U.S. government. Ignorance and skepticism of the UN should not have been surprising given that the alliance represented a conglomerate of almost four dozen countries spread across the globe—capitalist and communist, democratic and authoritarian, white and nonwhite—suddenly thrust together for no other reason than that they opposed common enemies. All the same, Assistant Secretary of State Breckinridge Long complained in May to Secretary of War Henry Stimson

President Roosevelt points at a world map to illustrate Allied strategy and interdependence during his 23 February 1942 Fireside Chat. Listeners followed along at home using maps published in *Fortune,* the *New York Times,* and other outlets. Bettmann Archive photo BE002874, © Corbis.

that Americans lacked sufficient "knowledge and appreciation of friendly countries." And the OFF study made the United Nations the top item for discussion at the 15 June meeting of the Committee on War Information, a panel composed of the nation's leading officials in the field that set U.S. propaganda policy. Committee members at various times included Davis, MacLeish, Nelson Rockefeller, Lowell Mellett, Robert Sherwood, Edward Barrett, and John J. McCloy, among others. These men considered the Intelligence Bureau's report and its recommendations for changing the public's attitude, which amounted to instituting a coordinated propaganda campaign that offered "informational encouragement" to Americans to broaden their worldview and find common cause with Britons, Chinese, and Soviets.[14]

It was left to OFF's successor, the Office of War Information (OWI), whose June 1942 foundation coincided with the committee's meeting, to implement the program. As the U.S. government's central propaganda clearinghouse, the OWI orchestrated a slate of multimedia propaganda campaigns that dealt with everything from conservation programs to the war's overriding moral principles. The United Nations initiative was a key part of that comprehensive strategy, helping to clarify why Americans fought by distinguishing their overseas friends. Mapping the world, moreover, which involved creating a taxonomy of peoples as allies or adversaries, provided an important intellectual service for Americans, whom officials understood to be relatively unfamiliar with the world beyond U.S. borders.

Moving pictures arguably served as the UN campaign's signature medium. OFF's Intelligence Bureau found insularity and xenophobia most prevalent among less educated and poorer Americans, a group that movies were well suited to reach insofar as they reduced complicated statecraft down to the lowest common denominator and rendered foreign relations understandable and meaningful to the widest possible audience. With some official guidance, film was capable of improving popular appreciation of friendly foreign powers. By applying a touch of its vaunted magic, Hollywood could "humanize and personalize" the Allies on-screen, thereby fostering emotional attachments and correcting viewers' "defective and abstract" knowledge of the outside world. That commercial cinema entertained customers only sweetened pro-UN propaganda and made the message of Allied unity more palatable to theatergoers.[15]

"We must hang together; or most assuredly we shall all hang separately." Benjamin Franklin's words, spoken to the colonies at the time of the American Revolution, made their way into the OWI's Government Information Manual for the Motion Picture Industry. First distributed to the Hollywood studios in June 1942, the primer delineated Washington's propaganda goals for the silver screen, including the prescribed divergent portrayals of the Allies and the Axis. "*We must understand and know more about our Allies and they must understand and know more about us,*" the manual stated, because "our hope for a decent future world lies in this understanding." Citing polling data indicating that Americans were generally ignorant about and critical of their major overseas partners, the OWI instructed filmmakers to "fight the unity destroying lies about England and Russia." Instead, studios were encouraged to "emphasize the might and heroism of our Allies, all the victories of the Russians, the incredible feats of resistance of the Chinese, and the stubborn resistance of the British after Dunkirk."[16]

In addition, the question was how, linguistically speaking, to tie the UN coalition together in such a way as to lend it a distinct identity as a single entity. Teamwork offered an obvious metaphor: "The American people are great at teamwork. They will be quick to realize that it is all-important that we and our Allies pull together to win this war." The OWI manual advised filmmakers that Lend-Lease, especially its component program of reciprocal aid provided by the Allies to the United States, could dramatize UN wartime interdependence and point toward peacetime international collaboration.[17]

Although Lend-Lease enjoyed wide support following its institution in March 1941, the program was not without critics. More than three-quarters of the public felt that the United States should be somehow compensated for its largesse, and strong disagreements about the program's scope, termination, and repayment terms plagued U.S. relations with its wartime partners for years to come. (A portion of the Soviet Union's debt remained unpaid at the time of the USSR's dissolution in 1991, for example.) Furthermore, fiscal conservatives likened the program to a global dole, a New Deal–style giveaway of American wealth to ungrateful, wasteful foreigners. Even the internationalist-minded *Time* magazine wondered aloud if Uncle Sam had become "Uncle Sucker."[18]

Cinema made Lend-Lease's benefits and UN interdependence alike more apparent to moviegoers. *Action in the North Atlantic* (1943), a Warner Bros. adventure starring Humphrey Bogart, followed the travails of an American merchant ship in a multinational convoy that navigated treacherous waters and avoided German U-boats to deliver crucial supplies to grateful Soviet citizens in Murmansk. The story "beautifully and effectively" exhibited the "United Nations idea," according to an OWI reviewer. *We Sail at Midnight* (1943), a short docudrama produced by the British Ministry of Information (MOI) and shown throughout the United States, illustrated how Anglo-American industrialists, sailors, and officials collaborated to ensure Lend-Lease's smooth functioning. After discovering that a British tank manufacturer lacked a critical American-made part, program administrators, deliberating under an OWI poster emblazoned with the words "Men Working Together," quickly responded and ordered its immediate shipment. The American manufacturer's management and staff—working together, naturally—then hurriedly produced and transported the necessary item to New York Harbor, where it was loaded onto a British vessel and shipped across the Atlantic via a multinational convoy, which arrived in the nick of time. Another short, *The Two-Way Street* (1945), a documentary commissioned by the OWI, portrayed the give-

and-take involved in reverse Lend-Lease. Such reciprocity, according to the voice-over narration, made the program a model for the future, as "all who have shared in the common defense must work together for better economic relations" in peacetime.[19]

More broadly, the United Nations was represented as a family of progressive peoples united by a common mission: remaking the world in such a way as to spread the Four Freedoms. The Allies aspired to create "a New World," a postwar utopia said by the OWI to encompass "a new and better life" for all, "democracy among nations as among individuals," and "a world community dedicated to the free flow of trade, ideas, and culture." During his 1941 annual address to Congress, President Roosevelt had declared that he looked "forward to a world founded upon four essential human freedoms": freedom of speech, freedom of religion, freedom from want, and freedom from fear. With help from cultural gatekeepers, the "Four Freedoms" came to represent the war's overriding moral principles in the popular imagination. FDR's words so moved Norman Rockwell that the folk artist translated their abstract articulation of liberty into four idealized scenes of everyday life. First published in the *Saturday Evening Post*, Rockwell's portraits became renowned when the Treasury Department employed them as centerpieces in its war bond sales drive. Drawing on the artist's work and the president's address, the OWI's propaganda guidance to the Hollywood studios associated the UN with the Four Freedoms: "If we hang together the United Nations are potentially stronger than the Axis in population, armed forces, raw materials, production capacity, and wealth. If we work together after the war as we have fought together during the war, the United Nations will have it within their power to establish 'for all peoples' and 'for future generations' a world in which there will be freedom of speech and freedom of religion, freedom from want, and freedom from fear."[20]

Marketing the United Nations as a collective force for "freedom" trafficked in inspirational fiction that overlooked some grim realities. Categorizing Stalin's Soviet Union as a liberal democracy was a stretch, to say the least. Great Britain still had its empire. African Americans were discriminated against in the United States. Indian nationalist leader Mohandas Gandhi pointed out the incongruity between the UN's words and deeds in a 1942 letter to President Roosevelt. The Allies' proclamation that "they are fighting to make the world safe for freedom of the individual and for democracy," Gandhi wrote, "sounds hollow, so long as India, and for that matter, Africa are exploited by Great Britain, and America has the Negro problem in her own home." African American civil rights activist A. Philip

Randolph also saw through the charade. "This is not a war for freedom. It is not a war for democracy," the leader of the March on Washington Movement said in May 1942; "it is a war to maintain the old imperialistic systems. It is a war to continue 'white supremacy' . . . and the subjugation, domination, and exploitation of the peoples of color."[21]

Still, the association of the Allies with benevolence contained a good deal of truth, particularly in comparison to the Germans, the Italians, and the Japanese. Contrasting the United Nations with what lay beyond its moral and ideological pale, the Axis Other, facilitated the development of a common Allied identity that the public could readily understand. Dehumanizing one's enemy, even to the point of portraying it as a savage, devilish beast, is a common if unfortunate by-product of war for the simple reason that doing so reduces the psychological barrier against killing other human beings. This tradition only grew during World War II, as the media had matured to the point where it offered more numerous and powerful avenues for replicating such imagery. Cultural authorities constructed the prime Axis powers, Japan and Germany, in the public mind as bêtes noires, monstrous creatures existing beyond the imagined community's bounds. Dragons to slay, they represented the exact opposites of everything that the fictive Allies held dear. If the United Nations stood for freedom, goodness, civilization, prosperity, and peace, the Axis stood for slavery, evil, barbarism, poverty, and war. What the idealized Allies upheld—human life, dignity, and diversity—the Axis destroyed. God was on the Allies' side, with official Soviet atheism conveniently ignored. However true or false these categorizations were (and they were both), they made for an effective public relations strategy, relying on standard tropes of heroes and villains to simplify and emotionalize complex geopolitical matters and thus enabling ordinary people to make some sense of the global war, to get on board, and to take sides even if they lacked full command of the particulars involved.[22]

"Properly directed hatred is of vital importance to the war effort," the OWI's Nelson Poynter explained to Hollywood studios. Starting from the proposition that Americans needed to "know our enemy—his philosophy, objectives, and tactics," the agency's information manual defined the adversary neither as a single person (Hitler, Japanese emperor Hirohito, or Italian dictator Benito Mussolini) nor as an entire people (Germans, Japanese, or Italians). Rather, just as the OWI fixed the UN's cause as a philosophical one (fostering the Four Freedoms), so too did it establish the enemy as an ideology—that is, "militarism—the doctrine of force—the age-old idea that people cannot co-inhabit the earth unless a few men dominate all others through physical force." A beastly creation, the "ruthless" Axis powers, unlike the peace-loving Allies, sought to bring the world under their tyrannical control "to exploit the peoples and monopolize the resources of the entire earth." Whereas the imaginary UN's overriding goal was the protection of human rights, the enemy subordinated the individual to the mass, enslaving it to the state's needs. "Under [the enemy's] system the individual is a cog in a military machine, a cipher in an economic despotism; the individual is a slave." Filmmakers were advised to hit that angle hard by portraying the adversary's "complete disregard for the inherent rights, the soul, of the people."[23]

That is not to say that the private media followed official directives to the letter. Slippage existed between official policy and commercial production with regard to portrayals of the Other, which often came out harsher than the state would have preferred. Just as Japanese wartime culture depicted Roosevelt and Churchill as demons and Americans as degenerates, the U.S. media produced Japanese caricatures. Anti-Japanese imagery sprang from the same combination of racial prejudice and post–Pearl Harbor anger that led to the internment of some one hundred thousand Japanese Americans. Racial slang—referring to Japanese as "Japs" or "Nips" (from Nippon, the Japanese reading of the country's name)—was part of the vernacular, even infecting the Warner Bros. cartoon *Bugs Bunny Nips the Nips* (1944). The stereotype of the bespectacled, bucktoothed Japanese, whether a simpleton or a sneak, was a staple of American wartime culture, barely raising an eyebrow until years later. In an advertisement for the RKO movie *Behind the Rising Sun* (1943), rapacious Japanese soldiers pawed semiclad, frightened Caucasian women as the text panted, "Jap brutes manhandling helpless women—by official proclamation!"[24]

Such racist representations delineated Us from Them by implying that Japanese were lesser beings unfit for membership in the normal family of nations because they were either too aggressive or too docile, depending on one's point of view. When U.S. ambassador Joseph Grew returned to the United States in April 1942 after having been under house arrest in Tokyo since the outbreak of hostilities, he publicly compared Japanese to sheep easily conditioned to serve the emperor. *Yank*, the U.S. Army's weekly magazine, also adopted this point of view, as did a sociologist who explained during a nationwide radio broadcast that Japanese were a "closely disciplined and conformist people—a veritable human beehive or ant hill." This characteristic alone, he claimed, disqualified Japan from the civilized world community insofar as its inhabitants formed a mass devoid of individual identity and incapable of independent thought. The brutal war in the Pacific only further inflamed anti-Japanese sentiment, making subhuman characterizations even more commonplace. Reality and image reinforced one another, with the one providing grounds for dehumanization and the other lending legitimacy to the commission of wartime atrocities up to and including the use of atomic weaponry against Hiroshima and Nagasaki in August 1945. In one telling example, the *New York Times*, in February 1945, ran an advertisement by a chemical company that showed a GI blasting a path "through stubborn Jap defenses" with a flamethrower. The ad bore the heading, "Clearing Out a Rat's Nest." So common were such comparisons that the OWI's Bureau of Motion Pictures warned filmmakers against referring "to the Japanese as 'little brown men' or 'yellow rats.' This is not a racial war. Many millions of our allies belong to the brown and yellow races and such references are offensive to them."[25]

War correspondent Ernie Pyle noted a difference when he transferred to the Pacific theater from Europe in February 1945. Whereas in the Pacific, Japanese "were looked upon as something subhuman and repulsive; the way some people feel about cockroaches or mice," he wrote, "in Europe we felt that our enemies, horrible and deadly as they were, were still people." When it came to Germany, state and media agreed that the adversary was Nazism for leading the country astray, a distinction that left cognitive space for differentiating "good Germans" from "bad" ones. The young lieutenant in the Twentieth Century–Fox movie *The Moon Is Down* (1943) was emblematic of the "good German," a humanist who expressed ambivalence about the Third Reich. Conversely, Nazis were cast as villains, a role for which they were well suited, as evidenced by Conrad Veidt's character, Major Strasser, in *Casablanca* (1942). Hollywood, whose trade was built in part on gangster movies, compared Nazis to criminals in Paramount's *The Hitler Gang* (1944) and to sexual offenders in RKO's *Hitler's Children* (1943). The studios were only following FDR's rhetorical lead. In his speeches, the president branded the Axis powers "crafty and powerful bandits" or "resourceful gangsters" who "banded together" to enslave "the whole human race."[26]

The media portrayed Nazism as an evil force, a remorseless, robotic killing machine that eliminated everything in its wake. A representative poster, inspired by tales of Nazi book burnings, showed a knife held by a swastika-marked fist impaling the Bible. Nazism threatened to destroy not just religion but also life itself, according to another graphic that depicted a giant swastika descending on a group of defenseless children, one clutching an American flag. Although the extent of the Nazis' crimes against humanity was not yet fully understood—that horrible realization would come only after the Allies' liberation of the extermination camps—a poster designed by artist Ben Shahn dealt with an atrocity that was known at the time. "This Is Nazi Brutality" featured a lone figure, hooded, shackled, and backed against a brick wall, an image contextualized by the words of a radio news report from the Czechoslovak village of Lidice, where in June 1942 German soldiers had massacred civilians and sent the survivors to concentration camps.[27]

Nazis were not, however, exempt from monstrous characterizations. One poster, "Lookout Monkeys," showed the sky thick with American warplanes about to take revenge on Hitler and the Japanese prime minister, General Hideki Tojo, shown as half-man, half-ape beasts that had ravaged the American countryside. In another image, reminiscent of Great War–era Anglo-American propaganda that commonly portrayed the Germans as rapacious, bloodthirsty Huns, two giants (again, Hitler and Tojo, the former armed with a Luger pistol, the latter holding a bloody knife) clutch a globe and leer hungrily at North America. Distributed by General Motors, this poster encouraged laborers to produce as a means of fending off the murderous would-be invaders, warning, "Our homes are in danger *now*!"[28]

Nightmarish visions of the Other gave Allied peoples the necessary visual language with which to express not only hatred for their enemies but also affection for their brothers in arms. A July 1941 David Low cartoon, for example, showed three servicemen, identified as representing the United States, Great Britain, and the Soviet Union, standing beneath a palm tree as they scanned the Pacific in anticipation of a Japanese attack. Unbeknownst to them, a monkey—labeled "Jap," wearing eyeglasses, and clutching a dagger—is suspended from the tree, preparing to stab the white men in the back. Hollywood director Frank Capra juxtaposed the Allies and the Axis on the big screen in *Prelude to War* (1942), the first installment of *Why We Fight*, his seven-part series that explained to American soldiers and civilians why, against what, and with whom they were fighting. As Capra saw it, the series, commissioned by the U.S. Army to orient GIs, had two main objectives that determined his representation of foreign powers. The first, stoking popular morale to win the war, led him to contrast "the enemy's ruthless objectives" with the Allies' fight "for the existence of our country and our freedoms." The second, cultivating an internationalist spirit conducive to peacemaking, Capra wrote, required pointing out the dangers of international outlawry on one hand and promoting a new world order based on "better understanding" and "democratic principles" on the other.[29]

Prelude to War became required viewing for millions of U.S. soldiers as well as civilians after Army brass permitted its commercial release in 1943. Winner of an Academy Award for Best Documentary, Capra's production is considered a cinematic landmark for its pathbreaking combination of style and service to the state. He communicated an officially prescribed worldview by skillfully assembling discrete aesthetic elements—authentic footage and staged scenes, animation, voice-over narration, and so forth—into a seamless, smartly paced, Oliver Stone–like whole that still overwhelms viewers to this day. Although *Prelude to War* was nothing more than one Hollywood director's take on reality, it came off as an authentic portrait of the world, a documentary that carried the U.S. government's seal of approval. It may have been even better than the real thing, as its impressive montage, moving at breakneck speed, made on-screen sense of a complex world. Perhaps Capra's real genius lay in his use of the enemy's own words. Confiscated enemy newsreels, documentaries, and commercial pictures—including scenes from Leni Riefenstahl's paean to Hitler, *Triumph of the Will* (1935)—were edited into *Prelude to War*, where they acquired anti-Axis meaning when juxtaposed against ideal imagery of the Allies. Capra described this technique as "Let the enemy prove to our soldiers the enormity of his cause—and the justness of ours." He continued, "Let our boys hear the Nazis and the Japs shout their own claims of master-race crud."[30]

Audiences received a geopolitical education without leaving their theater seats. From *Prelude to War*, they learned that the world war was caused by and their feelings of insecurity linked to obscure events in remote places, from Pearl Harbor to Poland to Manchuria. Viewers learned, too, that two worlds—one slave, one free—were engaged in a Manichaean struggle. The competing worlds, illustrated by animated drawings of a black globe and a white globe, mirrored one another. The slave Axis world was evil, demonic, barbaric, totalitarian, and aggressive; the free Allied world was good, godly, civilized, democratic, and peaceful. In Japan, Nazi Germany, and Fascist Italy, according to the voice-over narration, people surrendered "their rights as individual human beings and became part of a mass, a human herd," a statement seemingly backed up by what appears on-screen. Enemy documentary footage, recontextualized by Capra, shows row after row of uniformed Japanese obediently bowing to Hirohito, Germans repeatedly saluting Hitler, and Italians doing the same before Mussolini. Scenes intended to have one meaning in their original Japanese, German, or Italian contexts acquired altogether different connotations when repackaged in *Prelude to War*. Children pledging allegiance became a sinister plot to indoctrinate fascist youth. Adults saluting their head of state became "fanatical" worship of a diabolical totalitarian leader elevated to godlike status.

Moreover, the enemy sought "world conquest." Maps animated by Walt Disney Studios illustrated the enemy's plan, which entailed Japan conquering Asia before advancing east across the Pacific toward the United States. At the same time, the Germans would move from Europe to the Middle East to the Americas, where they would meet "their buck-toothed pals." If left unchecked, the Axis powers would ultimately end up in Washington, a potential calamity Capra represented by showing marching Japanese soldiers superimposed onto Pennsylvania Avenue, where they trample the U.S. Capitol and the White House, symbols of democracy and sovereignty. Over this scene, the narrator asks viewers to "imagine the field day [Japanese troops would] enjoy if they marched through the streets of Washington," having already raped Nanking, Hong Kong, and Manila.

Prelude to War's segue from the Axis to the Allies is striking. The animated globes reappear, and as the camera's focus shifts from the slave world to the free, the tone abruptly changes as well: the palette goes from dark to light, the instrumentation from heavy drums and brass to ethereal strings, the mood from gloomy to optimistic. In this sunny environment, John Q. Public could vote for whomever he pleased; attend the church of his choice; and speak, live, and work freely. Plus, the Allied world was peaceful, so much so that Americans had been slow to react to the gathering Axis threat, misled "by those who said we could find security through isolation."

Once disabused of that illusion, Americans had joined the United Nations. Capra's conclusion, a plea for collective security, begins with a visual tour of the Lincoln Memorial, a symbol of liberation since African American contralto Marian Anderson's 1939 performance there after she was prohibited from singing at another, segregated Washington venue. To the background strains of "The Battle Hymn of the Republic," the camera zeroes in on the portion of the Gettysburg Address in which Lincoln, speaking during the American Civil War, resolved "that these dead shall not have died in vain—that this nation, under God, shall have a new birth of freedom, and that government of the people, by the people, for the people shall not perish from the earth." Lincoln's words applied equally to World War II, according to the voice-over narration, representing "a free people's life and death struggle against those who would put them back into slavery." With a quick visual cut to the waving flags of the UN member states superimposed over footage of advancing Allied armies, the narrator reminds viewers that the Allies had "sworn that man shall remain free. This is the cause for which we fight." Here Capra, like Norman Rockwell, drew concrete links between foreign and domestic affairs, public and private matters. Through pictures and words, the director portrayed freedom, the abstract principle for which the Allies were said to be fighting, as a comfortable home, the safety of one's family, and the opportunity to earn a decent living. "Two worlds stand against each other—one must die; one must live," *Prelude to War* concludes as the animated globes make a final appearance, with the globe representing the free world moving forward to eclipse the globe symbolizing the slave world. That scene fades after a moment, replaced by a shot of a ringing Liberty Bell, backing the already ubiquitous "V for Victory" sign.

Hollywood features also projected the image of a diverse family of nations on the march toward a more liberal world order. Viewers were already conversant with such visions of international community, which corresponded with the impression of domestic tranquility left by wartime advertisers. Posters urged Americans from all walks of life to cooperate toward a common end. Distributed by the War Manpower Commission, one such image featured a photograph of black and white workers with the Stars and Stripes as a background. "United We Win," the text read, in case anyone missed the point. Movies did their bit by upholding the multicultural combat platoon as a model for American unity. In *Guadalcanal Diary* (1943), *Bataan* (1943), and *Gung Ho!* (1943), among many others, the platoon idealized wartime America in miniature, as its members—Catholics, Jews, and Protestants; easterners, southerners, and westerners; and Irish, Italian, and other immigrant Americans—forged a single unit via their demonstrated commitment to a shared national goal: battlefield victory.[31]

"Rick's Café Américain" provides the last refuge for Europe's beleaguered, polyglot victims of Nazism in *Casablanca*, the 1942 classic. What could pass as the war's signature movie is so artful that it is possible to overlook the fact that the film was made by Warner Bros. (and supervised by the OWI) for the explicit political purpose of lending support to the United Nations and American internationalism via a dramatization of the war in North Africa. (The movie was rushed to theaters in November 1942 to capitalize on news of Operation Torch, the successful Allied invasion of North Africa.) Exiled Americans, Britons, Czechoslovaks, Free French,

Norwegians, and Russians, bit parts played mostly by Hollywood's growing stable of refugee actors who had fled Nazi-dominated Europe, patronize the nightclub, a proto-UN menagerie. Like their fellow exiles, Victor Laszlo, a fugitive Czech resistance leader played by Paul Henreid, and his wife, Ilsa Lund (Ingrid Bergman), arrive in the capital of Vichy-controlled French Morocco in hopes of obtaining exit papers that permit safe passage to America. Their arrival sets in motion the film's politics and action, which takes place over two days in December 1941, as Laszlo rallies Rick's cosmopolitan patrons to do symbolic battle against Casablanca's fascist occupiers. When the film's villain, Major Strasser, leads Nazi officers in a rendition of "Die Macht am Rhein," Laszlo responds by conducting the house band in a performance of the French national anthem. Sung lustily by Rick's anti-Nazi clientele, "La Marseillaise" overwhelms the patriotic German song.

At the center of the brewing international maelstrom, of course, is the nightclub's owner, Humphrey Bogart's Rick Blaine, a hard-boiled New Yorker who stands in for America as it weighs the basic foreign policy choice put before it on the eve of Pearl Harbor. An idealist at heart who supplied guns to Ethiopia during its 1935 war versus Mussolini's Italy and fought in the Spanish Civil War against the Fascists, Rick nevertheless had an unfortunate formative experience with European affairs that left him, like his fellow Americans, disillusioned with and embittered toward the outside world. This being a Hollywood drama, Rick's cynical worldview stems from his failed whirlwind romance—in Paris, no less, site of the Treaty of Versailles, America's last serious foray into foreign power politics—with Ilsa, who had seemingly abandoned him as the Nazis marched into the city in 1940. His heart broken, the disillusioned Rick retreated to Casablanca, where, as a businessman catering to Nazis, Vichy officials, and refugees alike, he followed a strict personal code of neutrality and isolationism. Impatient with "causes" and global politics, Bogart's archetypal American sticks "his neck out for nobody," as he often summarizes his stance.

Yet *Casablanca*'s director, Michael Curtiz, and screenwriters, Julius and Philip Epstein and Howard Koch, framed the story so that the protagonist has to make a moral choice between aiding the Axis or the Allies. Having come into possession of two letters of transit that will guarantee their bearers' escape to America, Bogart's character must decide whether to do what is expedient (handing the papers over to Major Strasser and thereby aiding the Nazi cause) or what is right (providing the documents to Laszlo and Ilsa, an act that will assist the worldwide fight for freedom against Nazi tyranny). His political dilemma is complicated by a personal one—if he gives the letters to the fugitive couple, he will effectively forever bid adieu to Ilsa, his beloved, and assist his romantic rival, Laszlo. Rick struggles with his decision, and it is not at all clear which path he will choose. In the final reel, however, he famously opts for what is just, providing the letters of transit to Ilsa and Laszlo, who welcome him "back to the fight" before their hasty departure from Casablanca's airport ahead of the pursuing Major Strasser, shot dead by Rick to ensure the couple's successful getaway. The hero's tortured transition from cynical, selfish isolationist to committed, selfless internationalist—a shift that, within the film's context, comes on the eve of actual U.S. intervention—served as a morality tale that not only mirrored America's transformed worldview but also ennobled the Allied cause.

Bogart stepped from *Casablanca*'s airport into the sands of *Sahara* (1943), Columbia's dramatization of the North African campaign. Adapted by writer John Howard Lawson from a Soviet screenplay, *The Thirteen* (1937), *Sahara* managed to unify the U.S. Army and the United Nations at the same time. Bogart's character, Sergeant Joe Gunn, commands an American tank, nicknamed the *Lulubelle*, and its stereotypically diverse crew, whose members hail from Brooklyn to Texas. Separated from its unit and almost encircled by the enemy, the *Lulubelle* beats a hasty southward retreat across the desert. As it does, Sergeant Gunn's already motley crew swells with stragglers encountered along the way—a British medic, several Commonwealth troops, a Free Frenchman, and a Sudanese officer and his Italian prisoner of war—becoming a rolling microcosm of the United Nations. No effort is spared in singing the UN's praises. Desperate for water, the members of the *Lulubelle*'s ragtag outfit develop a sense of camaraderie as they scour the sands for wells, becoming a band of brothers struggling not just for survival but also for human dignity. The British medical officer voluntarily cedes authority to Sergeant Gunn, who runs the outfit firmly but democratically. Rather than leaving him to die in the Sahara, the group humanely welcomes into its fold the Italian prisoner, Giuseppe (a supporting role for which actor J. Carrol Naish earned an Academy Award nomination), redeemed by his expressed suspicion of fascism and his affection for America. Even Waco (Bruce Bennett), the white Texan at one extreme, forms a friendship with Sergeant Major Tambul (Rex Ingram), the black Sudanese at the other.

Tambul resides at the center of *Sahara*'s juxtaposition of the Allies and Axis. He is a full and equal member of the tank's team, even becoming the hero by virtue of his discovery of a water source that saves them all. In

Sergeant Gunn (Humphrey Bogart) leads an assemblage of the United Nations while Tambul (Rex Ingram) guards an enemy prisoner in *Sahara* (1943), Columbia's dramatization of Allied inclusivity. Photofest/ © Columbia Pictures.

contrast, a Nazi pilot, the film's requisite villain, rejects the African. When Gunn orders Tambul to search the pilot, downed and captured after firing on the crew and killing one of its men, the Aryan recoils at the prospect of being touched by what he calls a member of an "inferior race." Ever the democrat, Gunn proceeds with the search nonetheless.

Having found water, Bogart's men mount a defense of the precious re- source against an approaching battalion of thirsty German soldiers. Out- numbered, isolated, and short on supplies, the defense of some remote oasis appears to be a meaningless suicide mission. Yet the matter is put to a vote, and the members of the miniature UN unanimously elect to make a stand when Gunn puts things in broader perspective. In a melo- dramatic speech that reeks of OWI propaganda, Bogart's character ex- plains that even the defense of a lonely patch of sand serves the cause of victory insofar as it slows Axis momentum and buys time for the Allies to grow in strength. In that sense, his command's efforts were said to be analogous to those of Londoners during the Blitz, of Muscovites amid the German siege of that city, or of Chinese following Japan's invasion. Although most of the *Lulubelle*'s cosmopolitan crew (predictably including the saintly Tambul) die for the greater Allied good during the ensuing battle, *Sahara*'s story of international partnership ends on a happy note: Gunn and the few remaining survivors somehow hold out and capture their German counterparts just before the British Eighth Army arrives with news that the Second Battle of El Alamein has been won.[32]

Documentary films, too, demonstrated the rewards of international camaraderie. In 1942, the OWI commissioned *The Price of Victory*, a screen version of Vice President Henry A. Wallace's address before the Free World Association on 8 May 1942 in New York City. In his speech, Wallace envisioned the UN as a community of nations with a progressive mission to democratize the world. Intended as a rejoinder to publisher Henry Luce's 1941 editorial, "The American Century," read by some as a call for American empire, the vice president's talk instead styled World War II as a "people's revolution" to be shepherded by the United Nations in such a way as to bring about an egalitarian "century of the common man." A devout Episcopalian and social gospeler, Wallace imagined that new day as predicated on a Christian brotherhood of humanity and as characterized in the postwar era by national self-determination, human equality, and general economic improvement. Although Wallace's evangelism was not without critics—Connecticut's Republican representative Clare Boothe Luce (Henry Luce's wife) called his speech "globaloney"—his words nevertheless became a cornerstone of American wartime thought for their clear definition of the war's moral principles and bold expression of progressive internationalism. As such, Wallace's address emerged as the centerpiece of an OWI publicity campaign on behalf of Allied unity and the UN's stated aspirations. His words appeared on posters and inspired *The Price of Victory*, distributed by Paramount. Agency officials felt that the film would carry a "tremendous punch" abroad, where the vice president's vision of "a just, charitable, and enduring peace," punctuated by the spread of the Four Freedoms, would find a ready audience.[33]

Wallace's speech influenced *Democracy in Action* (1942), produced by the Department of Agriculture for farmers suspicious of foreigners and U.S. overseas activism. The short documentary encouraged growers to connect their labor to the health of America's allies no less than to that of the U.S. war effort. Agricultural produce acquired even greater importance during wartime, the film noted, as, under Lend-Lease, it fueled the

Allies' quest to make the world again safe for democracy. Cotton clothed Allied soldiers. Milk nourished "British kids." And canned vegetables, fruits, and meats fed all the United Nations, who "look to our pantry to keep them going."[34]

The vice president's message also infused *Oswego* (1943). Distributed theatrically via Hollywood's War Activities Committee, the OWI documentary promoted a catholic outlook by pointing out the many connections between an ordinary American town, Oswego, New York, and the wider world. The daily paper carried the latest world news. Family mailboxes contained letters from boys serving abroad. Local factories produced tanks for use by Allied forces. And each day, the city's harbor, a gateway to the Atlantic via Lake Ontario, witnessed the transaction of mutual Lend-Lease aid. (Directed by noted photographer and filmmaker Wilbur Van Dyke, *Oswego* was careful to note that what transpired in local waters represented a net benefit to Americans: bauxite arrived from Dutch Guiana (now Suriname) for transshipment to Canada, whose vessels off-loaded paper for use in the United States.)

The world was brought even closer to home during United Nations Week, when the town's residents hosted soldiers representing several Allied countries—Belgium, Britain, Canada, France, Greece, Norway, and Poland—as part of a community exercise in people-to-people diplomacy. Oswego took on "an international look" as the week began, with a plethora of public exhibits and a parade honoring its visitors, said to embody all "free peoples united in a common cause." Oswego's residents became better acquainted with their guests as each day passed. Romance bloomed between a local girl and a visiting Norwegian sailor. Catholics welcomed the Polish soldier, a coreligionist, into their fold for Sunday mass. Factory workers developed comradeship with the Allied troops, who offered assurances that the armaments made at the facility were being put to good use against the enemy.

By week's end, the small-town New Yorkers had become "old friends" with the Allied representatives. Over scenes of a good-bye dinner at the home of the local college president (a familial setting reminiscent of Rockwell's portrait of freedom from want), audiences heard that "foreign countries no longer seemed strange and distant: not Britain, Greece, France, and Norway, but Stephen, Jean, Alf, and Martin—friends sitting around a table." As a result, by the time the Allied soldiers departed to win the war and thus "make the image of peace and friendliness come true," according to the voice-over narration, both they and the town's residents better understood the pledge of the United Nations. *Oswego* closed with a recitation of that pledge, an oral acknowledgment of progressive world citizenship and its inherent rights and responsibilities: "We affirm our faith in the Four Freedoms essential to human happiness. We dedicate ourselves to that collaboration among men and nations that will establish security and lasting peace for all the peoples of the world."

Wartime visual culture reinforced the big screen's ecumenism. Mexican American caricaturist Miguel Covarrubias introduced viewers to their foreign friends in 1942 with *United Nations*, his family portrait of the alliance's leaders, fronted by the Big Four—Churchill, Jiang, Roosevelt, and Stalin. Posters distributed by both the OFF and the MOI that year each featured a photograph of an American, British, Chinese, or Soviet soldier along with text informing passersby, "This man is your FRIEND," as "He fights for FREEDOM." A 1943 OWI graphic took a more nuanced approach, illustrating in brilliant color the UN's hard power, combined industrial and military strength that would decide the war and usher in a peaceful tomorrow. Behind text reading "UNITED we are strong; UNITED we will win," long, steel gun turrets (or perhaps cement industrial smokestacks), each draped in a flag of a UN member state (with the flags of Britain, China, the Soviet Union, and the United States featured) fire their potent payload skyward, clearing the smoky clouds of battle and leading, one might assume, to a brighter, better, even heavenly future. Another 1943 OWI product conveyed a similar impression. Under a banner headline, "UNITED," the flags of the great Allied powers wave in the winds of certain victory as tanks, warships, and airplanes roll concertedly and inexorably forward. "The United Nations fight for freedom," the image's text reminded viewers.[35]

United Nations Day, an annual public festival first held on 14 June 1942, also commemorated a global outlook. In May, Roosevelt issued a proclamation turning the war's first patriotic holiday, Flag Day, held each June to mark Old Glory's adoption, into United Nations Day, organized by U.S. officials as a "springboard" for the entire UN campaign. The occasion fused Flag Day's customary homage to the prime symbol of national identity with a nod toward international belonging. As FDR stated, "We as a nation are not fighting alone. In this planetary war we are a part of a great whole; we are fighting shoulder to shoulder with the valiant peoples of the United Nations, the mass, angered forces of common humanity. Unless all triumph all will fail." Consequently, the president asked Americans to use the day when they traditionally honored their own country's

Office of Facts and Figures poster promoting China as one of the UN Allies, 1942. Item 44-PA-2097A, Still Picture Unit, National Archives and Records Administration II, College Park, Md.

"UNITED: The United Nations Fight for Freedom." Office of War Information poster, 1943. Item 44-PA-2195, Still Picture Unit, National Archives and Records Administration II, College Park, Md.

colors to pay heed as well to the flags of their UN allies, which he ordered displayed on all federal, state, and local government buildings. Private citizens were also encouraged to fly Allied standards at home as a show of international solidarity. A special poster created by the OFF to publicize the event featured the flags of the UN's greatest powers—Old Glory, the Union Jack, and the Soviet Hammer and Sickle—above those of the other Allies, all superimposed on an image of the Statue of Liberty and under the headline, "The United Nations Fight for Freedom."[36]

United Nations Day began with a morning radio program carried by the National Broadcasting Company (NBC) that took the ideas expressed by Vice President Wallace and President Roosevelt as its central themes. Written by Stephen Vincent Benét, the play reminded listeners that although the UN countries flew "many flags in many colors," they shared *"one hope, one aim, one unconquerable purpose*: freedom and justice for the common man, everywhere in the world. Freedom to think and to speak, freedom to worship; justice against the fear of force; justice for the unprotected, against the greed of a powerful few." Isolationism's moment had passed, discredited after creating the conditions for militarism's rise and war's return. Decent, ordinary people everywhere had now joined forces against international outlawry, requiring a new spirit of cooperation. To illustrate, the narrator quoted John Donne's "Meditation XVII" from *Devotions upon Emergent Occasions* (1624):

> No man is an island, entire of itself;
> Any man's death diminishes me,
> because I am involved in mankind,
> And therefore never send to know for whom the bell tolls;
> It tolls for thee.[37]

On that note, radio listeners heard tales of Allied unity. A Soviet spokesperson, for example, related the story of Peter, a fictional Red Army soldier who wrote a letter home before being killed on the battlefield. Although frightened on the eve of battle, Peter's fervent desire for freedom, "life," and "happiness" steeled his will. Peter's story reminded American audiences, safe in their living rooms, of their overseas brethren's sacrifices. The letter also suggested that the Soviet people were prepared to build Wallace's new century of the common man if only Americans would "take our hand" and "grant us understanding and forbearance." "We are your friends," the Soviet voice added. As the "Star-Spangled Banner" swelled in the background, the American, British, Chinese, and Soviet characters concluded the program with a joint call-and-response perpetuating the UN's image as a popular liberation army:

CHORUS: Unite!
NARRATOR: Unite in brotherhood—for a people's victory!
CHORUS: Unite!
NARRATOR: Unite in brotherhood—for a people's peace![38]

The dramatization complete, NBC broadcast FDR's keynote address. The day's festivities, he said, were held to "celebrate the Declaration of the United Nations—that great alliance dedicated to the defeat of our foes and to the establishment of a true peace based on the freedom of man." Here, Roosevelt directly linked the UN with the Four Freedoms, telling listeners that the Allies' shared belief in those basic human rights distinguished them from the enemy. He closed with a prayer written especially for the occasion, using his oratorical skills to link motifs of faith, family, and freedom with the Grand Alliance: "Grant us victory over the tyrants who would enslave all free men and nations. Grant us faith and understanding to cherish all those who fight for freedom as if they were our brothers. Grant us brotherhood in hope and union, not only for the space of this bitter war, but for the days to come which shall and must unite all the children of the earth." After requesting the "wisdom" necessary to craft a just and durable peace, the president asked to receive the following knowledge: "If our brothers are oppressed, then we are oppressed. If they hunger, we hunger. If their freedom is taken away, our freedom is not secure. Grant us a common faith that man shall know bread and peace—that he shall know justice and righteousness, freedom and security, an equal opportunity and an equal chance to do his best, not only in our own lands, but throughout the world. And in that faith let us march, toward the clean world our hands can make."[39]

People across the country marked United Nations Day. Patriotism no doubt moved the vast majority of revelers, but a spirit of international goodwill was in evidence, too. Churches hosted special services featuring prayers for UN victory. Some 20,000 residents of Columbus, Ohio, participated in a parade witnessed by another 150,000. Secretary of the Navy Frank Knox led a ceremony in Boston at which several Allied diplomats were present. Undersecretary of State Sumner Welles spoke in Baltimore, where he urged the UN members to reach a "new world understanding." More than 1,500 people gathered at Manhattan's Rockefeller Center, where the head of British Information Services, Sir Gerald Campbell, led

Allied soldiers in reciting, "We pledge our allegiance as United Nations. We confirm our unity." Afterward, Campbell bluntly told the crowd that the day's spirit of Allied unity must extend even beyond the armistice, when "our countries must cooperate with each other, or die."[40]

The biggest spectacle occurred in Chicago, where an estimated 585,000 people marched in a fifteen-hour parade, the largest in the city's history. A million spectators lined the route along Michigan Avenue, cheering on the passing "fantastic floats, marching men and women, cartwheeling youths, bicycle clubs, and all the neighborhood groups." Among those groups were the city's many ethnic associations, including those for people of Chinese, Mexican, and Polish descent, who, in lieu of actual foreigners, stood in for the United Nations, lending a cosmopolitan flavor to the festivities. Other marchers bore the standards of each of the UN's member states. The parade was but a prelude to the day's main event: an afternoon Soldier Field ceremony officiated by comedian Bob Hope. The *Chicago Tribune* described the celebration as "the Windy City's conception of the famous New Orleans Mardi Gras, with the serious overtones that brought the realization that this was more than a parade, more than a tribute to . . . the flag, or America's heroic allies: That it was also a re-iteration of the American belief in freedom and fair play and notice to the enemy that the people of the United States are ready for them."[41]

United Nations Day provided not only a forum to express support for the Allies but also a means of expressing hatred for the Axis. In Chicago's parade, American Federation of Labor members carried signs commanding, "Don't Be Saps. Help Lick the Japs." Ironworkers displayed a placard reading, "Hitler Will Never Cross Our Bridges." One lone man trudged along Michigan Avenue attired only in a barrel and holding a sign mocking "Hitler and His New Order." In Manhattan, one float, "Hitler—The Axis War Monster," portrayed the Nazi leader as an enormous mechanical skeleton, around which were strewn the mutilated bodies of women and children. Another float, "Tokyo—We Are Coming," showed a "big American eagle leading a flight of bombs down on a herd of yellow rats which were trying to escape in all directions." The "crowd loved it," a report noted. On a symbolic level, that float's juxtaposition speaks volumes about the Manichaean way of seeing the Allies and the Axis: the bald eagle representing individual freedom and technological superiority soaring, like a bomber, above the undifferentiated pack of yellow vermin, a racist image suggestive of Asian hordes devoid of humanity, individuality, and intelligence. As such, the float justified the UN's drive to destroy and establish dominion over the subhuman enemy.[42]

United Nations Day became a transnational event. Muscovites enjoyed a rare opportunity to watch British documentary films, browse an exhibit of American and British books, and hear lectures on the U.S. war effort. Allied flags flew alongside the Soviet standard on Moscow's streets. The display was meant to demonstrate the Allies' "common solidarity and their determination to throw all their means and strength into the struggle against their common foes," the enemies of "humanity," said the Soviet ambassador, Litvinov. Public endorsements of the UN were obviously stage-managed by Soviet authorities, but the U.S. press nevertheless reported them as fact, and they must have strengthened America's feeling of solidarity. A peasant from Kazakhstan was quoted as saying, "I see it this way. A poisonous snake came into our house. On the way it is eating up everything. While it is alive we can't live safely, nor can anybody else. Now we and our Allies are going to break its spine and head." According to a Red Army soldier, "The strengthening of fighting unity between us, Britain, and America is a knife struck at the vitals of the bandit Hitler."[43]

Britons turned United Nations Day into the United Kingdom's "greatest patriotic turnout" since the war's beginning. Church attendees prayed for victory. Parades wended through cities and hamlets draped with the flags of the UN's members. In London, a quarter of a million onlookers lined a parade route that carried a half-mile-long phalanx of laborers, farmers, and Allied, British, and Commonwealth troops up Whitehall, around Trafalgar Square, and past Buckingham Palace, where King George VI greeted them. The Soviet ambassador to London, Ivan M. Maisky, and his American counterpart, John G. Winant, were also on hand. Earlier in the day, Winant had read biblical passages at St. Martin-in-the-Fields, a service broadcast by the British Broadcasting Corporation, which carried FDR's keynote address as well. Statements by Churchill and Lord Halifax, ambassador to the United States, emphasized Allied unity. London's *Daily Mail* ran a cartoon heralding the celebration, later replayed in theaters via an MOI short, as physical evidence of the "United Will to Win."[44]

United Nations Day, Bogart's *Sahara* and *Casablanca*, Capra's *Why We Fight*, and other wartime phenomena asked Americans to reimagine the world, to see it anew. Whereas Americans once tended to be relatively insular, wartime experience taught them to be less parochial and more cosmopolitan. Soldiers left home to serve abroad in the armed forces. Civilians moved to Washington, D.C.; Detroit; Los Angeles; and other places to take defense jobs. Culture collected those individual experiences and contextualized them so that they acquired even broader

"OLD GLORY PARADES ON UNITED NATIONS DAY: American Army color guard marches through London's Trafalgar Square during the United Nations parade recently." Office of War Information photo, 1943. Item 208-AA-042M-5, Still Picture Unit, National Archives and Records Administration II, College Park, Md.

meaning. Americans learned that the world had fundamentally changed. It had become smaller—and more dangerous—thanks to technological innovation. Ships connected port cities and facilitated trade, but German submarines also could appear unannounced on the eastern seaboard. Airplanes quickened intercontinental travel, but Japanese bombers also could strike U.S. territory without warning. Newspapers, radio, and newsreels brought home information about faraway peoples and places but also bore witness to the Rape of Nanking, the Blitzkrieg, and eventually the Holocaust. What happened in Shanghai, Warsaw, and Kiev was no longer of merely local interest but now mattered to San Franciscans, Chicagoans, and New Yorkers. Safety, in turn, could no longer be obtained by isolating oneself from the outside world and its many dangers, as the fact that the globe was again engulfed in conflagration proved.

Rather, security came from looking outward, leaning forward, and organizing collectively. As such, Americans were taught almost overnight to become full members of the international community, a change codified in the Declaration of the United Nations. Hadn't Sir Gerald Campbell and Oswego's residents led symbolic recitations of global pledges of allegiance?

This broadened sensibility derived from several sources. *London Can Take It* and Edward R. Murrow's radio broadcasts during the Blitz viscerally linked American audiences to their British cousins. Listeners to Roosevelt's Fireside Chats received geography lessons when they unfolded their maps and followed along at home as FDR explained Allied strategy. Wendell Willkie perhaps best captured the new spirit, however. After losing the 1940 presidential election to Roosevelt, Willkie returned to private law practice but remained in the public eye, as in September 1941, when he defended the Hollywood studios against isolationist senators' charges of "warmongering." And he took liberal positions such as supporting FDR's foreign policies that marked Willkie as a maverick vis-à-vis the Republican establishment.[45]

With Roosevelt's blessing, Willkie departed from New York in August 1942 on what would be a forty-nine day, thirty-one-thousand-mile around-the-world journey that took him to Cairo, Khartoum, Ankara, Baghdad, Tehran, Moscow, and several stops in China. When he returned in October, an estimated 36 million radio listeners tuned in to hear him discuss his trip. The next year, Willkie published *One World*, a written account of his voyage. Willkie traveled by airplane, which taught him that the globe was interconnected as never before by transportation and communications systems. Whereas foreign peoples and crises once seemed distant and unimportant, they now appeared closer and pertinent to members of the emerging global community. "Distant points in the world" no longer existed, claimed Willkie, who learned from his travels "that the myriad millions of human beings of the Far East are as close to us as Los Angeles is to New York by the fastest trains." The author predicted that the problems of the people of the world would soon concern Americans "almost as much as the problems of the people of California concern the people of New York." "Our thinking in the future must be worldwide," argued Willkie, insisting that Americans were already becoming cosmopolitan by virtue of their wartime experiences: "This war has opened for us new horizons—new geographical horizons, new mental horizons," he wrote. "We have become a people whose first interests are beyond the seas. The names of Russian, Burmese, Tunisian, or Chinese towns command primary attention in our newspapers." Consequently, the United States was in the process of "changing completely from a young nation of domestic concerns to an adult nation of international interests and world outlook."[46]

The United Nations offered the clearest evidence to date of global connectivity. *One World* brimmed with enthusiasm for the UN's foremost powers—China and the Soviet Union, especially—and envisioned them developing into the core of a postwar international peacekeeping organization. "The United Nations must become a common council, not only for the winning of the war but for the future welfare of mankind," wrote Willkie. While doing battle, the Allies ought to "develop a mechanism of working together that will survive after the fighting is over." The author outlined a robust mission for the association of nations: it should simultaneously adjudicate international disputes and spread the Four Freedoms. Like Wallace, Willkie understood World War II as a "war of liberation" that would free people from not only fascism but also colonialism and "our own domestic imperialisms," by which he meant racism and poverty. Improved human welfare "throughout the world is interdependent," he argued.[47]

Willkie's internationalist message resonated among readers. *One World* sold more than a million copies within months of its March 1943 publication, eventually becoming the best-selling work of nonfiction in American history to that point. *Foreign Affairs*, the U.S. foreign policy establishment's journal of record, called the book "one of the hardest blows ever struck against the intellectual and moral isolationism of the American people." Protestant theologian Reinhold Niebuhr dubbed its author a "proponent of a wise internationalism."[48]

Internationalist Daryl F. Zanuck, who had campaigned for Willkie in 1940, planned to turn *One World* into a movie. (The fact that Willkie chaired Fox's board from 1942 until heart disease took his life in October 1944 may have influenced the executive producer's interest.) Though that project never reached the screen, Zanuck did produce *Wilson*, a biopic of the former president. Starring Canadian actor Alexander Knox, a relative unknown, in the title role, the Technicolor film sympathetically chronicled Wilson's life from his days as president of Princeton, through his tenure in the Oval Office, to his death in 1924.[49]

The most resonant episodes at the time of the movie's release in August 1944 dealt with Wilson's negotiation of the Treaty of Versailles, his origination of the League of Nations, and his effort to persuade the U.S. Senate to ratify the treaty and to join the League. His lengthy campaign ultimately ended in defeat in 1920, when the Senate rejected the treaty and League membership, a mistake for which the movie blamed isolationists in Congress, particularly Republican Henry Cabot Lodge (played by Sir Cedric Hardwicke), then chair of the Senate Foreign Relations Committee. Scholars have since shown that the story was a good deal more complicated than the movie's portrayal. Nevertheless, Zanuck's *Wilson*, which one advertisement hawked as "The Movie to Prevent World War III," taught a simple historical lesson intended to leave viewers with favorable impressions of the nation's twenty-eighth president and his expansive worldview: when given another chance to construct a stable world order, Americans should not repeat the mistake of allowing narrow-minded isolationists to block international cooperation, the only hope for a durable peace. During production, screenwriter Lamar Trotti wrote to Ray Stannard Baker, author of a Pulitzer Prize–winning eight-volume biography of Wilson, to express the hope that audiences would exit the theater more inclined to view the ex-president as "a great man who fought and died for a great ideal" as well as to oppose "the dangers of indifference, isolation, and reaction, so that the tragedy of the present war which the Wilson dream might have prevented, may never again be permitted to occur."[50]

In that vein, Zanuck somewhat enlivened a dull topic by personalizing Americans' complex foreign policy choice, presenting it as a head-to-head morality play. According to *Time* magazine, Knox's performance "sweetened, warmed, simplified, and softlighted" Wilson, "a famously cold and fiercely arrogant intellectual," whereas the president's nemesis, Lodge, came across as "a cold patrician" whose opposition appeared to stem less from a businesslike disagreement about the parameters of U.S. foreign policy than personal pique. *New York Times* senior film critic Bosley Crowther agreed, noting that Lodge had been cast as the requisite "villain" in Zanuck's dramatization of U.S. diplomatic history, with Hardwicke portraying the Massachusetts Republican as "a distillation of bitterness and icy contempt."[51]

By contrast, Knox's Wilson makes an impassioned defense of collective security, ultimately becoming a martyr for the cause. He returns to the United States from Versailles bearing an agreement to form the League of Nations, an organization that he believes will guarantee world peace for generations to come. Faced with stiff senatorial opposition, however, the president tours the country to rally the people behind his plan. On the stump, he declares that the age of American isolationism is at an end and predicts an even worse calamity if the Senate fails to ratify the treaty. Despite his efforts, Wilson loses the League fight. The picture's fallen hero, defeated and disabled by a stroke suffered while stumping for the League, nevertheless finds the strength to reassure his cabinet (and Americans watching in movie theaters in 1944) that the dream of collective security remained alive: he envisions a time when "it may come about in a better way than we proposed."

The filmmakers believed in the importance of getting every detail perfect to make it seem as if history were repeating itself, to remind Americans that they could not again make the mistake of shirking their global responsibilities. Trotti conducted extensive research while writing, Baker served as the film's historical consultant, and Zanuck spared no expense to make the movie seem authentic. To foster the illusion of verisimilitude, the film's set included careful re-creations of the White House, the chambers of Congress, and the Hall of Mirrors at Versailles. Los Angeles's Shrine Auditorium was transformed into a scrupulous likeness of the Baltimore hall that hosted the 1912 Democratic convention. Such touches led one wag to quip that Zanuck only "stopped short of resinking the *Lusitania*, refighting World War I and rebuilding postwar Paris." All told, *Wilson*'s budget totaled $5.2 million, making it the most expensive movie ever made at the time, easily besting its closest competitors, including David O. Selznick's extravaganza, *Gone with the Wind*.[52]

Wilson hit theaters backed by a million-dollar publicity campaign that included radio spots, nationwide billboard announcements, and full-page magazine and newspaper advertisements. Despite brisk ticket sales, the movie was a financial disaster. Its $3 million in receipts, while high, were not nearly enough to cover production costs, meaning that the studio lost some $2 million on the project. *Wilson*'s didacticism, its highbrow subject matter, and its two-and-a-half-hour length also undoubtedly turned off some viewers. Others, for their part, felt that the film, coming as it did on the eve of the 1944 presidential election, was little more than a campaign advertisement for FDR, Wilson's ideological heir.[53]

At the same time, however, it is clear that *Wilson*'s internationalist stance did not work against it at the box office. In fact, the film's sympathetic treatment of Wilson's fight to establish the League of Nations—and, by extension, Roosevelt's efforts to found its successor—received a warm reception. Audiences understood that the historical events described in *Wilson* applied to their own times. The film helped to spark a renewed scholarly interest in the former president, whose stature as a world statesman, previously at a nadir, underwent an apotheosis. Hailed by critics, the movie garnered numerous Academy Award nominations, including nods for Best Picture, Best Director (Henry King), and Best Actor (Knox), and won an Oscar for Best Screenplay. *San Francisco Chronicle* film critic Hazel Bruce learned one lesson from Zanuck's "Technicolor pageant of American history": "Wilson, it is now obvious, like Cassandra, spoke truth." Crowther wrote that *Wilson* gave viewers a "renewed appreciation of its subject's ideals and especially of his trials, which may be ours." The movie's message—"It must not happen again"—would put moviegoers in an "anti-isolationist frame of mind," he predicted. *PM Daily*, which serialized Trotti's screenplay, considered *Wilson* "without question, the most important picture of its time" because it had the potential "to save a new generation." *Time* praised its "worshipful sermon on internationalism." The *New York Post* opined, "This fine movie can play a great and important part in that long fight [for world peace], into which we have twice poured so much hope and so much blood." Columnist Lee Morris proclaimed on the front page of the *Philadelphia Record* that Zanuck's picture "may conceivably change the history of the world." Former secretary of the navy Josephus Daniels, who attended the movie's world premiere along with Willkie, Baker, Welles, Henry Luce, and others, wrote that the audience left "with the feeling that this generation must repair the errors which made possible the present holocaust." One GI surveyed by *PM* outside the Roxy Theater in New York said, "I believe in the United Nations. I think everyone should see this picture so we won't make the mistake again that we made in 1920. That's what I am fighting for." The *New Republic* interviewed patrons as they exited other theaters and found among them "a definite increase in cooperative spirit."[54]

Wilson made an impression on Roosevelt, in part because some viewers wrote to the White House. One New Yorker expressed "confidence in [FDR's] leadership," feeling "that under his direction attainment of victory and peace is a certainty." Zanuck found a willing pupil in Roslyn Van Hoven, a young resident of the Bronx. From his movie, she received "an education . . . and a lesson in American history" that taught her that isolationists were to blame for the outbreak of World War II since they had torpedoed President Wilson's peace plan. She wrote, "If the Republicans would have wanted to listen to President W. Wilson in 1918 and sign a League of Nations Treaty with France and Germany and England, your sons, their sons, and the sons of all America would be home now in the safety that they deserve. It took entirely too much young blood to make the Republicans see clearly. Although I am [only] 17½ years old, I don't think I shall forgive the Republicans. They have no right to help bring about this present *Wholesale Murder*." Americans could not afford to make another such mistake, continued Van Hoven, who advised Roosevelt to bring *Wilson* to the country's attention so that people could better "see the right from the wrong." Roosevelt himself screened the picture at the White House. After seeing how Wilson lost both his health and the League fight, FDR declared, "By God, that's not going to happen to me!"[55]

Wilson's message received support from unexpected sources. At the OWI's request, innumerable movies dealing with unrelated topics included segments or subplots about foreign affairs. *This Is the Army*, a patriotic adaptation of Irving Berlin's 1942 Broadway hit, is today remembered for Kate Smith's rendition of "God Bless America" and the musical's racial and sexual politics (there is a minstrel show, boxing champ Sergeant Joe Louis appears in a segregated scene, and some actors perform in drag). However, the Technicolor picture's international politics are seldom discussed. Starring Ronald Reagan, *This Is the Army*, which became Warner Bros.' highest-grossing 1943 production, traces the restaging of a World War I–era musical revue by U.S. soldiers. The film concludes with a straightforward but stirring lesson for World War II–era audiences: America was now fighting to complete the Great War's unfinished business, and only international cooperation would prevent World War III. Hundreds of choreographed men in uniform sing the chorus to Berlin's "This Time Is the Last Time" as the flags of UN member states unfurl onstage:

> And this time we will all make certain
> That this time is the last time;
> This time we will not say "Curtain"
> Till we bring it down in their own hometown.
> For this time
> We are out to finish
> The job we started then.
> Clean it up for all time this time,
> So we won't have to do it again.[56]

This Is the Army, like *Wilson* and *One World*, was part and parcel of the watershed in the American zeitgeist. To be sure, internationalism predated World War II, and isolationism would survive it: Wilson led the United States into battle in 1917 on the assurance that doing so would make the world safe for democracy; Americans wasted no time bringing their boys home once Japan surrendered in August 1945. But by any measure, isolationism, once the dominant mood, was eclipsed during the tipping point of World War II. After opting out of Wilson's League of Nations, Americans continued to oppose the idea of joining a reconstituted peacekeeping organization for the next twenty-plus years. Then things changed. The Japanese attack on Pearl Harbor had proven that neither geographical distance nor diplomatic isolation could guarantee peace and security. In fact, U.S. passivity in the face of international aggression arguably had worsened the situation by creating a power vacuum that allowed those threats to mature, eventually requiring an even bloodier, costlier confrontation to eliminate them. Though still doubtful about certain details, Americans became comfortable with the idea of collective security, a transformation best indicated by the newfound support for a postwar peacekeeping body. A February 1942 National Opinion Research Center survey showed that 86 percent of respondents favored U.S. participation in "a world police force to guarantee against future wars." Support diminished somewhat after the patriotic rush subsided and the complications of foreign entanglements set in. But backing for U.S. involvement in the world soon stabilized, with about three-quarters of people endorsing similar proposals for the remainder of the war.[57]

The 1944 elections served as a referendum on America's role in the world. The question before voters was no longer if but how the United States should be involved in foreign affairs, a shift in terms indicative of the extent to which internationalism had triumphed. American global activism enjoyed bipartisan political support, so much so that debate about U.S. participation in a postwar international peacekeeping body was virtually nonexistent. The Republican nominee, New York governor Thomas E. Dewey, did not question the need for the United States to meet its postwar responsibilities. Election Day marked a stark contrast from two years earlier, when conservatives and isolationists made whopping gains in the House and Senate. This time, voters, in addition to reelecting FDR to an unprecedented fourth term, turned out of office lawmakers saddled with isolationist voting records, including Republican senator Gerald P. Nye and GOP representatives Fish and Illinois's Stephen A. Day. Having missed their first chance to do so, Americans displayed a willingness to seize their second opportunity in a generation to perform the responsibilities of global leadership.[58]

With victory in sight, thoughts turned toward the peace. As they did so, attention naturally focused on the UN's Great Powers, which would be responsible for the world's welfare if and when they proved victorious. The UN, the best example of internationalism at work, came to be seen as the nucleus of a future peacekeeping organization. Not everyone got on board, of course: until Day's defeat in 1944, he and Senator Wheeler regarded such a body as a surrender of national sovereignty and a submission to Great Britain and the Soviet Union, potential future adversaries. And a variety of approaches existed to turning the UN coalition into something more permanent: the communitarian ideal as preached by one-worlders, balance-of-power politics as counseled by realists, and others in between. The first group included Willkie, who in *One World* raised the prospect of the coalition's major partners forming a common council to shepherd the planet from war to peace. Minnesota governor Harold E. Stassen similarly envisioned a "United Nations of the World." Speaking before the Minneapolis branch of the Foreign Policy Association, the young Republican outlined a plan for a world parliament led by an executive council composed of the major Allied powers. If such a world government were to become reality, Stassen promised, "the citizens of this state in the years ahead would be not only citizens of Minnesota, not only citizens of the United States of America, but also citizens of the United Nations of the World." Private lobbying organizations arose to work toward making the wartime coalition the seed of a permanent collective security organization. Beginning in 1942, the American Association for the United Nations sponsored model UN conferences in which student delegates practiced multilateral diplomacy. A similar group, the Chicago-based World Citizens Association, created a "Platform for World Citizenship" that upheld global congress in a "rapidly shrinking world" and foresaw world and national citizenship as involving no more conflict than federal and state allegiance.[59]

Turning the United Nations into the core of a world organization was a long, difficult process that began with broad statements by Allied leaders, continued with planning by foreign ministries, and ended with the foundation of the United Nations Organization at the 1945 San Francisco Conference. Public diplomacy was instrumental to that process, time and again propagating the ideal of collective security ahead of its realization. Roosevelt again took the stage, this time repeatedly characterizing the UN's major powers as "policemen" patrolling the world's beat to deter aggressors and keep the peace. Loath, as was his habit, to make commitments that would spark public debate and limit his flexibility, the president provided few details about his peace plan. Instead, he offered only vague generalities, likening the United Nations to a postwar constabulary force with the four Great Powers serving as regional law enforcers: China in Asia, Great Britain in Western Europe and the Mediterranean, the Soviet Union in Eastern Europe, and the United States in the Western Hemisphere. On New Year's Day 1943, the first anniversary of the UN Declaration, FDR called on the Allied "family of nations" to extend its ongoing fight against the enemy's international outlawry—or "barbarism" and "calculated savagery," as he phrased it—beyond the armistice.[60]

Talk of kinship was not solely for public consumption, either: the top Allied leaders regularly invoked it behind closed doors. During the November 1943 Cairo Conference, Roosevelt hosted a family-style Thanksgiving dinner for Anglo-American attendees, including Churchill. The president told the guests gathered at his villa "that large families are usually closer united than are small families; and that, this year, with the United Kingdom in our family, we are a large family more united than ever before." (No member of the Chinese delegation, which included Jiang and his wife, received an invitation, an omission that speaks to both the relative closeness of Anglo-American relations and the distance of East-West ties.) Days later, the feast moved to Tehran, where FDR opened the first plenary session, attended by Churchill, Stalin, and Soviet foreign minister Vyacheslav Molotov, among others, by noting, "We are sitting around this table for the first time as a family." The president welcomed "the new [Soviet] members to the family circle" and expressed his hope that the conference's subsequent meetings would be "conducted as between friends with complete frankness." Stalin, not generally given to such flowery language, responded in kind, urging participants to "take full advantage of this fraternal meeting."[61]

Scholars have overlooked the extent to which the UN shaped its own image via transnational publicity that helped make the realization of world government a self-fulfilling prophecy. A dedicated public diplomacy apparatus, the United Nations Information Office (UNIO), was organized in 1942, becoming not only the UN's maiden agency but also the first body to use the phrase "United Nations" as part of its title. Headquartered in both New York and London, the UNIO was an outgrowth of the Inter-Allied Information Committee, which since 1940 had distributed data in the United States about the developing anti-Axis coalition with an eye toward promoting American belligerence. After the UN itself came into being in 1942, the UNIO, directed by a board consisting of representatives of the alliance's member states, turned its sights first toward strengthening the wartime partnership and then toward generating public support, particularly within the United States, for the coalition's development into a permanent postwar peacekeeping body. Allied publicists wasted no time in shifting their focus: within days of the U.S. declaration of war, they agreed that preparing "the ground for postwar cooperation between the Allies and the United States" was now the imperative, and success depended on Americans taking an "interest in European and

Asiatic affairs after the war." Toward that end, UNIO programs sought to demonstrate internationalist principles and practices for the benefit of those who still harbored strong unilateralist sympathies.[62]

In collaboration with the OWI, the UNIO (rechristened the United Nations Information Organization in 1944) set about its work with gusto. It helped to organize United Nations Day each year as well as several film festivals, including one held at New York's Museum of Modern Art. The UNIO also established contacts with journalists—radio newsmen Lowell Thomas and H. V. Kaltenborn among them—and provided the broadcast and print media with a steady stream of photographs, press releases, and feature stories told "from a global point of view." (Independent radio stations and newspapers in medium or small markets were of special interest, and one study found that dailies in such cities as Fort Worth, Minneapolis, and Seattle regularly published the UNIO's canned material.) Traveling exhibitions—Kaufmann's department store kicked off Pittsburgh's commemoration of United Nations Week in June 1942 by hosting one such display—publicized the UN in various communities. Posters portrayed collective security as the best way to safeguard the world family's future, its children. Lecturers discussed the "united efforts of the Allies" with women's groups, chambers of commerce, and college students. A special United Nations educational kit, complete with maps and lesson plans, prepared in conjunction with the U.S. Office of Education became part of the curriculum in thousands of high school and college classrooms during the 1944–45 academic year. A reference library in New York allowed users to peruse a large collection of information about the Allies and/or postwar reconstruction. Perhaps most important, the UNIO publicized the work of related institutions—the United Nations Relief and Rehabilitation Administration and the UN's Food and Agriculture Organization—that instilled the habit of international cooperation even before the fighting had stopped.[63]

Publicity surrounding Allied summitry also served to concretize the abstraction of collective action in the public mind. The Moscow Declaration of 30 October 1943 put the UN's four major powers on record as being committed to an international organization. The document was equal parts diplomatic agreement and political theater. (The OWI's *United Newsreel*, which highlighted combined Allied efforts for overseas and domestic audiences, featured a segment on it.) The first summit meeting of Churchill, Roosevelt, and Stalin at Tehran, held 28 November–1 December 1943, marked a high point in perceptions of Allied solidarity. The OWI

"UNITED NATIONS. For all children a safe tomorrow—IF you do your part."
United Nations Information Organization poster, 1945, suggesting that
collective security safeguarded the world family's future generations.
Item 44-PA-2193, Still Picture Unit, National Archives and Records
Administration II, College Park, Md.

made sure that the public knew about the meeting, providing the press with background notes and photographs (including the iconic image of the British prime minister, American president, and Soviet premier) for maximum coverage. At the conclusion of the conference, the Big Three's leaders issued a widely published statement expressing their determination to work together in war and peace. The principals spoke only in generalities about the shape of things to come, outlining a "world family of democratic nations" open to all countries "dedicated . . . to the elimination of tyranny and slavery, oppression and intolerance." The declaration concluded, "We leave here friends in fact, in spirit and in purpose." Not long after his return home, President Roosevelt discussed his travels with the American people during a Christmas Eve Fireside Chat. FDR summarized Tehran's results and reminded his listeners not to be misled by isolationists, especially now that "the development of science" had made the world "so much smaller that we have had to discard the geographical yardsticks of the past."[64]

A coordinated public diplomacy push accompanied the Dumbarton Oaks proposals, the October 1944 agreements governing the makeup of the planned United Nations Organization's assembly and executive council. The UNIO organized a multimedia publicity campaign targeting the midwestern cities of Chicago, Milwaukee, and Minneapolis. The State Department printed more than two hundred thousand copies of the Dumbarton proposals and an informative, eight-page guide to the draft United Nations Charter. An edition of the OWI's *United Newsreel* was dedicated to the conference. State and the OWI collaborated to produce a short documentary film, *Watchtower over Tomorrow* (1945), that urged viewers to support the proposed UNO as a protector of future world peace and harmony.[65]

State Department officials hit the road as well, speaking before some five hundred groups across the country about the Dumbarton Oaks agreements. In an October address in Washington state, Assistant Secretary of State Adolf A. Berle Jr. expressed diplomats' basic thesis: the UNO would offer Americans increased security in a shrinking world. Perhaps "the most powerful argument" to be made on behalf of the new organization, according to Berle, was "the fact that air warfare puts this country out of the class of distant spectator and in the direct range of events." Newly appointed assistant secretary for administration Julius Cecil Holmes picked up that theme when he returned to his native Kansas to drum up support. Speaking before the Topeka Chamber of Commerce in February 1945, Holmes, who had just completed a tour of duty with the U.S. Army, declared that the age of easy security provided by America's two-ocean buffer was "gone forever. Oceans have ceased to exist as barriers. Aviation and robot bombs [German V-2 missiles], all the implements of modern warfare, have eliminated mere space as a factor in security." As a result, said Holmes, a self-described realist, an international peacekeeping body was an essential element of good national security. Collective security was feasible, he hastened to add, now that Americans and their Allied partners had gained invaluable experience in "working together."[66]

In his talks, Joseph Grew, now the undersecretary of state, reiterated the message that wartime experience had recast the American mind-set. Echoing Willkie, Grew told the Society of the Friendly Sons of St. Patrick in New York City in March 1945 that Americans had made "the discovery that the world is one." To be sure, it had taken "the wonders of the airplane and the radio" and "two world wars inflicted on mankind by the madness and greed of enemies thousands of miles from our shores" to come to that realization. Yet the "experience we have gained in cooperating for victory" also provided a tangible demonstration of what could be achieved through collective labors. Never before had "so many different nationalities worked together, day by day and month by month, with such closeness and comradeship and understanding as [had the United Nations] in the prosecution of this war," enthused Grew. Wartime practice—fighting alongside foreign comrades, jointly formulating military strategy, or negotiating peace plans at international conferences—had caused Americans to "think in world terms. It means that action and policy must be fashioned cooperatively in terms of its effect on the world community since the good of each nation and its individual citizens is bound up with the good of that community. It means, in short, a whole new set of intellectual and moral standards, not imposed by us but created by us to meet the challenge of our time."[67]

• • •

When President Roosevelt delivered his final inaugural address in January 1945, he spoke to a nation whose worldview had been fundamentally transformed over three-plus years of war. In his only wartime inaugural, FDR said that recent experience had taught several lessons, among them that "we cannot live alone, at peace; that our own well-being is dependent on the well-being of other nations, far away." Though trials awaited—the war in Europe was only then entering its final phase; the one in the Pacific was expected to last even longer—the American people had "learned to be citizens of the world, members of the human community."[68]

Though carefully chosen to lend legitimacy to the still unfinished work of peacekeeping, FDR's words reflected the revamped national zeitgeist. Americans now overwhelmingly supported U.S. membership in the proposed United Nations Organization. Internationalism ascended as a consequence of historical events, as a legacy of the unfinished business left by World War I, and as a reaction to the insecurities spawned by Pearl Harbor.

Its rise also owed a debt to the Allies' publicity campaign, through which cultural gatekeepers filtered wartime events and contextualized lived experience. The United Nations wartime alliance was by far the most extensive foreign entanglement in U.S. history. Consequently, 1 January 1942, the date of the United Nations Declaration's issuance, marked a significant departure from tradition—the birth of a new era—that took some getting used to. The big screen—from Capra's *Why We Fight* to Bogart's starring turns in *Casablanca* and *Sahara* to the OWI's *Oswego*—acclimatized audiences to the new reality. Working alongside Wallace's progressive rhetoric, the UNIO's publicity, United Nations Day's annual festivities, and many other factors, the movies introduced Americans to their overseas brethren and remapped the world in a way that shrank the imaginary space separating the home front from foreign battlefields. Pro-UN discourse modeled neighborly behavior by representing the alliance as a family of nations united to liberate the world: the arts frequently referenced the fraternity, friendliness, even fondness that ostensibly prevailed among the "world family of democratic nations," in the Tehran declaration's phraseology. A world war's worth of such talk, transnational in scope, revised geographic knowledge, plugged Americans into the global network, and connected them to their faraway allies, creating a sense of international kinship where none previously existed.

Clare Boothe Luce and other realists continued to deride such utopianism as hopelessly overoptimistic and even dangerously misleading. "Globaloney" calculated all of the benefits but none of the costs, including the limits that a world association could place on U.S. freedom of action. And FDR and other supporters' rhetoric featured generalities but failed to address the gritty details of membership, voting, and so forth that provoked debate. Furthermore, the "global family" discourse glossed over the hard facts of international life—the endurance of power politics, the timelessness of national rivalry, the inevitability of conflict—in the rush to exaggerate the blessings of goodwill. And, more to the point, it inflated expectations by giving false impressions of and minimizing America's outstanding differences with each of the foremost Allies—Britain, the Soviet Union, and China.

However utopian it may have been, internationalist culture also taught Americans to see the globe anew and to reimagine their place in it. Once relatively parochial and isolated, they emerged more cosmopolitan and engaged citizens of a planet that now seemed interconnected as never before. Whereas the world had previously appeared to consist of several discrete locales, it now seemed as one.

4

KISSING COUSINS HOW ANGLO-AMERICAN RELATIONS BECAME "SPECIAL"

A family—mother, father, and two small children—huddles in an underground bomb shelter buried in the yard of their English country home. The year is 1940, and the Battle of Britain rages overhead. The shelter's walls quiver, and debris falls as German bombs explode nearby. Although frightened, the members of the group survive the onslaught without serious injury. Others are not so fortunate, however, as is soon discovered: a close relative lies dead, and the family's home, a universal symbol of safety and comfort, suffers heavy damage. That memorable scene helped *Mrs. Miniver* (1942), MGM's portrait of a fictional English family's wartime travails, resonate among American viewers in a way few other films could match. Winner of six Academy Awards, including Best Picture, it was the highest-grossing movie in the studio's storied history to that point. Aside from its compelling narrative, stellar performances, and overall quality, *Mrs. Miniver's* political subtext earned it wide acclaim. Its central motif of family, symbolic of Great Britain and threatened by the Axis enemy, not only framed the Allies' war as a defense of that dear if vulnerable institution but also positioned the Anglo-American alliance as a community of kinfolk. An MGM promotional trailer spoke to precisely those themes, encouraging viewers to identify with their besieged transatlantic cousins by breathlessly proclaiming the Minivers "brave and decent people whose courage is the flaming spirit of a family of brave and decent nations."

The idea that Anglo-American relations were so uncommonly close as to be "special" acquired unquestionable currency in the popular culture of World War II, and Americans' embrace of Atlanticism was part and parcel of the broader sea change that occurred in their cosmology. That assessment is not mere sentimentality, and it neither denies that the alliance rested on corresponding national agendas—on realpolitik—nor suggests that it was devoid of conflict.[1] Rather, precisely those differences, which encompassed issues ranging from film trade to geopolitical strategy, necessitated a propaganda campaign, so closely coordinated as to be neither strictly American nor solely British but Anglo-American,[2] to foster an impression of international harmony. Propagandists charged cinema, a persuasive if slower medium, with taking the long view and situating diplomacy within a politicized context that would be meaningful, entertaining, and successful at the box office. Films romanticized the hard-boiled Anglo-American entente as a family of nations. All manner of wartime cinematic discourse—from Hollywood love stories to documentaries valorizing the fraternity of joint combat to newsreels highlighting President Franklin D. Roosevelt's intimacy with Prime Minister Winston S. Churchill—publicized bilateral affairs, which displayed "some of the tension and tortuousness of family relationships," according to historian H. C. Allen, a pioneering chronicler of transatlantic ties.[3]

In so doing, a sort of on-screen Anglo-American fantasyland emerged. Staged by Hollywood producers and vetted by government propagandists, it enlivened foreign affairs, interpreted reality, and framed the Allies' common interests in movie language—that is, as values shared among members of an extended family of peoples joined by ancestry, marriage, and/or friendship. The illusion proved salient and enduring. Indeed, the idea that Americans and Britons shared a "special relationship" was a direct outgrowth of the wartime experience—Churchill coined the term in 1943 and would go on to hail the "Grand Alliance" in his influential memoirs—and far outstripped any residual distrust to provide an intellectual basis for the postwar transatlantic alliance that still exists.[4]

Mrs. Miniver propagated the Anglo-American kinship narrative, a discourse nourished by the ongoing United Nations campaign. The movie originated as part of the interventionist lobbying effort prior to Pearl Harbor. Begun in October 1940 and filmed in the autumn of 1941, it was already in the pipeline when the United States entered the war in December and joined the UN in January 1942. Although the film's initial purpose may have been overtaken by events, *Mrs. Miniver*'s domestic drama reverberated all the more after its release in June, by which time Ameri-

Mrs. Miniver (Greer Garson) and Clem Miniver (Walter Pidgeon) head a British family, besieged but resolute, in MGM's *Mrs. Miniver*, the Oscar winner as 1942's Best Picture. Photofest/© MGM.

cans could better relate to their new overseas ally for having firsthand experience with the war's disruptive effects on family life. Paradoxically, the fictional Minivers, Hollywood's creations, enabled U.S. audiences to become better acquainted with their real-life British partners. The Minivers' tale, though invented, nonetheless seemed authentic, for it spoke to larger truths common to the wartime experience: fear and sacrifice, love and endurance, and, of course, family and the home. Moreover, the Minivers served as ideal characterizations of Britain. Middle-class and democratic, they were the kind of Britons whom Americans wanted Britons to be. (Or, put another way, the Minivers were the kind of Britons whom Britons such as Sidney Bernstein, the Ministry of Information [MOI] representative who advised MGM during production, wanted Americans to see.) What ordinary homemaker could measure up to Greer Garson, the London-born actor who played the film's eponymous matriarch? Resolute and attractive, the Minivers spoke to U.S. viewers who were welcomed to share and identify with the British family's home front struggles.[5]

Though maternal, Garson's Mrs. Miniver was no shrinking violet. Hers was the story of "a valiant woman, whose love and devotion shield her family" from destruction by the Nazi war machine, according to the movie's trailer. After all, she, not her husband (Walter Pidgeon), acts as the Miniver lodestone in that underground shelter. And she defends home and hearth from their gravest danger yet: a wounded German pilot whose plane is downed near the Miniver cottage. Desperate and half mad, the aviator holds our beloved heroine hostage at gunpoint while invading her home and ravaging her refrigerator. A similar—or worse—fate appears to await Mrs. Miniver and her children, asleep upstairs and unaware of the drama unfolding below. At the moment of most imminent danger, however, she wrestles the gun from the soldier's hands. Now in control, Mrs. Miniver could be forgiven if she punished him in some way. Instead, she ministers to his wounds, her actions meant to demonstrate the common decency of the British people. (Not incidentally, the German rejects her attentions, delivering instead a bombastic lecture on the inevitability of Nazi victory until local police arrive.)

No idealization of Great Britain would have been complete without addressing its domestic class system, given American criticism of it. *Mrs. Miniver* and the previous year's Best Picture, *How Green Was My Valley* (1941), about a Welsh coal mining family, departed from Hollywood tradition—of which playwright Noel Coward's *Cavalcade* (1933) is exemplary—in that they lavished attention on Britain's common folk rather than its aristocratic rich and famous. *Mrs. Miniver* paid homage to the "people's war," the MOI's central propaganda theme, which held that a new, more egalitarian and democratic Britain was being forged in the crucible of World War II. To convince Americans that such a social transformation was indeed under way, the MOI touted the Beveridge Report, a 1942 government paper outlining the creation of a comprehensive social security system, and *Listen to Britain* (1942), Humphrey Jennings's influential documentary about working-class Britons' daily lives. *Mrs. Miniver* did its part by applying a touch of Hollywood magic, dramatizing the change of heart undergone by the film's prototypical aristocrat, Lady Beldon, to convey the impression that Britain was evolving into a social democracy akin to that found in the United States. When the audience first meets Lady Beldon (portrayed by English stage star Dame May Whitty), she is grousing about weakening class distinctions. Her retrograde views begin to change, however, when her granddaughter, Carol, becomes engaged to the Minivers' eldest son, Vin, a pairing of which Lady Beldon eventually approves. Her transformation reaches completion during a rose competition. Top honors customarily go to Lady Beldon as a consequence of her social standing. But in this year's show, the first held during the "people's war," the village's working-class stationmaster, James Ballard, submits a clearly superior entry. The judges deliberate and, to no one's surprise, give first prize to Lady Beldon. But just as she is about to accept her award, Lady Beldon hesitates, takes one last honest look at the competing flowers, and declares Mr. Ballard the winner, a magnanimous act that earns applause from the crowd.[6]

In case audiences somehow missed the point, the movie's conclusion again framed the war as a fight for equality and liberty both at home and abroad. Residents gather in the same church where the vicar had interrupted a service to announce the outbreak of hostilities in September 1939. On that occasion, he put a certain spin on the situation: "Our forefathers fought for a thousand years for the freedom that we now enjoy, and that we must defend again." Now, the setting is the same but the context has changed: wounded soldiers sit in the pews, sandbags lie about, and the church itself is heavily damaged, its walls turned to rubble, its windows knocked out, a gaping hole in its roof. As the camera pans across the congregation, taking silent note of the empty seats, the reverend reads aloud the names of martyred local citizens, including Carol Beldon. Why had such innocents been sacrificed? Because, answers the vicar, "This is not only a war of soldiers in uniform. It is a war of the people, of all the people. And it must be fought . . . in the home and in the heart of every man, woman, and child who loves freedom." He adds, "This is the people's war. It is our war. We are the fighters. Fight it then. Fight it with all that is in us. And may God defend the right." At that, the congregation rises and sings "Onward Christian Soldiers." As the lyrics resound, the camera rises, as if looking toward heaven through the gap in the abbey's ceiling. RAF fighters flash across the sky, and the soundtrack dissolves into "God Save the King"—a most stirring if melodramatic ending.

Mrs. Miniver received almost unanimous praise. The year's top earner in both the United States and the United Kingdom, the picture swept the Oscars, including Best Picture, Best Director (William Wyler), Best Actress (Garson), and Best Supporting Actress (Whitty). A handful of critics came away unimpressed, questioning the sincerity of the "people's war" theme, but most welcomed the movie and its messages. The *Motion Picture Daily* lauded the climactic scene for articulating "the unconquerable spirit of the British people to save . . . freedom." Of the rose competition, *Variety* wrote, "Class distinctions . . . are seen to wear away." The U.S. Office of War Information (OWI), whose foundation coincided with *Mrs. Miniver*'s premiere, appreciated the film's presentation of "an idealized version of British life" that "downplayed class cleavages." Upholding the production as a model worthy of emulation, the OWI's Nelson Poynter pressed Hollywood studios to "give us a *Mrs. Miniver* of China or Russia, making clear to our people our common interest with [those nations] in this struggle."[7]

In the days to come, American theaters hosted many more pictures set in or dealing with Britain. They included *Random Harvest* (1942), an apolitical romance starring Garson that excelled at the box office and garnered seven Academy Award nominations; *Sherlock Holmes and the Secret Weapon* (1943), in which the famous detective (Basil Rathbone) kept a dangerous device out of Nazi hands; and *In Which We Serve* (1942), written and produced by Coward and directed by David Lean. Coward also starred in *In Which We Serve*, which dramatized the exploits of a fictional Royal Navy destroyer. A metaphor for wartime Britain, the ship's fortunes rose and fell on the common contributions and sacrifices of its crew—officers and enlisted men alike—a subtext suggestive of the new spirit of equality and dynamism said to be operative in the people's war. Lauded by reviewers as a "vibrant" testament to "British strength," *In Which We Serve* received two Oscar nominations, for Best Picture and Best Original Screenplay.[8]

Twentieth Century–Fox executive producer Daryl F. Zanuck, an ardent internationalist and onetime Fight for Freedom member, again came to

Britain's defense with *This above All* (1942). Production began in 1941, and, like *Mrs. Miniver*, the film started out as an attempt to hasten U.S. entry into World War II but became an argument for the British ally by the time of its May 1942 premiere. A classic love story, *This above All* involves Prudence Cathaway (British American actor Joan Fontaine), a rich young woman who falls for a poor soldier, Clive Briggs. Prudence's aristocratic family disapproves of her romantic choice, establishing a rift between the old England that the elder Cathaways symbolize and the younger, more democratic generation embodied by Prudence. The tension builds further when it is revealed that Clive is a deserter from the British army. Clive left after the debacle at Dunkirk because, as the antihero explains, he objected to being misled by "stupid, complacent, and out-of-date" officers with no qualifications for leadership other than "birth and class and privilege" and to the fact that innocent enlisted men were being asked to fight and die not for "a better England" but to preserve the "same rotten, worn-out conditions that kept [the officers'] class in comfort and [the soldiers'] in poverty." In other words, Clive, woodenly portrayed by American actor Tyrone Power, articulates some charges leveled at the British ruling class by contemporary American Anglophobes, setting up an on-screen debate with Prudence, who, although reform-minded herself, defends Britain, its establishment, and its wartime cause. Backed by Dover's white cliffs, she responds, in an overwrought speech, that despite its flaws, England has many things worth defending in its fight for survival against Nazi Germany: "Shakespeare and thatched cottages in the countryside . . . speakers in Hyde Park, free to say what they wish," and "the ancient dignity of our cities." Inspired by Prudence's words and redeemed by her love, Clive undergoes a transformation from conscientious objector to committed warrior akin to that of Gary Cooper's lead character in *Sergeant York* (1941). His faith in England restored, Clive vows to rejoin the army. Before he can do so, however, he suffers serious injuries while aiding London's Blitz victims. The movie closes with Clive, from his hospital bed, telling Prudence that she has been correct all along: "It's going to be a different world when all of this is over. . . . Some day, we're going to fight for what I believe in. But first, we've got to fight for what you believe in. You were right. We've got to win this war. We've got to!"[9]

Though preachy and overly sentimental, *This above All* was well received in the United States. Nevertheless, Americans remained critical of their overseas ally despite the pro-British, internationalist propaganda stretching back to 1939. Indeed, animosity toward John Bull resurfaced when the post–Pearl Harbor honeymoon ended, as traditional grudges joined with new concerns to increase Anglophobia. Though now on the defensive, diehard Anglophobes and isolationists remained vocal. "The money interests run England," an Irish American woman from Boston told interviewers in 1942, adding that those shadowy powers had conspired to "put pressure on Mr. Roosevelt to get us" into the war. Senator Gerald P. Nye remained on the warpath, publicly attacking Churchill's wartime strategy. Publishers William Randolph Hearst, the *Chicago Tribune*'s Robert McCormick, and Joseph M. Patterson of the *New York Daily News* continued to oppose any and all foreign commitments, including the wartime alliance with Britain.[10]

Liberals still identified Britain as an obstacle to global socioeconomic equity and national self-determination. As before, its domestic class hierarchy came under fire. Only this time, that critique, addressed by *This above All* and *Mrs. Miniver*, became intertwined with questions about Britain's military performance or perceived lack thereof. The surrender of two crucial strategic redoubts—Singapore in February 1942 and Tobruk in June—disappointed many Americans, who were further angered by reports that Lend-Lease materials had been left to waste in Singapore. Polls that year consistently ranked Britain at the bottom of the major UN powers in terms of battlefield prowess and the Soviet Union at the top. Zanuck, a key White House ally in Hollywood, wrote to FDR's press secretary, Stephen T. Early, lamenting that a "series of military defeats, vile rumors from the surrender of Singapore, and subtle Nazi propaganda [had] combined to develop almost overnight a violent, vicious hatred in this country for everything that is British."[11]

Some critics blamed the setbacks on Britain's domestic class system, which was perceived as preventing talented people of ordinary birth from rising to positions of authority. *Collier's* editors, for example, pointed to the "Colonel Blimps who still clutter up [Britain's] army" as the cause of Singapore's fall.[12] Others insisted that Britain's shortcomings—and its apparent reluctance to open a second front in Europe, a major intra-Allied irritant—stemmed from a misguided attempt to preserve its weakening global position at the expense of throwing its full weight against the Axis powers. It was said that SEAC, the acronym for Britain's Southeast Asia Command (whose commander had reportedly balked at reopening the Burma Road, the main supply line to China), actually stood for "Save England's Asian Colonies." And Hearst's newspaper chain printed an editorial in January 1942 alleging that Whitehall deliberately pursued a passive wartime strategy designed to bleed its allies to death so that it could emerge from the war in a position of relative strength. "England's plain policy seems to be to HAVE allies, but not to BE an ally," the piece concluded.[13]

The British Empire itself remained a sore spot, arguably further inflamed because it now so obviously contradicted the UN's stated purpose of fighting for worldwide freedom. That inconsistency was not lost on African Americans, many of whom suspected that the Western Allies' avowed support for postwar colonial independence was insincere. Blacks remained ambivalent about the United Nations. On one hand, African American patriots served their country with distinction, albeit in segregated units, partly out of a hope that victory over fascism abroad would produce a "double victory" over racism at home. Others, however, so associated their own domestic struggle for civil rights with the worldwide push for liberation by people of color as to engender a sense of transnational anti-imperial solidarity. A. Philip Randolph announced that his March on Washington Movement demanded freedom everywhere and linked "the interest of the Negro people in America to the interest of Negroes all over the world." The executive secretary of the National Association for the Advancement of Colored People, Walter White, combined support for Indian nationalism with denunciations of Britain's imperialism and America's domestic racism, declaring that "the struggle of the Negro in the United States is part and parcel of the struggle against imperialism and exploitation" elsewhere. Lester Granger, executive secretary of the National Urban League, took an even stronger line, accusing the Western Allies of seeking to uphold global white supremacy despite their statements to the contrary. A few African Americans went so far as to oppose the United Nations outright, and Elijah Muhammad and others were arrested in 1942 for expressing pro-Japanese sympathies.[14]

White liberals also did not overlook the empire's incongruity with the Four Freedoms, regarding the British as malevolent imperialists, "oppressors" who exploited and suppressed their colonies' wish for independence. In October 1942, *Life* magazine published "An Open Letter to the People of England," warning the addressees that if they tried to "cling to the Empire at the expense of a United Nations victory you will lose the war because you will lose us." Britain's stranglehold on India was "devastating for the United Nations," added the *New Republic*'s Michael Straight. *Christian Century* called British colonialism "the most divisive and morale-shattering question at issue before the United Nations" in that a "war to save freedom from the threat of totalitarian slavery has been turned by Mr. Churchill into a struggle to preserve imperialism from the menace of democratic self-rule."[15]

Churchill responded by remarking that he had not become prime minister "to preside over the liquidation of the British Empire." Official U.S. opposition to colonialism was harder to dismiss, however. For philosophic and even more important economic reasons, Washington—figuring that a freer world would lead to freer trade and that American goods would be able to best their competitors in an open international marketplace—pushed London to dismantle the imperial preference system, a trading bloc that also acted as a linchpin holding together the empire. And U.S. leaders possessed the leverage to make these efforts count as they demanded imperial preference's demise as payment in kind for Lend-Lease, a hard bargain that drove a wedge between the two countries' diplomats.[16]

Such differences generally did not produce calls to break up the wartime Anglo-American alliance. Nearly everyone recognized that despite its evident faults, Britain offered the best available partner—from the standpoints of corresponding interests and views—in the quest to defeat the Axis powers. However, observers raised questions about whether the partnership would endure beyond the Axis defeat and conducted a very public debate about the merits of Allied military strategy, which prioritized Germany's defeat over Japan's. Americans overwhelmingly regarded Japan, which had attacked U.S. territory, as their primary enemy. That viewpoint, combined with British missteps, encouraged Americans to direct their attention away from the European theater and toward the Pacific, where the United States could better master its own fate. In 1942–43, a "Pacific-first" movement gathered strength, lobbying for the reprioritization of U.S. strategy. The *San Francisco Examiner*, the *Chicago Tribune*, former U.S. ambassador to Japan Joseph Grew, most U.S. Navy officials, and a group of bipartisan lawmakers, including Democratic senators A. B. "Happy" Chandler and Burton K. Wheeler and Republican Styles Bridges, led the charge.[17]

Reports poured into Washington and London attesting to the public's disaffection. Although the American worldview was then undergoing a profound reorientation toward globalism, that process was not yet altogether evident even in 1944, when Edward R. Stettinius Jr., who replaced Cordell Hull as secretary of state in December amid intensified postwar preparations, warned Roosevelt that Americans still harbored "strong anti-British feeling" that presaged "a return to a stronger isolationism than ever." For their part, U.K. diplomats filed reports about everything from Americans' lingering "ancient grudge" against His Majesty's Government to their "hatred of 'British Imperialism.'" The former, "an inherited attitude reinforced by the story of the origins of the Re-' public and imbibed at school," predisposed "millions of Americans to criticism rather than praise of all things British." The latter, "almost universal amongst Americans," acted, according to Lord Halifax, as "a barrier to mutual confidence and [held] plain danger for future Anglo-American collaboration." Perhaps most important, Britons were viewed as "hidebound" Colonel Blimps who lacked "offensive spirit," leading to the widespread impression that the British lion had become a paper tiger ill equipped for partnership on anything approaching equal terms with the ever more powerful United States. Accurate or not, these perceptions combined to leave "British prestige . . . at low ebb," according to Harold Butler of British Information Services, the MOI's U.S. propaganda arm.[18]

Such analyses concerned U.S. and U.K. officials, and more decisive remedial actions were taken. To Europeanists in the Roosevelt administration, the pro-Pacific groundswell brought unwanted political pressure that if left unchecked could undermine the Western Allies' Europe-first strategy and decouple the United States from Britain. Speaking to that concern, Secretary of War Henry L. Stimson noted that "an intellectual effort" would have to be made to persuade Americans, who "really hated . . . Japan," to keep their sights on the European theater and Germany, "their most dangerous enemy." Stettinius had addressed a related worry: the public's continued distrust of Britain, which pointed to residual isolationism and difficult days ahead as the White House looked toward obtaining popular support for an international peacekeeping body. For those reasons and others, therefore, the Office of Facts and Figures concluded, "The American public does need a good selling job on the English." And when the OWI took over as the top U.S. propaganda ministry in June 1942, it spearheaded a pro-British information drive. Movies were integral to that effort, and the Hollywood studios were instructed to produce newsreels, shorts, and features that cast Britain and its dealings with the United States in a flattering light. Britain was waging a "magnificent" war against Nazi Germany, the agency's manual claimed, and combined military operations and Lend-Lease offered subjects ready-made for dramatizations of Anglo-American teamwork and harmony. Hollywood received word to hit those themes as well as to humanize Britons as "courageous and valiant people" who resembled Americans and cherished "the same hopes and aspirations that we do."[19]

British concerns ran even deeper. The U.S. obsession with decolonization remained a worry, as did the "Pacific pull" that Butler perceived as representing a "real danger" to Britain's war against its primary foe, Nazi Germany. In an influential August 1943 report that Minister of Information Brendan Bracken approved and forwarded to Churchill's War Cabinet for consideration, Butler outlined a worst-case scenario ending with the premature shift of U.S. resources to the Asian theater, the division of Allied strength, and Britain fighting alone in Europe. Greater stakes loomed ahead. Even if the Europe-first strategy remained operative, it was apparent that the war was virtually bankrupting the United Kingdom. Now mired in decline, even a victorious Britain would likely emerge with insufficient financial, industrial, and military wherewithal to remain a top-flight world power, administer its empire, or maintain domestic living standards. (Only a $3.75 billion loan from the United States in 1946 and Marshall Plan aid would keep Britain's economy afloat.) Looking across the Atlantic, British policymakers saw the United States, a friendly country on the rise, as a solution to their country's long-term ills. Were Anglo-American relations to be strengthened, ascendant U.S. power could be enlisted on the United Kingdom's behalf, better securing its worldwide interests and place in the global pecking order. All in all, British officials saw their fate as resting "very largely in American hands." Thus, as the Foreign Office wrote in 1944, the plan was "to make use of American power for purposes which we regard as good."[20]

At the same time, U.K. diplomats remained confident that any "prejudice" standing athwart good relations could be "softened and even eliminated by education and information." British Information Services head Sir Gerald Campbell urged Whitehall to "go as far as possible in the direction of revealing what Britain has done and is doing to prosecute the war against the Axis. We have everything to gain now by making known our effort and our sacrifices. We have everything to lose by silence." The key was to foster a sense of bilateral partnership cemented by the experience of coalition warfare and founded on common traditions, interests, and values as codified by the alliance's cornerstone texts, foremost among them FDR's Four Freedoms speech, the Atlantic Charter, and the Declaration of the United Nations. Propaganda needed to go far beyond rationalizing the empire to remind Americans of Britain's long "history of advancing liberalism and freedom" and "determination to work" for those ideals in the days to come, argued one Foreign Office U.S. expert, T. North Whitehead. Doing so, he wrote, would paint a clear portrait "of what we stand for and what manner of people we will prove to be in our future dealings." Furthermore, every opportunity should be taken to highlight "collaboration between the two countries," the MOI's publicity game plan pointed out.[21]

The U.K. initiative strove equally to draw the United States further into the international orbit and to orient the United States within that community. That is, British propagandists at the dawn of the American Century thought it essential both to feed and curb the U.S. appetite for global activism. And the language of Atlanticism, conceptually speaking, expanded U.S. horizons even as it tutored youthful U.S. exuberance and channeled U.S. power in directions that served British interests. High-level Britons imagined themselves as tutors, Greeks to America's Romans, as future prime minister Harold Macmillan expressed it in 1943. The trick was to make Britain's desiderata—Europe-first strategic thinking or post-war economic assistance—seem like they were America's, and success depended on developing an environment of Anglo-American teamwork in which Britain was regarded as a full and equal player rather than a junior partner dependent on U.S. largesse. "Unless the idea that Britain is 'indebted to the United States' can be eliminated," Butler and MOI American Division chief Robin Cruikshank agreed, "it will prejudice the discussion of all other postwar problems." Accordingly, the MOI decreed that one main message was Anglo-American "partnership, on equal terms."[22]

Propagandists worked as partners, so much so that distinguishing between U.K. and U.S. wartime propaganda is a fool's errand. It is more helpful to think of the propaganda as Anglo-American, a hybrid produced by a rich transoceanic exchange of people, ideas, and materials that speaks to the relative closeness of Anglo-American ties. (Although each of the four major Allied powers maintained some contact with its cobelligerents, Western authorities kept a certain distance from the Chinese and Soviets.) In 1942, top British and American officials established a Joint Committee that pooled resources, set policy, and coordinated efforts. The MOI and OWI routinely consulted: the MOI mentored its protégé and the OWI adopted many practices and themes tested by the more veteran service. British propagandists went about their business unmolested in the United States, and vice versa: barely an eyebrow was raised at the torrent of films, pamphlets, and press releases that spewed nonstop from British Information Services headquarters in Manhattan's Rockefeller Center, for example. The major American radio networks regularly carried BBC programming. Filmmakers produced joint documentaries. British advisers and actors shaped Hollywood features (*Mrs. Miniver*, for example), which dominated the U.K. and U.S. markets. And the major Hollywood studios owned production firms in the United Kingdom, meaning that pictures that appeared on the surface to be British-made were actually less so.[23]

A host of Hollywood pictures portrayed the Anglo-American alliance as an intimate relationship between kindred peoples. To some degree, all of them followed the narrative formula set by the pre-1942 Eagle Squadron films: a brash young American travels to Britain with negative stereotypes in mind and predictably clashes with his British hosts before finding common ground with and developing affection for them. That pattern was evident in MGM's comedy *A Yank at Eton* (1942), where Mickey Rooney's character ultimately befriended his elite school chums after getting off on the wrong foot. It held in *Eagle Squadron* (1942) as well. Independent producer Walter Wanger, the interventionist behind 1940's *Foreign Correspondent*, initiated *Eagle Squadron* late in the same year to encourage U.S. belligerence with a fictionalized account, reminiscent of *A Yank in the RAF*, of American pilots who joined Britain's air corps. Like Zanuck's picture, Wanger's featured a protagonist, Chuck Brewer (Robert Stack), who was a hotdog U.S. airman whose worldview underwent a reversal. Repeated are the genre's stock elements—the lead, a soldier of fortune who has enlisted only to settle a bet, initially refuses to play by the RAF's rules but eventually falls in line—as the on-screen American isolationist/Anglophobe matures into an international freedom fighter.[24]

Wanger's picture departed from the norm in one important respect: Brewer develops a romance with an Englishwoman that seals his embrace of the British ally. *Eagle Squadron*'s overall dramatic and political goal was to sweep away "the little barriers there are to intimacy between Americans and Englishmen," according to a treatment prepared by Wanger's production team. On film, Chuck falls for Anne Partridge (Diana Barrymore), an aristocratic Women's Auxiliary Air Force volunteer. Anne rejects Chuck's precipitous marriage proposal, however, citing the unprincipled, selfish American's failure to comprehend the war's larger stakes. Mere love is unimportant when everyone has a "job to do for England," Anne insists. Over time, though, the protagonist realizes the error of his ways, acquiring a deeper appreciation of Britons and their cause. "When this war started England didn't mean a thing to me," Chuck tells a colleague. Anne had told him that "there was something bigger than just us. I didn't get that. But now," he realizes, "Anne was right!" In the closing reel, the couple becomes engaged before the reformed American hero joins his RAF mates on yet another strike against German targets.[25]

Though it ought not to be mistaken for a great film, *Eagle Squadron* developed a cinematic method for projecting Atlanticism onto the big screen. Inspired by *Mrs. Miniver*'s critical and commercial success, Wanger's picture and other films represented the Western alliance as a community of nations joined by blood, marriage, or friendly experience. Likening foreign affairs to familial relations offered a natural analogy, if for no other reasons than that it appealed to theatergoers and proved a winning box office formula. In addition, cinematic stories of international kinship spoke to Americans' increased intimacy with their transatlantic relatives. A complex web of human relationships had for centuries connected the two countries. Many white Americans could trace their ancestral roots back to England, Scotland, or Ireland. Wedlock conjoined Anglo-Americans as well. Hundreds of British aristocrats had married wealthy American women over the preceding half century, including Lord Randolph Churchill (who married Jennie Jerome in 1874) and former King Edward VIII (who married Wallis Simpson in 1937). Transoceanic marriage occurred with much greater frequency during World War II, when some 3 million American GIs massed in the British Isles prior to the Allied invasion of Normandy. By the end of the war, U.S. soldiers, famously said to be "overpaid, oversexed, and over here" by resentful Britons, had married no less than forty thousand British war brides and fathered at least fourteen thousand children, numbers that underestimate Anglo-American intimacy since they count neither illegitimate births nor nonmarital social intercourse. Those marriages were undoubtedly the products of circumstance. But they also could be read as gendered signs of the changing bilateral power dynamic. Whereas British peers had wedded American debutantes during the age of U.K. supremacy, U.S. males took British brides now that the United States was ascendant.[26]

For these as well as nationalistic reasons, Americans no longer liked to think of U.S. relations with Great Britain, the "mother country," as those between child and parent, although that analogy remained in circulation. Rather, friendship, consanguinity, and especially matrimony seemed more appropriate, and celluloid romances such as *Eagle Squadron* and *Thunder Birds* (1942) characterized the Anglo-American alliance as a love story to win the hearts of wartime fans, the vast majority (70 to 80 percent, according to the industry's overestimate) of whom were women. Produced and written by Zanuck (under his nom de plume, Melville Crossman), *Thunder Birds* offered a fictionalized take on Allied pilots who trained in the United States. This forgotten Technicolor gem reversed the *Yank in the RAF* motif—"Tommy in the USA" was its working title—to underscore the human bonds forged at Thunderbird Field, an air base

"Discharged veteran, Robert Santini, was reunited with his British bride in New York City, when the former Olive Mason arrived in the USA, May 29th [1945]. The couple were married in Newbury, England, and are shown here being interviewed by [a] Red Cross worker." Office of War Information photo 208-AA-229-GG-1, Still Picture Unit, National Archives and Records Administration II, College Park, Md.

located deep in the Arizona desert. The trainees include Peter Stackhouse (performed by the British actor John Sutton), an earnest RAF pilot determined to earn his wings and thus carry on a long family tradition of national service. Here again, however, a problem arises: Stackhouse suffers from a fear of heights, a condition that threatens to frustrate his ambitions. Into this seemingly hopeless situation steps the base's American instructor, Steve Britt (Preston Foster), a crusty aviation legend with a heart of gold who, as luck would have it, flew with Peter's father back in World War I. Britt recognizes Stackhouse's still unrealized potential and resolves to help him pass the training regimen. More drama unfolds when the two men fall in love with the same woman, Kay Saunders, a beautiful Arizonan played by Gene Tierney. Steve holds Peter's future in his hands, and

U.S. Army staff sergeant Samuel Rochester holds hands with his "adopted" mother, Mrs. Norman Rawlence of Bremerton, England, at the American Red Cross Club's 1943 Mother's Day Tea Dance in London. Bristol's Pearl Phillips, Mrs. Rawlence's "adopted" daughter for the day, joins the clasp. Office of War Information photo, June 1943, 208-AA-40EE-1, Still Picture Unit, National Archives and Records Administration II, College Park, Md.

a rupture in Anglo-American relations appears at hand. Yet with common Allied interests in mind, Britt opts to set personal rivalry aside and continue his professional assistance to Stackhouse, who consequently performs—heroically, of course—the solo flight required to complete the training. Furthermore, Steve voluntarily takes a romantic backseat to the Briton, who has clearly won the American girl's heart. But there are no residual hard feelings; the love triangle is resolved amicably and to everyone's satisfaction. All parties involved remain on friendly terms in *Thunder Birds'* larger narrative of what Tierney's character refers to as "international solidarity." Indeed, the entire experience at Thunderbird—where American, British, and Chinese pilots "work together, study together, [and] play together," all the while "learning to know one another . . . to be friends," according to the narrator—comes off as one long Allied community-building exercise capped by Peter and Kay's engagement and a joint 4 July festival that confuses national and international identities.

Another wave of such movies hit theaters near the war's end, by which time attention had turned toward the future and whether the Anglo-American partnership would carry over into the postwar era. MGM released a parlor drama, *The White Cliffs of Dover* (1944), based on Alice Duer Miller's poem, that hearkened back to a previous era in Anglo-American marital relations. In the film, Irene Dunne plays a young American who travels to Britain, marries an aristocratic Englishman, and—despite some instances of Anglo-American misunderstanding along the way—comes to identify with her adopted country. Although the OWI panned *The White Cliffs*, predicting that its inclusion of snobby British and parochial American characters would cause hard feelings on both sides of the Atlantic, the film proved to be one of MGM's top earners that year.[27]

British-made features amplified the message of Anglo-American accord. The aptly named *Journey Together* (1945), an official RAF version of *Thunder Birds*, related a story of British pilots, including one played by a young Richard Attenborough, who train in the Arizona desert and are there befriended by Edward G. Robinson in the role of the base's top American officer. Director Anthony Asquith's *The Way to the Stars* (1945), supported by the MOI, explored the dense network of personal transoceanic ties that grew as U.S. Army Air Force pilots inundated an RAF base. Historian David Reynolds has detailed the uptick in anti-Americanism that accompanied the introduction of millions of often boisterous, cocksure, and sexually active American GIs into the United Kingdom ahead of the June 1944 D-Day invasion. (Antagonism arose despite the U.S. Army's attempt to moderate soldiers' behavior with instruction about Britain and its customs.) Asquith's picture—best thought of as a British take on Yanks, so many Yanks, in the RAF—alludes to this antagonism with scenes of obnoxious U.S. flyboys noisily intruding on the more reserved English. Rather than simply caricaturing the Ugly Americans, however, *The Way to the Stars* takes viewers on a journey of Anglo-American reconciliation. The foremost U.S. pilot, Johnny Hollis (performed by Douglass Montgomery, a Canadian), a sensitive, respectful guest, develops a close albeit platonic relationship with the widowed Toddy (Rosamund John) as well as a deep appreciation for her fellow townspeople. Meanwhile, the cast's RAF fliers, including Peter Penrose (star British actor John Mills), welcome Johnny and his colleagues into their fraternity after the Americans prove their mettle with strikes against the Luftwaffe. All told, Asquith, son of a former British prime minister, made a strong case for continued communion with "*our* American allies," as Toddy says, at the dawn of the postwar age. Among the most popular of all wartime British films, *The Way to the Stars*' lesson resonated with critics: Richard Winnington of the *News Chronicle* honored its "valuable . . . service" on behalf of Anglo-American harmony. The movie, renamed *Johnny in the Clouds*, premiered in the United States in 1946, with *Time* calling it "the most American film ever made outside the USA."[28]

Advertised as "a love story that bridges the Atlantic," director Herbert Wilcox's romantic drama, *I Live in Grosvenor Square* (1945) (a reference to the location of the U.S. embassy in London), cast American actor Dean Jagger as Sergeant John Patterson, a U.S. pilot who falls for an English-woman. Unbeknownst to John, however, the object of his affection, Lady Patricia Fairfax, played by the admired English actor Anna Neagle, is involved in a long-standing but stale relationship with his new British friend, Major David Bruce (Rex Harrison). The now customary love tri-angle follows, only to be resolved amicably, as in *Thunder Birds* and *Eagle Squadron*. Any wounded feelings begin to ease when John, a person of goodwill, volunteers for combat duty to avoid coming between Pat and David. But David, whose quality of character equals John's, sees that Pat truly cares for the American and arranges the estranged lovers' reunion. Giddy, John and Pat agree to marry and set up house in his native Flag-staff, Arizona, when the war is over. One final development ruins their plans, however: like the saintly Johnny Hollis in *The Way to the Stars*, John Patterson dies tragically in a plane crash, but not without taking action that spares the nearby village from harm. Lady Patricia is distraught, and the grateful townspeople posthumously honor Patterson for saving them, his British "friends," with a ceremony featuring an American flag salvaged from the wreckage. As the mayor of the village (a father figure whom John called "Pops") points out, the flag symbolizes the United States, a close "blood" relative of Britain's. The *Observer*'s film critic, C. A. Lejeune, wrote that *I Live in Grosvenor Square*, which toured U.S. theaters in 1946 under the tile *A Yank in London*, served as an effective advocate for alliance.[29]

Two masterpieces by Michael Powell and Emeric Pressburger—*A Canter-bury Tale* (1944) and *A Matter of Life and Death* (1946)—concluded the trend. Geopolitics is incidental to the former, a lyrical adaptation of Geof-frey Chaucer's fourteenth-century work. The motif of Anglo-American friendship is present all the same, evident in the easy rapport that grows among three modern-day pilgrims—two Britons, shopgirl Alison Smith (Sheila Sim) and Sergeant Peter Gibbs (Dennis Price), and an American, Sergeant Bob Johnson (John Sweet, a real-life U.S. Army soldier)—as they solve a mystery along their redemptive wartime journey to Canterbury Cathedral. Geopolitics is central to *A Matter of Life and Death*, encouraged by the MOI for its endorsement of good transatlantic relations. In it, an incipient romance between a member of the U.S. Women's Army Corps, June (Kim Hunter), and RAF squadron leader Peter Carter (David Niven) is interrupted by his apparent death in a May 1945 airplane crash. However, Peter miraculously survives the crash and reunites with June. A mistake has been made in the heavens, where the celestial powers that be are nonetheless determined to have Peter enter the afterlife, as their records indicate he must, while Peter is determined to remain alive with June. Caught in limbo, Peter appeals his case: although they were "born thousands of miles apart," he and June "were made for each other," he says. Argument is heard before a veritable United Nations in the sky, men and women of all colors and creeds representing the Allied nations. Peter's fate hinges on a question of international relations posed in cinematic language: can people of different nationalities really, truly care for one another? The appointed American prosecutor (played by Raymond Massey, a Canadian), an Anglophobic relic from the eighteenth century shot to death by a Redcoat during the American Revolution, thinks not, insisting that the Englishman, Peter, somehow manipulated June, a susceptible young woman of "good American stock." The modern, cosmopolitan defense counsel, a casualty of World War II, replies that the couple's "natural" attraction represents precisely the qualities—"love, and truth, and friendship"—needed to build a "new world today" and "a better one tomorrow." Powell and Pressburger's internationalist fairy tale ends happily enough when the court, persuaded that June and Peter's bond is genuine, allows them to remain together in peace on Earth.[30]

Another genre, feature-length war documentaries, projected instances of actual Anglo-American cooperation onto the big screen. The MOI's *Desert Victory* (1943) traced the Allies' North African campaign, which climaxed with the British Eighth Army's watershed victory over General Erwin Rommel's Afrika Korps at the Battle of El Alamein in 1942, a triumph that ended a string of British defeats stretching from Dunkirk to Singapore to Crete. Widely considered to be among the greatest works of its kind, *Desert Victory* changed perceptions when it reached U.S. theaters. By giving Britain's armed forces their due for the battlefield success, it corrected the impression that the United Kingdom made a poor

Peter (David Niven) and June (Kim Hunter) Carter are the Anglo-American couple happily reunited forever after in Michael Powell and Emeric Pressburger's *A Matter of Life and Death* (Archers, 1946). Photofest/ © Eagle-Lion Films.

military ally. That perspective, combined with the credit apportioned to the United States—the narrator, over shots of American-made goods being produced and shipped across the Atlantic to North Africa, pointed out that Lend-Lease aided the Eighth Army's push—lifted Allied spirits. Churchill was so pleased with *Desert Victory* that he personally sent a copy to FDR, who replied that it would do "great good" among American audiences. Winner of an Academy Award as the year's Best Documentary, the film served as an "unquestionable morale builder for [every] soldier and civilian of the United Nations," wrote *Variety*. In the words of the *New Yorker*, *Desert Victory* demonstrated "to the layman" that "this particular United Nation" could "wage one nifty campaign."[31]

Tunisian Victory (1944), a second North Africa documentary, took the notion of combined operations to another level. A joint Anglo-American project, the movie was plagued by rancorous behind-the-scenes disputes between its British and American directors—Hugh Stewart and

Frank Capra, with assistance from John Huston—over style and tone. Yet audiences remained blissfully ignorant of those internecine squabbles when *Tunisian Victory* arrived in U.K. and U.S. theaters in March 1944. The final product featured a fictional British soldier, George Metcalf (voiced by Bernard Miles), and his Yank counterpart, Joe McAdams (Burgess Meredith), who walked viewers through the campaign's major events from the joint planning by Churchill and Roosevelt in December 1941 to the liberation of Tunis in May 1943. George and Joe then engage in a dialogue, in which they agree to cooperate to create a more just and peaceful postwar world order. Over shots of soldiers representing the various UN powers, Joe asks, "Why can't we, after the war, keep on swinging together? Yeah, building things up instead of blowing things up. We can do it, I betcha." George responds in the affirmative: "Do all the jobs that need doing." "Boy, what a job," Joe replies hopefully. U.S. commentators generally praised *Tunisian Victory* for displaying the Allies' "collaborative spirit." From London, where some critics grumbled about the movie's overemphasis on American actions, U.S. ambassador John G. Winant nevertheless cabled Secretary of War Stimson of the film's "excellent reception here."[32]

Cinematic tributes to victory in North Africa were but preludes to the main event: a joint documentary memorializing the long-awaited Allied invasion of Europe. Officials expected D-Day to be a propaganda coup for the United States and Great Britain, a moment when the foremost Western Allies could rightfully bask in the glow of defeating Nazism and liberating Europe. As was the case with *Tunisian Victory*, British and American officials quarreled during production over which country should receive the most credit on-screen in *The True Glory* (1945). Yet again, however, those kerfuffles were nowhere to be found in the finished product, which bore a thick coating of bilateral amity. According to the leading authority on the movie, there is "no indication of the differences which existed between the Allies. The film's content transcends the vicissitudes of production."[33]

Directed by Carol Reed, who would become legendary for his work on *The Third Man* (1949), among other films, *The True Glory* recounted the Allied assault from the earliest preparations to Germany's final surrender. A quick-moving montage of documentary footage—there were no staged scenes, unlike in Capra's *Why We Fight* series—Reed's picture assigned the enemy full responsibility for the war's carnage, even to the point of including searing footage of the newly discovered German extermination camps, ghastly imagery that had the added effect of casting the Western

Allies as heroic liberators. And the film carefully apportioned credit to all those involved—British and American, enlisted soldier and officer, army and navy—for their sacrifices in destroying fascism: shots of bodies littering Omaha Beach attested to the high price paid by soldiers from all the Allied countries.[34]

Even more to the point, *The True Glory* framed the war as a crusade for freedom won as a consequence of Allied solidarity. Those themes became clear from the outset, in an on-camera introduction by General Dwight D. Eisenhower, supreme commander of the Allied Expeditionary Force. A proponent of psychological warfare throughout his career, Eisenhower took a personal interest in the project, so much so that Reed quipped that the general "got to be quite a pain in the neck after a while." Backed by the Stars and Stripes and the Union Jack, Eisenhower looks directly at the camera and extols Allied cooperation for the benefit of civilians back home: "Teamwork wins wars. I mean teamwork among nations, services, and men, all the way down the line from the GI and the Tommy to us brass hats." The Allies "were welded together by fighting for one great cause, into one great team—a team in which [viewers] were an indispensable and working member. That spirit of free people working, fighting, and living together in one great cause has served us well on the Western Front." In a nod to the future, he expresses confidence that the same "spirit of comradeship will persist forever among the free peoples of the United Nations."[35]

Anecdotes related by enlistees lend greater credence to Eisenhower's vision of enduring Allied brotherhood. A GI speaks of feeling like a "stranger" immediately after arriving in Britain, only to be so welcomed by his hosts as to become a member of an extended family. "All over the U.K., you'd see things that made you begin to realize that you were just part of a helluva big proposition," he says, his words cued to shots of Allied soldiers massing in Britain prior to the invasion. As footage shows German cities reduced to rubble, the voice of another participant states that victory invested the United Nations with an opportunity "to build a free world, better than before. Maybe the last chance." A propaganda film documenting the victors' wartime exploits might be expected to end on a triumphant, even hubristic, note. It does not. At the time of *The True Glory*'s September 1945 release, just one month after the end of the Pacific war, the United Nations still had unfinished business to which to attend: a stable peace awaited construction. Consequently, the documentary concludes on an anxious if optimistic note, as audiences learn the significance of its title, taken from a prayer by Sir Frances Drake spoken here over a montage of UN troops: "O Lord God, when thou givest to thy servants to endeavor any great matter, grant us also to know that it is not the beginning, but the continuing of the same, until it be thoroughly finished, which yieldeth the true glory."

Reed's masterpiece, winner of an Academy Award as 1945's Best Documentary, won critical praise on both sides of the Atlantic. *Time* and *Commonweal* endorsed the movie's portrayal of Allied solidarity, something that both magazines hoped would carry over into peacetime. The *New York Times* welcomed the evident "spirit of teamwork through which the final triumph was won." London's *Documentary News Letter* called it "an impressive record."[36]

Movies did not operate in a vacuum. Rather, they existed within a broader cultural environment where other media reinforced the narrative of transatlantic solidarity. U.S. radio listeners heard not only BBC broadcasts but also *Young Dr. Malone*, a popular daytime soap opera involving the title character's wartime adventures in Britain. OFF posters included one labeling a British soldier a "friend" to Americans in their fight for freedom. Fans reveled in the exploits of Joe Palooka, a comic book hero who gave Anglophobes the ribbing they deserved. And magazine readers came across a 1944 Coca-Cola advertisement that peddled soda pop and Atlanticism at the same time. Featuring a clutch of RAF pilots drinking Coke after a successful mission, the ad's text associated the beverage with international goodwill, a trademark of the company's sales campaigns: *"Have a 'Coke'* is a friendly greeting among RAF flyers back at early dawn from a night mission. It's a salute among comrades in arms that seals the bonds of friendship in Plymouth, England, as in Plymouth, Massachusetts. It's an offer as welcome on an English airfield as it is in your own living room. Around the globe, Coca-Cola stands for the pause that refreshes—[It] has become a happy symbol of good-hearted friendliness."[37]

No explanation of how Anglo-American relations became regarded as "special" could be complete without a word about Winston Churchill and his partnership with Franklin Roosevelt. Churchill emerged as perhaps the alliance's best publicist. Stage-managed by the MOI, he became nothing short of a media star in the United States, where he wormed his way into the American consciousness through countless radio speeches, newsreel appearances, and press accounts. Made larger than life, Churchill came to personify, in American eyes, Britain and its transformation from passive doormat to determined freedom fighter. His predecessor, Neville Chamberlain, had appeased Adolf Hitler at Munich in 1938, an action applauded by many Americans, FDR included, at the time but considered foolish and weak in retrospect. With Chamberlain, the ultimate Colonel Blimp, in the driver's seat, the nation seemed from a distance to be spineless and adrift. That perception changed when Chamberlain resigned in disgrace and Churchill arrived on Downing Street in May 1940. His stocky physique, immovable demeanor, and defiant speeches—he "mobilized the English language and sent it into battle," said broadcaster Edward R. Murrow, an authority on the subject—created the impression that Churchill possessed the energy and will needed to snatch victory from the jaws of defeat, an underdog tale if ever there were one. That impression arose in no small part as a consequence of his performance during the Blitz, when newsreels captured him giving what became his trademark "V for victory" sign while touring sites damaged by German bombs. Named *Time* magazine's Man of the Year for 1940, Churchill generated an air of vigorous optimism. And his V sign soon became ubiquitous in the United States—the OWI appropriated it for use in U.S. propaganda—giving Britons and Americans a mutual rallying point that lifted spirits in the war's bleak early period with the promise of better days ahead.[38]

Moreover, Churchill developed a close personal rapport with Roosevelt. Although they and their advisers disagreed, sharply at times, about military strategy and postwar policy, the two leaders exchanged almost two thousand messages in the five-plus years prior to FDR's death in April 1945, leading historian Warren F. Kimball, editor of their accumulated communications, to write that "no two national leaders ever corresponded on such intimate and personal terms." The friendliness and candidness that characterized their correspondence and their relationship as a whole cemented the Anglo-American alliance in the popular mind, creating a partnership that was not without conflict but was nevertheless quite close. The entente depended on more than just leadership, of course. Common language, traditions, values, and interests knitted it together, so much so that the Soviet Union and China seemed like associate powers by contrast. (All told, Churchill and Roosevelt met thirteen times, eleven of them without Soviet premier Joseph Stalin and twelve without China's President Jiang Jieshi.)[39]

In August 1941, Churchill and Roosevelt met aboard British and American warships anchored off Newfoundland's coast for the Atlantic Conference. The summit, carefully choreographed to foster an air of bilateral amity, began on 9 August, when the HMS *Prince of Wales*, its band playing "Stars and Stripes Forever," pulled alongside the USS *Augusta*. Fingers raised in the V sign, the prime minister boarded the *Augusta* as its musicians performed "God Save the King" and FDR greeted him with the words, "At last we've gotten together." The next day, the president visited the British battleship for a Sunday service. Churchill orchestrated the ceremony, personally selecting the prayers and hymns, which included "Onward, Christian Soldiers." The sermon, drawn from Joshua 1:5–6, emphasized themes of loyalty and cooperation in difficult times: "As I was with Moses, so will I be with thee: I will not fail thee, nor forsake thee." The congregants prayed for the success of their common purpose, asking God to "strengthen our resolve" to fight until "all enmity and oppression be done away, and the people of the world be set free from fear to serve one another." To the prime minister's secretary, the events seemed like "a sort of marriage service," a consummation of Anglo-American affinity. Churchill fondly recalled the affair as "a deeply moving expression of the unity of faith of our two peoples," symbolized by "the Union Jack and the Stars and Stripes draped side by side on the pulpit" and embodied by "the close-packed ranks of British and American sailors, completely intermingled, sharing the same books and joining fervently together in the prayers and hymns familiar to both."[40]

The Atlantic Charter codified the conference's unity of spirit and purpose. A statement of common war aims, the document committed Great Britain and the United States to the creation of a more liberal world order based on the Four Freedoms. Released to the world via telegram on 14 August, the Atlantic Charter called for national self-determination, liberalized trade, and worldwide freedom from fear and want. It also looked toward the establishment of a "permanent system of general security." The charter represented not only a diplomatic text but also an act of political theater that staked out the moral high ground for the Allies, established a collective identity, and conveyed an impression of solidarity, philosophic and otherwise.[41]

High-level interaction only intensified after the United States formally entered the war. Eager to cement the alliance and formulate joint strategy, Churchill rushed to Washington for another conference with the president. On 23 December 1941, he and Roosevelt held a joint press conference, though the prime minister was the main attraction. When Churchill stood on a chair so that the assembled journalists could better see him, his spunky departure from the norm earned "loud and spontaneous cheers" rarely heard among the otherwise jaded Washington press corps.[42]

A guest at the White House, the prime minister celebrated Christmas with the Roosevelts, inspiring veteran *Washington Evening Star* cartoonist Clifford Berryman to depict the entire conference, code-named Arcadia, as an exclusive family affair. That perception of intimacy deepened on Boxing Day, when Churchill addressed Congress, just the second time in U.S. history that a British prime minister had done so. Although not among Churchill's best, the speech, broadcast nationally by radio, was well received, owing in part to its reference to his American mother, Jennie. As cameras flashed, he concluded his talk by giving the V sign, a gesture reciprocated by the Supreme Court's chief justice, Harlan F. Stone. A thunderous standing ovation echoed throughout the House chamber. Lawmakers mobbed the prime minister, pumping his hand and slapping his back as he made his way up the aisle and out of the Capitol building, where a throng of well-wishers shivered in the wintry Washington evening to catch a glimpse of him.[43]

Churchill's triumphant Capitol Hill performance made the front pages of the morning papers. Newsreels replayed his address in movie theaters across the country over the days and weeks to come. *Newsweek* gushed that he had "made eyes glisten with his tender reference to his American mother." *Time* ran a photograph of Churchill captioned, "This was a man Americans liked," and accompanied by an article comparing his arrival to "a breath of fresh air, giving Washington new vigor, for he came as a new hero." *Life* estimated that the prime minister, who stayed in the city long enough to sign the Declaration of the United Nations on New Year's Day 1942, had "sold Washington on the war and on Britain. And he sold America on himself." An official report calculating his visit's net effect on the American psyche reached a similar conclusion: "Churchill's presence and actions here seem to have made real for the first time a sense of alliance between the United States and Britain." The document's author continued, "More than anything else, Mr. Churchill's words have fostered an awareness that the war is on a planetary scale. Editorial writers and broadcasters are now expressing [with] genuine conviction the concept that allied forces must be marshaled with the whole world conflict in view."[44]

The Atlantic and Arcadia talks were only the beginning, but they went far in establishing Anglo-American familiarity. Not incidentally, the prime minister returned to London and told King George VI that Britain and America were now "married" as a result of the meeting. (However, Churchill's subsequent characterization at the 1945 Potsdam Conference of the alliance as a marriage between an American "young lady" and a British gentleman must have struck President Harry S Truman as anachronistic.) That unifying narrative was so often repeated by the media that it became conventional wisdom. To be sure, Anglophobes and isolationists, once ascendant, existed still. Ambassador Halifax warned the Foreign Office in February 1945 that "old-fashioned isolationists," "America-firsters," and "anti-British hyphenates" could yet reemerge in force. But their numbers and influence now paled against those of the Atlanticists, who shared a common culture and interests with their not-so-distant British cousins. Polls showed that about three-quarters of Americans felt confident that Great Britain could be "depended upon to cooperate" after the armistice. One 1945 survey indicated that a solid majority agreed that the two countries should establish a permanent military alliance, a significant departure from the traditional aversion to foreign entanglements. That proposal received wide bipartisan support, most notably from New York's Republican governor, Thomas E. Dewey, who endorsed the idea during his 1944 presidential bid.[45]

On the other side of the Atlantic, Britons learned about the United States, for better or worse, via Hollywood's productions. American pictures were not novelties in the United Kingdom but had dominated the British market since World War I despite various restrictive measures imposed by Parliament and the Treasury. Hollywood further increased its market share during World War II as the domestic U.K. industry was hobbled by blackouts, supply shortages, and low investment. Whereas the major studios earned $52 million in the United Kingdom in 1939–40, that figure jumped to $88 million by war's end.[46]

Hollywood films exerted considerable influence on the 23 million people (nearly half of the total 1941 U.K. population of 48.2 million) who attended theaters each week. Cinema's ubiquity made it a primary means for acquainting Britons with their overseas brethren. "For the average moviegoer," Cambridge political scientist Denis W. Brogan observed in 1942, "America is the films," and the America shown on-screen was "an energetic, precedent-breaking, very amusing, fabulous country where anything goes and anything is possible." Impressions were generally but not always so favorable. Mass Observation, a private social research organization, found that the idea of Americans being "distant cousins," or "a rather eccentric kind of Englishmen," resided "at the back of many British minds."[47]

Movies united the Anglo-American relatives by bridging the physical and physic space that separated them. As early as August 1942, the *London Times* commented on the screen's success in building "up between the Allies that understanding which is the only true source of sympathy and confidence." For decades, movies had provided Britons with their most direct link to the United States. The result, according to the *Observer*'s Lejeune, was that "American speech and idiom is as familiar to the British as their own. British children whistle American tunes and use American slang. British boys pin up pictures of American stars in their bedrooms and billets. British girls fix their hair like Ginger Rogers." To another observer, Hollywood's encroachment on the nation's interior life might be less praiseworthy. But to Lejeune, Hollywood served up "a friendly picture" of "America as the land of freedom, opportunity, and comradeship" that attracted her to the United States: "If I had my wish, I would visit America tomorrow. Persuaded solely by the films, I should never be content until I had steamed into New York harbor past the Statue of Liberty, entrained at Grand Central Station, rubber-necked around Washington, stopped off in Chicago, done something, I don't care what, in Iowa, and seen the Golden Gate of San Francisco. . . . I want to be friends with the people whose pictures have given me so much pleasure for so long and who have advertised so warmly that their country is a haven for strangers."[48]

If Hollywood exerted what we today call "soft power" for the United States, then it could and did have counterproductive effects as well. Commercial cinema often exacerbated Anglo-American tensions. The British Library of Information's Richard R. Ford informed his State Department interlocutor that some of Hollywood's stock characters, including the gangster and the vamp, although popular, created "false and harmful impressions" of the United States. The MOI's Bernstein concurred, telling the *Hollywood Reporter* in 1942 that British theatergoers received "a steady stream of glamour boys and girls, and of spies, of crooks and millionaires" not at all indicative of "how the ordinary American lives." Thomas Baird of British Information Services echoed those remarks, reminding his U.S. counterparts that only "very few [Hollywood pictures] have contributed in any way to the Englishman's understanding of the ordinary American scene."[49]

U.S. officials, too, expressed a laundry list of complaints against Hollywood. Its productions presented "a distorted picture of American life with undue emphasis upon the cowboy, the gangster and extravagant playboys." Ambassador Winant cabled Archibald MacLeish of the OWI to protest movies that portrayed Americans as "idle and extravagant," an image that ran "counter to a sense of [common wartime] sacrifice." The OWI's Ferdinand Kuhn, a onetime London correspondent for the *New York Times*, singled out films that bred "irritation and annoyance" among Britons. Some, including *A Yank at Eton* and *Random Harvest*, contained inaccurate depictions of British society that did "great harm" when shown there. Others—notably *Objective, Burma!* (1945), a Warner Bros. combat drama pulled from U.K. circulation after its self-congratulatory tone led to protests—offended by exaggerating America's wartime accomplishments at the expense of Britain's. Of such pictures, Kuhn wrote, "we defeat our purpose, and create real ill will for ourselves abroad, whenever we brag about ourselves without reference to what our British and other allies have done."[50]

Authorities intruded on the transatlantic cultural conversation to better manage the U.S. image. The MOI targeted anti-Americanism by backing *The Way to the Stars* and *A Matter of Life and Death*. Whitehall implemented American studies programs in British schools and universities to counteract, in Reynolds's words, "the Hollywood image of America as a land of violence and corruption." In January 1943, the OWI established a British Division that distributed films and press releases and sponsored traveling exhibits and public lectures. And the Department of State conducted an educational film program as an antidote to Hollywood. Designed to "promote international goodwill," the program's short documentaries—about real-life cowboys, farmers, and Rosie the Riveters—were selected to give Britons who saw them (an estimated 22 million people in 1943 alone) "a true picture of America."[51]

Nevertheless, the Hollywood juggernaut rolled on unabated, and its omnipresence in British life fueled an anti-American backlash. Cultural conservatives blamed American pictures for a range of homegrown ills from juvenile misbehavior to the weakened national character, charges reminiscent of those leveled by U.S. reformers against the major studios. One paternalistic member of Parliament, for example, alleged in 1944 that British youths were being corrupted by American movies: "I am concerned with the effect upon the lives of our young people of too many films coming from Hollywood especially on Saturday afternoons when you can see thousands of young children, from working-class areas in particular, going to matinees and seeing films which they ought not to see." Furthermore, what was happening inside British theaters also became associated with questions about the United Kingdom's status in the world. Along with GIs, Hollywood's dominance was taken as tangible evidence of the United Kingdom's subordination to the United States. Despite all the talk about bilateral equality, it was now apparent that for the first time, Great Britain had become the junior partner in the Anglo-American relationship. For a country long accustomed to being a Great Power, the descent to middling status was discomfiting, to say the least.

And in that context, foreign movies made easy targets for domestic critics. Indeed, some claimed that Britain was being colonized by the ascendant United States and its movies. George Orwell, a onetime MOI employee, noted "an obvious growth of animosity against America," widely regarded as "a potentially imperialist country."[52]

In December 1943, the Board of Trade's Cinematograph Films Council impaneled a special committee, chaired by Albert Palache, to investigate charges of monopoly in the motion picture industry, including alleged collusion among the major Hollywood studios operating in Britain. While the Palache Committee's final July 1944 report found no evidence of wrongdoing, it did document how the "preponderating influence of American interests" had been "further accentuated" of late. Furthermore, the committee echoed a statement made by a similar body in 1938, expressing disturbance at this trend, for "the screen has great influence both politically and culturally over the minds of the people. Its potentialities are vast, as a vehicle for expression of national life, ideals and tradition . . . and as an instrument for propaganda."[53]

The Palache Committee's report served as an opening salvo in a renewed battle over the size of the American industry's stake in Britain's movie economy. Punctuated by import restrictions, revenue impoundment, and remittance controls, that extended fight began during the interwar period, as chapter 2 discusses. The disagreement simmered throughout the war despite the lip service paid to Allied harmony. One major issue had been the amount of Hollywood's remittable U.K. earnings. Two years of talks resulted in a December 1941 agreement whereby the studios could convert only $20 million of their annual earnings (pegged that year at $35 million). A new deal was reached in September 1942 that held maximum annual remittances steady but released the industry's accumulated impounded revenue, which totaled some $50 million at the time.[54]

Pressure mounted to rewrite the rules of the transatlantic movie game to better protect Britain's cultural, financial, and industrial interests. Finding it difficult to compete with Hollywood in their own backyard, British film producers and distributors (but not exhibitors, who profited from the bigger box office receipts typically earned by American movies) lobbied Parliament and the Board of Trade for heightened import protections. At the same time, the Treasury tightened exchange restrictions on all imported goods, films included. Under those circumstances, board member Rupert G. Somervell favored reducing "the amount of dollars [remitted] by the American film companies by diverting as large a proportion as possible to the Exchequer."[55]

Putting the screws to the American studios made good politics. A House of Lords member declared in 1944 that "the time has come to see that [Britain's domestic film] industry, so important for . . . the spread of prestige of this country, should grow in strength and vigor and take its place side by side with America." National prestige aside, some leaders thought it foolhardy to expend sterling on foreign movies, especially offensive ones, when the country lacked the wherewithal to acquire even the barest essentials. "If we have to ration imports of food, why in heaven's name pay over $20 million a year for stuff like *Objective, Burma!?*," the otherwise moderate *Daily Telegraph* asked. In Parliament, Tory Robert J. Boothby wondered how monetary and trade officials could abide spending precious specie on "second rate American films" in light of the "serious" dollar shortage. Boothby later amplified his views for the press: "I have a great admiration for Mr. Humphrey Bogart. . . . But if I were compelled to choose between Bogart and bacon, I am bound to say I would choose bacon at the present time."[56]

Such rhetoric fueled a nasty trade war, punctuated by Parliament's 50 percent increase in protective film quotas in early 1945. Americans pondered what the stricter regime portended, commercially and diplomatically speaking. London embassy staff warned Ambassador Winant about the "dangerous" anti-Hollywood climate prevailing in the United Kingdom as early as February 1944. In October, he, Hull, and Stettinius received an alarmist memorandum from Will H. Hays, the president of the Motion Picture Producers and Distributors of America (MPPDA), warning that any additional limits placed on the studios' profits in the United Kingdom—where they earned some 60-65 percent of their overseas revenue—represented "the most serious threat that the industry has faced since its inception." Hays even predicted that the movie business—employer of more than 250,000 people, holder of more than $2 billion in investments—would collapse if it lost access to its British receipts, perhaps slowing the entire U.S. economy as it converted to peacetime. And veteran MPPDA foreign envoy Fayette W. Allport advised studio executives about the "very strong and widely held" desire in London "to limit . . . the predominant part played by American pictures in British communal life."[57]

That festering dispute would worsen before it improved: in 1947-48, Parliament imposed a 75 percent ad valorem duty on imported movies, and Hollywood retaliated by boycotting the U.K. market, an unprecedented move that forced British authorities to compromise. The film trade battle exemplifies ongoing British and U.S. divisions—divides that movies not only failed to eliminate but also exacerbated—but hardly interrupted bilateral relations. Rather, Americans ended the war as citizens of the world who felt as if they were parties to a "special" relationship with their British cousins. Indeed, the U.S. worldview expanded remarkably quickly between September 1939, when Anglophobes and isolationists held sway, and August 1945, by which time Atlanticists and internationalists predominated.

To be sure, that transformation can be explained to a significant degree by facts on the ground. The United Kingdom and the United States shared an uncommon number of characteristics—interests, language, and beliefs. And their wartime collaboration, which brought Britons and Americans into closer physical and spiritual contact, defeated Nazism. Yet neither Anglo-American congruence nor the significance of events was immediately evident in the swirling confusion of global war, providing the opening through which propaganda entered the picture. Cultural and political authorities made a conscious effort to order chaos, frame reality, and perpetuate a myth of transatlantic kinship that defined mutual antagonism as characteristic of any close-knit family. Movies were central to that effort, for they were *the* cutting-edge technology of the day when it came to influencing consumers, who could be psychically transported across the Atlantic and brought into imaginative touch with their on-screen kinfolk via film's comprehensive sensory experience.

At the same time, the Hollywoodization of bilateral relations—idealized, sentimentalized, and enlivened by entertainers' touch—proved so persuasive precisely because it corresponded to a greater or lesser degree with lived experience. Britons and Americans were conjoined by extensive human relationships no less than common national interests. "Married," as Churchill put it, the United Kingdom and the United States, even in retrospect, enjoyed an usually close (albeit sometimes contentious) alliance. This state of affairs lent greater credibility to Anglo-American propaganda and explains why it worked so well. The same, however, could not be said for the other major Allied powers—the Soviet Union and China—geographically, ideologically, and/or racially separate from the Atlantic community. When movies tried to make the case for Soviets and Chinese as full and equal members of the UN's family of nations, the gap between fact and fiction was simply too vast, and propaganda fell mostly on deaf ears.

5

COURTING UNCLE JOE THE THEATRICS OF SOVIET-AMERICAN MATRIMONY

Following a sumptuous feast (and generous glasses of vodka), the guests, gathered around a Kremlin table in May 1943, toasted Soviet-American friendship. Soviet premier Joseph Stalin and foreign minister Vyacheslav Molotov praised the United Nations. Foreign trade commissar Anastas Mikoyan and ambassador to the United States Maxim Litvinov followed suit. The Americans present—including the sitting U.S. ambassador, Admiral William H. Standley, and his predecessor, Joseph E. Davies—reciprocated. What distinguished this reception from others that periodically honored Soviet comrades was that Davies had arrived as Franklin D. Roosevelt's special envoy and with a film that he and the president hoped would demonstrate American goodwill and help convince Stalin to act in concert with the major Allied powers throughout the war and beyond. After the toasts were complete, Stalin, a movie enthusiast, led his guests into his private Kremlin theater, where they watched the just-completed *Mission to Moscow*, a Hollywood-made, pro-Soviet picture based on Davies's diplomatic career. As the lights dimmed and the projector rolled, all awaited the dictator's reaction, on which the fate of this odd coupling of cinema and statecraft hinged.[1]

The film's Kremlin exhibition indicates that *Mission to Moscow*, among the most controversial movies ever, played a minor but significant role in Roosevelt's Soviet diplomacy. Having determined that the USSR held the keys to both wartime victory and postwar stability, FDR embarked on his equally controversial "grand design" to cultivate Stalin. *Mission to Moscow* served as one of several confidence-building measures that signaled U.S. friendship and films that prepared the American public for improved relations. Roosevelt's "courtship" or "wooing" of Stalin spawned legions of detractors, who employ such sexualized language to delegitimize the president's "political romanticism." FDR, a desperate suitor in this scenario, diligently attended to Stalin's every demand out of a naive belief that the tyrant's ardor could be won. However, proponents of this viewpoint insist, the president's courtship failed because his submissiveness only made him appear weak, emboldening the Soviet strongman to behave unilaterally and aggressively. Cold War conflict followed.[2]

To be sure, FDR has defenders, who point out, among other things, that he had few options for binding the United Nations other than his charm offensive, which gave Stalin nothing (Poland, for example) that the Red Army did not already possess.[3] But the point here is the common usage, witting or not, of familial phraseology to describe East-West affairs. The president "blurred the personal and the political," according to historian Frank Costigliola, and liked to think of his political allies, domestic or foreign, as honorary members of the extended Roosevelt clan. Whereas his critics adopted prematrimonial rhetoric when discussing the alliance of strange bedfellows, FDR welcomed Stalin into "the family circle" at the Tehran Conference, where he also referred to the murderous tyrant as "Uncle Joe."[4]

More to the point, U.S. propagandists and Hollywood filmmakers repeated such terms of endearment as they strained to naturalize the unnatural Soviet-American partnership for the moviegoing public, which remained uncertain that the alliance (unlike the "special" bonds of affection with the British cousins) represented anything other than a marriage of convenience. Optimistic U.S. diplomats often eroticized the distant, mysterious USSR as an "object of desire," Costigliola writes, and developed a "discourse of falling in love or of making love." MGM's *Song of Russia* (1944), appropriately enough, romanticized bilateral relations as a love affair between an American traveler and a Soviet woman, who was made to conform to U.S. sociopolitical norms. International matrimony involved extended family ties, the discourse held. *Mission to Moscow* insisted that brotherhood linked Soviets and Americans, two peoples who shared a common destiny. Director Frank Capra's *The Battle of Russia* (1943), another part of his *Why We Fight* film series, stood out among testaments to the "kinship" or "friendship" prevailing among the Allied family of nations, ostensibly united by their wartime experiences and peaceful aspirations.[5]

However foolish and ill-fated the big screen's portrait of Soviet-American matrimony may appear in retrospect, it did help initiate a constructive (if brief and, in the aftermath of the Cold War, forgotten) transnational dialogue that strengthened the fragile East-West coalition.[6] Constructive Soviet-American cultural engagement was virtually non-existent prior to World War II, in no small part because the Soviet Union had isolated itself from the outside world. The years after the Bolshevik Revolution had witnessed a cultural renaissance involving rich creative contacts with Western artists, intellectuals, and technicians. Stalin's rise to power, however, was accompanied by a cultural crackdown beginning in 1928 that built "socialism in one country" and its attendant mass social-ist consciousness by cleansing Soviet life of contaminating foreign and bourgeois influence. Among other things, the campaign targeted Holly-wood movies, which had accounted for 59 percent of all films exhibited in the USSR during the brief postrevolutionary window of openness. Foreign imports were banned, local film libraries were purged of alien pictures, and domestic productions deemed too experimental (that is, too West-ern) were suppressed on the orders of the Communist Party of the Soviet Union's Central Committee.[7]

Stalinism also dictated a party line requiring artists, intellectuals, and entertainers to denounce the Western capitalist powers, including the United States, in all forms of public communication. The basic story line of socialist realism, the official mode of artistic expression, involved ordinary characters (hence the misleading term "realism") who, under the party's tutelage, overcame various obstacles on their inexorable path toward a brighter socialist future. Foreign capitalists and their domes-tic ilk—kulaks, the bourgeoisie, and intellectuals—served as clichéd foils whose greedy aggression inevitably hindered the formula's plebeian heroes from attaining socialist nirvana. A governing strategy in the sense that mobilizing opinion against foreign and domestic enemies served as a means of social control, socialist realism's anticosmopolitanism con-tinued, with the major exception of the Popular Front era, until the Ger-man invasion in June 1941. It included such gems as *The Circus* (*Tsirk'*, 1936), among the most popular Soviet features ever. An attack on U.S. racial discrimination starring the beloved Liubov' Orlova, this musical drama followed the travails of a white American circus performer who eventually found solace in the USSR after giving birth to a biracial child and then being driven from her intolerant homeland.[8]

In light of those unpromising beginnings, it is remarkable that Moscow and Washington normalized cultural relations during the war. Once the United Nations coalesced in 1942, both powers hastened to improve communications. On the Soviet side, this relative openness stemmed from ongoing cultural liberalization. Foreseeing that the Soviet people would be more likely to defend family, home, and Mother Russia than socialism, the Kremlin loosened its restrictions for the duration of the wartime emergency, muting ideological themes and permitting public displays of Russian nationalism and Orthodox iconography. This crack in the Kremlin's exclusionary barrier also allowed Allied information and culture to be disseminated in the USSR, albeit on a strictly limited basis. Although sensitive to the long-term ideological dangers the changes posed, Soviet propagandists welcomed—for a time, anyway—such alien information for its ability to boost home front morale by demonstrating to the Soviet people that they were not alone in their struggle against Nazism.[9]

Once forbidden, American movies became prized as supplements to domestic screen propaganda. The Soviet motion picture industry, which even in peacetime succeeded in meeting only 20 to 30 percent of its production targets, had been further crippled by the German invasion. With one studio in Kiev lost and others relocated either beyond the Ural Mountains or to points in Central Asia, industrial disarray rendered the Central Committee's Upravlenie Propagandy i Agitatsii (Propaganda and Agitation Administration) powerless fully to exploit film, a key component of the Soviet propaganda machine in ordinary times. Receiving assistance from Hollywood, long regarded as a technological mecca by Soviet experts, offered a possible albeit imperfect solution.[10]

A conference on American and British film held in Moscow in August 1942 signaled the dawn of openness. Conference organizers—Ivan G. Bol'shakov, head of the Soviet film monopoly, the Council of People's Commissars' Komitet po Delam Kinematografii (Committee on Cinematography Affairs, KDK); and Vladimir S. Kemenov, chief of the Vsesoiuznoe Obshchestvo Kul'turnykh Sviazei s Zagranitsei (All-Union Society for Cultural Relations with Foreign Countries, VOKS)—hoped to acquaint Soviet industrialists with "modern American film production [and] with the technology of American film studios." Attended by Soviet journalists, officials, and filmmakers and organized in conjunction with the U.S. Office of War Information (OWI), the conference featured lectures and a photo exhibit on the American motion picture industry, screenings of several older Hollywood productions (including Charlie Chaplin's 1940 anti-Hitler send-up, *The Great Dictator*), and a floor display of movie equipment. Speakers endorsed greater cultural interaction. In his opening remarks, Bol'shakov said that the gathering sought to "strengthen the friendship and active cooperation" among Allied filmmakers with an eye toward making the "common cause of our great peoples" more readily apparent to moviegoers. "The peoples of our allied nations should know more about each other and it is the task of film workers . . . to bring this about," he declared. Kemenov and famed directors Vsevolod Pudovkin and Sergei Eisenstein praised Hollywood. Eisenstein, who had toured the movie capital in 1930 only to be criticized at home for his formal experimentation, noted happily that his "friendships" with American colleagues were being renewed.[11]

Ambassador Standley responded quickly to these overtures by holding discussions with Bol'shakov and Kemenov about developing "better understanding between the United States and the Soviet Union through the exchange of moving pictures, photographs, and printed material." A onetime U.S. Navy public affairs officer, Admiral Standley found his interlocutors to be "intensely interest[ed]" in his plan to institute an official U.S. information program in the Soviet Union. As he envisioned it, the program, to be administered by the U.S. embassy in Moscow, would rely on film, radio, and the press to acquaint Soviet audiences with the United States, its people, and its foreign policies. Cinema would lie at the initiative's core. As Standley explained in June 1942, the preparations under way for the Moscow movie conference indicated "that much could be accomplished in the development of goodwill and understanding between the United States and the USSR by making available technical, educational and propaganda . . . films to the Russians." To President Roosevelt and Secretary of State Cordell Hull, the ambassador expressed his view that by counteracting suspicion of U.S. motives bred by the USSR's self-imposed cultural exile, the initiative could be "of primary importance in our present and future relations with the Soviet Union."[12]

Standley's proposal received a favorable hearing in Washington. While there is no record of FDR's reaction, the ambassador's plan fit the president's general approach toward the USSR. In his eyes, Allied and Soviet fortunes were indivisible. The Red Army pinned down Hitler in Europe, and the president foresaw Soviet intervention in the Pacific as an asset against Japan. Looking ahead even farther, Roosevelt assumed that whatever peacetime world order developed would be unsustainable without constructive involvement on the part of Moscow. One sticking point arose, however. Roosevelt, like others, doubted the Kremlin's commitment to the United Nations, fearing that misgivings about Anglo-American resolve would lead Moscow to reach a separate peace with Berlin akin to the August 1939 Nazi-Soviet Pact. To allay any Soviet mistrust, FDR promised Molotov in May 1942 that the United States would open a second front in Europe. It soon became apparent, however, that the Western Allies could not meet that hasty pledge for some time, an inaction that only heightened White House anxieties about Soviet staying power. When Standley's proposal arrived, therefore, Roosevelt was amenable to using any and all means of demonstrating American goodwill to Moscow.[13]

The State Department offered qualified support as well. Elbridge Durbrow, a regional specialist who in 1944 would become chief of the department's Division of Eastern European Affairs, saw the benefits of ameliorating the USSR's cultural isolation, which in his view served to sustain Soviet xenophobia and anti-Americanism alike. According to Durbrow, "It was difficult for Soviet officials and the Soviet people in general to have an appreciation of the outside world" because "for over twenty-five years they have been almost completely isolated from any contact with other countries, and have been led by intensive propaganda to reach a warped picture of the situation outside the Soviet Union." Durbrow's comments implied that the Soviet worldview would have to become more balanced before the USSR could be a trusted partner and constructive member of the international community. Although unconvinced that cultural diplomacy alone could change Moscow's views, the department's Division of European Affairs nevertheless approved the ambassador's initiative.[14]

With official approval in hand, significant amounts of American culture and information flowed into the USSR for the first time in almost a generation. In 1943, Molotov permitted the OWI to establish an outpost in Moscow, and the agency took every opportunity to inform "the Russian people about American life, American culture, [and] America's part in the war." Readers snapped up two monthly magazines and an official information bulletin. Muscovites visited a U.S. information center, and an OWI subsidiary, the Voice of America, broadcast radio programming to Soviet listeners. The Soviet Information Bureau (Sovinformburo) and the Telegraphic Agency of the Soviet Union received U.S. press reports. Documentary films and *United News*, the OWI's newsreel series, publicized U.S. Lend-Lease aid and Anglo-American military activities, and the U.S. embassy held exhibitions for officials representing the Kremlin, foreign ministry, VOKS, KDK, and Sovinformburo.[15]

Despite these enormous strides, there was no indication that U.S. expressions of goodwill had reached Stalin, the man in charge. Nor had

American movies—aside from those occasions when Bol'shakov's committee incorporated portions of *United News* into its own serial, *Soiuz-kinozhurnal* (All-Union Newsreel)—yet achieved general distribution. Without clear signs of approval from above, lesser Soviet authorities remained unwilling to sanction the wide release of American pictures.[16]

Residual Soviet reticence became apparent when Standley, encouraged by the progress made, proposed public exhibitions of Hollywood movies. Toward that end, the ambassador and his cultural attaché held demonstrations of selected pictures for Soviet foreign ministry officials. Standley told the attendees, including Solomon A. Lozovskii, the vice commissar for foreign affairs and Sovinformburo chief, and Vassily Zarubin, head of the foreign ministry's American department, "The American people and the Russian people need to understand each other. Your people like our American films. They could teach your people a lot about America and Americans. We could learn much about Russians from your films. I hope to see good American films, both feature and educational pictures, screened every week in every movie theater in Soviet Russia." Early returns were positive. Waving "his hands excitedly," Lozovskii called the idea "wonderful" and publicly pledged his full cooperation. Kemenov did likewise. Molotov was said to be "enthusiastic." Standley then cabled Washington about the "considerable progress" made on a project that he believed could greatly "increase the knowledge and understanding of the United States in the Soviet Union." Despite these encouraging words, however, not a single Hollywood feature had appeared in public in the Soviet Union by May 1943. Disillusioned, Standley concluded, "It is well known that the Soviet Government has long followed a policy of giving the Soviet people a minimum of information concerning foreign countries and in my opinion any radical departure from that policy in the near future is unlikely."[17]

Mission to Moscow, originated to sell skeptical American audiences on the Soviet alliance, took the cultivation of the USSR to new levels. Produced with White House support, the picture illustrates the possibilities and perils of Roosevelt's courtship of Stalin. In late 1941, Davies, the president's longtime friend and political ally, published a memoir of his experiences as Roosevelt's handpicked ambassador to the Soviet Union from 1936 to 1938. Although the book, also titled *Mission to Moscow* and written, Davies claimed, to "get better public acceptance for aid to Russia . . . and [for] the Boss [Roosevelt] in his magnificent crusade," received heavy criticism for giving American readers an overoptimistic portrait of Stalin's Russia, it met with enormous popular success. Snapped up by readers hungry for insights about their new ally, it quickly sold more than seven hundred thousand copies and was serialized in the *New York Times Magazine*.[18]

The robust sales gave either Davies or Warner Bros. Studios copresidents Jack and Harry Warner the idea of turning the best seller into a Hollywood movie. Before proceeding, however, the newly successful author sought Roosevelt's endorsement. As with the book, the point, as Davies wrote to FDR's press secretary, Stephen T. Early, was to improve American understanding of the Soviets and "confidence in the integrity and honesty of . . . their desire to preserve future peace." The president evidently approved, and he kept abreast of the film's progress through occasional White House meetings with Davies in July, October, and November 1942. As the project neared completion in March 1943, Davies again went to the Oval Office, where he found Roosevelt "very much interested in hearing about the picture."[19]

Production began in July 1942 after Warner Bros. contracted with the ex-ambassador, a onetime corporate lawyer who insisted on having final approval of the screenplay and print. Clear about the messages "his" film should convey, Davies did not hesitate to invoke his contractual rights or the president, under whose authority filmmakers assumed Davies marched. After reading a draft of the script in September, for example, he promptly sent twenty-four single-spaced pages of comments to the producer and director, Robert Buckner and Michael Curtiz. Furthermore, Davies and his wife, Marjorie Merriweather Post, the cereal heiress and General Foods cofounder, were on the set almost daily from November 1942 through January 1943, annoying filmmakers with endless suggestions.[20]

The OWI also shaped the picture. Armed with opinion surveys indicating strong distrust of Moscow, Nelson Poynter of the Bureau of Motion Pictures (BMP) advised filmmakers to silence doubters. He was pleased, therefore, to discover that a draft screenplay demonstrated how "Russians are an honest people trying to do an honest job with about the same total objectives as the people of the United States."[21]

After reviewing the final script in November 1942, the OWI predicted that *Mission to Moscow* would "make one of the most remarkable pictures of this war" and would constitute "a very great contribution to the war information program." The film promised to "be a most convincing means of helping Americans to understand their Russian allies. Because it is a true story told by a man [Davies] who cannot possibly be accused of

Communistic leanings, it will be doubly reassuring to Americans." Moreover, the story

> *presents the Russian people most sympathetically.* Every effort has been
> made to show that Russians and Americans are not so very different
> after all. The Russians are shown to eat well and live comfortably—
> which will be a surprise to many Americans. The leaders of both coun-
> tries desire peace and both possess a blunt honesty of address and
> purpose. Both peoples have great respect for education and achieve-
> ment.
>
> One of the best services performed by this picture is the presenta-
> tion of Russian leaders, not as wild-eyed madmen, but as far-seeing,
> earnest, responsible statesmen. It is pointed out that essentially it is
> none of our business how they keep house—what we want to know is
> what kind of neighbors they will make in case of fire. They have proved
> very good neighbors, and this picture will help to explain why, as well
> as to encourage faith in the feasibility of postwar cooperation.

Government propagandists were equally enthusiastic about the completed print. Calling it "a magnificent contribution" to wartime morale,
the OWI expressed confidence that the picture would further "understanding of Soviet international policy in the past years and dispel the
fears which many honest persons have felt with regard to our alliance
with Russia." Moreover, "the possibility for the friendly alliance of the
Capitalist United States and the Socialist Russia is shown to be firmly
rooted in the mutual desire for peace of the two great countries."[22]

Completed in April 1943, the film was, in the words of Buckner, "an
expedient lie for political purposes, glossily covering up important facts
with full or partial knowledge of their false presentation." It whitewashed
Stalin's purges, rationalized Moscow's participation in the Nazi-Soviet
Pact and subsequent invasion of Finland, and portrayed the USSR as a
"normal" (that is, nontotalitarian) member of the UN's international community. In a prologue, the real Joseph Davies assured American audiences that he was no communist and that what they were about to see
was the truth as he had witnessed it during his diplomatic mission. Anxious studio publicists vouchsafed Davies's credibility: one advertisement
featured an ordinary family praising Warner Bros.' "so American" film;
another authenticated the former ambassador's story as "one American's
journey into the truth!" Davies's character (portrayed by actor Walter
Huston) travels to the Soviet Union in 1937 at Roosevelt's request. There,

according to the movie, citizens are well-fed and happy, the secret police "protect" people, and a consumer economy is emerging. In one scene, added at the last minute at the Davies family's insistence, Marjorie Davies (played by Ann Harding) visits the "USSR Cosmetic Factory," run by Polina Molotov, the foreign minister's spouse. Remarking on the shop's attractive window display of perfumes and beauty products, which resembled something one might find on New York's Fifth Avenue, Marjorie Davies expresses surprise that such luxury goods are available in the Soviet Union. Molotov, whom the *New York Times* found "suspiciously" aristocratic and "Elizabeth Ardenish," replies that the Soviets have "discovered that feminine beauty [is] not a luxury." Through such scenes, according to *Life* magazine, the Soviets were "made to look and act like residents of Kansas City, and the American standard of living appears to prevail throughout the Soviet Union."[23]

Davies's influence proved crucial with regard to the movie's handling of Stalin's purges. As in his book, draft screenplays remained equivocal about the state's charge that the show trial defendants were guilty of treason. During production, however, Davies insisted that the accused's guilt be made explicit, and he reportedly threatened to walk away from the unfinished project if filmmakers failed to do as he asked. The Warners relented, and the final version clearly portrayed Nikolai Bukharin, Marshal M. Tukhachevskii, Karl Radek, and others as participants in a plot, directed from abroad by Leon Trotsky in cahoots with Japan and Nazi Germany, to undermine the Soviet Union in advance of a foreign invasion designed to topple the Stalinist regime. Although the real Davies privately acknowledged the unlikelihood of such a scenario, his character says during the show trial scenes, "Based on twenty years' trial practice, I'd be inclined to believe these" charges.[24] *Mission to Moscow* thus assured audiences that the purges, far from being Stalin's bloodthirsty assaults on innocent victims, were necessary to eliminate quasi-fascist fifth columnists.

Finally, the production justified Moscow's foreign behavior, presenting the Soviet Union as a bellwether of prudent internationalism. It privileged Litvinov's prewar pursuit of collective security in the League of Nations. It showed, in a key scene, the cinematic Davies visiting Stalin (portrayed by character actor Manart Kippen), who expresses his desire for an antifascist alliance with the Western democracies. But the Soviet Union, he informs the envoy in a thinly veiled reference to the West's appeasement of Hitler at Munich in 1938, would not "be put in the position of pulling other people's chestnuts out of the fire. Either we must be able to rely on

"Uncle Joe" Stalin (Manart Kippen) explains Soviet foreign policy to U.S. ambassador Joseph Davies (Walter Huston) in *Mission to Moscow* (Warner Bros., 1943). Photofest/© Warner Bros.

our mutual guarantees with the other democracies or . . . well, we may be forced to protect ourselves in another way." The message was that the Soviet Union had cooperated with Nazi Germany from August 1939 to June 1941 only out of self-preservation after the West had reached its own accord with Berlin. In addition, claiming that he was privy to secret information, Davies insisted that filmmakers justify the Soviet Union's invasion of Finland in the winter of 1939–40, an action heavily criticized in the United States. As a result, the movie ultimately parroted Moscow's official line, which claimed that the Red Army had taken up "defensive" positions on Finnish soil in the face of Carl Mannheim's alleged collaboration with Hitler.[25]

Dubbed "Submission to Moscow" by one critic, *Mission to Moscow* would stir a storm of controversy and tank at the box office after it opened in American theaters on 30 April 1943. But when FDR and Davies previewed the film at the White House just before its public premiere, they were brimming with confidence. Moscow's geopolitical intentions preoccupied Roosevelt at the time. Following the Red Army's watershed victory at Stalingrad, the Office of Strategic Services, the wartime U.S. intelligence bureau, learned that Moscow had opened secret peace negotiations with Berlin. Opinions differed about how seriously to take the talks, which involved midlevel officials in Stockholm, but the mere existence of the discussions deeply concerned the president: the fortunes of the United Nations appeared to hang in the balance. Were Moscow and Berlin to make a separate peace, Hitler would be free to reconcentrate his forces in Western Europe, thereby making Anglo-American military operations much more difficult and costly. Furthermore, the prospect of a Soviet-German deal also raised longer-term questions about the Soviet Union's willingness to intervene against Japan in the Pacific and its fitness to participate in a postwar international peacekeeping body. U.S. popular opinion was a concern as well, because the American people would likely become even more skeptical about the wisdom of allying with Stalin if they were to learn about the still-secret Stockholm talks.[26]

Combined, these considerations further animated Roosevelt's stratagem of accommodating Stalin, who, the president reasoned, was not ideologically incapable of cooperating with Western capitalists. Roosevelt counted himself among the many convergence theorists—a group that also included Ambassador Davies and Texas Democrat Tom Connally, chair of the Senate Committee on Foreign Relations—who believed that Stalinist Russia, in the crucible of war, was developing into a postrevolutionary nation akin to the United States. Though mistaken, that scenario had some basis in fact. Stalin's institution of piecework and other incentives to encourage Stakhanovite industrial productivity was taken to mean that protocapitalism was emerging. His foreign policies—the nonaggression treaty with Nazi Germany and the wartime alliance with the Western democracies—seemed to indicate a leader guided by pragmatic national interest rather than ideological fervor. The Kremlin's rehabilitation of Russian nationalism and Orthodox worship, along with its dissolution of the Comintern in 1943, only added to the sense that Bolshevism was maturing.[27]

Convergence theorists believed that it was possible to do business with Stalin, and that line of wishful thinking provided an intellectual rationale for U.S. diplomacy and propaganda vis-à-vis the USSR. Safe in the knowledge that Stalin could be a viable negotiating partner, Roosevelt concluded that insecurity rather than socialist ideology impelled the Soviets to retreat behind a territorial buffer. If an atmosphere of mutual trust were established, he speculated, Stalin, confident that there was nothing to fear but fear itself, could be induced to come out of his shell and meet his Allied partners halfway. The announcement, made by Roosevelt and British prime minister Winston S. Churchill at their January 1943 Casablanca conference, that the Western Allies were committed to an unconditional, indivisible German surrender (an episode featured in a *United News* installment sent to Moscow) was meant in part to allay Soviet fears about a separate capitalist peace. Doing the White House's bidding, the OWI included creating "an atmosphere of cordial co-operation" among its key foreign propaganda goals in the spring of 1943. Yet Roosevelt placed the highest premium on personal diplomacy. Assured of his considerable powers of persuasion, FDR believed that if he could meet face-to-face with Stalin, the two men could forge a personal relationship like the one the U.S. president enjoyed with Churchill and could adjudicate any outstanding differences. FDR had tried to arrange a summit for almost a year, only to have the Soviet premier demur, citing his need to remain near the front. Davies was thought to be a useful asset in this regard, for the ex-ambassador's sanguinity about bilateral relations had earned him a benign reputation within the Kremlin. Roosevelt thus sent Davies on his second "mission" to Moscow with instructions to arrange a summit with Stalin and to make it clear that the United States was "on the level—had no axes to grind, and [was] concerned first with winning the war."[28]

In this context, the film version of *Mission to Moscow*, itself a meditation on convergence, became an integral part of Roosevelt's Soviet policy, which critics charged amounted to coddling Stalin. U.S. diplomats had learned that Stalin was a Hollywood movie buff. The marshal regularly watched bootlegged foreign pictures in his private Kremlin theater. During the Great Terror, for example, he reportedly enjoyed a Hollywood movie night with Molotov to wind down after a busy day signing 3,187 execution orders. Stalin's interest extended to overseeing Soviet motion picture production, as he regularly revised scripts and censored prints and sometimes called frightened directors at night with "suggestions" for improvement. Some observers have even claimed that the dictator was obsessed with cinema, in part because it was so much easier to create a socialist utopia on-screen than off. As he withdrew into the make-believe world, Stalin lost some touch with reality "in the sense of seeing actual factories, collective farms, villages, and even streets of Moscow," writes Peter Kenez, a foremost authority on Soviet film, and "more and more his view of the world was determined by what he saw on the screen."[29]

Although unaware of the full extent of Stalin's enthusiasm, Roosevelt and Davies hatched a plan after previewing *Mission to Moscow* in the White House: on his upcoming mission to Moscow, the former ambassador would show the movie to Stalin, Molotov, and other top Soviet officials. The Americans' motives extended beyond merely entertaining Stalin; rather, they hoped the movie's plot and unofficial status would demonstrate to the Kremlin that the U.S. people sincerely wished to cooperate. Prior to his departure, Davies asked the OWI to prepare an inventory of other pro-Soviet movies then in production. The list was long—including RKO's *North Star* (1943), MGM's *Song of Russia* (1944), and United Artists' *Three Russian Girls* (1944)—and the OWI reminded Davies to inform the Soviets just how significant it was "that private companies, *not just United States government*, films are being made to interpret Russia to the American people." FDR thus introduced *Mission to Moscow* into the diplomatic realm to persuade Stalin to remain with the United Nations. As historian David Culbert has noted, the film was among "the few examples one can point to of Roosevelt's being able to show Stalin that America had experienced a change of heart and that friendship and understanding were the new watchwords of the day."[30]

Days after his 20 May 1943 arrival on an airplane emblazoned with the words "Mission to Moscow," Davies went to the Kremlin, where Stalin had arranged a banquet in his honor. Deciphering the Soviet leader's response to the movie became a sort of after-dinner parlor game. Now disillusioned and critical of Roosevelt's Soviet policy, Standley had submitted his resignation as ambassador in April. Moreover, he resented Davies's encroachment on his turf. Standley privately expressed his disdain for what he saw as a mere publicity stunt: "To send a man 30,000 miles around the world using an American Army plane, a crew of nine men, gas and oil, the prestige of the U.S. Government, and the entire facilities of the American Embassy in Moscow to advertise and increase the box office receipts for Mr. Davies's movie doesn't sit so very well." Standley reported the Soviet reaction to the film as "glum curiosity." He

> doubted if the Hollywood treatment of events described in Davies's book met with the general approval of the Russians. They successfully refrained from favorable comments while the film was being shown, but Stalin was heard to grunt once or twice. The glaring discrepancies must have provoked considerable resentment among the Soviet officials present. Its abject flattery of everything Russian and the ill-advised introduction of unpleasant events in Soviet internal history that I am inclined to think the Kremlin would prefer to forget makes me believe that the Russians will not desire to give publicity to the film

at least in its present form. In any event I feel that the film will not contribute to better understanding between the two countries.[31]

Davies, however, came away with a very different impression. He ap-
prised Harry Warner of "the favorable and even enthusiastic comments
by some of the living characters portrayed in the film. . . . The Marshal
[Stalin] and Premier Molotov were generous in their praise of the picture." At the end of his journey, he informed Roosevelt that the Soviets
"feel kindly toward us" and that the "mission here could not have been
more satisfactory."[32] Wrong about so many other things, Davies was correct in this instance. Standley erred in thinking that Soviet authorities
would disfavor the movie's "abject flattery," "glaring discrepancies," and
depiction of "unpleasant events." While they may have been amused,
Stalin and his advisers also must have realized that *Mission to Moscow*
was tailor-made propaganda insofar as it lent credence to previous jus-
tifications for the purges and the Nazi-Soviet Pact offered by the party.
Largely for that reason, Stalin approved *Mission to Moscow*'s public release, making it one of the first Hollywood movies to receive general distribution in the Soviet Union in well over a decade. (Muscovites reportedly watched the trial scenes with "intense interest," according to a *New
York Times* correspondent who attended the picture's premiere.) And the
production's unintentional provision of support for Stalinism exposed a
weakness in Roosevelt's approach.[33]

FDR's use of *Mission to Moscow* evidently helped to coalesce the alliance. Neither Roosevelt nor the picture alone could persuade Stalin to
reconsider his core values or national security agenda, not that the dictator ever seriously considered permanently cooperating with the United
States. Nevertheless, those factors—along with the collapse of Soviet-
German peace talks, intelligence reports, and other bits of information—
helped convince him that entente was viable in the short term. Continued
albeit conditional Big Three collaboration (Stalin refused to deal with
Jiang Jieshi) offered the international climate best suited for achieving
Moscow's immediate geopolitical interests: Germany's defeat, aid and
breathing space for postwar reconstruction, and a security ring in Eastern Europe. He thus timed his own goodwill gesture—the Comintern's
dissolution—to coincide with Davies's visit. More important, he pledged
to attend the first tripartite summit, to be held that November in Tehran,
a promise he kept despite learning in June that there would be no second
front in 1943.[34]

Mission to Moscow enabled the Kremlin to prepare the Soviet people for that continued diplomatic tack. Although censors eliminated some material, scenes endorsing human and specifically Soviet-American kinship went unedited. Audiences heard Davies, in his subtitled prefatory remarks, say that "unity, mutual understanding, confidence in each other was necessary to win the war. It is still more necessary to win the peace." Sequences in which Litvinov told the League of Nations and Stalin told Davies of their hopes for Great Power cooperation also remained. So, too, did depictions of bilateral amity: Soviet youth admiring the Stars and Stripes; the Davieses' good working relationships with Stalin, Molotov, and the Litvinov family. The closing scene summarizing the movie's *One World*–like vision survived as well. In it, Huston's voice-over narration pledged to both the war dead—to the "heroes of the United Nations," whether they lay buried "beneath the snows of Russia, the warm desert sands of North Africa, the ancient soil of ravaged China, or in the deep green jungles of Guadalcanal"—and "unborn generations" that the Allies were fighting for justice and peace. His call for world solidarity ended with the question, "Am I my brother's keeper?" and an affirmative answer.[35]

Official reactions, carefully tracked by the Soviet Communist Party, indicated that *Mission to Moscow* was received in ruling circles as an expression of American friendship. Although Bol'shakov, like others, privately found its stereotypical displays of "enormous samovars, bearded men, dancing gopaks, sledges decorated with flowers and the like" laughable and "naïve," the Soviet press offered public praise. According to the Soviet newspapers *Komsomol'skaia Pravda*, *Vechernaia Moskva*, and *Izvestiia*, the movie, which played in at least six Moscow theaters, was "an act of friendly gratitude towards the Soviet Union and the Red Army." *Pravda* noted that *Mission to Moscow* sought "to promote mutual understanding and strengthen the bonds between two great countries." Official enthusiasm climaxed in early 1944, when the Soviet foreign ministry announced that it wished to bestow awards on the film's principals for their work in strengthening bilateral ties.[36]

Mission to Moscow had an even more far-reaching effect. It won a measure of the Kremlin's trust. Stalin's decision to release it further loosened the party's cultural strictures and paved the way for more Hollywood movies, a development that gave the United States a line of communication with the Soviet people. Within days, Andrei N. Andrievsky, head of Soiuzintorgkino, the agency in charge of foreign film trade, acted on this sign of openness from above and reached a cinematic exchange agreement with U.S. officials. Both Molotov and his aide at the foreign ministry,

Lozovskii, now thought it "advisable" to proceed with the May 1943 deal, which covered noncommercial shorts and newsreels.[37]

Soiuzintorgkino's purchase of *Mission to Moscow*'s distribution rights and its expressed interest in buying the rights to other pictures came as welcome news in Hollywood. The American motion picture industry's prior experience with the USSR had been unhappy. In June 1943, when Will H. Hays, president of the Motion Picture Producers and Distributors of America (MPPDA), spread the word that the Roosevelt administration was "very much interested in facilitating the distribution of suitable American films in the Soviet Union," executives saw an opportunity to make inroads into a vast untapped market underserved by the incapacitated Soviet industry. Hays advised MPPDA members to fulfill Washington's request for movies whose themes would help "solidify the amicable relations now existing between the Soviet Union and the United States," make "the peoples of the two countries better acquainted with each other," and increase bilateral "cooperation which will hasten the victory of our common cause." The studios agreed, and forty-eight features and thirty-seven shorts were made available to the U.S. embassy in Moscow for demonstration to Soviet officials.[38]

Up to twelve thousand Soviet elites—including, on occasion, Stalin and Molotov—saw each Hollywood import as a result of an extensive screening process in which the U.S. embassy hosted premieres for and/or loaned prints to Soiuzintorgkino, the KDK and foreign ministry, VOKS, Sovinformburo, and various party-controlled artists' clubs. More notable still, almost two dozen feature films were ultimately selected for public display. Most of the movies seen by popular Soviet audiences were apolitical comedies, romances, or musicals. Several others conveyed pro-Soviet sentiments by way of touting bilateral ties. MGM's *Song of Russia* received theatrical exhibition in 1944, and the Soviet-American romance won praise as "a tribute" to both "cultural collaboration" and "the warm feeling that is drawing the American and Russian people together." *North Star*, RKO's musical set on a fantastic collective farm, reportedly played to more than fifty thousand Siberians in less than three weeks. Vsevolod Pudovkin, a director who doubled as a VOKS official, welcomed the picture as "proof of the keen interest the American people take in our country and of their sincere desire to promote closer understanding between our two countries."[39]

Capra's *The Battle of Russia* also played in Soviet theaters, with an added preface informing audiences that it "was made by the American

Army to show its troops the quality of the Russian people, thus cementing the friendship between the two countries." The film, which documented the Red Army's progression of stunning victories culminating at Stalingrad in 1943, received hosannas from the Soviet press for doing just that. Writing in the periodical *Literatura i Iskusstvo* (Literature and Art), critic D. Zaslavsky echoed the claim that the documentary was "of great value in cementing Soviet-American friendship." As part of a VOKS-sponsored discussion of the film, director Georgii Vasiliev asserted that Capra had enabled Soviet and American audiences to "touch elbows" through the magic of cinema. Even Stalin, who watched the film in his private theater, "expressed himself favorably," according to W. Averell Harriman, Standley's successor as ambassador.[40]

Cosmopolitanism momentarily reemerged, and wartime references to the "international antifascist family" or the "family of humanity" were surprisingly common in the liberalized USSR, writes Soviet historian Jeffrey Brooks. Author Ilya Ehrenburg used language reminiscent of Wendell Willkie's in his 1943 description of war's universalizing effects: "The Siberian understands the grief of Greece, the Ukrainian understands what France has endured; the suffering of the Norwegian fisherman is close to that of the Belorussian peasant." Stalin spoke of Tehran as a "fraternal meeting," and Muscovites celebrated United Nations Day. Such celebrations were not necessarily genuine, and Standley resigned after calling attention to the fact that the Soviet media failed to publicly acknowledge the full extent of U.S. aid. Nevertheless, posters and editorial cartoons touted the USSR's united front with Great Britain and the United States against Nazi Germany, and *Soiuzkinozhurnal* and *Pravda*, among other newspapers, regularly included reports about the activities of the Western Allies, news that connected Soviet citizens with their overseas comrades and, in Brooks's words, lent the United States and Britain "a legitimacy and authority that contrasted with the xenophobia of the 1930s."[41]

All of these movies were commissioned to counteract deep-seated U.S. antipathy toward communism and the Soviet Union. The Soviet experiment had won a number of outside admirers during the "Red Decade," when the dynamism sparked by Stalin's five-year plans so starkly contrasted with capitalism's gravest crisis during the Great Depression of the 1930s. Moreover, Nazi Germany's ascendance led the USSR to be regarded—even among U.S. foreign policy makers—as a potential counterweight, with fascism temporarily displacing communism atop Americans' list of ideological enemies during the late 1930s. Popular Front groups flourished, including the Hollywood Anti-Nazi League, in the movie capital, and membership swelled in the local chapter of the Communist Party of the United States of America (CPUSA), which attracted screenwriters in particular.[42]

Whatever goodwill the Soviet Union had earned, however, crumbled under the weight of troubling events that made U.S. headlines, the Great Terror and the Nazi-Soviet Pact chief among them. The full scope of Stalin's crimes was not yet known, and what little news trickled out of the Soviet Union bred confusion regarding the purges' cause and meaning. Davies, who as U.S. ambassador to Moscow at the time was best positioned to interpret, sent contradictory dispatches to Washington: some claimed that Stalin was ruthlessly eliminating his political opponents; others contended that he was eradicating actual enemies of the state. From either perspective, it was clear that something abnormal was happening in the Soviet Union. Stalin's terror conjured memories of Hitler's earlier attack on the Sturmabteilung. To the *Kansas City Star*, Stalin's actions revealed "the real basis of power in every dictatorship, whether Communist or Fascist." Liberal philosopher John Dewey, who cochaired an independent inquiry that found the purge victims to be innocent of treason, compared Stalin's internal repression to Hitler's, writing of the Soviet Union that any "country that uses all the methods of Fascism to suppress opposition can hardly be held up to us in a democracy as a model to follow against Fascism."[43]

The Nazi-Soviet Pact further soured Americans, splintering the Left and marking the end of the Popular Front. Noncommunists from liberals to socialists to Trotskyites denounced Stalin for cooperating with Hitler and bolted the coalition, leaving only CPUSA members to defend Moscow. The mutual nonaggression treaty fostered the impression that the Soviet Union was untrustworthy, a reputation it never fully shed, and further inclined the general public toward the view that the USSR differed little from Nazi Germany. Commentators adopted "totalitarian" as a catchall term to describe the new kinds of states that had emerged in the Soviet Union, Fascist Italy, and Nazi Germany, as all such dictatorships shared some traits. "Communism and Fascism are essentially alike, for each means the exaltation of force, the suppression of liberties, [and] a regimentation . . . which subordinates the individual to the demands of the State," the *Christian Science Monitor* concluded. The Nazi-Soviet Pact, according to *Collier's* magazine, removed "all doubt, except in the minds of incurable dreamers, that there is any real difference between Communism and Fascism."[44]

Germany's invasion of the USSR in June 1941 and the Red Army's impressive resistance went a long way toward cleansing the Soviet Union of its perceived sins. Yet Americans remained unprepared fully to accept the Soviet Union as a friendly power. Anticommunism, concerns about Stalin and his domestic excesses, and distrust of Moscow did not end overnight. At one extreme, some observers proposed that the United States should tailor its actions to enable fascism and communism to consume one another. As Harry S Truman, then a little-known senator from Missouri, put it, "If we see that Germany is winning we ought to help Russia and if Russia is winning we ought to help Germany and that way let them kill as many as possible." "Let Us Hope," a cartoon published in the *Chicago Tribune* just two days before Pearl Harbor, graphically illustrated this line of reasoning. The first of two panels depicts two stags—one labeled "Vicious Nazis," the other "Deadly Reds"—locked in combat. The second panel shows the scribe of history, finding only the combatants' remains, recording the results: "Two Dangerous Beasts Have Destroyed Each Other!"[45]

Opposition continued to flow from all corners even after events—Barbarossa and Pearl Harbor—suddenly turned the USSR and the United States into awkward allies. Anticommunists led the charge. Radio personality Gerald L. K. Smith and his followers, dubbed the Committee of One Million, mobilized against the "military alliance with communistic Russia." Nevada senator Pat McCarran and Texas representative Martin J. Dies were opposed as well, with Dies, the chair of the House Un-American Activities Committee (HUAC), adding that he and his constituents opposed communism "as much in 1942 as we did in 1938." At the other end of the spectrum, the noncommunist Left was less than pleased about cooperating with Stalin. Labor leader David Dubinsky and Norman Thomas, the Socialist Party's perennial presidential candidate, worried that by partnering with the USSR, the United States would only abet the Soviet dictator's quest to "become lord over most of Europe and Asia." Offended by the Kremlin's customary suppression of religion, Catholics viewed Stalin as the Antichrist and railed against America's unholy alliance with "atheistic communism." *Catholic World* and the sitting U.S. ambassador to Spain declared that the "pagan" USSR posed an even graver threat to "Christian civilization" than did Nazism.[46]

Many Americans did not trust the Soviet Union to be a faithful partner throughout the trials of war, not after the diplomatic somersaults the Soviets had already turned. This mistrust revealed itself in the belief that Moscow would again sign a separate peace with Berlin, thereby leaving the Western Allies holding the bag. A May 1942 poll showed that more than one-third of the public shared FDR's concerns on this point. These worries were also manifested in a feeling that even if the Soviets remained true for the time being, they would betray the United States after Hitler was defeated. A February 1942 survey found that only 38 percent of respondents trusted the Soviets to cooperate with the United States once victory was achieved, with another quarter remaining ambivalent. Ill will toward the USSR moved James "Scotty" Reston, then a young reporter for the *New York Times*, to warn readers that such "carping" was "not only plain bad manners and a free gift to the goons we are fighting against, but it is bad politics and bad strategy and it can help lose the war."[47]

Roosevelt would have agreed with Reston's analysis, for the president's Soviet diplomacy depended on adequate domestic support. Early returns indicated that he had little room for maneuverability, however. The extension of Lend-Lease aid to the USSR in 1941 had been a slog: only 38 percent of the public initially supported the proposal, whose passage required a concerted lobbying effort by the White House. In 1942, the OWI summarized the problem that lay before the administration: "There is still widespread distrust and misunderstanding of Russia. To win the war and to make a lasting peace we must overcome this feeling."[48]

Hollywood was employed to educate the public and augment FDR's political capital. Currying public support for a communist dictatorship in a capitalist democracy presented a genuine creative challenge; meeting it required the performance of intellectual gymnastics. If the war represented a crusade to spread the Four Freedoms, as the president's rhetoric and the OWI's marketing insisted, then doing so required allies who somehow contributed to that liberalizing mission. Therein lay the rub, for only dishonest propaganda could depict Stalin's USSR as a beacon of liberalism, and U.S. publicists had vowed to follow a "strategy of truth."

Here again, convergence theory came to the rescue. If the USSR were in fact becoming a mature state akin to the United States, then it could be plausibly said that the Soviets made suitable allies insofar as they now had interests and values similar to those of Americans. Accordingly, Hollywood received guidance from the OWI to the effect that movies were expected to underscore Soviet-American commonality. The two countries' "aims" were "the same" in that each anticipated the "betterment of worldwide economic relations . . . and cooperation in safeguarding peace and security for all freedom-loving peoples after the war." Furthermore, Moscow's Popular Front–era pursuit of collective security—no nation "worked harder to preserve" an antifascist coalition than the USSR, according to the agency—also boded well for Allied harmony. The official line also held that no one shared Americans' desire for global improvement more than the Soviet people, who were reputed to be on the front lines of the United Nations' "people's war" to extend the Four Freedoms by ridding the world of fascism. All things considered, then, Soviets appeared not unlike Americans (an important motif in the imagination of Allied familiarity), and the OWI encouraged Hollywood to do what it did best: translate the war's kaleidoscopic events and abstract principles into recognizable, human terms. American viewers had yet to come to know their Soviet allies on a personal level, a shortcoming that film could correct, or so U.S. propagandists believed: "We can see them, dramatically and heroically, through the medium of pictures. We can see them as people, as one of us. We can see into their lives, their homes. We can suffer with them in their hardships and gain strength from their strength. This is a war for the anonymous individual and his inalienable rights. We want to know this anonymous individual, because he and we are one and the same."[49]

"Americans reject Communism. *But we do not reject our Russian ally,*" OWI guidance summarized. Cinema, operating under that formula, performed a sleight of hand with regard to dramatizing the Soviet ally. American movies, both documentaries and features, typically upheld ordinary Soviet heroes: partisans, rank-and-file Red Army soldiers, and the like. Official symbols of Soviet authority—Stalin or other Communist Party figures, say—remained mostly in the wings. Such casting enabled the screen to bypass divisive topics such as ideology and politics in the name of building unity. To the extent that that narrative strategy bent the truth, glossed over inconsistencies, and belittled the complexities of bilateral relations, it also preached goodwill, constructed Allied identity, and fostered international kinship.[50]

Documentary films familiarized American moviegoers with their Soviet comrades. If documentaries were important for the way in which they viscerally connected American audiences to the authentic sights, sounds, and feel of wartime Britain, they were doubly important with regard to the USSR, a comparatively mysterious, exotic place about which Americans knew little. The USSR's war with Nazi Germany on the Eastern Front provided a case in point. Western photographers were rarely on hand to record the action. And although the press devoted coverage, the theater's basic narrative (What was happening? Who was winning?) remained unwritten until Stalingrad. Transnational exchange helped bring developments into sharper focus. The Soviet state film authority, the KDK, exported footage shot by Soviet cameramen to the United States, where it enabled millions of American moviegoers to better visualize and understand the Russo-German war. Installments of *Soiuzkinozhurnal* were shipped to the OWI, which pooled the footage for use by the American newsreels: MGM's *News of the Day, Paramount News*, Twentieth Century-Fox's *Movietone News, Universal News*, Warner Bros.' *Pathé News*, and Time-Life's *The March of Time*. Soviet footage also provided the raw material for dozens of short- and feature-length documentaries that played in U.S. theaters, helping to fill the emotional, intellectual, and geographical voids between American viewers and the Soviets. Taken together, these pictures made "fine tribute[s]" to the USSR and demonstrated "the strength of the Russian people," according to the OWI.[51]

Despite their apparent objectivity, wartime documentaries subjectively re-created reality. Editorializing as they dramatized, actuality films imposed clear, emotionally charged narratives on complex, chaotic real-time events that helped viewers tell friends from foes. Just as *London Can Take It* created bonds of affection between American viewers and the beleaguered inhabitants of the English capital during the Blitz of 1940, the short documentary *City of Courage* (1942) brought moviegoers closer to Muscovites besieged by Hitler's armies in 1941–42. A sympathetic portrait derived from Soviet footage, the film left the impression that Muscovites, like Londoners, could "take it" and were remarkably similar to Americans. "But for the space of two oceans, these people might be citizens of Moscow, Idaho, fighting for their lives," intoned the narrator over scenes of the city's brave residents taking cover in subway stations.[52]

Moscow Strikes Back (1942), a retelling of the successful defense of the Soviet capital, provided American audiences with their first sustained glimpse of the brutal war on the Eastern Front. Actor Edward G. Robinson narrated the English-language version of the Soviet-made film, whose portraits of Soviet victimization and strength curried American favor. Produced by the Soviet Central Newsreel Studio and distributed in the United States by Republic Pictures, a midsized studio, *Moscow Strikes Back* opens with images of a prewar Red Square festival—a Labor Day–like affair, Robinson says—introducing Muscovites as a peaceful, familiar, likable people. Having established its collective hero, the film moves on to its corresponding villain, Nazi soldiers, who besiege Moscow after invading in June 1941. All seems lost; Moscow is sure to capitulate. Yet against all odds, the Red Army relieves the capital and pushes back the enemy.[53]

Cameras follow the victorious Red Army as it advances, establishing a documentary record of the enemy's cruelty, gruesome evidence that engendered sympathy for the USSR as a victimized but resolute agent for the Four Freedoms. On-screen Soviet citizens welcome the Red Army as it liberates their villages from the Nazis' clutches. In one memorable scene, an elderly woman—weeping and repeatedly crossing herself—greets and blesses each soldier who passes through her newly freed village. Another peasant showers the troops with gifts of food. When we (the audience) see visual proof of the by-products of the German occupation, we better understand why the on-screen villagers are so relieved. "Degenerate" Nazi soldiers, Robinson says, raped Soviet women, words confirmed by a shot of a tearful adolescent girl, her face bloodied, her stockings down below her knees, being led to presumptive safety by a Red Army soldier. Scores of frozen corpses litter the snow-covered earth. Schools, libraries, and cultural institutions—including the homes of composer Pyotr Tchaikovsky and authors Anton Chekhov and Leo Tolstoy—have been reduced to rubble, empirical evidence meant to represent the Nazis as barbaric enemies of civilization.

Moscow Strikes Back would not have been complete without an explicit appeal for Allied unity. Robinson does not disappoint when he concludes, over scenes of the Red Army marching westward toward Berlin, that the people of the United Nations could take heart from the Soviets' travails. "The fighting unity of China, England, the United States, the Soviet Union, all the other free peoples must, can, will insure final victory. On all of us rest the mission of world liberation." Coming when it did—the picture premiered in the United States in August 1942, to which point Allied forces had generally been on the defensive—*Moscow Strikes Back* buoyed Allied morale and inspired confidence in the USSR. It "lifted the spirit with the courage of a people who have gone all-out," according to the *New York Times*. The *Hollywood Reporter* saw it as "the sturdy, gory record of the magnificent days . . . when stouthearted Russians" stopped the Nazi advance. Tennessee Valley Administration director David E. Lilienthal saw the film at a January 1943 reception given by the Russian Purchasing Commission in honor of Edward R. Stettinius Jr., the Lend-Lease administrator and future secretary of state. Also in attendance at the event, held at Washington's Shoreham Hotel, were an assortment of governmental and business leaders involved in supplying the Soviet Union with war materials. In his diary, Lilienthal noted that even this worldly crowd erupted in "vigorous applause. Imagine watching the former chairman of the United States Steel Corporation, who sat two seats from me, pounding his hands, together with the Russians and all the rest of us, for good old Joe [Stalin]."[54]

The U.S. government got into the act with *The Battle of Russia*, the pro-Soviet entry in Capra's *Why We Fight* series. Just as *Prelude to War* and *The Battle of Britain* instructed American GIs and civilians in how to view the war, their enemies, and their British friends, *The Battle of Russia* taught them how to regard their awkward Soviet bedfellows. Capra and director Anatole Litvak, a Russian émigré whose credits included the seminal anti-Nazi drama *Confessions of a Nazi Spy* (1939), mixed staged scenes and Soviet film clips into a fast-paced sensory experience that informed even as it entertained and editorialized. Told with an air of official authenticity, the combat docudrama retraced the trajectory of the war on the Eastern Front, beginning with the German invasion and ending with the successful Soviet defenses of Moscow, Leningrad, and Stalingrad. It sold the Soviet alliance in part on practical grounds, arguing that it contributed to U.S. national security. An introduction features written tributes to Soviet heroism by U.S. military authorities: Secretary of War Henry L. Stimson; General George C. Marshall, the army chief of staff; and General Douglas MacArthur. Brief geography, sociology, and history lessons follow, combining to form a kind of on-screen *National Geographic* profile attesting to the USSR's strategic importance. Viewers learned that the Soviet Union was vast (covering one-sixth of the earth's surface, it was adjudged the largest nation in the world), rich in natural resources (notably oil, coal, and timber), and great in population (some 193 million). Political discussion is largely absent; Stalin receives only a few seconds of screen time.[55]

The Battle of Russia makes emotional appeals on behalf of the Soviet alliance as well, as is evidenced when the focus turns to a less controversial matter, the ordinary Soviet people, who are made out to be heroes cut from the same cloth as Americans. Capra's Soviets worship a Christian god. A clip of the exterior of St. Basil's Cathedral appears on-screen. The camera takes viewers inside, where a crowded Russian Orthodox service is under way, a scene meant to dispel the specter of atheistic communism. The film audience listens as the congregants intone a hymn, the purported text of which scrolls over the scene. It is a prayer for victory written by Moscow's archbishop, one that befits Capra's clear taxonomy of the world, separating the good Allies from the evil Axis powers: "Oh, merciful Lord . . . crown our efforts with victory . . . and give us faith in the inevitable power of light over darkness, of justice over evil and brutal force, of the cross of Christ over the fascist swastika." Like Americans, Capra's Soviets are diverse. As in *Moscow Strikes Back*, old newsreel footage of peacetime festivals shows smiling representatives of the USSR's many national and ethnic groups, who, according to the narrator, are "citizens of one country" despite the fact that they are "of every race, color, and creed" and speak different tongues. And, like Americans, they are sturdy, for these hardy souls, not Stalin or his underlings, are hailed for turning the tide on the Eastern Front. "Generals may win campaigns; but people win wars," the narrator says over a montage depicting soldiers and guerrillas, workers and farmers, young and old rushing to save the country from certain defeat.

It all makes for a good Capraesque story about a likable, plucky underdog, a modern-day David who overcomes impossible odds and defeats a seemingly invincible Goliath. Here, the role of Goliath is played by the Nazis, made-to-order Hollywood villains. Many of the resonant images of the Nazi occupation first shown in *Moscow Strikes Back* are repeated here: shots of women lavishing their Red Army liberators with smiles, food, and blessings; of people returning home only to find the corpses of their loved ones, disfigured, frozen, and piled unceremoniously in the snow; of the smoldering ruins of Tchaikovsky's, Chekhov's, and Tolstoy's homes. Replayed, too, is the charged footage of Soviet rape victims. "These are the things that Russians can never forget," the narrator explains.

Nor, it was hoped, could American audiences. Capra and Litvak's dramatized episode of Allied victory was calculated to inspire unity, for which *The Battle of Russia*'s rousing conclusion appeals. Once defeated, the Axis powers will be held to account for their crimes by the "united people of these United Nations," the narrator promises. The scene then dissolves into a parade of marching soldiers and billowing flags representing the UN member states, those of the Great Powers in the lead. The procession moves to the sounds of "The United Nations (Victory Song)," composed by Dmitri Shostakovich and first performed by Paul Robeson in 1942. An ode to Allied unity, the song, reportedly sung by schoolchildren in the United States and Britain throughout the war, expresses common hopes for a brighter future:

> Make way for the day called Tomorrow,
> Make way for the world that is new,
> Fight on for the dawn of Tomorrow,
> Together we'll all see it through.

The song and the film reach a simultaneous conclusion, as the visual elements dissolve into the "V for victory" symbol backed by an image of the ringing Liberty Bell.[56]

The Battle of Russia left a lasting impression on one sophisticated viewer, Alfred Kazin, the son of Russian immigrants who saw it while serving in the U.S. armed forces. More than three decades later, the author and literary critic still clearly recalled his viewing experience:

> Nothing [brought home] the torment of the Russians in the Hitler war as did those scattered shots from captured Nazi newsreels and Soviet sources which I saw on a snow-soaked day at a camp in Illinois. Sitting in the post theater, embracing Russia as my parents had not been allowed to embrace it. . . . The movie [made] it easy to sit in southern Illinois and to accept that lovely Russian sacrifice in my behalf. I lose all separateness, feel absolutely at one with the soldiers in that dark theater.
>
> It was a physical shock, walking out of the theater in the gray dripping twilight, watching the men plodding back to their barracks in the last slant of light, to realize how drained I was, how much I had been worked over, appealed to.

Originally intended for exhibition only to Kazin and other servicemen, *The Battle of Russia* proved persuasive enough that officials approved its release to the general public in November 1943. Most reviewers praised its contribution to Allied unity. *Variety* announced that the net effect of the "story of a people who will not be dispossessed of its native land or its freedom to govern itself" was "to hearten the people massed behind the increasing drive of the United Nations." A "document of inestimable value," the film would "unquestionably help foster a closer kinship and spiritual bond between the U.S. forces and their fighting ally." Senior *New York Times* film critic Bosley Crowther agreed, writing that the picture commanded "respect and admiration" for the Soviets.[57]

Hollywood came to the USSR's aid more slowly. The dearth of pro-Soviet features led the BMP's Poynter to publicly rebuke the major studios in June 1942 for failing to clarify "to our people our common interest with the Russians . . . in this struggle." Hollywood's silence can be ascribed to worry among filmmakers about the possible ill effects of taking Moscow's side. There was little to indicate that pro-Soviet propaganda would be well received by anti-Soviet moviegoers. In fact, experience indicated quite the opposite: such pictures were likely to exact a price. If anything, the major studios had previously taken a mildly anti-Soviet on-screen position despite the progressive political atmosphere that prevailed in the industry. Two romantic comedies of the Nazi-Soviet Pact era, for example—director Ernst Lubitsch's *Ninotchka* (1939), starring Greta Garbo, and King Vidor's *Comrade X* (1940), with Clark Gable—poked fun at communism for its alleged denial of human romantic and material instincts.

Even so, William Randolph Hearst's newspaper syndicate had accused Hollywood of being a communist hotbed. Moreover, in 1938, Dies's HUAC launched an aborted investigation of subversive activity in the movie community and a year later leaked an indiscriminate list of suspected communists to the press that included stars Humphrey Bogart, James Cagney, and Melvyn Douglas. California's version of Dies, state senator Jack Tenney, chair of the legislature's Joint Fact-Finding Committee on Un-American Activities, opened a probe of "Reds in movies" in July 1941. Although interrupted by the war, that inquiry only highlighted the latent political dangers involved in supporting the Soviet Union.[58]

The reception accorded *Mission to Moscow*, Hollywood's maiden voyage into pro-Soviet waters, did nothing to dispel that impression. Whereas the Warner Bros. production exceeded expectations in the Soviet Union, it fell disastrously short of them at home. The film caused an uproar following its premiere despite the anxious studio's lavish half-million-dollar advertising budget. To be sure, the picture had defenders across the political spectrum, from the CPUSA's *Daily Worker* to the American Legion, which argued that better Allied unity hastened U.S. military victory. Numerous film critics, including Crowther of the *New York Times*, the *San Francisco Chronicle*'s Dwight Whitney, and *PM*'s Jack McManus, similarly lauded the movie's alliance-building intentions. According to the *New Yorker*, "If the greater part of the public is startled by the information it offers and is sympathetic to its message, it is a good picture. If it attracts the notice of high social circles and in some way allays congressional anxieties about Russia as an ally, it is a good picture . . . because those congressional anxieties need allaying, and quick."[59]

Most others, however, were disturbed by the movie's departures from both the historical record and Davies's book. Manny Farber of the *New Republic* declared himself prepared to bestow the "booby prize" on *Mission to Moscow* for inventing "its own facts" and indiscriminately praising all things Soviet. Henry R. Luce's *Life* magazine, normally an internationalist bellwether that had dedicated its cover to Stalin only weeks earlier, claimed that the movie "whitewashed" the USSR "to a degree far exceeding Davies' book." John Dewey and Suzanne La Follette, cochairs of the independent inquiry into the Moscow show trials, published an influential letter in the *New York Times* claiming that the movie's many inaccuracies made it "the first instance in our country of totalitarian propaganda for mass consumption." "If the purpose of the picture was to improve" bilateral relations, wrote journalist Quentin Reynolds, "it was completely defeated by the obvious inaccuracies shown on the screen." Reynolds, who attended a special screening for diplomats and correspondents held at the U.S. embassy in Moscow, argued that Warner Bros. had succeeded only in creating an on-screen fantasyland that bred false expectations: "The film portrayed a Russia that none of us had ever seen. This would have been all right except that the picture purported to be factual and the Russia shown in the film had as much relation to the Russia we all know as Shangri-la would have to the real Tibet."[60]

The harshest critics represented an odd assortment of the non-Stalinist Left, Catholics, and the anticommunist Right. "Grotesque," *Mission to Moscow* took "Stalin-Worship" to new depths, according to Eugene Lyons. Trotskyites in Los Angeles and New York organized mass protests against the production's claim that the exiled Bolshevik had engineered a conspiracy against the Soviet Union. *Commonweal*, a Catholic periodical, called the movie "straight propaganda" as a result of its silent passage of official Soviet atheism and published a letter from one irate filmgoer observing that the wartime alliance obliged Americans neither to condone "the spreading of communist propaganda" nor to "love Stalin, his judicial and political system and his international diplomacy." Anticommunist member of Congress Marion T. Bennett, a Missouri Republican, charged that Hollywood had "lost its head and gone completely overboard in its attempt to make communism look good. Our temporary military alliance with Russia must not make us forget that . . . there is no difference between communism and Nazism as it affects the common man."[61]

The box office told the sad tale. Regarding the film as procommunist propaganda, just plain boring, or both, general audiences did not care for *Mission to Moscow*. *Variety* listed it eighty-fourth of the top ninety-five gross earners for 1943. Warner Bros., which spent $1,500,000 on production (a high but not unprecedented figure), lost about $600,000 on the project. Several disgruntled viewers voiced their displeasure by writing letters to the studio. Orville F. Grahame of Worcester, Massachusetts, regretted the liberties "taken with truth in . . . *Mission to Moscow*. It is unfortunate that a film on Moscow should have to be in accord with the traditional attitude of American Communists and hew to their line. The American people admire the Russian people and their fight, and perhaps even the realism of their leaders. But we admire most our own attitudes towards life and truth." W. F. Flowers of Encino, California, sardonically congratulated the studio "on a very open faced piece of communistic propaganda. I believe you have done a good job from the standpoint of propaganda work, but a work that is going to backfire . . . on Warner Bros. I am convinced that a great many people will do as my family are going to do and . . . attend theaters only where Warner Bros. films are *not* being shown." And with more than a hint of xenophobia (the Warner brothers were Jewish and Harry had been born in Poland), Alice McCarthy of Jackson Heights, New York, a self-described "*native-born* American citizen," submitted "a violent protest against [the studio's] propaganda film *Mission to Moscow*." Jackson, who took pro-Soviet movies to be "subversive," closed by suggesting that the Warners "go to Russia and stay there."[62]

Despite its poor reception, *Mission to Moscow* marked the first of some two dozen pro-Soviet features produced by Hollywood studios at the behest of the U.S. government. The slate included *Action in the North Atlantic* (1943), an adventure whose screenplay was written by CPUSA member John Howard Lawson. Having survived the Dies Committee's accusations, Bogart starred as the captain of an American merchant ship that runs a gauntlet of German U-boats on its way toward delivering Lend-Lease goods to the USSR. When the vessel reaches Murmansk, it is welcomed by Soviets flashing the "V for victory" sign and shouting "Tovarich," the Russian word for comrade. Reactions varied. Poynter welcomed *Action in the North Atlantic*'s support for "the cause of the United Nations." But *Los Angeles Times* conservative columnist Westbrook Pegler objected that the movie somehow provided "a stupendous plug" for the National Maritime Union, alleged to be a "hostile" labor union that followed "a strict Party-line."[63]

In mid-1942, FDR confidant Harry Hopkins approached playwright Lillian Hellman, a CPUSA member whose credits included *The Little Foxes* (1939), an exposé of capitalist greed, and the antifascist *Watch on the Rhine* (1941), about writing a screenplay salute to America's Soviet ally. Hellman agreed, envisioning the project as another piece of political theater: a documentary illustrating the heroic struggles of real-life defenders of the USSR from fascist invaders. However, her views clashed with those of the film's producer, Samuel Goldwyn, a conservative loath to champion the workers' state on-screen and a renowned skeptic when it came to "message" pictures. His approach generally prevailed in the final product, *North Star*, released by RKO in 1943. Far from being the sort of gritty drama favored by Hellman, *North Star* emerged instead as a lavish Hollywood production so divorced from reality as to strain credulity. A compromise of sorts, it resorted to fantasy to paint an attractive portrait of the Soviet ally, crafting an alternative reality that existed only on the studio's back lot, the make-believe Soviet village of North Star. (During production, the *Los Angeles Times* published a report on "Hollywood's first Soviet collective," the movie set erected by RKO designers at the corner of Santa Monica Boulevard and Formosa Avenue. The ersatz village felt so familiar as to "be in the North Dakota wheat lands," director Lewis Milestone said.) Whereas *Mission to Moscow* tackled uncomfortable subjects head-on, *North Star* took an oblique approach. Stalin? Not shown. The Great Terror? Never happened. A man-made famine in which millions perished? Not in this revision of recent Soviet history. RKO's peasants are well fed and happy.[64]

Those imaginary peasants steal the spotlight. Divided into two acts, the movie introduces viewers to the hardy inhabitants of North Star, a fictional Ukrainian village, in the carefree, bounteous days of spring 1941. (The fact that many actual Ukrainians, victimized by that collectivization-caused famine and Stalin's terror, initially welcomed Hitler's armies as liberators seems to have been lost on those involved in the film.) Here the genre is musical comedy, a kind of *Hee Haw* set on a kolkhoz, with the centerpiece an outdoor community festival. Marina (played by Anne Baxter), Kolya (Dana Andrews), Dr. Kurin (Walter Huston), and the town's other peasants, who could be mistaken for farmers from the American heartland were it not for their phony accents and stereotypical costumes, eat, drink, tell corny jokes, play balalaikas, perform traditional Ukrainian dances, and sing. (Aaron Copland composed the music, Ira Gershwin the lyrics.)[65]

North Star's thesis emerges in the second act, when Germany's armed forces descend on the village. Shifting from musical comedy to drama, the movie distinguishes between Nazi foes and Soviet friends, said to be motivated by the same liberal goals as Americans. Faced with the choice of collaborating with or resisting the invaders, the film's villagers choose the latter course to remain free "from fascist slavery." The able-bodied men arm themselves and head for the hills, from whence they wage guerrilla warfare; everyone else remains behind and destroys everything of value before the Germans can use it. The partisans eventually liberate the village, proving once again that things usually work out for the better in Hollywood's alternate reality. North Star is but a shell of its former self, however, and so the villagers decide to continue the struggle elsewhere. As the kolkhoz smolders in the background, one of the protagonists, speaking as if reading from talking points prepared by the OWI, says that her people will continue to fight for "a free world for all men. The earth belongs to us, the people, if we fight for it. And we will fight for it."

Not surprisingly, the OWI endorsed the picture's portrait of Soviet freedom fighters. It suggested no revisions to the script, which in officials' view made "a tremendous contribution to our understanding of our Russian allies. We see them as people—like ourselves." "In this presentation of the suffering and courage of the Russians," the OWI's review continued, "we are shown that the strength of Russia lies in its people, who are willing to give their lives to keep their countrymen from fascist slavery and to ensure a free world for all men." And the agency numbered *North Star* among Hollywood's "most outstanding films" from the standpoint of advancing "American understanding and appreciation for the courage and sacrifices of an ally." In a letter to Goldwyn, the BMP's Ulric Bell praised the picture's dramatization "of the part plain people are playing everywhere in the fight for the right to freedom." Some critics agreed: *Life* named *North Star* picture of the year; *Motion Picture Herald* editor Martin Quigley welcomed its "story of people" for humanizing the Soviet ally.[66]

MGM did its bit with *Song of Russia*. CPUSA members Paul Jarrico and Richard Collins wrote the screenplay, and the opening scene establishes the motif of Soviet-American community. As the movie opens, the audience in a major U.S. concert hall awaits an orchestral performance led by celebrated American conductor John Meredith, a fictional character played by Robert Taylor, who has just returned from a musical tour of the USSR. The concert begins with a rendition of "The Star Spangled Banner." As the orchestra plays, the scene dissolves into a flashback set in Moscow, where a Soviet ensemble greets Meredith with the same tune at the beginning of his tour. A throng of cheering Muscovites welcomes the conductor, American flags waving against a backdrop of Soviet political iconography. A celebrity among the Soviet people, Meredith's evident popularity would, OWI officials hoped, counteract Americans' negative impression of the rough-and-tumble revolutionary proletariat with that of "a peaceful and constructive people" interested in artistic and technological achievement.[67]

Romance, *Song of Russia*'s central metaphor for Soviet-American reconciliation, also emerges as Nadya Stepanova, a beautiful young pianist played by Susan Peters, pushes through the crowd to meet Meredith, her idol. The couple falls in love, and the audience participates in their whirlwind romance, gaining a better appreciation for the USSR and its people in the bargain. Fellow tourists, viewers see the country anew through Meredith's eyes. In one scene, he and Nadya dine at an upscale Moscow restaurant, where they enjoy a fine meal and an elaborate floor show of traditional Russian song and dance. John, his preconceptions about Soviet Sparta disproved, expresses his surprise: "I can't get over it. Everybody seems to be having such a good time. I always thought Russians were sad and melancholy people." Nadya then shepherds him (and Ameri-

Aspiring Soviet musician Nadya Stepanova (Susan Peters) meets American conductor John Meredith (Robert Taylor), starting an international romance that transcended politics in MGM's 1943 feature, *Song of Russia*. Margaret Herrick Library, Academy of Motion Picture Arts and Sciences, Beverly Hills, Calif. © MGM.

can viewers) on a sightseeing tour of her country, an excursion made to seem more realistic by the inclusion of documentary footage of Moscow's ultramodern subway and major attractions and the countryside's factories and collective farms. Such sights, OWI reviewers believed, would "dispel the impression of many Americans that Russia is composed solely of bleak, snow-covered plains and grubby, primitive villages. Such distorted ideas breed a natural reluctance to accept Russia as a fully responsible partner in the war and in the peace; but the knowledge that Russia is a vast, progressive industrial-agricultural community, not unlike our own, engenders confidence in this powerful ally."[68]

Soviet-American rapprochement via Nadya and John's romantic liaison seems at hand. "If I didn't know I met you in Moscow, you might be an American girl," he says, an intended compliment that brightens his companion. And the two kiss on a veranda with Moscow silhouetted in the background. But their budding relationship is troubled, and in that respect *Song of Russia* is a conventional Hollywood romance about a couple whose love faces challenges. What sets this international romance apart is the kind of obstacles its lovers confront. Whereas family, class, or ethnicity typically keep apart Hollywood's Romeos and Juliets, country, politics, and ideology do so here. Still on the veranda, for example, a troubled Nadya tries to tell John about their "serious differences—socially, culturally, we haven't even discussed—." Hearing none of it, Meredith cuts her off with a kiss before she can utter the words "politics" or "communism," topics so divisive as to be unspeakable.

Rather than stumbling into the political minefield, *Song of Russia* frames the couple's differences in sexual terms, a wise move that makes for an entertaining story about foreign relations in the fullest sense. Feeling her distance from John to be insurmountable, Nadya retreats alone to her home village following the scene on the veranda. And our Soviet protagonist appears in different guise when we next see her: unlike her Western and glamorous Moscow self, who sports stylish hair, a modern wardrobe, makeup, and jewelry, she has resorted to the trappings of peasantry on the collective farm, unadorned save for a traditional blouse and kerchief. Dirty faced, she labors on the farm, plowing the fields at the wheel of a tractor and manhandling a machine gun as part of mandatory civil defense training. These visual clues convey the impression that Nadya, the movie's representative for all things Soviet, has gone native or communist and in the process has become less feminine, as measured against the classic Hollywood ideal. Nadya confirms as much when she tells John, who arrives to reclaim his beloved, that mere emotion cannot conquer all that keeps them apart. Traditional gender roles have been flipped, and we are left with a Soviet woman (or Hollywood's version thereof) whose dubiousness about romantic love and disinterest in fashion are among the markers of her Otherness.

Song of Russia drew on a common stereotype holding that collectivism unsexed Soviet womanhood and thus represented a larger threat to Western order, sexual and otherwise. Anticommunists took it for granted that the Marxist-Leninist-Stalinist experiment in social engineering had rendered the family (along with its attendant institutions of courtship and marriage) into a productive unit attuned to the state's needs and drained of all sentimentality. Capitalism's defenders also were predisposed to the view that human material needs typically went unfulfilled in a production-oriented economy, adjudged inferior to the free market with regard to satisfying consumer desires. That idea, in turn, laid the groundwork for American popular culture, which took emotion and consumption as gender signifiers, to represent Soviet females as unfashionable, unloving, asexual beings denatured by communism. *U.S. News and World Report* described Cold War–era Moscow as a city of "hard-working women who show few of the physical charms of women in the West. Most Moscow women seem unconcerned about their looks. . . . [Y]oung women [stride] along the streets purposefully, as though marching to a Communist Party meeting." *Song of Russia*'s most direct antecedents, *Ninotchka* and *Comrade X*, featured unsexed Soviet leads, Greta Garbo's title character and Hedy Lamarr's aptly named Theodore, who won Westerners' hearts only when they reversed course and embraced romance, consumerism, and femininity.[69]

Peters's characterization of a strong, independent woman in *Song of Russia* spoke to the wartime gender disorder in the United States, where women were expanding their horizons as they entered the paid workforce in greater numbers. The image of a mannish proletarian—Nadya Stepanova or Rosie the Riveter—was something else altogether, however, for she embodied sexual revolution. So when Nadya was inevitably put back in her place, the 1944 movie both reconstituted the traditional U.S. gender order and domesticated the USSR to welcome the Soviets into the UN's family of nations. John ultimately convinces Nadya to believe in the power of love, and the two marry, exchanging vows in an Eastern Orthodox church, a ceremony that symbolized the Soviet-American alliance (and of course counteracted the image of godless communism). Through matrimony, Nadya has been domesticated and sexual order reestablished. The larger point made by such a tale about an "ideologically committed Russian female [who] melts like butter in the embrace of some westerner's arms," according to scholars Michael J. Strada and Harold R. Troper, was that "in the tussle between Marx and marriage, marriage always wins out. The relevant subtext message reads that ideology is only skin deep. Given the right inducements, such as a handsome American or reasonable facsimile, Russian women become starry-eyed romantics."[70]

Their honeymoon cut short by the German invasion, the newlyweds rush to the defense of Nadya's kolkhoz only to find it in ruins. (Moviegoers heard a re-creation of Stalin's actual postinvasion radio address. According to the OWI, the speech, which labeled the war as a fight for freedom from fascist tyranny, demonstrated that Soviets and Americans shared a common aim "for a free and peaceful world.") Here, the film, as scripted, was to have ended with Nadya, shot by the Germans, dying in

John's arms. This ending was considered uninspiring, too melodramatic, or both, and the screenplay was revised and the movie concluded on a more positive note: back in the smoldering village, Nadya's brother, Boris, insists that she and Meredith can be most helpful by drumming up U.S. support for the Soviet people's fight for freedom. As Boris dreamily outlines his plan, the audience sees that scene dissolve into another one of John and Nadya—she again elegantly dressed—performing in New York as part of a concert benefiting Russian war relief.[71]

In *Song of Russia*, MGM had discovered a formula for making diplomacy entertaining, repackaging the official version of Soviet-American relations into a marketable international love story set against the backdrop of war. The majority of viewers found *Song of Russia*'s pro-Soviet message more palatable since the lesson was sweetened with amusement. "MGM's contribution to the fostering of a better understanding of the Russians is fundamentally a grand, appealing, romantic film . . . with the war and the Russian system emerging as minor actors," said the *Motion Picture Daily*. The *New York Times* assured fans that unlike the typical message picture, *Song of Russia* was "a honey of a topical musical film, full of rare good humor, rich vitality and proper respect for the Russians' fight in this war." The musical score and love story alone were "sure to have wide appeal." The OWI admired the picture's contributions to Soviet-American "community" and bilateral "goodwill and understanding."[72]

All told, *Variety* noted, Hollywood had put the Soviets "through the wringer, and they have come out shaved, washed, sober, good to their families, Rotarians, brother Elks, and 33rd Degree Masons." Movies were not the only elements of wartime American popular culture to preach the gospel of Russia redux: advertising, graphic design, radio, and the printed word also evangelized on behalf of Soviet-American community, part of a vast outpouring of support for the USSR. In March 1942, the *Treasury Star Parade*, a radio program produced by the U.S. Department of the Treasury and carried by stations across the country, featured a segment about a fictional Soviet infantryman who ended a letter by writing, "Across many lands and many oceans, I clasp your hand, my American friend." One year later, *Life* magazine dedicated a special issue to the USSR, describing the Soviets as "one hell of a people" who "look like Americans, dress like Americans, and think like Americans." *Time* reinforced the impression of solidarity in a January 1943 cover story: "The two peoples who talk the most and scheme the biggest schemes are the Americans and the Russians. Both can be sentimental one moment, blazingly angry the next. Both spend their money freely for goods and pleasures, drink too much, argue interminably. Both are builders. The U.S. built mills and factories and tamed the land across a continent 3,000 miles wide. Russia tried to catch up by doing the same thing through a planned program that post-pioneer Americans would not have suffered. The rights as individuals that U.S. citizens have, the Russians want and believe they eventually will receive."[73]

Whether on screen or off, the cultural offensive's net effect altered the Soviet Union's reputation to a degree. The Bolshevik beast was domesticated, its perceived threat to the Western socioeconomic order tamed. One beneficiary was Stalin, an erstwhile bête noire whose image underwent an extreme makeover. Known both before and after the war as diabolical—a wild-eyed Bolshevik, Hitler's coconspirator, a butcher—Stalin transmogrified into "Uncle Joe," a close member of the Allied family. Convergence theorists came to see him not as an incorrigible madman but as a mere strongman who had forcibly modernized his backward nation. Although his methods were harsh, the results were evident: the quickly industrialized Soviet Union had bested Nazi Germany and won the European war for the Allies. Success bred success, and Stalin's (and by extension the USSR's) stock rose. *Time* named him its Man of the Year for 1942, hailing the Kremlin's straight-talking "tough guy" as a worthy ally. Stalin served as the USSR's public face, and he became a media celebrity even though he never set foot in the United States. Gruff yet avuncular, he graced the covers of magazines and appeared in innumerable newsreels and photographs, so many that he came to personify the Soviet Union and its war effort. Even Hollywood gave him the star treatment, casting him as a leading man in *Mission to Moscow*. Ambassador Davies described Stalin to millions of *Reader's Digest* subscribers as a "quiet" and "kindly" man who lived simply, worked hard, and conducted business "with complete honesty." In *Collier's*, Quentin Reynolds described the Soviet leader's appearance as that of a "kindly Italian gardener."[74]

Public opinion also moved to some degree. Pollsters periodically asked whether Russia could be trusted to cooperate with the United States after the war ended. In February 1942, only 38 percent of respondents answered affirmatively. Moscow's poll numbers climbed steadily, if unspectacularly, thereafter. Forty-six percent trusted the USSR in early 1943, when German forces surrendered at Stalingrad. That number grew to 51 percent in December 1943 when it was announced that Stalin, Roosevelt, and Churchill would hold their first summit meeting at Tehran. Public confidence reached its zenith, at 55 percent, in February 1945, when the Allied leaders met again at Yalta.[75]

However, the information blitz did not come close to matching social engineers' expectations. The relatively meager results become clearer in light of the watershed that occurred in the American outlook elsewhere: a September 1943 Gallup Poll indicated that while most Americans endorsed a permanent U.S. military alliance with Great Britain, only 39 percent favored a similar arrangement with the Soviet Union. Still deeply anticommunist, the public maintained only lukewarm confidence in the USSR, and any inevitable political complications could cause that confidence to plummet. Only a bare majority ever found Stalinist Russia dependable despite a years-long barrage of pro-Soviet movies, radio programs, posters, and the like. Every poll showed that about one-third of respondents distrusted the Soviets, while one-fifth expressed no opinion. And people's reasons for distrust remained basically the same: the U.S. and Soviet "political and social systems [were] too different"; the Soviets were "treacherous by nature"; the USSR was out "for all she can get"; Stalin was duplicitous; or the Kremlin was uninterested in "justice and the legal rights of [its] own people." The American people added the new concern that Stalin, with the Red Army now astride Europe, had at his disposal a "mighty instrument" for communizing the world, in the words of the *New York Times*' Anne O'Hare McCormick, and *Fortune* magazine's September 1945 snapshot of the mood on the street looked unchanged from pictures taken four years earlier, save for a greater feeling of kinship with ordinary Soviet folk: "Foremost among the bad points Americans see in Russia is communism, followed by Russian hostility to religion and various aspects of Russia's dictatorial government and lack of personal freedom. A number of Americans believe that Russia's foreign policy is purely selfish and acquisitive. Objections to Russia, however, concentrated on matters of government and policy—only 1.8 percent had any hard words to say about the Russian people."[76]

A significant and vocal minority of viewers developed oppositional readings of pro-Soviet movies. *Commonweal* opposed *Mission to Moscow* and every other such film for implying that religious freedom was alive and well in Stalinist Russia. *Time* found "serious weaknesses" in *The Battle of Russia*, including "figure-skating around the Russian Revolution and the German-Soviet Pact which Sonja Henie could envy." And *Newsweek* saw *North Star*'s focus on "simple, peace-loving farmers" as a smokescreen that allowed Soviet ideology and policies to be sidestepped "in favor of local color" and "melodramatic resistance." Part of the Hearst chain, the *New York Daily Mirror* called for a boycott of what it referred to as "pure bolshevist propaganda" written by Hellman, describing her as "a partisan pleader for communist causes." *Newsweek* called *Song of Russia* a "Red herring" and announced that MGM had gone "overboard" in "presenting the Russians as a simple, industrious, religious folk who relax from a day's work in night clubs that would put the Rainbow Room to shame, and who love peace, music, their country, and Americans."[77]

In addition to being unpersuasive, pro-Soviet propaganda helped trigger a backlash against the Roosevelt administration and Hollywood for their alleged softness on communism. This anticommunist reaction, which metastasized during the Cold War, had its roots in World War II. Business leaders, Republicans, and southern Democrats accused the administration of misusing the wartime emergency to install socialism in the United States. "The New Dealers are determined to make the country over under the cover of war if they can," alleged "Mr. Republican," Ohio senator Robert A. Taft. As evidence, critics pointed to everything from Roosevelt's alliance with Stalin to the proliferation of wartime federal agencies to FDR's unprecedented fourth election to the presidency in 1944, which revived portrayals of him as a leftist dictator in the making.[78]

As a left-leaning official propaganda ministry, no agency made an easier target for criticism than the OWI. A 1942 congressional report revealed that CPUSA members served on the agency's payroll, and director Elmer Davis was pressured to fire about a dozen employees. Unappeased, New York's John Taber, the ranking Republican on the House Appropriations Committee, claimed in March 1943 that Davis's outfit distributed "insidious propaganda" that followed "communist lines" on behalf of FDR's "fourth term," among other things. Another GOP appropriations committee member, Pennsylvania's John Ditter, described the agency's staff as "starry-eyed zealots out to sell their particular pot of gold to a bewildered people." Opposition reached a crescendo that summer in the wake of a Voice of America broadcast implying that the Allies' Italian occupation policies had departed from their stated antifascist principles. In the midst of the contretemps, *New York Times* columnist Arthur Krock characterized the OWI, the Voice of America's parent agency, as a communist hothouse that spoke with an "ideology" more in tune with Moscow's than Washington's. Such accusations animated that year's decision by Congress to slash the OWI's budget, severely crippling its domestic operations forevermore.[79]

At the same time, allegations of communist infiltration rocked the movie world. Hollywood's pro-Soviet output helped provoke those charges. So, too, did the Soviet-American cultural exchange, which permitted Soviet cultural diplomats to operate in the United States. Just as their American counterparts promoted both national and multinational interests in the USSR, Soviet propagandists used the opportunity to spread good word about the USSR and the UN alike. Press officers at the Soviet embassy in Washington provided journalists with Soviet government dispatches and distributed an official *Information Bulletin.* An illustrated magazine, *Soviet Russia Today,* appeared on American newsstands.[80]

Soviet cultural diplomats trained their sights on Hollywood as well. In October 1942, Vladimir Bazykin, the embassy's VOKS representative, proposed to take full advantage of Hollywood's pro-Soviet "turn" by setting up a system through which Soviet officials could regularly advise the studios regarding the proper on-screen representation of the USSR. Back in Moscow, another VOKS official recommended Bazykin's proposal to Grigorii Aleksandrov, a member of the Central Committee's propaganda arm, the Upravlenie Propagandy i Agitatsii. Advising the studios offered "huge propaganda possibilities" since the "power of American film is well known. If a film appears on the big screen, [tens of millions of] viewers see it." Sympathetic Hollywood movies thus could be "one of the most powerful means of our propaganda in the USA."[81]

Soviet diplomats shaped Hollywood's portrait of the USSR from behind the scenes. Ambassador Litvinov and Vassily Zarubin, the foreign ministry's top American expert, approved the supply of extensive documentary footage to Warner Bros. for use in *Mission to Moscow,* described as a "sympathetically made" picture sure to "have an enormous influence in bringing about a better [bilateral] understanding." Hellman received unspecified "cooperation" from Litvinov and Molotov when she conducted background research in Moscow for *North Star.* The OWI invited Bazykin to review the screenplays for both *North Star* and *Song of Russia,* and his suggested revisions affected the final product.[82]

Mikhail Kalatozov, already an established director who would go on to make *The Cranes Are Flying,* winner of the top prize at 1958's Cannes Film Festival, arrived in Los Angeles in 1943 on a special movie mission. Kalatozov, whom the press dubbed "Stalin's film ambassador," had a stated purpose of strengthening bilateral cultural relations. His mission, as he put it, sought to enlist Hollywood "in the establishment of an enduring peace and [the promotion of] understanding and tolerance." His actual aims generated hostile responses from his American hosts, however. The first, expanding Soviet film exports to the United States, resulted in a 1944 trade agreement between RKO and Soiuzintorgkino. RKO canceled the deal, however, under heavy pressure from the State Department, which objected that the agreement would have given Moscow a guaranteed

American outlet, beyond Washington's control, for the dissemination of communist propaganda.[83]

Kalatozov's second goal involved instructions he received from Vsevolod Pudovkin. The director, who headed the VOKS Film Section, ordered Kalatozov to establish "contact between the workers of Soviet and American cinematography," including screenwriters, reputed to be Hollywood's most radical craftspeople. The directive is open to interpretation, and it is unclear how Kalatozov carried it out. Did he establish a network among sympathetic film artists merely to share tradecraft and promote Allied goodwill? Or did he recruit party members and fellow travelers to advance the USSR's agenda? Some evidence indicates that Soviet agents tried to recruit American filmmakers. Posing as an engineer, one intelligence officer participated on a U.S. tour by a delegation of Soviet film experts, but he reported that he had been unable to "penetrate" the film community. The Federal Bureau of Investigation (FBI) kept close tabs on Kalatozov. In 1944, the bureau's director, J. Edgar Hoover, informed Assistant Secretary of State Adolf A. Berle Jr. that the Soviet emissary had "been in contact with a number of individuals who are engaged in Communist activities in the United States." And the Department of Justice tightened its enforcement of the Foreign Agents Registration Act, requiring Kalatozov and other Soviet officials to register as foreign propagandists with law enforcement officials, a decision that Moscow protested.[84]

By that time, the FBI saw connections among Soviet activities, those of domestic radicals, and Hollywood's pro-Soviet output, taken as ipso facto evidence that the film colony had been infiltrated by communists, who, it was presumed, sought to use the screen to indoctrinate American moviegoers in Marxism-Leninism-Stalinism ahead of a socialist takeover of the United States. After all, party members Lawson, Collins, Jarrico, and Hellman had been involved in *Action in the North Atlantic*, *Song of Russia*, and *North Star*. As a result, the FBI monitored suspected radicals in Hollywood. In 1943, the bureau's Los Angeles agent reported that communists had penetrated the movie community. The alleged takeover had begun in earnest in 1941, the agent wrote, when the local CPUSA chapter capitalized on the Soviet Union's wartime "prestige" to recruit members and "develop a new crop of fellow travelers and sympathizers." Party leaders allegedly found willing recruits in the motion picture industry, staffed by a "different type of individual"—a thinly veiled catchall reference to Jews, the foreign-born, and first- or second-generation Americans—whose "ideas and culture" were "much closer to the land of their birth or extraction" than to "the ideals and traditions of America." And the agent harbored "no doubt that the national origins and inherited 'ideologies' of those now in control of the motion picture industry are determining [domestic political trends] and bending them in a direction unfavorable to American ideals and customs—and it can be said, in the long run, democracy." In sum, foreign agents and domestic radicals had managed to turn movies into "a medium for carrying out the Communist Party line and glorifying the Soviet Union as a democratic, progressive state and economy which could well be adopted elsewhere and, by implication, right here in the United States."[85]

Anticommunists went on the offensive against the supposed takeover of Hollywood. Congressional conservatives took the first step in late 1943, when they called for an investigation of pro-Soviet movie propaganda and of the Roosevelt administration's links with Hollywood, a proposal reminiscent of the 1941 probe of the industry's warmongering. Momentum built in February 1944 with the formation of the Motion Picture Alliance for the Preservation of American Ideals, a coalition of conservative screen artists. Led by its first president, Sam Wood, director of *Goodbye Mr. Chips* (1938), among other pictures, the alliance's membership included studio head Walt Disney; directors Clarence Brown and King Vidor; actors Gary Cooper, John Wayne, and Robert Taylor; gossip columnist Hedda Hopper; and labor leader Roy Brewer. Appalled by Hollywood's leftward turn, the group issued a statement objecting to the industry's apparent domination by "Communists, radicals, and crackpots" and pledged "to fight, with every means at our organized command, any effort of any group or individual, to divert the loyalty of the screen from the free America that gave it birth." In March, the alliance sent a letter to Senator Robert R. Reynolds inviting the conservative North Carolina Democrat to investigate the "flagrant manner in which the motion picture industrialists of Hollywood have been coddling Communists" and "totalitarian-minded groups" determined to disseminate "un-American ideas and beliefs" via the screen. Then, in the summer of 1945, Mississippi Democrat John E. Rankin, who had become acting chair of HUAC after Dies's retirement, informed his fellow lawmakers that California state senator Jack Tenney had reopened his probe, stalled for four years by the wartime Soviet-American alliance, into the "widespread Marxism" in Hollywood that purportedly threatened nothing less than "the Constitution and the American way of life."[86] Although HUAC did not launch its notorious Hollywood investigation until 1947, the Second Red Scare had already begun.

A similar process—of international contact and goodwill giving way to miscommunication and unilateralism—occurred in the Soviet Union at the same time. Things had seemed to be going well there—the U.S. charm offensive featured public showings of pro-Soviet movies, which were received as evidence of American friendship. U.S. diplomats were therefore surprised to learn that some viewers clandestinely took a derivative message from even *Mission to Moscow*. Frederick C. Barghoorn, a junior officer stationed at the Moscow embassy, spoke with several Soviet citizens, all of whom described the film's depictions of life in the Soviet Union as "funny." Specifically, his interlocutors found the window display at the "USSR Cosmetic Factory" and the on-screen ubiquity of food, modern automobiles, and high fashion "fantastically luxurious." Rather than dismissing the American production as hopelessly parochial, however, Barghoorn's contacts confided that such scenes revealed to them Americans' greater expectations, born of higher U.S. living standards. Barghoorn had that view confirmed by a conversation with a woman who found American movies "depressing" because they so obviously contrasted the material quality of life in the Soviet Union with that in the United States. Other Soviet reactions made more sense in light of these revelations. Stefan Sharff, a Moscow correspondent for the *New York Times*, for example, reported that Muscovites were "amused" by a scene showing Tania Litvinov, the ambassador's daughter, and other Russians ice-skating in a fabulous "Alpine resort atmosphere." In short, viewers, operating in the unique context of Stalinist Russia, disassembled *Mission to Moscow*, taking from it imagery of capitalist lifestyles that fulfilled personal desires and, according to Barghoorn, sustained quiet opposition to the Kremlin. If this episode illustrates the inability of propagandists, even Stalin's, to regulate the popular mind, it also shows that even a Stalinist apologia could be an engine of American influence.[87]

The U.S. offensive also included ostensibly apolitical Hollywood features. Only on the surface did they appear so, however, since such movies almost always presented the United States as a prosperous, free, and pleasant country and thus articulated on a deeper level a profound ideological argument. By detailing what one reviewer called the Horatio "Algeresque" tale of inventor Thomas Edison's mythical rise from obscurity to world renown, MGM's *Edison, the Man* (1940) suggested that the American Dream was alive and well, permitting everyone to achieve fame and fortune by virtue only of talent and hard work. The Jack Benny comedy *Charley's Aunt* (1941) and the Sonja Henie musical film *Sun Valley Serenade* (1941) conveyed the impression that the good life of personal fulfillment and pleasure was within reach of most Americans, who appeared to posses the necessary means and leisure time to pursue it. *Sun Valley Serenade* and *Cabin in the Sky* (1943), a musical with an all-black cast led by Lena Horne, featured performances by Louis Armstrong, Duke Ellington, and Glenn Miller that contributed to a jazz craze in the Soviet Union. Those and other pictures, including the Deanna Durbin musical *His Butler's Sister* (1943) and *Appointment for Love* (1941), starring Charles Boyer, were set in relatively opulent surroundings—a winter resort, a swanky Manhattan apartment, the estate of a Broadway playwright. Even as they entertained, these films empowered Soviet audiences to compare ideal Western standards of living with their own. One American review of *Sun Valley Serenade*, for example, noted that its presentation of people enjoying "luxuries in one of the world's most magnificent winter resorts" was a "visual delight" and a "poor man's substitute" for being there.[88]

Propagating that outlook was neither more nor less calculated than the Soviets' spreading of communism in the United States. The American Way was an article of faith, and the war revivified confidence in it. Popular and persuasive, Hollywood movies became vehicles for projecting American ideals into the USSR, where cultural liberalization permitted imports but Soviet law, although sporadically enforced, still criminalized personal contact with foreigners. The MPPDA's president, Hays, spoke to that point of view when he added a twist to his old refrain, proclaiming that in the USSR, Hollywood pictures could present "the American way of life and our democratic ideals, and at the same time serve as constant advertising for American products." Finding "the conditions of the common people" in the Soviet Union to be "very low," Ambassador Standley wanted to improve their lot by paternalistically teaching them "about America and Americans, about our ideals, our standards, the way we think, the way we live, [and] our wants and needs in this modern world." Movies, he concluded, could "educate the Russian people to the better things of life." Harriman, who replaced Standley in October 1943, also arrived at the conclusion that commercial cinema served as a useful "instrument" for "for publicizing the American point of view . . . in the Soviet Union."[89]

U.S. diplomats came to appreciate cinema as a valuable soft power agent in the USSR. Hollywood movies were in great demand, reported the Moscow embassy—so much so that a staff member had been "offered bribes by various organizations desirous of borrowing pictures." Ambassador Harriman lauded films for raising interest "in our country" among the "opinion forming audience in Moscow"; his subordinate, Edward Ames, emphasized their mass appeal. The introduction of American pop culture counteracted Soviet isolation and fostered cosmopolitanism, the junior embassy official argued, causing consumers to "acquire a great craving for things foreign, go to the American movies, and attempt to do things as they are done abroad." Motion pictures in particular made "it possible for the Russians to get an idea of how people in other countries looked, dressed, and acted. Admitting the inadequacies of the Hollywood film as a picture of American life, still the movie has been a great eye-opener."[90]

American culture had penetrated so deeply that some State Department experts thought they detected a growing rift between the Soviet people and the Kremlin. Calling ordinary citizens the party's "Achilles Heel," Barghoorn claimed that the United States had emerged as a popular but still subterranean symbol of opposition to authoritarian rule. George F. Kennan argued in his influential "long telegram" that the Soviet public, "remarkably resistant in the stronghold of its innermost thoughts," stood "emotionally farther removed from [the] doctrines of [the] Communist Party" in February 1946 than ever before. In a separate "long cinematic telegram," the architect of containment claimed that the wartime introduction of Hollywood movies had helped to expose that divide. And he insisted that movies be part of any postwar U.S. cultural diplomacy initiative, providing a friendly "exposition of American life" and counteracting the impression, fostered by party propaganda, that the Soviet people were "surrounded by enemies, that they are in the midst of a crisis, which must culminate in war with the capitalist west."[91]

Thus, the United States had established a cultural toehold in the Soviet Union by the end of World War II. Soviet visitors took advantage of the OWI's Moscow information center. Listeners heard Voice of America broadcasts. Viewers saw two dozen Hollywood movies, which represented only the tip of the iceberg: some 150 American newsreels, 50 shorts, and 73 features crossed Soviet borders during the war years. Those numbers may seem meager except in comparison to the weakened Soviet motion picture industry, which produced only 25 features in 1944 and a record-low 19 the following year.[92]

Understanding the situation, Soviet authorities withdrew from the cultural exchange that enabled the American invasion. Their departure became evident in the summer of 1944, when despite previous assurances to the contrary, the KDK refused to include coverage of the Normandy landings in *Soiuzkinozhurnal*. (Harriman learned that the Soviet people would not be informed of the full "scope and magnitude" of the Anglo-American invasion of Europe.) Although plans called for Soiuzintorgkino to purchase distribution rights to fifteen more Hollywood features, only one more (the explicitly pro-Soviet *Song of Russia*) received the go-ahead. Moreover, the U.S. embassy received word that Soiuzintorgkino was under new orders to buy only those movies that somehow portrayed "American life and society in an unflattering light." Pictures already in circulation were to be altered to create the "impression that an inferior product is being shown with a consequent implication that the Russian industry has little or nothing to learn from abroad." Andrievsky explained that Soviet cultural authorities elected to restrict contact because the people had acquired "a taste" for Hollywood's product, a development that posed all sorts of ideological and industrial dangers. In June 1944, the Soiuzintorgkino chief told an owi representative that "films contrary to Russian ideology were not acceptable, no matter how good technically they might be."[93]

Moscow's disengagement was but a first step in a general cultural cleansing. Beginning in early 1946, Andrei A. Zhdanov, the party's chief ideologue and head of the Upravlenie Propagandy i Agitatsii, directed a campaign intended to purge Soviet culture of bourgeois and alien influence and to reduce contact with the outside world. During an April Upravlenie Propagandy i Agitatsii meeting, Zhdanov detailed Hollywood's evils, most notably its tendency to undermine authority figures and sow civil disobedience. As examples of this iconoclastic spirit, he pointed to Hollywood Westerns and comedies that characterized law enforcement officials as corrupt or inept. The Soviet Communist Party ideologue suggested that U.S. cultural diplomats plotted to touch off civil unrest with such "aggressive" imagery, and he expressed regret that those impressions had been permitted to circulate during the war. Henceforth, Zhdanov declared, "Party principles" would govern cinema, purified of outside influences to better shape "the character of the Soviet people."[94]

For Western diplomats, who took openness as an indication of the ussr's normality and willingness to cooperate, the Kremlin's disengagement signaled a worrisome shift in Soviet foreign policy. Harriman, now wary of Soviet intentions and critical of fdr's conciliatory approach, reported that he was "considerably disturbed by evidence . . . of the apparent reversion in the Soviet film industry to the earlier policy of isolationism." Combined with his analysis of Soviet behavior in other areas, the trend toward insularity caused the ambassador to speculate about the future of Soviet-American relations. He cabled his concerns to Washington in September 1944:

These developments in the motion picture field, which are parallel to a greater or lesser extent in other fields of Soviet-American relations, reflect a development in the Soviet Union which is far greater in its implications than the mere dissemination of American motion pictures. I can see it only as a reflection of a trend toward increasing restrictions on foreign influence and contact within the Soviet Union and at least partially as a return to earlier attitudes and policies. I have no way at the moment of knowing whether this trend is temporary or one that may expand and develop in the coming months. It is, however, something that should be borne in mind in our relations with the Soviet Union and will be watched with the utmost care.[95]

Harriman's pessimism about Soviet-American prospects heavily influenced Truman as he reevaluated U.S. policy and adopted a tougher stance toward the USSR after succeeding Roosevelt, who died in April 1945. The ambassador's staff was no less disillusioned. The typical U.S. diplomat arrived in Moscow like a suitor eager to court the exotic Soviet mistress. Some acted on that impulse and, as did John Meredith in *Song of Russia*, wooed musicians and ballerinas, relationships that served as physical manifestations of the discourse of Soviet-American family. More often than not, however, that same diplomat ended the war as a "disappointed lover," in the words of Elbridge Durbrow. Or, as writer and OWI employee Samuel Spewack phrased it in a novel about his Moscow experiences, American envoys "came with love, and left with fury." They did so in part because their Soviet friends, lovers, and wives were subjected to increased harassment, including arrest, torture, and exile, by Stalin's secret police.[96]

To the extent that it was ever happy, Soviet-American matrimony appeared headed for divorce, all that pillow talk destined for the ash heap of history. Though well intentioned, Roosevelt's courtship of Stalin, cinematic and otherwise, failed to achieve a lasting union. Having set out to reconcile the strange bedfellows, film ultimately only further estranged the United States and the Soviet Union. Not even Hollywood's vaunted magic could make the reality of Stalinism disappear, despite what spin doctors thought possible. The more film strained to make over Stalinism's image, the less plausible and more propagandistic pro-Soviet movies seemed, exposing an obvious and unbridgeable gap between fact and fiction.

The audience remained the ultimate, mostly ungovernable arbiter of meaning. American moviegoers, predisposed against the Soviet experiment, were left feeling unconvinced and, worse, manipulated by Hollywood's love affair with Moscow, which animated an anticommunist backlash that would metastasize into a Second Red Scare purge of the motion picture industry. At the same time, that gulf between the transmission and reception of prescribed meaning only widened when pictures like *Mission to Moscow* crossed international boundaries. When given the rare opportunity to view Hollywood movies, Soviet fans exerted an unexpected amount of interpretive agency, teasing out procapitalist imagery from pro-Soviet films. The denouement—the Kremlin's reimposition of its cultural freeze to stop the contaminating inflow and Washington's perception that such stoppage of intercourse signaled Cold War—point to the uncertainties that arose when cinema and statecraft met.

6

NEGOTIATING THE COLOR DIVIDE

RACE AND U.S. PATERNALISM TOWARD CHINA

An American scientist known to be at work on a top-secret project for the U.S. military has been murdered. His research is missing, stolen by the killers, Nazi agents, whose nefarious plan is to spirit it to Berlin. Not to worry, though: Charlie Chan saves the day. The Chinese American detective was quite familiar to moviegoers by the 1944 release of *Charlie Chan in the Secret Service*. He had first appeared in a 1925 novel by pulp fictionist Earl Derr Biggers, inspired by tales of real-life Honolulu detective Chang Apana. Chan became a pop culture fixture over the ensuing two decades, headlining five more Biggers novels and thirty Hollywood pictures as well as comic strips, radio series, and even a board game. In all his manifestations, the humble Chan invariably exercised his superior investigatory skills and used Confucian wisdom to solve puzzles that befuddled lesser sleuths. *Charlie Chan in the Secret Service* departed from the expected in only one important respect. In this, the second of seven wartime entries in the series, which would continue until 1949, Chan worked as a special U.S. agent in Washington, D.C., where totems of the Sino-American alliance—portraits of President Roosevelt and Republic of China (ROC) leader Jiang Jieshi—decorated his office. Otherwise, he still got his man: the Nazi plot was foiled, and America's secrets were kept. As was his habit, Chan expressed—in pidgin, fortune-cookie English—aphorisms and anti-Japanese views. And, most important, a white man—in this case, actor

Detective Charlie Chan (Sidney Toler) does his bit for the Allies in *Charlie Chan in the Secret Service* (Monogram, 1944), thwarting an Axis plot with the help of actors (left to right) Arthur Loft, Marianne Quon, Benson Fong, and Mantan Moreland. Photofest/© Monogram Pictures.

Sidney Toler—played the Chinese American character, wearing yellow-face makeup, as was true of every Chan movie produced since 1931.[1]

Edward Said paid mind to neither Charlie Chan nor American pop culture in *Orientalism,* a pathbreaking exposition of how nineteenth-century middle- and highbrow Europeans produced a binary intellectual universe that framed the Orient as the Occident's inferior Other and thereby legitimated the purportedly modern, masculine, and paternal West's imperial authority over the presumably backward, feminine, and childlike Middle East. If he had looked at twentieth-century American culture, Said might well have found that Hollywood served as a major conduit of Orientalist knowledge about Asia. A manufacturer of what historian John Kuo Wei Tchen has termed "commercial Orientalism," the American movie industry trafficked in racial stereotypes—Fu Manchu, the sinister would-be master-of-the-universe who embodied the "yellow peril" scare at the turn of the century; the exotic, conniving, and sexually manipulative Dragon Lady; the docile and sacrificial Madame Butterfly.[2]

Hollywood's Orientalist characterizations and plot lines depended, in turn, on its discriminatory casting practices. During the transition to talking pictures, an informal guideline developed among the major studios against casting Asian American actors in lead roles, based on the theory that foreign-sounding accents spelled trouble at the box office. The imposition of the Production Code in the early 1930s formalized that rule of thumb, including an antimiscegenation clause that banned on-screen interracial lovemaking. Combined, those two directives effectively marginalized Asian American performers, forced out of lead roles and into bit parts. A Jazz Age fashion icon and international celebrity who appeared opposite Douglas Fairbanks in *The Thief of Baghdad* (1924), Chinese American actor Anna May Wong decamped from Hollywood when suitable work stopped coming her way. Other performers eked out their livings in Hollywood's studio system as extras or supporting actors playing typecast characters with extremely limited agency, and a generation of actors—including Marianne Quon, Keye Luke, Victor Sen Yung, and Benson Fong, perhaps best known as Charlie Chan's meddlesome daughter and sons 1–3—spent its entire career in the background, lending on-screen touches of Oriental flavor, to use the day's parlance.[3]

Charlie Chan owed his long and successful movie career precisely to the industry's exclusionism. A trio of Asian actors—George Kuwa, Sojin Kamiyama, and E. L. Park—played the detective in the first three Chan movies, released in the late 1920s. None of those films achieved much commercial success, however, in no small part because majority-white moviegoers objected to a "Chink" playing the assertive Chinese American lead, as *Variety* wrote of Sojin's turn. (Sojin was Japanese, in fact.) The franchise did not take flight until Warner Oland, a Swedish character actor whose Mongolian roots had given him steady work depicting Asian villains, assumed the part in the fourth film, *Charlie Chan Carries On* (1931). Both Oland's takeover and his method of performing Chan (yellowface) were part and parcel of Hollywood's anti-Asian bias. An egregious building block of Hollywood's Orientalism, yellowface was a form of racial performance in which white actors masqueraded, or passed, as East Asian characters with the aid of makeup, costuming, affected speech, and the like. Common to American theatrics in the late nineteenth and early twentieth centuries, yellowface, like blackface, was a form of racial parody that exaggerated features deemed "'Oriental,' such as 'slanted' eyes, overbite, and mustard-yellow skin color," partly to demean Chinese, mark them as inferior and foreign, and thus sharpen the various racial (non-white versus white), geographical (East versus West), and national (Chinese versus American) distinctions that sustained Western supremacy. In other words, yellowface performance served in part to put Asians in their place, since white actors could use it to pass as Asian, but Asian actors could not use it to pass as white.[4]

Modern critics have rightfully condemned Charlie Chan, a stereotypical figure created and depicted by white men. Novelist and playwright Frank Chin has denounced Chan for fathering the stereotypical "good Chinaman"—passive, angelic, and unthreatening to the racial status quo—and the forty-four movies with him in yellowface for serving as "parables of racial order" that insulted Asians and insisted on their "assimilation by whites." Author Gish Jen has similarly identified the sleuth as "the original Asian whiz kid" and a foundation of the "model minority" stereotype. Furthermore, his on-screen depiction by a series of white performers—Oland from 1931 until his death in 1938, followed by two European Americans, Toler until 1946 and then Roland Winters—recalled blackface minstrelsy, rendering Chan a yellow Uncle Tom who accommodated white supremacy. "Don't worry, he seems to say, no one's going to go making any trouble," Jen writes. Antidefamation groups organized a 2003 letter-writing campaign that forestalled the planned television broadcast of a Charlie Chan movie festival. Collectively, the films served as "a painful reminder of Hollywood's racist refusal to hire minorities to play roles that were designed for them," wrote the Organization of Chinese Americans. Instead, the character was "inaccurately depicted by Caucasian actors, who wore face paint to act out stereotypical images of Asians as slant-eyed, bucktoothed, subservient, and non–English speaking." The National Asian American Telecommunications Association's letter categorized Charlie Chan as among "the most offensive caricatures of America's cinematic past." In *Charlie Chan Is Dead*, the evocative title of a 1993 anthology of contemporary Asian American fiction, Elaine Kim called for the permanent burial of the "fake 'Asian' pop icon" whose "obsequious manner, fractured English," and "absurdly cryptic, pseudo-Confucian sayings" left a stereotypical legacy as demeaning as Stepin Fetchit, Sambo, or Aunt Jemima.[5]

All of these criticisms are correct. Nevertheless, precisely the attributes—his fortune-cookie aphorisms, humility, and appearance—that appall Chan's critics today appealed to fans during World War II, when the veteran pop icon received a new mission. U.S. propagandists enlisted him and his fellow "Chinese" figures to serve as the on-screen spokespersons for a promotional campaign that strove to introduce and acculturate Americans to their new Chinese ally. Acting as Sino-American interpreters, these characters implicitly asked moviegoers to rethink their Orientalist preconceptions—race was a daunting obstacle blocking better bilateral understanding—and to see Chinese as the Other no longer. Rather, with the Japanese enemy now categorized as the sole villain in the Pacific, Toler and other yellowface masqueraders (Katharine Hepburn among them)—as well as the actors (Gregory Peck, for one), directors (Frank Capra), and publishers (Henry Luce) who led viewers on authoritative if vicarious tours of China—encouraged the white majority to embrace Chinese as Us, like-minded friends in the worldwide struggle against the Axis and for the Four Freedoms. In short, such Sino-American mediators, both imagined and real, worked to incorporate Jiang's republic (Mao Zedong's communists complicated matters and were thus conveniently ignored) into the United Nations' body politic, upholding the "new China" said to be emerging as a potentially great Americanized power destined to become the fourth global policeman.

Paradoxically, however, such boosterism relied on Orientalist staging—yellowface, paternalist plotlines, gendered romance narratives, and so on—to humanize and welcome Chinese into the Allied family of nations. Scholars who have refined Said's framework and studied its U.S. variant have rediscovered Orientalism's dynamism, its fungibility. Pro-Chinese propaganda illustrates Said's point to the effect that Western interpretations could have the curious effect of transforming Orientals "from a very far distant and often threatening Otherness into figures that are relatively familiar," even as such mediations obscured "the fact that the audience [was] watching a highly artificial enactment of what a non-Oriental has made into a symbol for the whole Orient." U.S. perceptions of China underwent a major reevaluation at midcentury, as the United States developed greater geopolitical capability and Americans discussed race relations more openly. New Deal liberals—and most of those who staffed the Office of War Information (OWI) or produced Hollywood movies fit that description—prized, in theory, racial tolerance, social inclusiveness, and international brotherhood. As a result, they—like author Pearl S. Buck, whose bestselling novel *The Good Earth* (1931) was remade into a 1937 blockbuster MGM movie—embraced the East with cultural productions that sentimentalized and romanticized the Orient in such a way as to transcend East-West difference. If that "China mystique" advanced a more pluralistic vision of the global community, scholars Karen Leong, Mari Yoshihara, and Christina Klein have observed, then it also sustained

Orientalist logic that gendered and stereotyped China, thereby legitimating paternal U.S. intervention to guide that country's proper modern, Americanized development.[6]

Even yellowface minstrelsy, perhaps Orientalism's worst error, could be compatible with the promotion of Sino-American solidarity, at least from the perspective of non-Asian producers and consumers. Krystyn R. Moon has written that "allure and repulsiveness coexisted in these performances," which reflected a degree of white attraction to and desire for Chinese. Yellowface performers borrowed techniques developed by blackface minstrels since the 1830s. Blackface worked both for and against racial stereotyping, according to W. T. Lhamon Jr. Lhamon's subjects, working-class ethnic minstrels, rehearsed racial parody because they possessed the power to belittle blacks and the wish to reinforce color boundaries. But they passed also to transgress fixed racial identities, satirize social norms, and signal their identification with African Americans as opposed to the powers that be who enforced and profited from the status quo. Michael Rogin reached a similar conclusion in his study of Hollywood's blackface tradition, likening on-screen minstrels to crossdressing performers in that both masqueraded as someone else partly to express affiliation with another and/or to question established racial (or gendered or sexual, as the case may be) identities. Moreover, Rogin's analysis of such films as Elia Kazan's *Pinky* (1949) reminds us that cinematic minstrelsy could coexist, if uncomfortably, with a pro-civil-rights stance.[7]

The "racial ventriloquism" performed by Toler, Hepburn, and Gene Tierney as well as others who attempted to pass as Chinese on the silver screen occupied a middle ground between East and West. Within the context of wartime culture meant to valorize Sino-American unity, such portrayals, reprehensible as they may be, interpreted Asians for Westerners, deracinated and whitened Chinese, and thus redrew the boundary that once delineated Them from Us to include Chinese in the Allied community. Charlie Chan's Honolulu residence, pidgin English, and Western attire marked him as a cosmopolitan figure straddling two worlds. The detective acknowledged his hybridized identity in *Keeper of the Keys*, Biggers's final novel, published in 1932. He explained that he could not fully understand the mind of Ah Sing, a Chinese criminal, because the Chinese American Chan bore "the brand—the label—Americanized." He continued, "Am I an American? No. Am I, then, a Chinese? Not in the eyes of Ah Sing." Chan's thoroughly acculturated children—fluent in youthful

American slang, they say "Gee whiz" in wonderment and address their father as "Pop"—further attest to the character's immigrant credentials.[8]

To some degree, yellowface provided wider interpretive latitude that licensed enactment of "Chinese" heroism on screen, for everyone knew that a white face resided just below the makeup's surface. And Chan was supremely talented, to the point of being either an admirable figure or a stereotypical "model minority," depending on one's point of view. He continues to occupy his customary position in *Charlie Chan in the Secret Service*: a recognized senior expert, a famous sleuth who, because of his unusual and acknowledged investigatory skill, can and does exert authority over others. He interrogates Caucasian suspects. He fingers the Nazi culprits. He solves the crimes that Westerners cannot. His less adept peers defer to him, the smartest person in any drawing room mystery. And he is made to appear courageous and consequently worthy of a higher position in the racial order than Birmingham Brown (Mantan Moreland), his frightened, wide-eyed, Stepin Fetchit–like African American sidekick. Oland's and Toler's yellowface portrayals gave rise to a new, positive, stereotype of Chan as the "good Chinaman" that deviated from the extant bad one embodied by the sinister Fu Manchu. And that positive if stereotypical image resonated among Americans and Chinese alike. T. K. Chang, the ROC's Los Angeles consul, who regularly advised Hollywood on cinematic depictions of his country, endorsed the American series, which was so popular in China as to inspire several Chan knockoffs.[9]

Chan merits close scrutiny because as the most recognizable symbol of China in contemporary American pop culture, he best exemplifies the tensions that beset that culture, trapped in an Orientalist mindset. Toler's characterization, enabled by the industry's discriminatory labor practices, also contained Chan's evident talents and reduced the challenge he otherwise would have posed to the established racial hierarchy—for, again, everyone understood him merely to be a white actor working under a yellow mask. Avuncular and humble, Chan was beloved precisely because he was assimilated, deferential, and unthreatening to the system, as Frank Chin and Gish Jen have ascertained. So obviously offensive to modern eyes, yellowface (as well as the Orientalist stereotypes, jokes, and narratives that littered these avowedly pro-Chinese movies) hardly raised a Caucasian eyebrow at the time. All such practices were still credible and would remain standard until the 1960s. Although otherwise hawkeyed OWI staffers worked diligently behind the scenes to improve Hollywood's output—and their correspondence with the studios offers rich insight into the difficulties of humanizing Chinese allies amid the predominant Orientalism—they took yellowface for granted, neither mentioning Toler's depiction nor pressuring Monogram studio to recast any of the seven wartime Chan movies.[10]

American views did indeed become more tolerant and inclusive during World War II, as evidenced by the 1943 repeal of the exclusion acts that since 1882 had generally barred Chinese from immigrating to or becoming naturalized citizens of the United States. Aside from correcting what FDR called that historic "injustice to our friends," however, the mid-century white majority remained locked in the day's racial logic, which sustained Jim Crow segregation, Japanese internment, and continued Chinese exclusion. Congress followed its repeal of complete exclusion by restricting legal Chinese immigration to only 105 persons annually, a miniscule quota that rendered "openness" virtually meaningless.[11] For all of its complicated meaning, yellowface ultimately if quietly upheld that supremacist ideology by putting Chinese in their place and restricting their assimilated passage into either the American or UN melting pots, as the case may be.

Operating from a presumed position of white racial and U.S. national superiority, most Americans approached Sino-American relations as paternalists with a missionary responsibility to Christianize, democratize, modernize, and generally uplift China according to a prescribed American model. For proof one need look no further than the writings of Luce, who spoke of the brilliant dawning of an American Century about to unfold in China and elsewhere. Whereas Britons were considered cousins, Chinese were thought of as children, extended wards of the U.S. state. Historian T. Christopher Jesperson has observed that "paternalism, and all it implies about treating adults as children," lay "at the root of the American attitude toward . . . China." Regarding China as a "less-than-sovereign" entity and Chinese "as childlike" provided "convenient rationale[s] for policies that necessitate[d] involvement or interference in the affairs of" that nation, actions ostensibly taken "under the guise of 'benevolent' intentions . . . for the good of the recipient. Paternalism, evoking as it does familial relations, most notably those between father and child," aptly describes the U.S. frame of reference during World War II, "when the United States tried to assume the role of a father, implicitly, and sometimes explicitly, casting China as a child." Like contemporary photography, any number of the era's movies—from John Wayne's *Flying Tigers* (1942) to *China* (1943), starring Alan Ladd, to *The Keys of the Kingdom* (1944), with Gregory Peck as Father Francis Chisholm, a Catho-

Assuming the role of a surrogate parent, an American soldier stationed in China wipes a local child's face. The GIs treated the youths to a New Year's feast. Office of War Information photo, n.d., 208-AA-13V-6, Still Picture Unit, National Archives and Records Administration II, College Park, Md.

lic missionary—featured narrative arcs in which white, usually male, Americans, motivated by the "China mystique," intervened altruistically to protect and guide their Chinese dependents along a foreordained developmental path.[12]

A component of Orientalism, paternalism worked to gender Sino-American relations as well. Gina Marchetti has shown how, prior to World War II, Hollywood occasionally told miscegenation stories—about white women raped, seduced, or held captive by "Asian" men, usually in yellow-face—that stoked fears about the "yellow peril" supposedly emanating from the East by framing it as a threat to racial purity. Movies reversed that narrative during the war, however. No longer was white woman-hood, as representative of the race, endangered on-screen by the lascivious Fu Manchus of the world. (However, if the Fu Manchu in question happened to be Japanese, the old rules still applied, as the ad for RKO's *Behind the Rising Sun* [1943] showing enemy soldiers assaulting Caucasian women suggests.) Rather, international, interracial love emerged as a metaphor representing the transcendence of difference and the establishment of Sino-American harmony. Here again, cinematic romances such as Twentieth Century–Fox's *China Girl* (1942) and *Blood on the Sun* (1945), released by United Artists, sentimentalized bilateral ties but added a twist. Unlike such Anglo-American love stories as *Thunder Birds* (1942) or *The Way to the Stars* (1945), which occasionally linked American women with British men, Sino-American romances invariably featured U.S. males engaged with "Chinese" females, who symbolically feminized China and signaled its exotic sexual availability. More than two decades after the fact, a *Chicago Daily News* correspondent still nostalgically remembered the wartime alliance as a "happy union," a "shotgun marriage" consummated after an "overlong engagement."[13]

Whereas those major studio productions negotiated the color line and broke the miscegenation taboo by having Caucasian actors such as Tierney and Sylvia Sidney pass in yellowface as "Asian" objects of desire, sex and race operated to ghettoize Anna May Wong, limiting her opportunities to enact Chinese volition to a couple of B movies. Even during her heyday, Wong bristled at being typecast in Madame Butterfly or Dragon Lady parts, and her options as a leading lady narrowed still with the Production Code's imposition. Matters came to a head over MGM's casting of its screen version of Buck's Pulitzer Prize–winning novel *The Good Earth*. Wong coveted the role of O-lan, the story's figurehead, who promised to be Hollywood's most visible and three-dimensional such character yet despite her stereotypical servility and self-sacrifice. And as the industry's top Chinese American actress, there was reason to believe the rumors that Wong would get the part. Irving Thalberg's production team thought otherwise, however; his assistant considered Wong most suitable as a bit player to lend "atmosphere" to the production. When the studio announced that Paul Muni had been cast as Wang Lung, the male lead, it was clear that O-lan would go to someone other than Wong, whose only consolation was to be offered a supporting role as Lotus, the unsympathetic home wrecker. In short, producers refused to gamble on the movie-going public's enlightened willingness to accept an Asian American lead and deemed Wong too Chinese to play Chinese. To add insult to injury, MGM's *The Good Earth* became a hit with Caucasians headlining, and Luise Rainer won the Best Actress award for playing O-lan in yellowface.[14]

Having declined MGM's offer, an embittered Wong decamped Hollywood for a spell, touring war-torn China during her sabbatical. She returned as a patriot who raised funds for United China Relief, among other activities. With less money at stake than major productions, B movies could afford to take risks, and they served as Wong's only outlet for displaying on-screen her newfound political commitment and underutilized talent for playing strong, proud Asians. A pair of otherwise forgettable 1942 flicks from Producers Releasing Corporation distinguished themselves in one respect: each featured a Chinese American in a powerful headlining role, the era's only Hollywood pictures to do so. Whereas mainstream Hollywood productions featured American men rescuing Chinese, *Lady from Chungking* flips the narrative so that Wong's character, a resistance leader who spearheads an uprising that frees two American pilots from Japanese captivity, takes action that saves U.S. males. *Bombs over Burma* casts her as a Chinese schoolteacher/secret agent who foils an Axis plot to disrupt the Burma Road, the Allies' primary supply line to China. Both cheap thrillers promoted Chinese capability and internationalism alike. She receives crucial assistance from Soviet and American accomplices. Her American helpmate in *Bombs over Burma* gains firsthand Asian experience that allows him to see the internationalist light. As a result of his epiphany, the bus driver declares, somewhat unhelpfully, that he now numbers "coolies" among his "blood brothers" because they, too, are just ordinary guys who, like underdogs everywhere, must fight back against the "big boys" of the global block.[15]

The only problem was that Wong remained marginalized, laboring in relative obscurity. To whatever extent these two B movies were empowering, they did not carry equal weight with A-list productions, the arena in which U.S. propagandists trained their energies. The June 1942 Office of Facts and Figures (OFF) study of U.S. attitudes regarding the United Nations found the public well disposed toward China. Chinese were liked almost as much as Japanese were hated. More than 80 percent of those surveyed trusted Chongqing to cooperate with Washington even beyond the armistice. That astonishing figure, which outpaced Moscow's (51 percent) and even London's (77 percent) popularity ratings, held constant throughout the war.[16]

However trusted China may have been, it remained an afterthought in the American mind. Survey after survey showed a disregard for China's military capability and geopolitical significance. She (China was typically feminized in U.S. discourse) was considered to be by far the least important of the UN's four major powers, and two-thirds of those polled speculated that Japan could be defeated without Chinese involvement. All told,

China's image amounted to that of a "trustworthy, but not very important, ally." The public did not "regard the Chinese as Allies comparable in importance to the Russians and the British," concluded OFF researchers, adding that "the American mind" had not yet "grasped the concept of China as an important world power."[17]

To be fair, China did not yet have power equal to any of the Big Three. Nevertheless, benign paternal neglect led Americans to undervalue the country's worth. Despite China's vast size, two-fifths of respondents to the 1942 OFF survey could not place the country on a map. Less was known about Jiang than about Winston Churchill or Joseph Stalin, even though the Chinese ruler appeared on *Time*'s cover no fewer than six times during the war years. Misperceptions abounded in that information-free zone. Critics commonly listed China's shortcomings as "backwardness," "disunity," and passivity, ailments historically said to afflict developing nations throughout Asia, Africa, and the Americas.[18]

Such "stereotyped conceptions" and doubts about China's "real importance" must be counteracted, U.S. propagandists insisted, to establish a spirit of Sino-American "unity." Instrumental in winning the war, feelings of East-West solidarity also instilled "essential foundations of mutual respect, confidence, and understanding" conducive to the "cooperative solution" of postwar problems. With that goal in mind, publicists strove to increase U.S. appreciation of the ROC, elevate its stature to that of a fourth world policeman alongside the UN's three other great constables, and foster Sino-American partnership, all with an eye toward integrating China into Americans' developing cosmology.[19]

Portraying the ROC as democratic, modern, and especially unified was a tall order, and the OWI would experience trouble filling it without violating the agency's "strategy of truth." Undaunted, the OWI's Government Information Manual declared that America's "traditional patronizing attitude" must be overcome. The screen had yet to acquaint moviegoers with their new Asian allies. It had clarified China's importance neither to the Allies' immediate fortunes nor to the future maintenance of peace and security throughout the Pacific. Toward that end, the OWI called on the Hollywood studios to dramatize the "might," "heroism," and "incredible feats of resistance" displayed by the Chinese. More important, Washington entrusted filmmakers with a special mission to humanize Chinese— within the narrow confines of contemporary racial views, that is. By applying a touch of movie magic, the film capital could allow viewers to "see [Chinese] as people, as one of us. We can see into their lives, their homes. We can suffer with them in their hardships and gain strength from their strength. This is a war for the anonymous individual and his inalienable rights. We want to know this anonymous individual, for he and we are one and the same."[20]

At the same time, Washington cautioned Hollywood not to fall prey to the enemy's "divide and conquer" strategy by thoughtlessly perpetuating divisive and "timeworn stereotypes." Filmmakers were asked to discontinue their habit of portraying Chinese as "comic" laundrymen, "houseboys," or "menials." "This is not a racial war," they were reminded. "Many millions of our allies belong to the brown or yellow races and such references are offensive to them." The OWI added high-minded instruction: "Our allies are human beings like ourselves. They have the same hopes and aspirations that we do. Despite superficial differences of language and custom, essentially we are all alike." Accordingly, entertainers received word to depict Chinese as underdogs, "as great and courageous fighters" who somehow managed to stymie Tokyo's modern war machine despite having only "outdated" equipment.[21]

Despite that injunction, U.S. culture stooped to racism in introducing Americans to and differentiating among the peoples of Asia. Americans needed little help identifying Japanese as their enemy in the Pacific. Even U.S. citizens of Japanese descent were considered security threats and were interned in the wake of Pearl Harbor. Less clarity existed with regard to Chinese. Were these unfamiliar people of color from the other side of the world friends or foes? How could one tell? Helpfully, *Life* magazine published side-by-side photographs of Ong Wen-hao, China's economic minister, and Japan's prime minister, Hideki Tojo, to demonstrate how to "distinguish friendly Chinese from enemy alien Japs." Careful analysis of the subjects' divergent facial features proved, the magazine claimed, that Japanese "and Chinese are as closely related as Germans and English." If that assessment left room for confusion, the U.S. Army distributed a 1942 *Pocket Guide to China* to soldiers destined for the Pacific. The guide included a comic strip, "How to Spot a Jap," illustrating the physical characteristics said to distinguish Japanese from Chinese. Whereas the graphic pointed out the traits that purportedly marked Japanese as alien from and inferior to Westerners, it demonstrated the ways in which Chinese resembled Americans. Unlike his Japanese counterpart—said to be shorter and bucktoothed and to have legs "joined directly to his chest!"—the typical Chinese man was "about the size of an average American," smiled easily, and possessed eyes "set like any European's or American's."[22]

Hollywood features provided additional taxonomic instruction that contrasted Asians in such a way as to categorize Japanese as Them, the dangerous Other, and Chinese as Us, members of the extended Allied family. In the comedy *They Got Me Covered* (1943), Bob Hope, playing a reporter who found himself in a jam after stumbling onto an Axis spy ring, dials a random phone number and pretends to report a kidnapping to the Federal Bureau of Investigation. A surprised man answers and insists, "I no kidnap nobody. Only wash laundry. FBI? You want Japanese. Me Chinese. Hundred percent American!"[23]

Incorporating Chinese into the imagined Allied community took a more serious turn in movies that stylized the actual war in the Pacific. *Thirty Seconds over Tokyo* (1944), MGM's venerated account of April 1942's Doolittle Raid—the audacious attack on Japan, the first U.S. response to Pearl Harbor, was authorized, in part, to raise American morale, and its inherent drama translated easily to the screen—anticipated a time when the United States would really give the Japanese "a dose of their own medicine," as one character puts it. After dropping their payloads on Japanese industrial and military targets, most of the sixteen B-25s return to China as planned, including one piloted by Ted Lawson (Van Johnson), whose memoir had inspired the screenplay by Dalton Trumbo, later one of the Hollywood Ten. At that point, *Thirty Seconds over Tokyo*, starring Spencer Tracy as James H. Doolittle, pivots from an anti-Japanese to a pro-Chinese position. Lawson's bomber runs out of fuel just shy of its destination and crash-lands in Japanese-occupied China, where the resistance rescues the injured crew members and spirits them to hospital for treatment. The theme of Sino-American amity is laid on pretty thick. "Jiang Jieshi, we're his friends," declares Lawson to gain the trust of Charlie (Ching Wah Lee), the guerrilla leader. Schoolchildren serenade the recuperating soldiers with "The Star-Spangled Banner." Grateful, noble peasants (the picture suffers from patronizing depictions) bestow gifts on the airmen for their bravery. And in the penultimate scene, Lawson, recuperated and U.S.-bound, bids adieu to Benson Fong's Dr. Chung, the Westernized, English-speaking physician who has nursed the Americans back to health, with the words "You're our kind of people" and a wish for greater Sino-American cooperation in the future. According to *Thirty Seconds over Tokyo*—widely acclaimed at the time as Hollywood's best Pacific war film, far outclassing RKO's *Bombardier* (1943), Warner Bros.' *Destination Tokyo* (1943), and Twentieth Century–Fox's *Purple Heart* (1944)—Americans could find common ground with Americanized if stereotypical Chinese like Dr. Chung.[24]

Producer Walter Wanger's *Gung Ho!* (1943) recapitulated an event whose renown has faded with time: Carlson's Raiders' August 1942 guerrilla attack on Makin Island, among the first U.S. offensives in the Pacific. Randolph Scott starred as Colonel Thorwald, a character based on Colonel Evans Carlson, who forged, as would Lee Marvin in *The Dirty Dozen* (1967), a misfit collection of U.S. soldiers (including one played by Robert Mitchum) into an elite fighting unit for an unconventional raid on the Japanese stronghold. A caricature of the enemy emerged, as was customary in such pictures about the Pacific theater. Japanese were said to be "crafty" and "tenacious," and Thorwald readily found volunteers eager to fight them. One recruit joined to right the wrong of Pearl Harbor; another, a Filipino American, signed on to avenge the memory of his sister, ravaged and killed back in Manila; a third did so because, he said, "I just don't like Japs."

Chinese, conversely, provided Carlson's men with "gung ho," their esprit de corps. An Anglicization of *gong he*—translated literally as "work" and "together," the phrase was the slogan of Chinese Industrial Cooperatives, a Western-led body that organized grassroots Chinese resistance and inspired Carlson to form his raiders—"gung ho" entered the American lexicon and became a morale-boosting motto for the U.S. Marine Corps during World War II. The movie was largely responsible for the phrase's adoption, and Scott's Thorwald, Carlson's cinematic equivalent, learned it while fighting alongside America's Pacific ally. Impressed that poorly equipped but highly motivated Chinese guerrillas had outlasted the Japanese invaders, the colonel appropriated their fighting spirit and schooled his troops in it. And thanks in part to their gung-ho attitude, the U.S. raiders staged a successful surprise landing on Makin that took the island and eliminated most of its occupying forces, suffering only minimal casualties in the process. Although *Gung Ho!* enjoyed a mixed critical reception, Wanger's "tribute" to China's fighting spirit earned plaudits from the OWI, which praised it for fostering "better understanding of one of our allies."[25]

Documentaries familiarized Americans with China, serving as travelogues that oriented viewers to that faraway, unknown place. Director Frank Capra's *Prelude to War* (1942) began the lesson with a geopolitical introduction that distinguished among the major players in the Pacific theater. Whereas Tokyo's dictatorial "gangsters" had targeted China as part of their plan for world conquest, the otherwise peaceful people of the ROC, rallying under Jiang's "inspired leadership," bravely fought for freedom despite suffering serious harm. Education continued with the penultimate installment in Capra's *Why We Fight* series, *The Battle of China* (1944), an hour-long study of Chinese geography, history, and society done for the benefit of U.S. GIs slated for service in the Pacific. Just as other entries in the series recorded British or Soviet suffering at the hands of Nazi Germany, this one documented Chinese victimization by the Japanese, a theme sure to win American hearts. Capra recounted the dead at Shanghai, where Japanese bombers had "slaughtered" tens of thousands of "defenseless civilians" back in 1937, an event famously summarized by H. S. Wong's photograph of a solitary orphaned baby crying next to Shanghai's train station. A Chinese national who worked as a Hearst newsreel cameraman, Wong's iconic photo widely appeared in U.S. newsreels and newspapers, where it left an indelible image of the Second Sino-Japanese War. Shots of dead bodies and burning buildings in *The Battle of China* further attested to Tokyo's "deliberate mass murder" of Shanghai's people.[26]

The Nanking Massacre, shorthand for the atrocities committed by Japanese forces during their 1937–38 sacking of the republic's onetime capital, received coverage as well. At least two hundred thousand Chinese civilians or prisoners of war were killed and tens of thousands of women raped during one of history's worst crimes against humanity. Although Tokyo denied the massacre's occurrence and claimed that it was merely a figment of Chongqing's imagination, American correspondents reported the event, which in the United States became known as the Rape of Nanking and associated with Japanese cruelty and Chinese victimization, generally speaking. *The Battle of China* included shocking visual evidence of executions and mass burials: the voice-over informed listeners that during the Rape of Nanking, Japanese forces "outdid themselves in barbarism. Soldiers raped and tortured. They killed and butchered." The Chinese thus deserved U.S. aid. Capra's was not the only film to reference what had transpired at Nanjing and Shanghai. Although they did not name the events, several Hollywood features—Republic's *Flying Tigers* and Fox's *China Girl* and *The Keys of the Kingdom*—included Chinese orphans cared for by American soldiers or missionaries. Warner Bros.' 1943 Stalinist apologia, *Mission to Moscow*, featured a scene in which Ambassador Davies toured a fictional Soviet hospital overflowing with Chinese children maimed by Japanese invaders. Paramount's *China* and MGM's *Dragon Seed* (1944) had plotlines in which girls and women were raped. Such dramatizations of the Pacific theater engendered sympathy among on-screen U.S. paternalists, converting those metaphorical Americans into internationalist missionaries committed to China's salvation and defense.[27]

A common thesis pervaded American portraits of China. Advanced by Luce's Time-Life media empire, United China Relief's fund-raisers, and Capra's orientation films in addition to Hollywood's features, this thesis held that a "new China" was arising, phoenixlike, from the ashes of the Second Sino-Japanese War. The war had given birth to a revitalized nation, the argument went, fully united under Jiang's able guidance and mobilized against Japan. (Optimists consistently overestimated the generalissimo's capabilities and popularity and underappreciated his ongoing internal power struggle with Mao's communists.) According to this brand of wishful thinking, moreover, the ROC had embarked on a redevelopment project that, with appropriate U.S. tutelage, would someday result in an economically modernized, politically liberalized, and socially reconstructed country modeled on its American benefactor. An Americanized China would remain closely allied with the United States, serving U.S. interests as a crucial recipient of American products and expertise and as a friendly, stable, peaceful outpost (the fourth policeman) in the Pacific's reconfigured postwar power grid. Accordingly, Americans had a paternalistic duty to see to it that their Chinese charges were shepherded along a responsible path leading toward both wartime victory and a Christianized, democratized, and modernized future. When Jiang's spouse, Mayling Soong, made a successful monthlong goodwill tour of the United States that took her from Washington to Hollywood in 1943, the *New York Times* commented that readers could take a "certain paternal pride" in hosting the dignitary, for she, like *Thirty Seconds over Tokyo*'s Dr. Chung, embodied Americanized Chinese. According to the *South Atlantic Quarterly*, the American-educated, English-speaking Madame Jiang demonstrated during her travels that the Chinese were "more nearly kin to ourselves . . . than many a European nation of 'our own race.'"[28]

The "new China" thesis was predicated on a theory of Sino-American convergence postulating that the two countries and their peoples were becoming more alike in the crucible of war. Rather than imagining convergence as a dialogical process in which Chinese and Americans borrowed from one another to forge hybridized customs, theorists saw it as a recipe in which Chinese, exemplified by Madame Jiang, adapted to prescribed American norms. For example, Luce, born in China to Protestant missionary parents, made much of Jiang Jieshi's 1929 conversion to Christianity, which seemed to portend a Christianized future for the entire republic. Jiang was portrayed as a modernizer as well, and Capra's *The Battle of China* compared Shanghai's skyscrapers with Manhattan's as evidence of progress. China's present was analogized with America's past in such a way as to suggest that the ROC occupied a historical stage of development likely to lead to a positive outcome. Speaking in 1945, Minnesota congressman Walter Judd, a China lobbyist and onetime medical missionary, equated Jiang with George Washington and insisted that the republic, undergoing a rebirth akin to the American Revolution, should be judged "in terms of conditions as they were . . . 20 years ago and 200 years ago." Physiological and psychological similarities also were said to be operative. The teachings of *Life* and the U.S. Army on "How to Spot a Jap" informed readers that Chinese and Americans shared certain physical and mental traits. The Allied peoples "think alike, react alike, and hold much of the same ideals," added United China Relief speakers. Partnership rested on common wartime interests and peacetime aspirations, or so U.S. publicity claimed. *The Battle of China* concluded that Chinese security and American security were interdependent and that hope for a better postwar world depended on cooperation. "China's war is our war," the voice-over narration declared. Footage of Jiang, Roosevelt, and Churchill conferring at November 1943's Cairo summit, a major propaganda event, spoke to the republic's inclusion in the innermost sanctum of Allied power. Scenes of ROC pilots training at bases in the American Southwest and discussing aeronautics with their U.S. comrades confirmed that the Allies fought "side-by-side . . . in the struggle of freedom against slavery, civilization against barbarism, good against evil."[29]

A 1942 OFF poster labeled the Chinese as "friends" to Americans in their fight for the Four Freedoms. And the OWI called on filmmakers to give the public more stories of cooperation with its "brothers-in-arms." Producer Daryl F. Zanuck's *Thunder Birds* depicted Chinese aviators training alongside their American and British allies at an Arizona airbase, where everyone learned "to know one another" and became fast "friends" in such close quarters. An official documentary, *The Stilwell Road* (1945), recapped the arduous multinational effort—"never was there such a polyglot army," observed narrator Ronald Reagan of the involved American, Australian, British, Burmese, Chinese, Indian, and New Zealander troops—to reopen an overland supply line to China after Japan had severed the Burma Road in 1942.[30]

Flying Tigers applied to Sino-American friendship the same formula developed by *A Yank in the RAF* (1941) and its ilk to illustrate closer Anglo-American ties. Featuring John Wayne, whose star was rising thanks to his roles in war movies and John Ford's Western, *Stagecoach* (1939), the B movie ripped a page from the headlines, further sensationalizing the already legendary exploits of Claire Chennault's American Volunteer

Group. Republic dramatized the maturation of one fictitious flier who, after being attracted only by the "dough" to be made in the Pacific, comes to understand that, in the OWI's words, "China's fight means something more." As the enterprising U.S. pilot in question, Woody Jason (John Carroll), says when the audience meets him, China "is not our home. This is not our fight." Taking only a businesslike approach to Sino-American relations, Woody's selfish individualism, a stand-in for isolationism at large, manifests itself in his refusal to play by Volunteer Group rules, and his poor discipline contributes to the deaths of two comrades.

Lectures from Wayne, his commanding officer, about the necessity of teamwork fall on deaf ears. Woody begins to amend his ways only after he encounters a refugee camp and is moved to shelter its wounded orphans from further injury by Japanese forces. His metamorphosis into a committed internationalist—a transformation akin to those experienced by Robert Stack's Chuck Brewer in *Eagle Squadron* (1942) and Dean Jagger's John Patterson in *I Live in Grosvenor Square* (1945)—reaches its conclusion on 7 December 1941, when he learns to appreciate the indivisibility of American and Chinese security. The antihero confesses his past sins, admitting that he boyishly volunteered for service "just for laughs" and that, like any other "kid," his mien had been limited to his hometown street, which encompassed "his whole world." At that time, Chongqing, Hong Kong, and Shanghai were nothing more than "just a lot of names in a geography book." But firsthand experience in China has taught Woody otherwise. Now a self-described "man," those Chinese cities where "millions of people are being maimed and killed" mean as much to him as Texas, Maine, or Michigan. Duly converted to the civic religion of *One World*, Carroll's character joins Wayne's in performing the film's final heroic act, the destruction of a key link in Japan's supply line, buying time for Jiang's forces.

However fondly John Wayne fans may regard *Flying Tigers*, the OWI felt otherwise. The agency's commentary speaks to some shortcomings typical of Hollywood's pro-China presentations. Officials duly credited Republic for making a genuine attempt "to portray the Chinese sympathetically," citing the orphans and a prologue in which Jiang paid written tribute to Chennault's airmen. A major trafficker in paternalistic imagery that bred serious misunderstanding, the OWI predicted that the sight of adorable, wounded children—the movie's primary characterization of Chinese—would be "irresistible" to American audiences and would inspire their "sympathy." But the office objected to the B movie's stereotypical depictions of its few Chinese adults, who fell into two categories: deferential peasants or simpletons. (Two bit parts—wide-eyed, subservient restaurateurs who spoke pidgin English and provided comic relief—were singled out for criticism.) Furthermore, the OWI noted the lack of Chinese subjectivity apparent in the film. Unlike, say, Zanuck's *A Yank in the RAF* or Wanger's *Eagle Squadron*, in which Americans and Britons met on common ground, *Flying Tigers* failed to reference a commensurate Chinese ally suitable for U.S. partnership. Although set in China, *Flying Tigers* was really an American story about U.S. soldiers who exercised American power in the Pacific. The tension involved in Woody's conversion was almost entirely internal, bearing little relation to the external Asian ally. Nor did that nearly invisible ally display any capacity for self-sufficiency. "No Chinese fighting men are shown. There is no evidence of cooperation between the Chinese forces and the American volunteers," concluded the OWI, adding that Republic had missed a golden "opportunity to play up the might and heroism of our Chinese allies, to demonstrate that they have been fighting our battle for almost a decade, to correct some of the misconceptions concerning the Chinese which are prevalent."[31]

All of these Pacific war dramas dealt primarily with the U.S. war against Japan. Supporting China was only incidental to *Flying Tigers*, *Thirty Seconds over Tokyo*, and *Gung Ho!* Not one major production with China as its central topic appeared in theaters until 1943. The dearth led the OWI's Nelson Poynter to complain in May of that year that Hollywood had not done enough to close the "big gap in our knowledge and understanding of China." "Give us a *Mrs. Miniver* of China," he implored.[32]

As was the case with regard to Britain and the Soviet Union, international commerce eventually motivated studio executives to act on China's behalf. Hollywood had no China market to speak of during wartime, although executives dreamed of establishing one. Language and cultural differences inhibited free and easy communication even in the best of times, and war was not those times. Japanese forces occupied a vast swath of the country, and Tokyo eliminated American productions from that jurisdiction as yet another step in its lengthy anti-Hollywood protectionist campaign. The system of distribution and exhibition in unoccupied China functioned far below its normal capacity, with only about thirty topflight theaters remaining operational. If the Chongqing embassy's reports are to be believed, the moviegoing experience there was not altogether pleasant. U.S. diplomats found the capital's best theaters "uncomfortable" places where ill-maintained sound equipment and projectors, operated by disinterested "underlings," garbled dialogue and ruined film stock. Distribution, moreover, had nearly ceased. Only a handful of imported film canisters per month could be flown over the Himalayan hump or driven from Burma. Disrupted rail and road networks slowed internal shipment to a crawl. These factors gave rise to a thriving black market. Pirates made unauthorized copies of the few imports that did arrive and peddled them, at cut rate, to Chinese theater owners. Indeed, piracy served as the industry's top complaint about the China market. In May 1944, Motion Picture Producers and Distributors of America (MPPDA) president Will H. Hays sent the head of the State Department's Telecommunications Division a twenty-four-page memorandum cataloging the various foreign injustices done against Hollywood exports. The document's section on China noted the "absence of copyright protection" that "encourages the pirating of films whose exhibition now and in the postwar period presents a serious problem to the industry."[33]

Although the companies opposed the black market, the demand indicated that Hollywood might someday discover riches among China's half billion potential customers. In May 1943, Richard H. Davis, a foreign service officer assigned to the Chongqing embassy, filed a report that suggested as much. Despite wartime dislocations, patrons continued to pack what few theaters remained open. Ticket buyers numbered "several million," a figure certain to grow during peacetime. "The average motion picturegoer sees one or two pictures a week," and some paid to watch even more, continued Davis, adding, "Cinemas are attended by everyone regardless of age, sex, [or] class." Furthermore, Chinese fans, especially middle- and "higher-class" ones, reportedly preferred Hollywood's movies to their competitors. Domestic production had come to a virtual halt, and what few films emerged fell "far short of American technical standards." Davis believed that Moscow's industry, though saddled with challenges, represented Hollywood's likeliest foreign challenger, and he conceded that some "excellent" Soviet pictures had generated some deserved buzz. However, he observed, interest in them had declined of late, a slackening he attributed "to the fact that Soviet films contain more propaganda than entertainment whereas American producers have cleverly combined the two with good results in many cases." The diplomat harbored no doubts that "American films are the most popular with Chinese audiences." They were so popular, in fact, that they raised U.S. stature and increased Allied solidarity. The few American features, shorts, and newsreels that trickled in "increased the knowledge of the average Chinese picturegoer as to events in other parts of the world" and gave a clearer "realization of the powerful allies who are fighting on China's side."[34]

By all appearances, then, vast financial and political opportunities beckoned in postwar China: an OWI functionary foresaw a "worthwhile" market there once victory was won, and U.S. Chamber of Commerce head Eric Johnston, who would succeed Hays as MPPDA president in 1946, predicted "mutual profit" after the war. Yet the companies found their ability to capitalize on those opportunities hindered by such obstacles as piracy and Chongqing's taxation scheme. To raise revenue, the insolvent ROC placed a series of national, provincial, and municipal taxes and surcharges on theater admissions that almost quadrupled the average ticket price to ninety-five yuan (equivalent to about fifty U.S. cents). The add-ons not only artificially priced some customers out of the market, thereby reducing ticket sales and the studios' box office take, but also, according to industry insiders, supplied an extensive slush fund drawn on by Jiang's corrupt bureaucracy. United Artists foreign manager Walter Gould notified Carl E. Milliken, director of the MPPDA's Foreign Department, that the taxes and surcharges enabled ROC officials and quasi-officials to "live on the fat of the land, with this particular fat being furnished by American pictures."[35]

Currency exchange restrictions provided a third stumbling block. To conserve its foreign currency supply, Chongqing, taking a page from London's playbook, limited the amount of the American industry's earnings that could be converted into dollars from yuan and remitted to the United States. The control regime, established in May 1942, was initially lenient insofar as it permitted the U.S. firms to remit 50 percent of their earnings at a favorable twenty-to-one exchange rate. (The remainder, as in Britain, was placed in an account on which the companies could draw only for local expenditures.) Dollar reserves dwindled, however, leading to a Chinese press campaign against the "overly generous" terms granted to Hollywood, which needlessly drained precious foreign currency. In March 1945, the ROC finance ministry proposed a severe cutback: allowable remittances were to be reduced by more than 90 percent, thereby permitting the companies to transfer only 4 percent of their net local earnings.[36]

Troubled, Hollywood again turned to its corporatist partner in Washington for help. As payment in kind for its extensive wartime services on behalf of the United States, the MPPDA expected—almost demanded— State Department intervention to create a more favorable and liberalized postwar Chinese marketplace. Time and again, the trade association's Hays, Milliken, and other leaders called on U.S. officials to address Chinese exchange limits, piracy, and taxation, the latter of which was described as a "racket," an "organized method of graft" that required elimination if the industry were to "see the light of day." In so doing, the MPPDA repeated its customary argument that what was good for Hollywood was good for America. More movies in China, as elsewhere, would benefit not only the film business but also the United States and its private manufacturers, for Hollywood's pictures served as "animated catalogues which familiarize distant peoples with an extensive range of American products" as well as with the American way of life. If the barriers inhibiting cinema's free movement into China were lifted, then 500 million Chinese could be magically rendered into admirers of America, practitioners of democracy, and purchasers of "American gadgets and appliances, new furniture, new kitchen stoves, new automobiles, new radios, new phonographs, and a thousand other products of American factories or farms."[37] The possibilities were limitless, the MPPDA implied.

Diplomats ignored the piracy issue and made little if any headway in changing ROC fiscal policies but did negotiate reduced currency controls. In July 1945, in part as a consequence of the State Department's involvement, including that of Ambassador Patrick J. Hurley, a compromise was reached whereby the Chinese finance ministry agreed to set annual allowable remittances at 15 percent, with a fixed exchange rate of twenty yuan to the dollar—a nice sweetener, given that the prevailing rate had suddenly inflated to an estimated three thousand to one by that point.[38]

To curry Washington's favor, the industry participated in an information program jointly conducted in China by the State Department and the OWI. Launched in January 1942, the program featured film exhibitions, radio broadcasts, and academic exchanges that were supposed to "acquaint Chinese . . . with various aspects of American life, institutions, and war effort," thereby buoying Chinese morale and strengthening Allied harmony. In that way, the initiative closely resembled its companions targeting the Soviet Union or Great Britain. Only an aim to modernize China, to train it in and uplift it to American standards, distinguished U.S. public diplomacy in the East. As the department's directive to its embassy in Chongqing stated, the program "sought to assist China" and contribute to its war effort by demonstrating the "many different ways in which American scientific, technical, social, educational, industrial, and other experience may be of use to China in raising its standard of living, improving the condition of its rural population, [and developing its] educational, social, and administrative programs."[39]

Educational films had a special mission to perform in that respect, for on-screen illustrations of U.S. agricultural and industrial achievements, medical and technical procedures, and defense and social programs could "stimulate the imagination of the Chinese and arouse their hopes for the future economic development of their country with American aid." Planners, in other words, hoped that moving pictures could effect Luce's much-anticipated American Century by inspiring Chinese to emulate U.S. models. The program featured three short documentaries—*Democracy in Action* (1942), Pare Lorentz's *The River* (1938), and *The Heritage We Guard* (1940)—that provided tutelage in political behavior, flood control, and soil conservation, respectively. *Power and the Land* (1940) recapped the New Deal's rural electrification program, and *Tanks* (1942) displayed U.S. military and industrial might integral to the UN's war effort. *Oswego* (1943) attended to alliance building, with Chengdu's *Central Daily News* reporting that "thundering handclaps" erupted when photographs of Jiang, Roosevelt, and Churchill appeared on screen to the strains of their respective national anthems prior to an outdoor screening. Audiences did not always receive the intended messages, however. Wilma Fairbank, the Chongqing embassy's cultural attaché and spouse of noted Chinese historian John K. Fairbank, came away from another outdoor exhibition with an altogether different impression. Instead of inculcating "admiration" for U.S. techniques, she reported that the film in question, about Iowa's hog industry, provoked open disbelief among Szechuan farmers, who found the depicted American animals too huge to be true. Miscommunication resulted, she concluded, because what appeared on-screen was "too remote" from everyday experience "in a society where hogs were raised on refuse and wheeled to market on wheelbarrows by manpower."[40]

Fox was the first to answer Poynter's call for an Asian *Mrs. Miniver*. Zanuck wrote the story for *China Girl* (under his customary pseudonym, Melville Crossman), conceiving it as a Chinese version of *A Yank in the RAF*. One of the project's working titles was "A Yank in China," and in early 1942, Zanuck instructed screenwriter Ben Hecht to pattern its protagonist after Tyrone Power's character in that 1941 drama of Anglo-American conviviality. Johnny Williams (George Montgomery), an American newsreel cameraman working in occupied China in late 1941, emerged as Power's analogue. Jaded and selfish, Johnny declines an invitation to join Chennault's Flying Tigers, unwilling to risk his life for China whose fight is not his concern. "Let [China] burn. It ain't our bonfire," he tells a friend, an American Volunteer Group pilot, who responds, to little effect, "I can't see it that way, [Johnny]. It's savages [Japanese] against civilization." Suspicious Japanese authorities nonetheless detain Johnny and offer his release in exchange for footage of the Burma Road's operation. Before deciding whether to help Tokyo, however, Williams escapes with the help of a fellow Westerner and makes his way to Mandalay, where he encounters Gene Tierney, in yellowface, as Haoli Young, a beautiful Vassar-educated, English-speaking Chinese woman who, with her father, operates a Kunming orphanage. Haoli, patterned after Madame Jiang, and Johnny fall madly in love, and Tierney, whom the *New York Times* dubbed a "wan Madonna," uses her considerable charms to lure Williams to China's side. After discovering that the "friendly Westerner" is actually a spy for Tokyo, Williams bests the agent in a slugfest and then races to Kunming to save his beloved Haoli, her father, and the orphans from the Japanese, who, he has learned, plan to bomb the city. Johnny arrives as the bombs fall. Flames already engulf the orphanage, and the father and some of the children lie dead inside. Haoli is alive, and the couple are reunited briefly before their unlikely romance is tragically cut short as she is killed attempting to rescue the survivors. Distraught, the hero completes his reformation into a committed internationalist warrior. Johnny shoulders an unattended machine gun and avenges his "China girl" by strafing Japanese planes.[41]

This "East-West romance," as the *Los Angeles Times* called it, symbolized and lent emotional sustenance to the actual Sino-American partnership. In that respect, *China Girl* resembled *Song of Russia* (1944), *I Live in Grosvenor Square*, or any other such Allied love story. Zanuck took a significant departure from custom, however, by featuring an interracial romance. The antimiscegenation rule enforced by the Production Code Administration (PCA) prohibited nonwhite performers such as Anna May Wong (who was never considered for the part) from appearing opposite white males as the object of their desire. Only the casting of a Caucasian actress in that role licensed Fox to skirt the Production Code in the name of meeting its wartime obligation to promote Allied unity.[42]

While *China Girl* may have been the first to test the strange discursive waters, it was not the last film where interracial romance, enabled by yellowface, bridged the East-West divide. *Blood on the Sun* (1945) starred James Cagney as Nick Condon, a fictional American newspaperman working in interwar Tokyo who discovered the Tanaka Memorial. Although a forgery, as Tokyo claimed at the time, the memorial was taken to be an authentic document authored by the onetime prime minister, Baron Tanaka Giichi, outlining Japan's plan for world domination beginning with the conquest of China and ending with the defeat of the United States. The Tanaka Memorial figured prominently in Capra's orientation films. *Blood on the Sun*, produced by Cagney's brother, William, also took

Gene Tierney in yellowface as Haoli Young, the Eurasian object of the affection of Johnny Williams (George Montgomery) in Daryl F. Zanuck's Sino-American romance, *China Girl* (Twentieth Century–Fox, 1942). Photofest/© Twentieth Century–Fox.

the plan as genuine and traces Nick's effort to spirit the memorial out of Japan to publish it and raise international awareness of Tokyo's plot. After several socks to Japanese jaws administered by the ever-pugnacious Cagney, his character exposes the plan before the world court of public opinion.

Nick receives critical help from Iris Hilliard, a beautiful Eurasian spy (biracial, she was described as having Chinese and American parentage) working on China's behalf. Iris is played by Sylvia Sidney, a Caucasian actress in yellowface, one of several white performers in chinoiserie in *Blood on the Sun*. The part represented a comeback for Sidney, who had not appeared on-screen in four years. A specialist of sorts as a result of what one critic described as her "slightly Oriental features," Sidney drew on her previous experience performing Cio-Cio San in *Madame Butterfly* (1932) opposite Cary Grant. Mesmerized by her exotic charms, Cagney's Nick falls head over heels for Sidney's Iris. Here again, yellowface provided flexibility that enabled the Cagneys to negotiate the PCA's miscegenation ban and depict a transcendent interracial romance analogizing, normalizing, and sentimentalizing bilateral ties. Furthermore, Iris's phony appearance, combined with her pro-Allied politics and biracial biography, permitted audiences to accept her union with a white American male, for it was apparent that white skin lurked just below the yellow makeup. That racial mask, in other words, enabled Iris/Sidney to pass between East and West and claim membership in the Allied community as defined by Americans. No longer the Other, Iris, like Haoli and Charlie Chan, is neither Chinese nor American but a cosmopolitan, hybridized wanderer among worlds.

As one might imagine, Zanuck's and the Cagneys' sharp detours from convention—their films were rare exceptions to the accepted rules—provoked considerable comment when each premiered at Grauman's Chinese Theatre in Los Angeles, *China Girl* in January 1943 and *Blood on the Sun* in June 1945. Grauman's, which hosted the wartime premieres of most pro-China movies, must have facilitated flights of fancy among audiences, with its Orientalist design and the statue of Wong that graced its lobby. There, film critic Margaret Thorp believed that viewers could imaginatively travel to "the Place de la Concorde, Broadway at midnight, the Himalayas, or any one of a dozen South Sea islands." Establishment critics professed openness to and fascination with the yellowface romances. The *Los Angeles Times* supported the "transcendent passion" evident between Haoli and Johnny in *China Girl* for reducing Sino-American differences and commingling Allied identities. To date, OWI officials believed, Fox had done "the best job of promoting China's cause" because its film's "Chinese" characters contradicted negative, Orientalist preconceptions of the "mysterious East." *China Girl* was certain to "boost" U.S. confidence in China since it featured allies who demonstrated "fortitude." Tierney's Haoli was deemed a far cry from "the slant-eyed Oriental siren" all too common to the screen, and her father, a Westernized scholar, offered a refreshing corrective to the stereotypical "Chinese laundryman" familiar to moviegoers.[43]

To be sure, some observers expressed coded disapproval of *China Girl*'s interracial coupling even if it was mediated through Tierney's yellowface masquerade. *PM* printed a letter from an irate reader who objected to Haoli's manipulative, sexual appeal to Johnny and by extension to the viewing public. Yet although *China Girl* was judged a major "disappointment" that fell short of what viewers expected of Zanuck, Hecht, and director Henry Hathaway, critics objected on aesthetic rather than moral grounds. The *Washington Post* damned Fox for giving theatergoers an "inconsequential" love story. The *New York Mirror* panned Tierney's "unconvincing Asiatic part." And the *Los Angeles Times* remained of two minds: the same Sino-American romance that transcended boundaries and built bilateral understanding also appeared manufactured and thus unmoving, not least because it was doomed from the start. Those versed in the rules of the cinematic game knew well in advance that Haoli must die because she had transgressed the Production Code and the PCA simply "would not permit her to live and marry an American." (Interestingly, however, Sidney's Iris was permitted to live and remain united with her white love interest, perhaps because she was presented as Eurasian rather than Chinese.)[44]

Although modern critics may rightly deplore Tierney's and Sidney's characterizations as degrading racial parodies, fascinated contemporary whites welcomed them as progressive depictions that dignified Chinese, promoted racial tolerance, and advanced Sino-American understanding. However, wartime liberals could adopt this position only because yellowface perpetuated Orientalist stereotypes that sustained white supremacy and assigned Chinese figures to a subordinate position in the customary racial hierarchy. Various reviewers described Sidney's Iris as a "beauteous Eurasian girl," a "bewitchingly mysterious Chinese-American spy," or a "Eurasian Mati Hari [*sic*]." *New York Times* fashion writer Barbara Berch carefully recounted for interested readers the daily on-set makeup and hairstyling regimen that magically transformed Sidney into character. (The part, not incidentally, briefly restarted the actor's career, and she went on to star in several more films over the next few years.) The *Christian Science Monitor* commended the production team's makeup artists and Caucasian bit players for bringing realistic Asian characters to the screen. And the *Los Angeles Times* applauded the Cagneys for being "enlightened" enough to put Nick Condon's romantic "interest in the half-caste girl" on display. The San Francisco Press Club found *Blood on the Sun*'s thesis of international harmony so compelling that it recommended the movie for showing at the United Nations Organization conference then ongoing in the city.[45]

Yellowface made a final ignominious appearance in *Dragon Seed*, MGM's foremost pro-China contribution. Based on Pearl S. Buck's 1942 novel by that name, MGM's production can be thought of as either *The Good Earth* retrofitted to wartime or a Chinese companion to *North Star*, the studio's pro-Soviet picture. The film looked back at the beginning of the Second Sino-Japanese War though the eyes of Ling Tan (Walter Huston, *Mission to Moscow*'s star) and his family, stereotypically simple, decent peasants who desperately clung to their land as Japan's invaders encroached. Ling Tan and his brood (wife, sons, daughters-in-law, and grandchildren) at first approached the enemy with equanimity, reasoning that the Japanese could be treated as but the latest in a long line of foreign barbarians who came and went. Isolated and independent—like farmers everywhere, by implication—the Tan family remained blissfully ignorant of the world beyond their little valley and felt unconnected to people in the next village, much less across the sea. They dismissed speculation, for example, that some unseen "stranger" tended the other side of the land beneath their feet, supposed to be a humorous take on the old "dig to China" joke.

When the OWI invited ROC consul T. K. Chang to review the script, he responded with a thirteen-page memorandum enumerating his many concerns. Chang's objections included inauthentic dialogue and the characterization of China's peasantry as passive, "stubbornly stupid," and "totally ignorant to the impact of the war" and of the wider world. The OWI concurred with his analysis, and the agency advised MGM to make revisions that accentuated both Chinese subjectivity and Sino-American solidarity.[46]

MGM made many of the recommended adjustments, with the result that the final product traces the intellectual development of *Dragon Seed*'s protagonists, a journey that begins with their awakening to the enemy's cruelty. Cartoonish, the brutish, sneering Japanese "devils" descend on and lay waste to Ling Tan's village, indiscriminately raping

women, slaughtering innocent peasants, and virtually enslaving survivors. What is to be done? Should the family shelter in place and collabo-
rate with the evildoers? Or is active resistance the best course? Daughter-
in-law Jade Tan influences the decision. A protofeminist, as one would
expect from a Katharine Hepburn character, Jade bristles at her station in
the traditional, patriarchal countryside. A free thinker, she desires nothing more than to expand her horizons by reading the books denied to her.
A freedom fighter, she convinces her neighbors to resist the Japanese to
win liberty, regain dignity, and improve the world for future generations.
Persuaded, Ling Tan, a peaceful man with no appetite for mindless ven-
geance, sets his crops ablaze and abandons his land—his precious plot
of good earth—to join his countrymen's westward trek toward the republic's new capital in Chongqing. Jade and the others escape to the hills to
become part of the guerrilla resistance. The OWI subsequently praised
MGM's "inspiring presentation of the people of Fighting China," which
was sure to raise U.S. confidence.[47]

More important, Jade, the foremost representative of the "new China"
rising from the war's ashes, encourages the village elders to widen their
gaze and see themselves in league with others. Under her tutelage, Ling
Tan comes to understand that there is, in fact, another human being on
the other side of his earth, an American ally who cherishes similar aspirations. Before departing his farm, Huston's character delivers a lengthy
soliloquy expressing his newfound feeling of interdependence with that
American "stranger," who although unseen seems palpable and familiar.
Speaking proverbially, as did all the film's "Chinese" characters, Ling Tan
recalls the words of a wise man: "There is one sun and one moon for all. If
that is true, all share the sun and moon. Why should we not also all share
the earth? This valley is not the world, but only part of the world. And
there are others like me whose faces I have never seen. Elsewhere, there
are men who love peace and long for good and who will fight to get these
things. So the stranger is no longer a stranger to me but a man like me."
Lamenting only that he could not speak with his faraway friend, Huston's
Ling Tan receives assurance from Hepburn's Jade that face-to-face contact is incidental to international congress, as decent people everywhere
speak the same language of peace. Huston agrees, adding, "Somehow
tonight, I feel that there is a power sweeping around the world bringing us all together with that stranger." In sum, within the context of the
1940s, Hepburn and Huston—in yellowface—deliver a message of color-
blind brotherhood meant as a statement against racial prejudice and in
favor of interracial harmony.

Two years of negotiations had produced what the OWI perceived as an outstanding product. Completed in mid-1944, *Dragon Seed* showed Americans that "the common people of China are akin to ourselves" and demonstrated to the "fighting peoples of the United Nations that we are all bound together by a unity which transcends differences in customs and language." A handful of critics were equally impressed. *Dragon Seed* struck Buck, an interested observer, as proof that motion pictures could exert "leadership in sowing the seeds of greater understanding between Asia and the West." And the picture performed well enough at the box office: *Showmen's Trade Review*, a trade publication, ranked it among the year's most popular attractions.[48]

The OWI had badly misjudged the situation, however, and again demonstrated its talent for making bad pictures worse. Perhaps no movie other than *Mission to Moscow* fell further short of its propaganda objectives. Most critics savaged *Dragon Seed* when it premiered in July 1944. A small minority objected on principle to its reliance on yellowface, a device that in this case inhibited genuine Sino-American understanding. Declaring *Dragon Seed* an "unimaginably bad movie," James Agee disliked the fact that European Americans, dressed in "pajamas" and appearing "with their eyes painfully plastered in an Oriental oblique," played Chinese parts. Their strange wardrobe and makeup not only created an air of artificiality (the exact opposite of what MGM had intended) but also stifled the actors, leading to lumbering performances. The otherwise conservative *Wall Street Journal* ruled that whites should not "take Oriental parts." Hepburn's and Huston's ill-advised use of yellowface "badly handicapped" the "art of make-believe" in *Dragon Seed*, a movie that despite the best efforts of the studio's makeup department stood not a "Chinaman's chance of [making] most of the featured actors look much like Chinamen."[49]

Most others accepted yellowface as a given. Chang made no reference to it in his extensive remarks. Alice MacMahon earned an Academy Award nomination for her supporting role as Ling Tan's wife. Indeed, the majority of critics attacked *Dragon Seed*'s yellowface performances not on principle but on the grounds that the performances themselves, aside from MacMahon's, were poor, unconvincing, and injurious to the illusion of authenticity on which good theater depended. Chang and others objected to the artists' phony accents and speech patterns—what he called the "queer expressions imputed to the Chinese." His long list of objectionable dialogue included characters who spoke of having "big news in my mouth," directed others to "wait 500 heartbeats," or addressed their elders as "my father" or "my mother." "Honestly," Chang wrote, "Chinese do not talk like that." MGM and the OWI ignored his advice, however, leading the *New York Times* to complain that the words of Akim Tamiroff, a Russian-born actor who played a supporting "Chinese" role, fell "upon the ear as resonantly as the sound of gefilte fish banged against a temple gong." The leads received near unanimous condemnation. Hepburn's accent struck listeners as if it came from an elite northeastern college (she had attended Bryn Mawr) rather than the Chinese countryside. Huston's penchant for "poetic" phraseology rang a false note as well. Their verbal tricks, adopted in an apparent attempt "to suggest the Chinese language," sounded contrived, as if they were drawn from "an international grab bag," according to the *Chicago Tribune*. The whole effect—the sound of the actors' awkward speech; the sight of them wearing strange makeup and clothes, which chief *New York Times* film critic Bosley Crowther found "something of a shock"—ruined the illusion of verisimilitude. Given a "jolt," audiences un-suspended their disbelief. It was difficult to identify with on-screen foreigners, Crowther summarized, when one so easily realized that they were just "popular stars dressed up." At nearly two and a half hours long, *Dragon Seed* was a tortuous experience that "pretzeled" backs and benumbed other body parts "beyond medical repair."[50]

Paramount's *China* starred Alan Ladd as David Jones, an unprincipled American oil salesman in occupied China who expressed no qualms about trading with Japan. An "apostle of isolationism," according to the OWI, Jones—a Pacific analogue to another expatriate capitalist, Humphrey Bogart's Rick Blaine in *Casablanca* (1942)—sticks his neck out for no one because nonneutrality interferes with the pursuit of commerce. It is possible to do business with Tokyo, and business is good. The oilman, interested only in the almighty dollar, considers Japanese good paying customers but regards the Chinese refugees who clog the road to Shanghai, where another big business deal awaits, as mere livestock. "This is not my war," declares Jones, sounding much like Johnny in Zanuck's *China Girl*, and adding that he has some "pretty good friends" in Tokyo. Heartless, he even resents the fact that his more humane employee, Johnny Sparrow (William Bendix), harbors a rescued orphan, an adorable infant who appeals to "every ounce" of human emotions, wrote the *New Yorker*.[51]

Yet over time and incrementally, Jones comes to see the error of acting as a merchant of death whose petroleum fuels the Japanese war machine against China, for whose people he develops paternalistic affection. Jones's worldview begins to change when his path crosses that of

Carolyn Grant (Loretta Young), an American missionary-teacher shepherding her Chinese students to safety as the Japanese encroach. Lovely and willful, Grant leverages the playboy's romantic interest in her to convince him to see the herd astride the road as human, as "poor, frightened" people "bombed out of their homes." In addition, the schoolgirls in her care speak early and often about their aspirations to "build a new China" through education. The scales fall from Jones's eyes, and his vehicle, now overloaded with Grant, her students, and the orphan, detours to the country home of Tan Ying (Quon), one of Grant's pupils, where the group shelters overnight. After departing the next morning, Grant and Jones discover that Tan Ying has remained behind. Fearing for her safety, they return, only to find that Japanese forces have descended on the farm, murdered the orphaned child and Tan Ying's parents, and raped the girl. Face-to-face with the enemy's brutality, which is reminiscent of the Rape of Nanking, Jones undergoes his final change of heart, mowing down the offending Japanese soldiers with a machine gun and joining local Chinese guerrillas, who welcome him into their fold as a "brother." No longer dubious of his character, Grant professes her love for the reformed hero, who gives a speech about his newfound solidarity with "millions of little guys" everywhere before leading a successful if sweaty guerrilla offensive. Although martyred during it, the erstwhile Sinophobe has done his bit for the Allied cause.

China's conversion narrative, Hollywood's standard motif for bringing Allied solidarity to the big screen, ends, predictably enough, with an American hero's alignment with the ROC. However, Paramount's tale of Sino-American harmony rested on paternalistic foundations. It reinforced the impression given by U.S. culture, generally speaking, that bilateral engagement entailed an American parental responsibility to altruistically protect and rescue Chinese dependents threatened by external aggressors and largely incapable of independent action. Granted, the Chinese resistance depicted on-screen demonstrated some capacity for self-sufficiency, and the movie avoided yellowface characterizations. And critics praised director John Farrow for casting Chinese American performers—Quon, Yung, Philip Ahn, and Richard Loo, among others—in supporting roles that lent greater authenticity to the film. But those nonwhite characters, realistic though they may have been, only served as window dressing for and as helpmates to the white leads, who stood at the center of the action and made all the decisions. Ladd's David Jones, like Woody in *Flying Tigers*, amends his mien as he develops sympathy for and becomes determined to save downtrodden Chinese subordinates. He mows down the Japanese rapists and takes charge of the climactic offensive that decimates enemy forces. Even the OWI, which expressed confidence that Jones's internationalist transformation would improve Sino-American "friendship and understanding," remained concerned about *China*'s typecasting of "simple" and "ineffectual" Chinese figures who looked to Americans for salvation. The schoolgirls whose safety appeared entirely dependent on Grant gave officials the most pause. Worried that such depictions combined to create a "subtly disparaging treatment," the agency advised Paramount to make revisions that strengthened Chinese agency.[52]

Aside from the guerrillas, however, the OWI's recommendations had little discernible effect on the final product, a corny, "absurd," and "cheap" thriller that received a chilly critical response. While the *Brooklyn Eagle* endorsed the film's "sympathetic portrayal" of Chinese, *PM* wrote that Paramount had given the public a phony "Hollywood view of China." The magazine urged moviegoers who insisted on seeing *China* to adopt a "bifocal attitude" that would enable them to enjoy the action but filter out "all the bad, the stereotyped, and the silly."[53]

Fox's *The Keys of the Kingdom*, the war's last major pro-China release, had a long and troubled production history that points to Orientalism's endurance. In 1941, megaproducer David O. Selznick purchased the screen rights to A. J. Cronin's best seller, whose protagonist was Father Francis Chisholm, an early-twentieth-century Scottish missionary often at odds with Catholic Church authorities as a consequence of his unorthodox beliefs and methods. When Selznick took the PCA's temperature prior to production, he found Hollywood's internal censor lukewarm at best. Led by lay Catholic Joseph I. Breen, the PCA opposed the story's portrayal of the church as rigid and doctrinaire. Selznick suspended the project and in November 1942 sold his property to Fox, which for some reason had fewer qualms about touching that third rail of moviemaking. The OWI had since become operational and previewed a synopsis of Nunnally Johnson's script. Appalled, the OWI registered serious concerns about the story's handling of not only the church—which indeed served as the villain—but also China. Father Chisholm came off as a religious imperialist who "invades a foreign land, with the avowed purpose of forcing [his] way of thinking" on Chinese, stereotyped as "ignorant heathen[s] who must be shown the light" by a Westerner. The plotline negated China's freedom to worship, one of the Four Freedoms for which Americans and their allies were said to be fighting. Were it to come to fruition, the movie also would not improve U.S. understanding of the "new" China; rather, its focus on the "old" China seemed likely to perpetuate misconceptions of and even hostility toward America's modern ally. For example, the synopsis featured warlords who mistreated Westerners, thereby introducing a racial wildcard likely "to arouse American antagonism to the Chinese" and counteract U.S. propaganda, which strove "to unite all races in a fight against a common enemy." The OWI demanded major rewrites and lectured the studio on its obligation to uphold Allied goodwill: "There is great need today for a more thorough comprehension of present-day China's united, intelligent, courageous contribution to the war." Fox's presentation of "Chinese as ignorant, fear-ridden, and disunited can only confuse and retard our understanding" and "cause resentment among the Chinese," allies who deserved some "consideration."[54]

Another year of rewrites supervised by producer Joseph L. Mankiewicz only worsened the situation. The revised screenplay submitted in January 1944 suffered from "serious problems" that, if left uncorrected, would render the film unsuitable for either domestic or foreign consumption. "Chaos," "confusion," and backwardness still reigned in the historical drama set amid the Qing Dynasty's fall and the ROC's rise. Scripted locals treated illness with exorcisms, patriarchs sold unwanted girls into sexual slavery, and peasant "heathens" stoned Western missionaries. Bandits continued to plague the land, and whatever nationalist forces opposed them appeared directionless and dispirited: a young officer complained bitterly about dying for a "ridiculous dream to be called the Chinese Republic."[55]

Worse still, Mankiewicz's script added derogatory dialogue. One character, Dr. Willie Tulloch (played in the film by Thomas Mitchell, better known as Uncle Billy in 1946's *It's a Wonderful Life*), joked about his Chinese laundryman back home. Another, Mother Maria Veronica (Rosa Stradner, Mankiewicz's wife), characterized Chinese as the "lowliest subjects of God's kingdom." Vincent Price's Monsignor Angus Mealy wondered aloud about Chinese racial inferiority and the "inscrutable Oriental mind." All such contradictions of the UN's stated aspirations for international equality struck the OWI as potential fuel for "antagonism between the white and yellow races." Little wonder, then, that the OWI again called for significant amendments, as Fox's project disserved Sino-American goodwill. The agency reiterated that "China is today taking her place" among "the four great United Nations of the world. She is contributing immeasurably toward the defeat of our Japanese enemy, and is destined to play an important role in the peace to come. To portray the Chinese people as backward, superstitious, ignorant, cowardly, and malicious is to insult one of our most important allies in a manner which would be deeply resented."[56]

Eager to begin shooting, Fox, having just announced that Gregory Peck would headline, hurriedly revised and resubmitted the screenplay less than a month later. The minor alterations left the OWI's concerns unmet, however. Government publicists again registered their opposition in no uncertain terms: the negative presentation of "heathen" Chinese as "dirty, cowardly, and dishonest people" would not only "cause tremendous resentment among our Chinese allies" but also obstruct the mutual understanding considered so "fundamental" to "a better postwar world." The OWI played its trump card, warning Fox that if the movie were not amended, the U.S. Office of Censorship would classify the movie as a "derogatory picturization of one of the United Nations" and refuse it an export license.[57]

For its part, the ROC embassy lodged an official protest with Fox, and the consulate's Chang sent a letter to Breen alerting the PCA to the "serious distortion" plaguing Cronin's book, the project's source. Studio president Wendell Willkie received a complaint from China Defense Supplies, a private aid group with strong ties to the White House. Now faced with united and determined opposition, Fox finally relented. Wishing to avoid "any international embarrassment," the studio hired a Chinese national and a Catholic priest to serve as technical advisers who vetted the picture and provided the studio with political cover. Many of the problematic characterizations, scenarios, and dialogue—including the line about the "ridiculous dream" of a republic—were eliminated, leading Father Albert O'Hara, the Catholic adviser, to report that the church's and China's good reputations survived intact. Fox added a foreword informing audiences that the history about to unfold on-screen was far removed from conditions in wartime China. And as a confidence-building measure, the studio invited a top OWI official to tour the set. He came away impressed that the movie would ultimately demonstrate China's progress over the three decades depicted, from the first set's "primitive" village of rudimentary straw-thatched shacks to the third set's town of brick houses that bespoke the arrival of "civilization" and evoked middle America.[58]

With the authorities' preliminary blessing in hand, production raced ahead, and a rough cut was completed by December 1944. Although not entirely satisfied, the OWI gave its approval. Whatever offensive dialogue remained—the laundryman joke and the reference to Chinese as God's "lowliest" children were among the most egregious examples—was mitigated, the agency felt, by the missionaries' evident acceptance of racial equality in the Lord's eyes. Told in flashback, *The Keys of the Kingdom*, released in U.S. theaters that holiday season, reviewed Father Chisholm's thirty-year mission to China. The narrative endorsed East-West cooperation, as Chisholm's steadily growing flock of Chinese converts attested. That congregation, led by Joseph (Fong), Chisholm's longest-serving and most devoted follower, mirrored the republic's development. And although the subject was not explicitly addressed, the movie drew on Jiang's conversion to Christianity, which many U.S. observers, Luce included, took as proof of Sino-American spiritual convergence.[59]

At the same time, *The Keys of the Kingdom* exemplified the paternal missionary spirit embedded in the culture at large. To its credit, *Keys* did not repeat the yellowface mistake committed by *Dragon Seed, China Girl*, or the Charlie Chan movies. Rather, it followed Hollywood's customary casting of Asian Americans, here Fong and others, in secondary roles, where they (literally) supported and acted as helpmates to white leads. True, nonwhite performers could bring dignity to those parts, and Fong's portrait of Dr. Chung in *Thirty Seconds over Tokyo* provided an outstanding case in point. More often than not, though, such characterizations succumbed to racial stereotyping. And in *Keys*, Fong's Joseph loyally and stereotypically served Peck's Father Chisholm as a "devoted Chinese [house]boy," observed the *New York Times*. Discursively speaking, Father Chisholm acted as a surrogate parent who, like *China*'s Carolyn Grant or Woody in *Flying Tigers*, effectively adopted and saved Chinese orphans from that metaphorical Shanghai station. Peck's character unapologetically addressed even his adult congregants as his "children," and the good priest saw fit to uplift and Christianize his local charges. He and his colleague, Dr. Tulloch, modernized China by spreading the blessings of Western medicine.[60]

The majority of moviegoers applauded the film's paternalistic outlook. Although *Keys* received mixed reviews, Peck—gifted with a distinctive, fatherly demeanor—won praise for his "arresting" performance and was anointed overnight as a new star. Only his second movie (after the 1944 pro-Soviet drama *Days of Glory*), *Keys* earned Peck his first Academy Award nomination as Best Actor.

In retrospect, propagandists and filmmakers strove to humanize and win support for America's wartime ally but ended up perpetuating gross misperceptions of China and its relationship to the United States. The owi and Hollywood had received an impossible mission. The more they

Father Francis Chisholm (Gregory Peck) heals a Chinese boy with modern Western medicine in *The Keys of the Kingdom* (Twentieth Century–Fox, 1944), Peck's breakthrough picture. Photofest/© Twentieth Century–Fox.

strained to depict Jiang's China as democratic, modern, and united, the less believable that portrait became. If opium dens and white slavery rings no longer marred Hollywood's China, then another kind of fantasy-land emerged, one that helps to explain the surprise, disappointment, and anger that would follow Mao's revolution in 1949 and lead some observers to ask, "Who lost China?," a question that took America's paternal responsibility for China's welfare as a given. The big screen obfuscated the running political battle between Jiang's nationalists and Mao's communists, conspicuous by their absence from wartime films, and inflated expectations that the former could not fulfill. Jiang appeared less and less capable of meeting the unrealizable standards Hollywood set for him even before the war ended. Whereas 56 percent of Americans had supported a permanent U.S. alliance with China in November 1943, that figure plummeted to only 42 percent in April 1944, not much greater than the minority (35 percent) who favored such an arrangement with the distrusted Soviet Union.[61] To be fair, such lukewarm support stemmed from the fact that the ROC, despite FDR's insistence to the contrary, was not a world power, a fourth policeman on a par with the United States, Great Britain, and the Soviet Union. In reality, China was a middle power and would remain so until the People's Republic's rise decades later.

Somewhat paradoxically, American disregard for Chinese capability also rested on a presumption of racial hierarchy that insisted on Western supremacy over Asian subordinates, be those imaginary subalterns domestic or foreign. The white majority simply was not yet prepared to see Chinese as full and equal members of the human race, much less of the Allied family. Hollywood movies reinforced the prevailing racial norms that underwrote Chinese exclusion. When given an opportunity to do so, filmmakers never considered taking a courageous stand by truly dignifying the Chinese ally. Instead, Hollywood fell back on conventional stereotypes and demeaning characterizations that let the status quo go unchallenged and belied UN pretensions to equity. However exemplary Charlie Chan may have been, Sidney Toler's yellowface portrayal, like Katharine Hepburn's or Gene Tierney's performances elsewhere, more than counteracted positive images. The major studios cast Chinese American actors exclusively in supporting roles. Anna May Wong's performances as powerful, independent Chinese protagonists in a couple of low-budget B movies stood as the exceptions that proved the rule. And the rule, in this case, was set by Hollywood's box office calculations, personnel policies, and PCA, whose antimiscegenation clause necessitated racial masquerade to negotiate the color line when dramatizing Sino-American romance, movie language that ordinarily bespoke internationalism when unburdened by race. Fox's *Keys*, Paramount's *China*, Republic's *Flying Tigers*, and their ilk illustrated the acceptable view of East-West relations—that is, as a family indeed, but a patriarchal one in which the United States acted as the parent tutoring the childlike ROC on its journey toward maturation within the confines of the American Century. However comforting that Orientalist narrative may have been, it militated against genuine intercultural understanding and ultimately disserved Americans by blinding them to China's complexities.

CONCLUSION

Together, Hollywood and Washington projected an image of the United Nations as a family of nations. A term of endearment, the analogy normalized the otherwise unnatural alliance, personalized each of the UN's Great Powers, and emotionalized the linkages among them. It had the added advantage of making easy sense to moviegoers, enabling filmmakers to reinterpret the UN's constituent diplomatic partnerships as international romances or household dramas. A linguistic big tent that accommodated the Allies' obvious differences, the comparison also implied trust and permanence, suggesting (in vain, it turned out) that the unbreakable bonds of kindred nations would remain intact after the war's last shots had been fired.

Testaments to international familiarity accumulated as victory neared, and they bespoke the extent to which the language of kinship resonated. They came from Yalta, site of the penultimate Allied summit in February 1945, whose prime, valedictory image of the war's conquering heroes—Churchill, Roosevelt, and Stalin—bookended Tehran and reaffirmed the final communiqué's optimistic words to the effect that the same multilateralism that had won the war would secure the peace as well. FDR put a positive spin on Yalta's intense internal "atmosphere" by likening it to that which often prevailed within "a family," thus confirming author Basil Mathews's observation that the Allies' evident disagreements were to be expected among kin.[1]

They came from the Elbe River, where divisions of the U.S. Army and Red Army met in April on their respective paths toward Berlin. It was hardly accidental that newsreel cameramen and photographers were present to record the symbolic event. Sensing a photo op, Soviet and American propagandists arranged events beforehand and directed the action, instructing their soldier-subjects to pose for the cameras to make the most of the made-for-media moment. One staged shot featured a couple of ordinary Joes, one American, the other Soviet, locked in fraternal embrace, mugging for the camera to their buddies' amusement. *The True Glory*, the documentary about the Normandy landings that premiered in September, replayed that and other images of Allied brotherhood, narrated by the off-screen voices of enlisted people. A GI recalled the moment when his unit arrived at the Elbe and was warmly greeted as comrades by the "Rooskies." "We did okay, but I'd hate to think where we'd have been without those guys," he added.

They came, as well, from the victory celebrations that erupted in Moscow, London, New York, and elsewhere following Germany's surrender on 8 May. While revelers commemorated national triumphs, they also paid homage to the United Nations alliance, whose endurance defied expectations and made success possible. London's celebrations were the most cosmopolitan, since so many foreign dignitaries and soldiers were stationed there. Britons sought out the some four hundred thousand U.S. servicemen and -women who remained in the United Kingdom on V-E day to bask in the glory of their shared accomplishment. The Union Jack, Stars and Stripes, and Hammer and Sickle flew alongside one another in Piccadilly Circus, where "American sailors and laughing girls formed a conga line," wrote English novelist Mollie Panter-Downes. Amid the chaos, a jubilant American GI hugged an English matron, another moment of transatlantic kinship captured by an official photographer. Similar scenes took place around the country. Recuperating soldier Christen T. Jonassen and a friend were strolling the streets of Sherborne, Dorset, when pubgoers invited the Yanks inside for a celebratory round of drinks. After several toasts, more drinks, and choruses of British and American songs, the revelers poured into the streets, where GIs, Britons, and assorted UN service people "all marched and sang, linked tightly together." Jonassen recalled the "infectious" feeling of losing one's individual identity amid the festivities and becoming part of a multinational crowd: he lost "consciousness of the 'I' and became one with the other, and like one joyous, free being [we] went sweeping through the streets of old Sherborne."[2]

The fact and fiction of globalism also sprang from the United Nations

Allied cameramen and photographers cover the Soviet-American linkup at the Elbe River in April 1945. Signal Corps photo 111-SC-203902-S, Still Picture Unit, National Archives and Records Administration II, College Park, Md.

Conference on International Organization held in San Francisco. It was there that the seed of the ad hoc UN alliance finally blossomed into a world association, the family of nations long envisioned by all manner of wartime political talk. Sponsored by the four Allied powers, the conference welcomed delegations representing forty-six other countries that subscribed to the principles embodied in the Declaration of the United Nations. The meeting itself demonstrated how modern transportation and communication drew the international community together. Delegations traveled to California by sea, rail, and air. An intricate on-site voice communication system allowed conferees to negotiate with their counterparts or to confer with their home governments. An enormous international press corps reported events to audiences worldwide. According to a breathless account by the United Nations Information Organization (UNIO), more than 2,500 print journalists cabled more than 150,000 words per day from San Francisco. Radio commentators "were

An American GI and a Soviet soldier share a fraternal embrace after the Elbe linkup. The sign behind them reads, "East Meets West." Signal Corps photo 111-SC-205228, Still Picture Unit, National Archives and Records Administration II, College Park, Md.

constantly on the air giving accounts and interpretations of [the] latest developments." Newsreel cameramen shot some 160,000 feet of film, and still photographers took thousands of pictures.[3]

The conference, which began in April, served as a family reunion of sorts. Delegates spent a significant portion of the next two months in San Francisco discussing which countries—Soviet republics, Latin American states, defeated enemies—were eligible for admittance to the "family of nations," a phrase that frequents the documentary record. That debate ended with the Charter of the United Nations Organization (UNO). Infused with the optimism so overabundant in the air, the charter's preamble styled the UNO as a utopian international community, where members "practice tolerance and live together in peace with one another as good neighbors." Residents would have to patrol the community, for aggressors would inevitably interrupt the idyll. But if the UNO's good neighbors fulfilled their collective security obligations, peace would prevail,

"Jubilant American soldier [Private First Class Melvin Weiss] hugs motherly English woman and victory smiles light the faces of happy service men and civilians at Piccadilly Circus, London, celebrating Germany's unconditional surrender." Signal Corps photo, 7 May 1945, 111-SC-205398, Still Picture Unit, National Archives and Records Administration II, College Park, Md.

"standards of life" would rise, and "faith in fundamental human rights" would spread. The "century of the common man" prophesied by Henry Wallace appeared to be at hand.

To become reality, the long-dreamed human cooperative only awaited the document's signature and ratification. As such, the conference—indeed, the entire internationalist movement—culminated on 26 June, when delegates of the fifty participating nations, representing more than 80 percent of the earth's population, signed the UNO Charter. As the delegations, led by those of the sponsor countries, entered the specially designed futuristic stage of the San Francisco Opera House to sign the text, the act of political theater fostered the impression that a brave new world was beginning. A white circular table stood at center stage, bathed by klieg lights and backed by all the flags of the member states plus the UNO's new emblem, a globe cradled by olive branches resembling dove-like wings of peace. Like any number of wartime events—Tehran, the Elbe linkup, Yalta—the UNO's birth provided a photo op orchestrated for the media, specifically the print journalists, photographers, and newsreel cameramen who perched on scaffolding to witness and record the seminal procession for worldwide audiences and posterity alike.[4]

Those and other snapshots, arranged sequentially, tell a story of the United Nations that plays like a Hollywood movie. Its plotline, which could have inspired the *Star Wars* chronicle, pitting the benign Rebel Alliance against the evil Galactic Empire, followed a now-familiar trajectory: as a result of foreign aggression, the Allies, an odd assortment of flawed but noble misfits, necessarily went to war against seemingly invincible adversaries, the Axis powers. Early on, the protagonist UN, in real life and on film alike, suffered a string of dispiriting setbacks. At lowest ebb, however, the plucky underdog picked itself up by its own bootstraps. Much like the multiethnic military unit in a prototypical World War II–era combat drama, the heroes united in the crucible of war, found a common identity as a family of nations, and turned the tide. Like any Hollywood rags-to-riches tale, this picture ended happily when Japan surrendered on 15 August 1945, and the United Nations, having snatched victory from the jaws of defeat, reestablished peace for the good citizens of the world. Fighting for self-defense and freedom, the Allies' motives appeared beyond reproach. God was on their side. Whereas the enemy's leaders (Hitler, Mussolini, and Tojo) came straight from central casting as tyrannical embodiments of villainy, the UN's good guys (Churchill, Jiang, Roosevelt, and even Stalin) became media darlings. All the while, ordi-

Newsreel cameras roll as the Republic of China's delegation, led by V. K. Wellington Koo, signs the United Nations Charter at the San Francisco Conference, 26 June 1945. UN photo 236035, United Nations Photo Library.

nary Americans, Britons, Chinese, and Soviets acted as a cast of millions and participated as consumers in the romanticized narrative of Allied affection that unfolded on-screen.

That narrative helped the Allies win the war and the peace. Words did not do it alone. Boots on the ground supplied by industry won the war. Facts—including that the Allies needed one another's strengths to realize their common ambition of defeating the Axis—determined why the UN arose and endured. And material conditions—the desire of the foremost Allied powers to consolidate their supreme positions and forgo a debilitating third world war—gave birth to the UNO. Yet images made invaluable contributions at each step along the way because, as Richard Overy has pointed out, they staked the moral high ground for the Allies, unified them behind a common endeavor, and fueled their will to win a cause that, to all appearances, seemed fully justified, liberative, and noble. The

Allies won the battle of ideas, and cinema acted as a major weapon in their propaganda arsenal.[5]

Motion pictures exerted a profound effect on home front Americans, most of whom watched the war unfold from a safe distance. Art met life through the magic of the movie of the United Nations, a cinematic *Reader's Digest* that gave viewers a simplified, unambiguous, and appealing summary of what was in reality a messy, complex geopolitical situation of unprecedented scope. This narrative lent moral clarity to the "good war," framed as a fight between good and evil. It defined the Allies as a close-knit family of nations—a band of brothers, an international romance, or a paternal guardianship—that aspired to free the world and secure the peace. Its overarching narrative raised morale, inspiring confidence that the saga would end victoriously. Seeing that movie play on an endless loop for a half decade helped transform the worldview of the 85 million Americans who attended theaters each week. The big screen transcended distance and bridged divides, creating an impression of American proximity to and harmony with overseas British, Chinese, and Soviet kith and kin. To be sure, differences endured, some destined to grow: generally speaking, whites refused to see Chinese as full and equal partners; anticommunists never reconciled with Stalin; nationalists were skeptical about world government. The change is nonetheless unmistakable. By any measure, the U.S. intellectual and political landscape of 1945 differed fundamentally from that of 1941 with regard to the wider world and America's place in it. A transformation had taken place, marked by internationalism's rise and isolationism's fall. A new cognitive geography developed, mapping the globe as indivisible and interconnected as never before. Peoples and nations seemed so joined in spirit and by technology as to make it appear that there was just *One World*, as Wendell Willkie had claimed. By war's end, the question was no longer if but how the United States should participate in an international peacekeeping federation. Having crossed an intellectual threshold and grown accustomed to rubbing shoulders with fellow citizens of the world, Americans joined the UNO with remarkably little debate about the wisdom of doing so.

That transformation arguably came about without reference to culture and solely as a consequence of historical events: the shock of Pearl Harbor, the experience of fighting a world war, and the thrill of victory achieved alongside foreign allies demonstrated the value of collective security. But facts do not speak for themselves; they are subject to interpretation. And the big screen, backed by Washington's authority at a time when people still trusted the government, interpreted events to mean that the international era had opened. No less than General Dwight Eisenhower, the architect of victory in Europe, told viewers of *The True Glory* that Allied cooperation caused Hitler's defeat. Frank Capra's official *Why We Fight* documentaries provided a world geography lesson whose message was that America needed to fight but could not win alone. And *Mission to Moscow*, based on the memoirs of a U.S. ambassador, was one of several commercial productions that in one way or another sugar-coated propaganda with plotlines that taught Americans to stop worrying and love the world like family. These movies starred on-screen role models such as Humphrey Bogart, Greer Garson, and John Wayne, who demonstrated how to court the Soviets, embrace British cousins, or lavish parental affection on China.

Contemporary academic research supported the view that movies had helped remake the American worldview. World War II served as a gigantic laboratory in which to test the "magic bullet" theory of social engineering, and postwar behavioral scientists reentered the ongoing debate about the media's effects armed with a vast store of data yielded by the U.S. government's various orientation programs. Some scholars, including Yale psychologist Carl I. Hovland, concluded that cinema exerted strong influence on U.S. perceptions of the wider world. With support from the Carnegie Foundation, Hovland headed a team of War Department researchers who set out to measure propaganda's precise impact on soldiers' beliefs. Hovland and his colleagues' landmark study, published in 1949 as part of a four-volume series that revisited the GI's psychological experience, focused on Capra's orientation films. Questionnaires administered to two groups, one that had seen Capra's work and a control group that had not, revealed that *The Battle of Britain* had "marked effects" on "the men's knowledge of factual material" and opinions regarding specific issues. The picture heightened soldiers' understanding of and appreciation for certain aspects of the UN's war effort, including Britain's contribution to Allied victory. A similar pattern was found to be at work with *Why We Fight* as a whole: those who saw the series came away with a better grasp of some matters. After watching *Prelude to War*, for example, interviewees reported being more convinced that the Allies would improve the world.[6]

Hovland's postmortem showed that wartime cinema did in fact influence human subjects, a finding that lent empirical weight to behaviorism. Thus sustained, pop behaviorism flourished in the postwar era, reappearing periodically in public panics about movies, television, and later video games as the root causes of the scourge of the day—radicalism, youthful rebellion, teen violence. The ever more sophisticated behavioral sciences—and Americans were optimistic that science, partially credited for winning the war, could produce a brighter future—strove to develop "magic keys," encoded messages said to be capable of determining human behavior. While Vance Packard's *The Hidden Persuaders* would someday reveal how midcentury advertisers applied such technology to stimulate consumption, the Rockefeller Foundation foresaw a civic use, reporting in November 1944 that "social engineering" could promote group cohesion during the difficult transition to peacetime.[7]

Wartime propaganda proved effective enough to lead Washington to institute public diplomacy, with film performing a key part, as a fixture of U.S. foreign relations. Previously skeptical of cultural diplomacy, State Department officials argued in 1945 that winning hearts and minds world wide should remain a matter of prime concern even after the fighting had stopped. Newly appointed assistant secretary of state for public affairs Archibald MacLeish asserted in January that official outreach should be considered essential to the proper functioning of the nascent "Parliament of Man." Departmental consultant Arthur W. Macmahon submitted an influential memorandum in July calling for the establishment of a U.S. international information service to replace the OWI, a temporary agency not expected to survive long past V-J day. His report concluded that "international information activities are integral to the conduct of foreign policy" insofar as they increased the chances of the United States receiving a "full and fair" hearing abroad. Macmahon recommended that motion pictures, decided outsiders at the war's outset, play instrumental roles in giving voice to American views before the world court of public opinion. To illustrate his stance that movies exerted "massive influence . . . in building background impressions about the United States" across the globe, the Columbia University political scientist quoted the *Public Opinion Quarterly* to the effect that World War II had witnessed "the long-awaited recognition of the motion picture as a primary source of public information and education. A tremendous power for good or evil has attained maturity. A new industry, a new medium for mass appeal, a new technique of child and adult instruction is being perfected. Its influence on . . . the subsequent transition from a war to a peace economy will be profound. Its effect on the future is incalculable."[8]

As a result, U.S. foreign propaganda, unlike its home front counterpart, continued when President Harry S Truman did as expected and abolished the OWI in a cost-cutting move on 31 August 1945. The OWI's overseas functions and staff simply passed, albeit in reduced form, to the

State Department and its Office of International Information and Cultural Affairs. State retained primary responsibility for public diplomacy until the U.S. Information Agency, the country's first peacetime propaganda ministry, was founded in 1953. As Macmahon predicted, movies served as prime tools in the U.S. Cold War campaign to win hearts and minds. The U.S. Information Agency distributed educational films as part of its mandate to improve America's global image and buoy anticommunist spirits worldwide. Cinema helped not just U.S. occupation authorities reorient German and Japanese cultural life but also Economic Cooperation Administration publicists develop transatlantic support for the Marshall Plan. And State Department diplomats continued to repay their corporatist partners in Hollywood by endeavoring to lower protectionist barriers wherever they hindered the free trade of American film exports. Such locales included those behind the Iron Curtain, where George F. Kennan hoped to extend wartime gains in insinuating American views and values.[9]

Despite its impressive achievements, however, cinema never fully convinced moviegoers that nations could peacefully coexist as one big happy family. Audiences were far too sophisticated to swallow that line. Hovland's study also concluded that movies exerted less impact on viewers' attitudes than expected. Capra's documentaries had little discernible effect on "motivation to serve as soldiers, which was considered the ultimate objective of the orientation program." Although *The Battle of Britain* improved knowledge, it did not cause GIs to rethink their general impression of the United Kingdom. Researchers offered several explanations for this finding: individual spectators' states of mind, variable viewing conditions, and the like. By implicitly identifying the audience as an active participant in the determination of meaning, these observations helped set the parameters of modern media scholarship. Hovland's research contributed to a quantum leap forward in social scientific knowledge. Along with similar conclusions reached by Paul Lazarsfeld and Joseph Klapper, Hovland's work questioned the prevailing behaviorist consensus and gave rise to more nuanced theories about how the media worked. One, the "limited effects" model, a direct outgrowth of Hovland's work, postulated that the media could motivate the masses but to a lesser extent than had previously been thought.[10] Whereas the old Payne Fund studies imagined juvenile delinquents to be movie-made, in other words, Hovland established that soldiers were not entirely so.

As if to illustrate that wisdom, the big screen's one-worldism proved to have a short shelf life. Familiarity was an accurate enough characterization of wartime geopolitics, which saw the Allies put aside their differences in pursuit of a common objective. But that image was discredited, overtaken by events, when the Great Powers pursued divergent national interests in the postwar period. To be sure, consanguinity remained an apt description of Sino- and Anglo-American relations. (U.S. officials continued to speak of their paternal responsibility for the welfare of Chinese "youths"; Churchill proposed a "fraternal association" with the United States in 1946.) Fraternity on a grander scale soon lost some of its luster, however. The practice of collective security quickly and inevitably departed from its utopian ideal at San Francisco, where even as the UNIO touted the new world order, news reports documented heated exchanges among conferees regarding Security Council voting procedures and General Assembly membership. Disillusionment followed, inadvertently fostered by wartime internationalist propaganda that had exaggerated cooperation and obscured conflict among the world's policemen, giving rise to inflated, unrealizable expectations that all such future congress would be equally collegial and successful. The American appetite for internationalism diminished over time, as Roosevelt's New Deal gave way to Truman's Fair Deal and Eisenhower's Modern Republicanism and as the UNO itself proved resistant to U.S. designs, stymied by Soviet veto and/or Second or Third World voting blocs. U.S. superpower interests had expanded, and rather than retreating from an unwelcoming world behind safe national borders, as had been the case during the interwar period, midcentury Americans reconfigured their worldview once more, adopting nationalist globalism as the perspective most suitable to forging the American Century. That is, they welcomed robust engagement with the outside world but did so only on a semi-independent basis and on terms demonstrably advantageous to the United States. World government emerged as a bogeyman, either an ineffectual debating society that constrained U.S. freedom of action or a sinister big brother that limited Americans' sovereign right to choose. Cinematically speaking, Alfred Hitchcock's *North by Northwest* (1959) reflected the latter view, featuring Cary Grant as an innocent U.S. business executive mistakenly caught in the crosshairs of an international plot springing from a meeting of the UNO.[11]

Mere words of support for the family of nations were powerless to prevent the world from splitting in two. The brief marriage of convenience between the Soviet Union and the United States ended in bitter divorce by 1947, the year U.S. diplomat Charles E. Bohlen lamented, "Instead of unity among the great powers . . . after the war, there is complete disunity between the Soviet Union and its satellites on one side and the rest of the world on the other. There are, in short, two worlds instead of one." As "Yalta" became a Cold War–influenced memory signifying not bilateral goodwill but FDR's alleged sellout to Stalin, movies that had worked to familiarize the Allies suddenly reversed course and constructed the other superpower as the archenemy. *Encounter at the Elbe*, a 1949 Soviet feature directed by Grigorii Aleksandrov and starring his spouse, Liubov' Orlova, revisited the historic linkup, portraying it as a moment when the United States rejected the USSR's outstretched hand of friendship and embarked on a nefarious project to reinstall fascism in occupied Germany. Hollywood released a string of anticommunist pictures, beginning with *The Iron Curtain* (1948) and *The Red Menace* (1949), that sustained the ongoing Second Red Scare of the late 1940s and early 1950s by demonizing the USSR, legitimating the hunt for domestic radicals, and equating one-worldism with subversion. When China was "lost" to communism via Mao Zedong's revolution in 1949, Hollywood reflected Washington's ostracism of the People's Republic with a handful of films distinguished by John Frankenheimer's brainwashing tale, *The Manchurian Candidate* (1962).[12]

Some pictures portrayed communism as a danger to the normative American family, unwittingly mirroring the Cold War rhetoric of U.S. diplomats. Postwar statesmen excluded the USSR from the "family circle" that FDR had widened at Tehran to include Uncle Joe. During the Cold War, the circumference of that circle was reduced considerably to encompass only the Western, anticommunist alliance. Headed by the patriarchal United States, that alliance was said to be composed of Western European states that World War II had left weakened, feminized, and vulnerable to penetration by the Soviet Union, styled as a competing alpha male home wrecker. U.S. and European diplomats, for example, discussed sensitive issues on the assurance that the information would remain safe "within the family." W. Averell Harriman and Kennan issued warnings about the danger of "Marxian penetration," phraseology suggesting that Moscow's threat was considered not only ideological and political but also sexual, as historian Frank Costigliola notes, and familial. Paramount's Cold War drama *My Son John* (1952) put a twist on such portrayals of the Soviet menace by depicting a mother's worry that communism had perverted her prodigal son. *I Was a Communist for the FBI* (1951) hinted at the strain fighting Reds put on the home life of an undercover federal agent.[13]

Anticommunist productions served as professions of Hollywood's loyalty, questioned by the House Un-American Activities Committee (HUAC). HUAC's infamous investigation of the motion picture industry is widely thought to have been rooted solely in the cultural politics of the Cold War, but it was a legacy of World War II as well, for Hollywood was called to account for its recent pro-Soviet past. Executives had cooperated with the federal government in part to wrap themselves in the flag as a prophylactic against future right-wing attacks. They miscalculated. The latest act in an extended saga involving Hollywood and its critics—including the Dies Committee and the 1941 Senate isolationists—opened on 20 October 1947, when HUAC, revitalized under chair J. Parnell Thomas, began its hearings on Capitol Hill. A "heady marriage of show business and politics," the well-publicized proceedings, writes historian Thomas Doherty, "blended the hoopla of a gala premiere (floodlights, microphones, celebrity appearances, and starstruck spectators) with the drama of courtroom ritual." In the midst of the media frenzy, Thomas gave an introductory statement explaining his committee's interest in Hollywood. Evidently a lay behaviorist, the chair took for granted "the tremendous effect which moving pictures have on their mass audiences." "We all recognize that what the citizen sees and hears in his neighborhood movie house carries a powerful impact on his thoughts and behavior." Since Hollywood offered "such a tremendous weapon for education and propaganda," the New Jersey Republican stated, subversives "would strive desperately" to subvert and control it. He and his fellow committee members were determined to root out any communists or fellow travelers who had infiltrated the industry to protect the public from brainwashing and prevent a stealthy radical takeover of the United States.[14]

Jack L. Warner was the first witness to testify, and the committee grilled him about *Mission to Moscow*. HUAC's chief investigator, Robert Stripling, read aloud testimony given by Warner during a preliminary investigation conducted in Los Angeles the previous May. At that time, investigators had asked if the studio executive considered *Mission to Moscow* to be "pro-communist" propaganda. Warner conceded that the movie condensed actual events here and there, an artistic license routinely invoked by filmmakers, but insisted that he did "not consider that film pro-communist at the time." Furthermore, Warner expressed bewilderment about how a picture made at the behest of the U.S. government to aid the nation's war effort could in retrospect be labeled subversive. "We were at war at that time," he reminded the chair, adding that the studio had only tried to do its patriotic duty.[15]

Thomas and Stripling continued to badger Warner. Who wrote the screenplay? Was it Howard Koch, suspected of and eventually blacklisted for harboring procommunist sympathies? Who ordered the film? President Roosevelt? Perhaps sensing a trap set by investigators to elicit politically damaging testimony indicating that New Dealers were soft on communism, Warner answered only that a "general feeling" existed in 1942 that friendly gestures should be made toward the Soviet ally. Stonewalled, Stripling returned to the characterization of *Mission to Moscow*. The ensuing exchange speaks to both the fluidity of interpretation and the consequences of politicized entertainment after circumstances had changed:

> STRIPLING: Would you consider it a propaganda picture?
> WARNER: A propaganda picture—
> STRIPLING: Yes.
> WARNER: In what sense?
> STRIPLING: In the sense that it portrayed Russia and communism in an entirely different light from what it actually was?
> WARNER: I am on record about forty times or more that I have never been to Russia. I don't know what Russia was like in 1937 or 1944 or 1947, so how can I tell you if it was right or wrong?
> STRIPLING: Don't you think you were on dangerous ground to produce as a factually correct picture one which portrayed Russia—
> WARNER: No; we were not on dangerous ground in 1942, when we produced it. There was a war on. The world was at stake.
> STRIPLING: In other words—
> WARNER: We made the film to aid in the war effort, which I believe I have already stated. . . . How did I, you, or anyone else know in 1942 what the conditions were going to be in 1947?[16]

Louis B. Mayer was the next mogul on the hot seat. Who commissioned *Song of Russia*? Mayer could not recall. In response to an investigator's observation that two suspected radicals, Paul Jarrico and Richard Collins, had written the screenplay, Mayer assured the committee that studio and industry censors had vetted projects at each stage of production so as to excise any potentially objectionable material before it reached the public. Stripling called *Song of Russia* "communist propaganda"; Mayer insisted otherwise. Although Soviet-American relations had since undergone a U-turn, he conceded, when "viewed in the light of the war emergency at the time, it is my opinion that [the film] could not be construed as anything other than for the entertainment purpose intended and a pat on the back for our then ally, Russia."[17]

A stream of witnesses subsequently contradicted Mayer's testimony, however. Robert Taylor, *Song of Russia*'s male lead, saved his reputation by blaming the studio for forcing him to appear in "communist propaganda" over his objections. Russian-born anticommunist writer and philosopher Ayn Rand gave HUAC a scene-by-scene interpretation of the film, after which she questioned the wisdom of Hollywood's idealization of Stalinist Russia: "We are discussing the fact that our country was an ally of Russia, and the question is, what should we tell the American people about it—the truth or a lie? If we had good reason, if that is what you believe, all right, then why not tell the truth? Say it is a dictatorship, but we want to be associated with it. Say it is worthwhile being associated with the devil, as Churchill said, in order to defeat another evil which is Hitler. There might be some good argument made for that. But why pretend that Russia was not what it was?" When Representative John S. Wood of Georgia wondered aloud if such a warts-and-all approach would have raised popular morale, she responded, "I don't believe that the morale of anybody can be built up by a lie. If there was nothing good that we could truthfully say about Russia, then it would have been better not to say anything at all."[18]

Other witnesses spoke to the communist infiltration of Hollywood, alleged to have accelerated under cover of the wartime Soviet-American alliance. The Motion Picture Alliance for the Preservation of American Ideals, an anticommunist body that encouraged HUAC to investigate the industry, took Hollywood's pro-Soviet record as prima facie evidence of an upsurge in radical activity. Director Sam Wood, the group's founding president, and members Taylor, Walt Disney, and Gary Cooper, along with Screen Actors Guild president Ronald Reagan, among others, testified to radicalism's rise and named the names of accused Communist Party members and fellow travelers active in Hollywood. Those so named were blacklisted, unable to find work in the industry after the studios' trade association, rechristened the Motion Picture Association of America under the leadership of former U.S. Chamber of Commerce head Eric Johnston, issued its Waldorf Statement promising not to employ known party members or sympathizers. That statement was released in November, just days after the Hollywood Ten—witnesses who refused to testify before HUAC, including John Howard Lawson, Albert Maltz, and Dalton Trumbo, whose respective screenwriting credits listed *Action in the North Atlantic*, *Moscow Strikes Back*, and *Thirty Seconds over Tokyo*— were cited for contempt of Congress.[19]

Together, the HUAC hearings and their progeny—the Hollywood Ten, the blacklist, and the Waldorf Statement—provide a fitting if unhappy coda to this story, as they helped draw the curtains on both Hollywood's golden age and its corporatist partnership with Washington. Although the American motion picture industry and the U.S. government would continue to trade content for commerce, the duo would never again be as dynamic as they were during World War II, whose peculiar correlation of forces soon weakened. That partnership had coalesced in 1940, when the Roosevelt administration interceded on the industry's behalf in an antitrust suit brought by the Justice Department, engineering a consent decree that temporarily relieved the major studios from litigation in exchange for their discontinuance of certain anticompetitive practices. Federal prosecutors reopened the lawsuit several years later, however, when they discovered the firms had not lived up to the letter of that decree. Without White House patronage, the case, *United States v. Paramount Pictures, Inc., et al.*, reached the Supreme Court. In a landmark 1948 decision, the Court found the major studios in violation of the Sherman Antitrust Act and required their divestiture of theater chains and stoppage of those unfair practices, a ruling that effectively brought an end to the studio system, the engine of classic Hollywood. Technological change hastened Hollywood's decline as well. Having made a public splash only a few years earlier, at the 1939 New York World's Fair, television soon outshone movies as the lodestar of postwar popular culture. Though the studios attempted to compete by making the big screen even bigger—enticing midcentury fans with musicals in brilliant Technicolor, thrillers in three dimensions, and epics in wide-angle Cinemascope—TV captured the public imagination with an intimacy, immediacy, and convenience that movies could not match. By the 1950s, television's golden age had dawned; Hollywood's had passed. Consequently, postwar policymakers frequently tapped the small screen when the need arose to educate the public about foreign affairs.[20]

The movie of World War II, undoubtedly the most filmed event in human history, continues to play in our collective memory and on those screens, big and small, filling them with indelible images of Allies and Axis. We can draw usable lessons from that mediated tradition, which teaches not only that spin doctors manipulated the American people, albeit on behalf of a defensible cause, but also that the people, less gullible than presumed, proved equally sophisticated. In some respects, World War II's transnational cinematic history may feel familiar since we are living in a moment of intensified global interconnectivity and proliferating information technology. Yet that movie was made during a bygone era when people were still coming to grips with cinema's power to shape worldviews, Hollywood still reigned supreme, and citizens still trusted authorities and took what was said largely on faith. At that time, control of the mass media, relatively small and monolithic by our standards, rested in the hands of a few kingpins who aspired to be members of the establishment. With a few phone calls made, some meetings held, and a little horse-trading done, moviemakers could be brought more or less on board to endorse the bipartisan foreign policy consensus. No comparable consensus exists now that we are in a partisan, cynical age when authorities are distrusted and the media are segmented and somewhat democratized. Perhaps that is all to the good, but it makes a repeat performance of World War II's synchronized coverage unlikely in the foreseeable future.

NOTES

Abbreviations

BC	Bosley Crowther
FDRL	Franklin D. Roosevelt Presidential Library and Museum, Hyde Park, New York
FOR	Foreign Office Records, National Archives, Kew, United Kingdom
FRUS	U.S. Department of State, *Foreign Relations of the United States*
GARF	State Archive of the Russian Federation, Moscow
LAO	Los Angeles Office, Overseas Operations Branch, Office of War Information Records, RG 208, National Archives and Records Administration II, College Park, Maryland
LAT	*Los Angeles Times*
LC	Library of Congress, Washington, D.C.
MIR	Ministry of Information Records, National Archives, Kew, United Kingdom
MP	Lowell Mellett Papers, Franklin D. Roosevelt Presidential Library and Museum, Hyde Park, New York
MPAA	Motion Picture Association of America General Correspondence, Academy of Motion Picture Arts and Sciences, Beverly Hills, California
MR	Lowell Mellett Records, Bureau of Motion Pictures, Domestic Operations Branch, Office of War Information Records, RG 208, National Archives and Records Administration II, College Park, Maryland
NARA	National Archives and Records Administration II, College Park, Maryland
NYT	*New York Times*
OF	Official File, Franklin D. Roosevelt Presidential Library and Museum, Hyde Park, New York
PCAC	Production Code Administration Collection, Academy of Motion Picture Arts and Sciences, Beverly Hills, California
RG 59	Department of State Records, RG 59, National Archives and Records Administration II, College Park, Maryland
RG 84	Department of State, Foreign Service Posts Records, RG 84, National Archives and Records Administration II, College Park, Maryland
RG 208	Office of War Information Records, RG 208, National Archives and Records Administration II, College Park, Maryland
RGASPI	Russian State Archive for Social and Political History, Moscow
WBA	Warner Bros. Archives, University of Southern California, Los Angeles
WHH	Will H. Hays
WP	*Washington Post*

Introduction

1. Photo LC-USZ62-32833, n.d., PRES File—Roosevelt, F. D.—International Conferences—Tehran, Prints and Photographs Division, LC. Variations of the Tehran portrait appeared in the *LAT*, 7 December 1943, B3; *NYT*, 7 December 1943, 1; *WP*, December 7, 1943, 1. For historians' documentation of the diplomatic, military, and economic aspects of the Grand Alliance, see, for example, Stoler, *Politics of the Second Front*; Stoler, *Allies and Adversaries*; Perlmutter, *FDR and Stalin*; Bennett, *Franklin D. Roosevelt*; Louis, *Imperialism at Bay*; Thorne, *Allies of a Kind*; Kimball, *Churchill and Roosevelt*; Woods, *Changing of the Guard*.

2. Photo 61-158 (5), 29 November 1943, Motion Pictures File, box 19, Photographs of FDR, FDRL; Trachtenberg, *Reading American Photographs*.

3. A lengthening list of works deal with Allied cultural relations or propaganda: see, for example, Parks, *Culture, Conflict, and Coexistence*; Brewer, *To Win the Peace*; Cull, *Selling War*; David Reynolds, *Rich Relations*; Jesperson, *American Images*, 59–81.

4. Calls for wider approaches to the war's cultural or social histories include Kimball, "Incredible Shrinking War"; Loyd E. Lee, "We Have Just Begun," 369, 378.

5. Over the past three decades, historians have addressed the cultural dimension of U.S. foreign relations. Leading examples include Ninkovich, *Diplomacy of Ideas*; Rosenberg, *Spreading the American Dream*; Hunt, *Ideology and U.S. Foreign Policy*; Gienow-Hecht, *Transmission Impossible*; Mark Bradley, *Imagining Vietnam and America: The Making of Postcolonial Vietnam, 1919–1950* (Chapel Hill: University of North Carolina Press, 2000).

Although it has had a major impact on the subfield, some diplomatic historians remain unconvinced, arguing that the "cultural turn," dismissed by one critic as the "intellectual equivalent of the Big Mac," fails to establish convincing empirical links to power, defined as a nation's ability to achieve its interests. See Bruce Kuklick, "Confessions of an Intransigent Revisionist about Cultural Studies," *Diplomatic History* 18 (January 1994): 121–24; Robert Buzzanco, "Where's the Beef?: Culture without Power in the Study of U.S. Foreign Relations," *Diplomatic History* 24 (Fall 2000): 623–32; Thomas Alan Schwartz, "Explaining the Cultural Turn—Or Detour?," *Diplomatic History* 31 (January 2007): 143–47.

6. Recent and competing treatments of interwar U.S. foreign policy include Doenecke and Wilz, *From Isolation to War*; Margot Louria, *Triumph and Downfall: America's Pursuit of Peace and Prosperity, 1921–1933* (Westport, Conn.: Greenwood, 2001); Benjamin D. Rhodes, *United States Foreign Policy in the Interwar Period, 1918–1941: The Golden Age of American Diplomatic and Military Complacency* (Westport, Conn.: Praeger, 2001). In addition to the four Great Powers, the original twenty-six signatories of the Declaration of the United Nations were Australia, Belgium, Canada, Costa Rica, Cuba, Czechoslovakia, Dominican Republic, El Salvador, Greece, Guatemala, Haiti, Honduras, India, Luxembourg, Netherlands, New Zea-

land, Nicaragua, Norway, Panama, Poland, South Africa, and Yugoslavia. Twenty-one other countries added their names over the next two and a half years: Mexico, Philippines, Ethiopia, Iraq, Brazil, Bolivia, Iran, Colombia, Liberia, France, Ecuador, Peru, Chile, Paraguay, Venezuela, Uruguay, Turkey, Egypt, Saudi Arabia, Lebanon, and Syria.

7. For examinations of anti-Soviet attitudes, see Gleason, *Totalitarianism*, 31–50; Mark, "October or Thermidor?"; Adler and Patterson, "Red Fascism"; Maddux, "Red Fascism, Brown Bolshevism"; Levering, *American Opinion*.

8. Said's *Orientalism* has spawned a large body of work on American Orientalism. See, for example, McAlister, *Epic Encounters*; Klein, *Cold War Orientalism*; Yoshi-hara, *Embracing the East*; Little, *American Orientalism*; Leong, *China Mystique*; Roan, *Envisioning Asia*.

9. See Allen, *Great Britain and the United States*, 17–29, 133–40, 150, 153; Perkins, *Great Rapprochement*; Charles Soutter Campbell, *From Revolution to Rapproche-ment: The United States and Great Britain, 1783–1900* (New York: Wiley, 1974); Dimbleby and Reynolds, *Ocean Apart*, 28–49.

10. Moser, *Twisting the Lion's Tail*, documents the rise of interwar conflict. On African Americans' views, see Meriwether, *Proudly We Can Be Africans*, 59–68; Von Eschen, *Race against Empire*, 22–43.

11. Anderson, *Imagined Communities*, 4, 6. Overy, *Why the Allies Won*, 15, 22–23, 286, 325, credits propaganda. Divine, *Second Chance*, recalls the lessons learned from Wilson's shortcomings. U.S. World War II propaganda both facilitated victory and prepared for peace, according to Brewer, *Why America Fights*, 4, 10.

12. According to Brewer, *Why America Fights*, 1, 277, U.S. propaganda histori-cally has associated war with freedom's advance. Scholars suggest that mass cul-ture can serve as a sensual prosthetic, enabling individuals to participate in events that they did not experience firsthand. See Burgoyne, *Film Nation*, 14, 105; Gabler, *Life*, 114. Blum, *V Was for Victory*, 16, argues that Americans fought the war "on imagi-nation alone," and popular nostalgia for the "good war" was a by-product of the state's careful management of home front culture (Adams, *Best War Ever*, xi, 2, 9–15; Roeder, *Censored War*).

13. For more on the war's encroachment on civilian life, see Sherry, *In the Shadow of War*, 40, 89. Roan, *Envisioning Asia*, discusses how films marketed as being shot "on location" transported theatergoers to and produced knowledge of foreign locales.

14. U.S. Bureau of the Census, *Historical Statistics*, 400, 796; Cantril, *Public Opin-ion*, 957.

15. Roan, *Envisioning Asia*, 2, 11. Lary May deconstructs Hollywood's wartime conversion narratives in *Big Tomorrow*, 148–57.

16. Bender, *Rethinking American History*.

17. Qualter, *Opinion Control*, 122, 124; Brewer, *Why America Fights*, 5, 7, 11.

18. Denis Morrison, "Russian Characters in Yank Films Are Now Dignified and Gallant," *Variety*, 28 October 1942, 15.

19. A rich literature explores Hollywood's distortion of world politics and history. See, for example, Vasey, *World According to Hollywood*; Rosenstone, *Visions of the Past*; Toplin, *History by Hollywood*; Toplin, *Reel History*. Cinematic communication is decoded by Metz, *Film Language*; Bordwell, *Narration*; Kaplan, *Looking for the Other*.

20. Dower compares Japanese and American imagery in *War without Mercy*, 73, 259.

21. Costigliola, "Nuclear Family"; Christina Klein, "Family Ties and Political Obligation: The Discourse of Adoption and the Cold War Commitment to Asia," in *Cold War Constructions*, edited by Appy, 36–38. Familial discourse figures into imagined nationhood, according to Zaretsky, *No Direction Home*; Silber, *Romance of Reunion*; Elaine Tyler May, *Homeward Bound*.

22. Elaine Tyler May, *Homeward Bound*, 47, 59–63, 69–72, 75; Hartmann, *Homefront and Beyond*, 38–39; D'Emilio, *Sexual Politics*, 23–39. Several works discuss gendered conceptualizations of international politics, including Scott, *Gender and the Politics*, 42–49; Costigliola, "'Unceasing Pressure'"; Marchetti, *Romance and the "Yellow Peril."*

23. David Reynolds, *Rich Relations*, 413, 420–22; Burk, *Old World, New World*, 553–59.

24. Mathews, *United We Stand*, 11.

25. Gerstle, *American Crucible*, 9. The cultural production of place, space, or landscape—that is, how people understand and represent the world—has been variously described as cognitive mapping, moral geography (McAlister, *Epic Encounters*, 4), or imaginative geography (Roan, *Envisioning Asia*, 214 n. 6).

26. Akira Iriye, "Internationalizing International History," in *Rethinking American History*, 53–56. Examinations of preexisting internationalism include Ninkovich, *Global Dawn*; Iriye, *Cultural Internationalism*. Several historians identify World War II as a tipping point in the American worldview, including Divine, *Second Chance*; Borgwardt, *New Deal for the World*; Engerman, "American Knowledge," 600, 607–10.

27. Engerman, "American Knowledge," 607; *FRUS 1945*, 2:80; Luce, "American Century." For the midcentury production and export of the American Way ideal, see Belmonte, *Selling the American Way*, 3–4, 179; Wall, *Inventing the "American Way."*

28. According to Bodnar, *"Good War,"* 6–7, humanitarianism shone brightly until 1945 but was soon eclipsed by resurgent nationalism. Fousek, *To Lead the Free World*, provides a trenchant analysis of U.S. nationalism's postwar reemergence. For competing views on how elites viewed movies, see Decherney, *Hollywood and the Culture Elite*; Ninkovich, *Diplomacy of Ideas*, 2–3, 63. Vasey, *World According to Hollywood*, 175–93, catalogs diplomatic incidents caused by insensitive Hollywood movies.

29. Applications of the corporatist model to international history include Hogan, *Marshall Plan*; Maier, *Recasting Bourgeois Europe*; Wilson, *Ideology and Economics*, ix–xi. For a critique, see Gaddis, "Corporatist Synthesis," 359–60.

For the argument that corporatism characterizes Washington's ties with Hollywood, a "chosen instrument" of the U.S. government, see Kitamura, *Screening Enlightenment*, xi; Trumpbour, *Selling Hollywood*, 20, 26–27; Jarvie, *Hollywood's Overseas Campaign*, 16–17, 319–20, 324, 326, 354; Thompson, *Exporting Entertainment*, 93–99, 111–12, 117–18; Rosenberg, *Spreading the American Dream*, 7–8, 202–6, 230.

30. Staiger, for example, concedes that the "controlling conventions" of cinema "win out over illusionary variety. Not everything is possible at every time" (*Interpreting Films*, xi, 8, 10, 21). Helpful works on the gap between the transmission and reception of meaning include Staiger, *Perverse Spectators*, 1, 5, 23; Fiske, *Understanding Popular Culture*; Cayton, "Making of an American Prophet"; Judith Mayne, *Cinema and Spectatorship* (London: Routledge, 1993); Linda Williams, ed., *Viewing Positions: Ways of Seeing Film* (New Brunswick: Rutgers University Press, 1995); Shaun Moores, *Interpreting Audiences: The Ethnography of Media Consumption* (London: Sage, 1993); Reeves, *Power of Film Propaganda*, 239–41.

31. U.S. Bureau of the Census, *Historical Statistics*, 400, 840; Rosten, *Hollywood*, 374, 378–80; Lowry, "Trade Follows the Film."

32. On soft power, see Joseph S. Nye Jr., *Bound to Lead*, 31–32, 267n; Joseph S. Nye Jr., *Soft Power*, x, 5–8. Salesman, writer, and self-help guru Dale Carnegie's *How to Win Friends and Influence People* (New York: Simon and Schuster, 1936) remained a best seller a decade after its publication.

33. de Grazia, *Culture of Consent*, 151–52, 159–60, 168, 187; de Grazia, "Mass Culture and Sovereignty," 53–56, 72–81; Thompson, *Exporting Entertainment*, 133; Kitamura, *Screening Enlightenment*, 1–21.

34. Scholars have explored the robust Anglo-American competition within the "special relationship" regarding, among other things, propaganda (Brewer, *To Win the Peace*), military strategy (Stoler, *Allies and Adversaries*; Thorne, *Allies of a Kind*), economics (Woods, *Changing of the Guard*), and even aviation (Engel, *Cold War at 30,000 Feet*).

35. Blum, *V Was for Victory*, 6.

36. On foreign receptions of American culture, see Kroes, Rydell, and Bosscher, *Cultural Transmissions and Receptions*; Kuisel, *Seducing the French*; Pells, *Not Like Us*; Wagnleitner, *Coca-Colonization*, xi–xiii; Ambler, "Popular Films." For an overview, see Gienow-Hecht, "Shame on U.S.?"

37. For the argument that ideology was central to superpower competition, see Caute, *Dancer Defects*, 1; Gould-Davies, "Rethinking the Role of Ideology"; Gaddis, *Cold War*, 83–118; Odd Arne Westad, *The Global Cold War: Third World Interventions and the Making of Our Times* (Cambridge: Cambridge University Press, 2007), 4.

Chapter 1

1. Peter H. Odegard, *The American Public Mind* (New York: Columbia University Press, 1930), 197; C. H. Hamlin, *The War Myth in United States History* (New York: Vanguard, 1927), 91. For a full discussion of British propaganda in the United States, see chapter 2.

2. I. F. Stone, "Creel's Crusade," *Nation*, 9 December 1939, 647. For discussions of the CPI and its critics, see Vaughn, *Holding Fast the Inner Lines*, xi–xii, 233–38, 347–50; Kennedy, *Over Here*, 41, 59–66.

3. William Henry Chamberlin, "Russia's Goldbrick Constitution," *American Mercury*, October 1937, 184. Normally associated with the Cold War, the term "totalitarianism" was already in vogue by the late 1930s, when commentators used it to describe a new kind of utopian state that sought not only to govern but also to forcibly remake and coordinate society by insinuating itself into citizens' private lives. See Alpers, *Dictators, Democracy, and American Public Culture*, 136–41; Gleason, *Totalitarianism*, 10, 31–50, 92–94, 108–42. Pertinent Cold War–era scholarship includes Hannah Arendt, *The Origins of Totalitarianism* (New York: Harcourt, Brace, 1951); Merle Fainsod, *How Russia Is Ruled* (Cambridge: Harvard University Press, 1953); Carl J. Friedrich and Zbigniew K. Brzezinski, *Totalitarian Dictatorship and Autocracy* (Cambridge: Harvard University Press, 1956).

4. "22,000 Nazis Hold Rally in Garden; Police Check Foes," *NYT*, 21 February 1939, sec. 1, pp. 1, 5; letter to the editor, *Nation*, 27 May 1939, 626; Gertrude Quitman and William H. Allen, *Dictator Isms and Our Democracy: Nazism, Fascism, Communism: "Made in America" Brands* (New York: Institute for Public Service, 1940), 10–45; MacDonnell, *Insidious Foes*, 123–36.

5. Gordon Carroll, "Dr. Roosevelt's Propaganda Trust," *American Mercury*, September 1937, 1–31; Dorothy Thompson, "Stopping Propaganda: The Democracies Have the Jitters," *Vital Speeches of the Day*, 1 June 1939, 494–95; John T. Flynn, "Mr. Flynn on War Hysteria," *New Republic*, 11 September 1940, 660. See also Dallek, *Franklin D. Roosevelt*, 140, 159; Freidel, *Franklin D. Roosevelt*, 239, 276–77, 343.

6. John Dewey, "Creative Democracy: The Task before Us (1939)," in *Later Works*, 14: 226–27; John Dewey, *The Public and Its Problems* (New York: Holt, 1927), 208, 139, 169; Westbrook, *John Dewey*, xv. An outstanding study is Gary, *Nervous Liberals*, 25–26, 29–33.

7. *Journal American* quoted in Roeder, *Censored War*, 13; William Henry Chamberlin, "Do We Want a Gobbels in America?," *Christian Century*, 22 April 1942, 524–26. Prior to U.S. intervention, the White House rejected a proposal for a central propaganda agency on the grounds that it would be too controversial. See Harold L. Ickes to FDR, 28 April 1941, Lowell Mellett to FDR, 5 May 1941, both in White House—1941 file, box 5, MP; Harold L. Ickes, *The Lowering Clouds, 1939–1941*, vol. 3 of *Secret Diary*, 426.

8. John Marshall and Donald Slesinger quoted in Gary, *Nervous Liberals*, 91, 95; *Congressional Record*, 75th Cong., 3rd sess., 1938, 83, pt. 7, pp. 8021–22.

9. Lasswell, Casey, and Smith, *Propaganda and Promotional Activities*, 60–61; Ivan P. Pavlov, *Conditioned Reflexes: An Investigation of the Physiological Activity of the Cerebral Cortex*, translated by Gleb V. Anrep (London: Oxford University Press, 1927). In Watson's experiment, a once-fearless small child ("Little Albert") learned to fear a rat through negative reinforcement (John B. Watson and Rosalie Rayner, "Conditioned Emotional Reactions," *Journal of Experimental Psychology* 3 [February 1920]: 1–14). Though Watson's study remained a fixture within the discipline into the 1940s (see Robert S. Woodworth, *Psychology*, 4th ed. [New York: Holt, 1940], 379), its methodology and ethics came under increasing scrutiny (see Ben Harris, "Whatever Happened to Little Albert?," *American Psychologist* 34 [February 1979]: 151–60).

Neobehaviorist touchstones include Edward Chace Tolman, *Purposive Behavior in Animals and Men* (New York: Century, 1932), 371–414; B. F. Skinner, *The Behavior of Organisms: An Experimental Analysis* (New York: Appleton-Century, 1938), 19–21, 438–40. For an overview, see John A. Mills, *Control: A History of Behavioral Psychology* (New York: New York University Press, 1998), 1–8.

10. Quoted in Gary, *Nervous Liberals*, 87; Sproule, *Propaganda and Democracy*, 64–65.

11. *War of the Worlds*, Orson Welles, CBS broadcast, 30 October 1938 (in author's personal collection); "Radio Listeners in Panic, Taking War Drama as Fact," *NYT*, 31 October 1938, 1; Cantril, *Invasion from Mars*, 47–55, 154, 159–60, 190, 203.

12. Lasswell *Propaganda Technique*, 4, 10–12, 15, 220–21. See also Harold D. Lasswell, "The Developing Science of Democracy," in *The Future of Government in the United States*, edited by Leonard D. White (Chicago: University of Chicago Press, 1942), 43; Sproule, *Propaganda and Democracy*, 154–70. Walter Lippmann was a veteran advocate. See Lippmann, *Phantom Public*, 14, 20, 69; Lippmann, *Public Opinion*, 236, 248–49.

13. Edgar Dale and Norma Vernon, introduction to *Propaganda Analysis* (Columbus, Ohio: Bureau of Educational Research, May 1940), i; Gallup and Rae, *Pulse of Democracy*, v–vi, 6–15; Bernays, *Crystallizing Public Opinion*, 14, 21–32, 56–57; Bernays, *Propaganda*, 9–10, 12–14, 20–23, 25, 28, 113–14; Bernays, *Speak Up for Democracy*, viii–ix; Bernays, *Democratic Leadership*, [1–6]; Tye, *Father of Spin*, 195–97.

14. Peter Odegard, "Public Opinion and Propaganda in Wartime America," 5 May 1942, Speeches and Articles file, box 31, Peter Odegard Papers, FDRL; Brewer, *Why America Fights*, 5, 7, 11.

15. Robert Sherwood to Harry Hopkins, 17 December 1941, Propaganda file, box 213, Harry L. Hopkins Papers, FDRL; Francis Biddle to FDR, 22 April 1942, OF 4734; MacLeish quoted in Blum, *V Was for Victory*, 29. Even the CPI's reputation underwent an apotheosis, as contemporary historians came to regard it as a viable blueprint for "Tomorrow's Committee" (Mock and Larson, *Words That Won the War*, vii, 338, 346).

16. Executive Order 9182, 13 June 1942, in Roosevelt, *Public Papers*, 11:274–83.

For OWI deviation from the "strategy of truth," see Shulman, *Voice of America*, 95, 99–100, 107–9, 152; Winkler, *Politics of Propaganda*, 1–7, 66–72, 104–9.

17. Lasswell, Casey, and Smith, *Propaganda and Promotional Activities*, 17–18; Donald Slesinger, "The Film and Public Opinion," in *Print, Radio, and Film*, edited by Waples, 88–89, 98.

18. "The Movies: Entertainment *Plus* Education," *Christian Century*, 27 April 1938, 521; Sklar, *Movie-Made America*, 135–40.

19. Charters, *Motion Pictures and Youth*, 13, 25–35, 60–61; Blumer, *Movies and Conduct*, 47, 109.

20. Frank K. Shuttleworth and Mark A. May's study is summarized in Charters, *Motion Pictures and Youth*, 20–21, 23; Peterson and Thurstone, *Motion Pictures*, 64–66. See also Holaday and Stoddard, *Getting Ideas*, 76–80.

21. Thorp, *America at the Movies*, 13, 80.

22. Ibid., 62–63, 71, 76–77.

23. Ibid., 24.

24. Cantril and Gordon Allport quoted in Pells, *Radical Visions*, 265; Archibald MacLeish, "Poetry and the Public World," in *Time to Speak*, 88.

25. Bernays, *Propaganda*, 156; Davis quoted in Koppes and Black, "What to Show the World," 88–89; OWI, *Government Information Manual for the Motion Picture Industry*, 8 June 1942, Manual Material—Hollywood Office file, box 1438, Records of the Chief of the Domestic BMP, RG 208.

26. This paragraph and the following one are based on Koppes and Black, *Hollywood Goes to War*, 63, 100–103; Schatz, *Boom and Bust*, 271; Samuel Goldwyn quoted in Daniel J. Leab, "Introduction: Politics and Film," *Film History* 20, no. 4 (2008): 395.

27. WHH quoted in Thorp, *America at the Movies*, 160–61; Vasey, *World According to Hollywood*, 3–9, 128, 225–27; Black, *Hollywood Censored*, 244–88. See also Doherty, *Hollywood's Censor*.

28. Nugent quoted in "Movies: Entertainment *Plus* Education," 520–21; MacLeish quoted in Thorp, *America at the Movies*, 162–63. The motion picture industry's slump coincided with the so-called Roosevelt Recession. Studio earnings plummeted 41.6 percent in 1938 and another 11.4 percent in 1939 (Rosten, *Hollywood*, 377).

29. Harry M. Warner, "Hollywood's Obligations in a Producer's Eyes," *Christian Science Monitor*, 16 March 1939, 3; Roddick, *New Deal in Entertainment*, 65–67, 119.

30. Wanger, "120,000 American Ambassadors," 45–47.

31. Wanger, "Role of Movies."

32. WHH quoted in Thorp, *America at the Movies*, 161–62.

33. Birdwell, *Celluloid Soldiers*, 3, 13, 17–19; Doherty, *Projections of War*, 39–40; Gabler, *Empire of Their Own*, 338–47.

34. Jarvie, *Hollywood's Overseas Campaign*, 105–6, 126, 151–58, 162, 171–72; Thompson, *Exporting Entertainment*, 105–11, 155–58; de Grazia, *Irresistible Empire*, 316–31.

35. Harry Warner to Harry Hopkins, 6 March 1939, Motion Pictures file, box 117,

Hopkins Papers; Jack Warner to FDR, 25 November 1940, box 4, OF 73. Producers used distribution practices to compel theater owners to rent B movies along with higher-quality and more marketable A productions. Blind booking required exhibitors to accept B movies sight unseen to receive an A feature. Block booking meant that theater managers had to accept a predetermined block of B movies to receive an A picture. The consent decree provided only a temporary reprieve. The case would be reopened. Without White House protection, the U.S. Supreme Court found the major studios in violation of antitrust law in 1948 and required them to sell their theaters.

36. Lowell Mellett for FDR, 23 December 1940, White House—1940 file, box 5, MP; Mellett, draft memorandum, [1941], White House—1941 file, box 5, MP; Harry and Jack Warner to FDR, 20 May 1940, White House press release, 27 February 1941, both in box 4, OF 73; Culbert, *News for Everyman*, 5–7; Steele, *Propaganda*, 25–27, 33–34, 98, 100, 142–43.

37. Koppes and Black, *Hollywood Goes to War*, 80–81, 105–12; Sweeney, *Secrets of Victory*, 4.

38. Ulric Bell to Robert Riskin, 22 December 1942, Riskin file, box 3510, Records of the Chief, LAO; Ulric Bell to Nelson Poynter, 19 May 1943, Poynter file, box 16, MP; survey by the Los Angeles Office of the Overseas Operations Branch, 15 September 1944, Chief's Office file, box 3509, Records of the Chief, LAO.

39. Robert Riskin to Ulric Bell, 22 October 1943, Riskin file, box 3510, Records of the Chief, LAO.

40. State Department to American Diplomatic and Consular Officers in the American Republics, 25 October 1940, 111.46 Advisory Committee/75A, Departmental Order 768, 28 July 1938, 111.46/1, both in RG 59. For discussions of American interwar cultural initiatives, including those of the Division of Cultural Relations, see Costigliola, *Awkward Dominion*, 167–83; Ninkovich, *Diplomacy of Ideas*, 13–25; Rosenberg, *Spreading the American Dream*, 108–21.

41. Irene A. Wright to Charles A. Thomson, 7 June 1941, Interdivisional Committee file, box 163, Records Relating to International Information Activities, RG 59; minutes, "Meeting Regarding Non-Theatrical Film Program," 4 November 1942, Miscellaneous Meetings file, box 164, Records Relating to International Information Activities, RG 59.

42. For the controversies surrounding these films, see Vasey, *World According to Hollywood*, 75–103.

43. Richard R. Ford to John Begg, 21 October 1941, 841.4061 Motion Pitures/327, RG 59; Sklar, *Movie-Made America*, 174; Lary May, *Big Tomorrow*, 1–4, 12, 44, 57–65, 75, 87.

44. Richard L. Strout, "Now 'Mr. Capra Goes to Washington' but the Senators Are Not Amused," *Christian Science Monitor*, 27 October 1939, 3; Pete Harrison quoted in Frank Nugent, "Capra's Capitol Offense," *NYT*, 29 October 1939, 5. Favorable com-

mentary included Frank Nugent, "Capra Cuts a Caper," *NYT*, 22 October 1939, 13; advertisements, *WP*, 22 October 1939, 3, 26 October 1939, 16.

45. Joseph P. Kennedy to WHH, 12 November 1939, Joseph P. Kennedy to FDR, 12 November 1939, both in 840.6 General, Department of State Post (London) Records, RG 84; memorandum of conversation, 21 March 1940, Miscellaneous Meetings file, box 164, Records Relating to International Information Activities, RG 59.

46. Luce, "American Century," 63–65; C. P. Holway, "Fight Fire with Fire," *Nation*, 11 January 1941, 55; Baughman, *Henry R. Luce*, 129–33. For discussions of reinvigorated American confidence, see Dallek, *American Style*, 125–26, 134–37; Smith, *America's Mission*, 114; Warren Susman, "Introduction," in *Culture and Commitment*, edited by Susman, 9–16, 20, 23; Wall, *Inventing the "American Way,"* 105.

47. Carl E. Milliken for WHH, memorandum, 19 September 1944, State Department file (reel 10), MPAA. On postwar market conditions, see Guback, *International Film Industry*, 3–5, 91–95; Jarvie, *Hollywood's Overseas Campaign*, 373–93.

48. WHH to Cordell Hull, 21 October 1943, 800.4061 Motion Pictures/332, RG 59; WHH, memorandum, 29 September 1944, State Department file (reel 9), MPAA.

49. WHH, memorandum, 5 October 1943, Foreign Relations—Russia file (reel 10), MPAA; WHH to Cordell Hull, 21 October 1943, 800.4061 Motion Pictures/332, RG 59.

50. Spyres P. Skouras to Francis Colt de Wolf, 1 February 1944, 800.4061 Motion Pictures/398, RG 59; Edwin Schallert, "Zanuck Sounds Call for Better Pictures," *LAT*, 13 May 1945, B1–2; Goldwyn quoted in Kouwenhoven, "Movies Better Be Good!," 538–39.

51. Wallace Murray to Sumner Welles, Adolf A. Berle Jr., and Breckinridge Long, 1 February 1941, 800.4061 Motion Pictures/130, RG 59; G. Howland Shaw, memorandum, 8 November 1943, 800.4061 Motion Pictures/333A, RG 59; "The Non-Theatrical Motion Picture Program Abroad," *Bulletin*, 18 September 1943, 198–99.

52. Adolf A. Berle Jr. to FDR, 8 September 1944, Publicity, Press Releases, Coordination file, box 163, Naval Aide's Files, Map Room Papers, FDRL; *Bulletin*, 24 September 1944, 316; Berle, *Navigating the Rapids*, 466; Kimball, *Juggler*, 10, 18–19, 102, 182, 186–87, 191, 198.

53. Adolf A. Berle Jr., draft memorandum, January 1944, Leroy D. Stinebower, memorandum, 11 January 1944, both in 800.4061 Motion Pictures/408, RG 59.

54. Adolf A. Berle Jr., memorandum, 22 February 1944, 800.4061 Motion Pictures/409A, RG 59; Arthur L. Loew to Louis Cowan, 24 August 1945, New York Office file, box 3509, Motion Picture Division, LAO; Schwarz, *Liberal*, vii, ix.

55. Carl E. Milliken to WHH, 29 January 1944, State Department file (reel 10), MPAA; Mori Krushen, "D.C. Aid to Film Biz Abroad," *Variety*, 6 September 1944, 3; Kouwenhoven, "Movies Better Be Good!," 534–40; Lowe, "Washington Discovers Hollywood." The reorganization produced the Motion Picture and Radio Division, which unlike its predecessor, the Division of Cultural Relations, utilized the mass media in overseas information programs. The reshuffling also resulted in the Tele-

communications Division, responsible for the international mass media trade. Executives considered it a stronger advocate for their interests than its predecessor, the Division of International Communications.

56. Nelson Poynter to Lowell Mellett, 17 May 1943, Poynter file, box 16, MP.

Chapter 2

1. Gerald P. Nye, "War Propaganda."

2. Ibid., 720–22.

3. For historians' treatments of overt and covert British propaganda in prewar America, see, for example, Cull, *Selling War*; Brewer, *To Win the Peace*; Mahl, *Desperate Deception*. The voluminous scholarship on pro-British wartime cinema includes Birdwell, *Celluloid Soldiers*; Glancy, *When Hollywood Loved Britain*; Aldgate and Richards, *Britain Can Take It*; Chapman, *British at War*; K. R. M. Short, "Cinematic Support for the Anglo-American Détente, 1939–1943," in *Britain and the Cinema*, edited by Philip M. Taylor, 121–43.

4. Discussions of the antebellum American mind-set include Cole, *Roosevelt and the Isolationists*, ix, 6–9; Doenecke, *Storm on the Horizon*, x, 1–8; Moser, *Twisting the Lion's Tail*.

5. FDR's moving of public opinion in an internationalist direction is a source of academic controversy. His management style has variously been characterized as passive (Marks, *Wind over Sand*, 3), cautious (Casey, *Cautious Crusade*, xxxii), and proactive but devious (Douglas M. Charles, *J. Edgar Hoover and the Anti-Interventionists: FBI Political Surveillance and the Rise of the Domestic Security State, 1939–1945* [Columbus: Ohio State University Press, 2007]).

6. H. C. Engelbrecht and F. C. Hanighen, *Merchants of Death: A Study of the International Armament Industry* (New York: Dodd, Mead, 1934).

7. For discussions of Anglo-American détente, see Allen, *Great Britain and the United States*, 17–29, 133–40, 150, 153; Perkins, *Great Rapprochement*; Charles Soutter Campbell, *From Revolution to Rapprochement: The United States and Great Britain, 1783–1900* (New York: Wiley, 1974); Dimbleby and Reynolds, *Ocean Apart*, 28–49.

8. Lavine and Wechsler, *War Propaganda*, 118; Cantril, *Public Opinion*, 274; Plummer, *Rising Wind*, 71–73.

9. James M. Read, *Atrocity Propaganda, 1914–1919* (New Haven: Yale University Press, 1941), 201–8; James Duane Squires, *British Propaganda at Home and in the United States: From 1914 to 1917* (Cambridge: Harvard University Press, 1935); Horace C. Peterson, *Propaganda for War: The Campaign against American Neutrality, 1914–1917* (1939; Port Washington, N.Y.: Kennikat, 1968), 4; Lavine and Wechsler, *War Propaganda*, 14, 17, 22–31, 89–92, 171–216.

10. Minute, [1940], A 538/26/45, FOR 371/24227.

11. Lord Lothian to Lord Halifax, 28 September 1939, A 7053/7052/45, FOR 371/22839; David Reynolds, *Lord Lothian*, 58.

12. Stephen Lawford Childs, memorandum, July 1940, A 3772/26/45, FOR 371/24231; Cull, *Selling War*, 83; Krome, "'Weapon of War,'" 39, 58.

13. Lord Lothian to Lord Halifax, 28 September 1939, A 7053/7052/45, FOR 371/22839; F. R. Cowell, minutes, 7 November 1939, A 7720/7052/45, FOR 371/22840, 20 December 1939, A 9056/7052/45, FOR 371/22841; Aldgate and Richards, *Britain Can Take It*, 21–24; Chapman, *British at War*, 59–65.

14. "Air Lion," *Time*, 20 November 1939, 80; Philip T. Hartung, "All of the People All of the Time," *Commonweal*, 22 December 1939, 206; *Variety*, 24 January 1940, 14.

15. Powell quoted in Cull, *Selling War*, 84; *Variety*, 5 November 1941, 8.

16. Sir Alfred Duff Cooper for Winston S. Churchill, 3 July 1940, Sir Alexander Cadogan for Winston S. Churchill, memorandum, 3 July 1940, both in A 3561/26/45, FOR 371/24230; Stephen Lawford Childs, memorandum, July 1940, A 3772/26/45, FOR 371/24231; Brewer, *To Win the Peace*, 11, 36, 43–44, 48–50.

17. Donor Lists, California Organizing Committee to Ulric Bell, 10 September 1941, Motion Picture Industry file, box 32, Fight for Freedom Papers, Seeley G. Mudd Manuscript Library, Princeton University, Princeton, N.J.; Birdwell, *Celluloid Soldiers*, 3, 13, 17–19; Doherty, *Projections of War*, 39–40.

18. Sidney Bernstein to Frank Darvall, 10 July 1940, A. W. Jarratt, report, 24 November 1940, both in F 109/9/4, MIR 1/600.

19. Cordell Hull to Joseph P. Kennedy, 16 October 1939, 841.4061 Motion Pictures/189, RG 59; Jarvie, *Hollywood's Overseas Campaign*, 105–6, 126, 151–58, 162, 171–72; Thompson, *Exporting Entertainment*, 105–11, 155–58.

20. Joseph P. Kennedy to Cordell Hull, 9 October 1939, in *FRUS 1939*, 2:218; Jarvie, *Hollywood's Overseas Campaign*, 182–88, 342–47; Woods, *Changing of the Guard*, 9.

21. Joseph P. Kennedy to Cordell Hull, 13 October 1939, 841.4061 Motion Pictures/189, RG 59; Frederick L. Herron to George S. Messersmith, 27 November 1939, 841.4061 Motion Pictures/210, RG 59; Koskoff, *Joseph P. Kennedy*, 27–36, 79–81.

22. WHH to Cordell Hull, 16 October 1940, 841.4061 Motion Pictures/253, RG 59; Alan N. Steyne to Joseph P. Kennedy, 25 October 1940, 841.4061 Motion Pictures/255, RG 59.

23. Adviser on International Economic Affairs, memorandum, 3 June 1941, 841.4061 Motion Pictures/288, RG 59; memorandum of conversation for Thomas Burke, 26 March 1941, 841.4061 Motion Pictures/276, RG 59; WHH to Sumner Welles, 19 March 1941, 841.4061 Motion Pictures/279, RG 59; WHH, memorandums of conversations, 11–12 March 1941, Foreign Relations—Great Britain file, MPAA.

24. WHH, memorandums of conversations, 11–12 March 1941, Foreign Relations—Great Britain file, MPAA; Long, *War Diary*, 217–18.

25. WHH, memorandums of conversations, 11–12 March 1941, Foreign Relations—Great Britain file, MPAA; Cordell Hull and Lord Halifax, memorandum of conversation, 24 May 1941, 841.4061 Motion Pictures/284, RG 59; Sir Gerald Campbell and

Breckinridge Long, memorandum of conversation, 2 April 1941, 841.4061 Motion Pictures/282, RG 59.

26. WHH, memorandums of conversations, 11–12 March 1941, Foreign Relations—Great Britain file, MPAA; John G. Winant to Secretary of State, 11 September 1941, Sir Kingsley Wood to John G. Winant, 4 October 1941, Cordell Hull to John G. Winant, 30 August 1941, all in 840.6 Motion Pictures—General, Department of State Post (London) Records, RG 84.

27. John Balfour to Sir Frederick Whyte, 26 July 1940, A 3581/26/45, FOR 371/24230.

28. WHH and Cordell Hull, memorandum of conversation, 12 August 1941, WHH to Fayette W. Allport, 18 September 1941, both in MPAA.

29. Oscar Deutsch to Jack Beddington, 15 July 1940, F 14/2, MIR 1/568; minutes, 14 February 1940, A 231/26/45, FOR 371/24227; Nicholas Pronay, "The News Media at War," in *Propaganda, Politics, and Film*, edited by Pronay and Spring, 186–91.

30. Sir Frederick Whyte to Lord Lothian, 1 January 1940, A 709/26/45, FOR 371/24227.

31. Fielding, *March of Time*, 4, 92–94, 254, 267–69. On Luce's views, see Baughman, *Henry R. Luce*, 3, 116–22; Herzstein, *Henry R. Luce*, 128–32.

32. Calder, *People's War*; Calder, *Myth of the Blitz*; Sonya O. Rose, *Which People's War?*; Jose Harris, "Great Britain: The People's War?," in *Allies at War*, edited by David Reynolds, Kimball, and Chubarian, 233–59.

33. Murrow, *This Is London*, 182, 186–87; MacLeish, Paley, and Murrow, *In Honor of a Man*, 7–8. For discussions of broadcasters' foreign politics, see Horten, *Radio Goes to War*, 33–38; Culbert, *News for Everyman*, 5–7, 86–89, 111, 116–17, 136–42. Isolationists bemoaned on-air internationalism. See "Internationalist Hall of Fame," *Scribner's Commentator*, November 1940, 17; Samuel E. Romer to Sidney Hertzberg, 6 December 1940, in *In Danger Undaunted*, edited by Doenecke, 385.

34. BC, "The War on the Screen," *NYT*, 27 October 1940, sec. 9, p. 5.

35. Cull, *Selling War*, 18.

36. BC, review of *Foreign Correspondent*, *NYT*, 28 August 1940, sec. 1, p. 15; *Motion Picture Herald*, 31 August 1940, *Motion Picture Daily*, 28 August 1940, both in *Foreign Correspondent* file, Production Code Files, PCAC.

37. "Foreign Correspondent," *Life*, 26 August 1940, 42–45; *Variety*, 28 August 1940, 16; Eugene Lyons, "The Truth about Foreign Correspondents," *American Mercury*, November 1940, 358–62; Goebbels quoted in Leslie Halliwell, *Halliwell's Film Guide*, 7th ed. (New York: Harper and Row, 1989), 367.

38. Devere Allen, letter to the editor, *Christian Century*, 16 October 1940, 1284–85.

39. Seton I. Miller, *The Sea Hawk* (draft screenplay), 13 May 1939, Seton I. Miller and Howard Koch, *Sea Hawk* (final screenplay), [1940], both in Story file, *The Sea Hawk* Collection, WBA. For more on the "Merrie England" pictures, see Roddick, *New Deal in Entertainment*, 235–48.

40. *Fire over England*, dir. William K. Howard (London Film Productions, 1937); Seton I. Miller to Walter MacEwen, 26 March 1940, Story file, *Sea Hawk* Collection, WBA.

41. Glancy, *When Hollywood Loved Britain*, 100–103. DVD versions include the queen's speech.

42. Publicity Pamphlet, July 1940, Publicity file, *Sea Hawk* Collection, WBA; Herman Lissauer to Jack Kelly, 21–22 June 1940, Research file, *Sea Hawk* Collection, WBA.

43. Philip T. Hartung, "The Screen," *Commonweal*, 23 August 1940, 371; "New Pictures," *Time*, 19 August 1940, 78; Kenneth McCaleb, "Swashbuckling Fight It Out in *Sea Hawk*," *New York Mirror*, 10 August 1940, Clipping file, *Sea Hawk* Collection, WBA; BC, review of *Sea Hawk*, *NYT*, August 10, 1940, sec. 1, p. 16; "Swashbuckling on the Warner Sea," *Newsweek*, 19 August 1940, 46; A. W. Jarratt to Jack Beddington, 18 August 1941, F 109/9/4, MIR 1/600; Roddick, *New Deal in Entertainment*, 268, 281.

44. Korda, *Charmed Lives*, 138–39; R. C. Sherriff, *No Leading Lady: An Autobiography* (London: Gollancz, 1968), 335–36; Winston S. Churchill to David B. Cunynghame, 22 October 1937, in Churchill, *The Coming of War, 1936–1939: Companion Documents*, vol. 5, pt. 3, edited by Martin Gilbert (Boston: Houghton Mifflin, 1983), 810–11. For more on Korda's official ties, see Richards, *Age of the Dream Palace*, 135–37; Philip M. Taylor, *British Propaganda*, 96. John M. MacKenzie examines Korda's imperial portraits in *Imperialism and Popular Culture* (Manchester: Manchester University Press, 1989), 152–54. Korda's clandestine service is exposed in Mahl, *Desperate Deception*, 67–68, 180.

45. Alexander Korda, "Imagination vs. Microphone: Alexander Korda Cuts Shackles," *New York Herald Tribune*, 16 September 1940, quoted in Cull, *Selling War*, 179.

46. Otis Ferguson, "The Admiral and the Lady," *New Republic*, 21 April 1941, 533.

47. Olivier, *Confessions*, 91; Otis Ferguson, "The Admiral and the Lady," *New Republic*, 21 April 1941, 533; Short, "*That Hamilton Woman*."

48. Roscoe Williams, review, *Motion Picture Daily*, 24 March 1941, in *That Hamilton Woman* file, Production Code Files, PCAC; "Movie of the Week," *Life*, 7 April 1941, 41; BC, review, *NYT*, 4 April 1941, sec. 1, p. 25. See also *Variety*, 20 March 1941, 3.

49. War Cabinet Defense Committee, minutes, 19 May 1941, A 3893/118/45, FOR 371/2618/; British Press Service to MOI, 21 May 1941, Richard R. Ford, notes, 21 March 1941, both in F 14/2, MIR 1/568; British Library of Information, "Films from Britain," September 1941, British Films file, Records Concerning Film Subjects (1941–43), box 1536, RG 208; David Reynolds, *Creation of the Anglo-American Alliance*, 197.

50. Short, "RAF Bomber Command's *Target for Tonight*," 194.

51. *One Night in Lisbon*, dir. Edward H. Griffith (Paramount, 1941); Glancy, *When Hollywood Loved Britain*, 111–12, 128.

52. Zanuck quoted in Glancy, *When Hollywood Loved Britain*, 118.

53. Review, *NYT*, 14 November 1941, 28; Vaughn, *Ronald Reagan in Hollywood*, 102–3.

54. "*Yank RAF* Fine $16,500," "Storm Socks Omaha," "*Int'l Squadron* Hefty $24,000 in Healthy L.A.," all in *Variety*, 5 November 1941, 11; review of *International Squadron*, *NYT*, 14 November 1941; BC, review of *A Yank in the RAF*, *NYT*, 27 September 1941, sec. 1, p. 11; "The New Pictures," *Time*, 13 October 1941, 94; "Blond Blitz on the RAF," *Newsweek*, 6 October 1941, 59–60.

55. Cantril, *Public Opinion*, 409–11, 967, 971, 973–74; Cantril, *Gauging Public Opinion*, 222; Gallup, *Gallup Poll*, 1:212, 233, 237–38, 240, 243, 250–51, 262.

56. Cantril, *Public Opinion*, 957. For able analyses of *Sergeant York*, see Doherty, *Projections of War*, 100–103; Koppes and Black, *Hollywood Goes to War*, 37–39; Toplin, *History by Hollywood*, 87, 98–99.

57. Burton K. Wheeler to WHH, 13 January 1941, President's Personal File 1945, FDRL. Roosevelt's 29 December 1940 Fireside Chat dealt with national security.

58. Philip T. Hartung, "You Takes Yer Choice," *Commonweal*, 25 April 1941, 16; John T. Flynn to R. Douglas Stuart Jr., 4 August 1941, in *In Danger Undaunted*, edited by Doenecke, 383–85; U.S. Congress, Senate, Committee on Interstate Commerce, *Propaganda in Motion Pictures*, 116–18.

59. Margaret Frakes, "Why the Movie Investigation?," *Christian Century*, 24 September 1941, 1172–74; Don Herold, "Seat at the Cinema," *Scribner's Commentator*, December 1941, 105–6.

60. U.S. Congress, Senate, Committee on Interstate Commerce, *Propaganda in Motion Pictures*, 1–2. See also Moser, "Gigantic Engines."

61. U.S. Congress, Senate, Committee on Interstate Commerce, *Propaganda in Motion Pictures*, 6, 11, 33, 38, 41, 48; Gerald P. Nye, "War Propaganda," 720–22.

62. U.S. Congress, Senate, Committee on Interstate Commerce, *Propaganda in Motion Pictures*, 57, 73, 105, 108.

63. Charles Kupper to Universal Pictures, 23 February 1940, MPAA; [illegible] to FDR, 27 July 1941, Wheeler file, OF 4453; Alice C. Reyhner to FDR, 14 September 1941, OF 73; Margaret Frakes, "Why the Movie Investigation?," *Christian Century*, 24 September 1941, 1172.

64. Daryl F. Zanuck to Ulric Bell, 14 August 1941, Motion Picture Industry file, box 32, Fight for Freedom Papers; Moser, "Gigantic Engines," 741; Mahl, *Desperate Deception*, 60–61.

65. Daryl F. Zanuck to Ulric Bell, 14 August 1941, Motion Picture Industry file, box 32, Fight for Freedom Papers; Lowell Mellett for FDR, 27 August 1941, memorandum for Mrs. Dennison, 28 August 1941, both in box 5, OF 73.

66. Daryl F. Zanuck to Stephen T. Early, 28 November 1941, Z-misc. file, box 22, Stephen T. Early Papers, FDRL; Moser, "Gigantic Engines," 742; Mahl, *Desperate Deception*, 173.

67. U.S. Congress, Senate, Committee on Interstate Commerce, *Propaganda in Motion Pictures*, 4, 18–22, 338–39.

68. Ibid., 57–61, 81.

69. Gerald P. Nye, "War Propaganda," 721, 723; U.S. Congress, Senate, Committee on Interstate Commerce, *Propaganda in Motion Pictures*, 11–12, 17.

70. "Senate Isolationists Run Afoul of Willkie in Movie 'Warmonger' Hearings," *Life*, 22 September 1941, 21; Berg, *Lindbergh*, 427; Cole, *Charles A. Lindbergh*, 162, 175.

71. Michael Straight, "The Anti-Semitic Conspiracy," *New Republic*, 22 September 1941, 362–63; Philip Dunne, "Propaganda or History?," *Nation*, 20 September 1941, 241–42; "Senate Isolationists Run Afoul of Willkie in Movie 'Warmonger' Hearings," *Life*, 22 September 1941, 21–22; Barnet Nover, "On Propaganda: Witch Hunt on Capitol Hill," *WP*, 10 September 1941, 11.

Chapter 3

1. Declaration of the United Nations, 1 January 1942, in *FRUS 1942*, 1:25–26.

2. Mathews, *United We Stand*, 358; *Bulletin*, 3 January 1942, 3–4; David Low, "Vigorous Youngster" (illustration), 29 December 1941, *London Evening Standard*, British Cartoon Archive, University of Kent, Canterbury.

3. Borgwardt, *New Deal for the World*, 5–8; Divine, *Second Chance*, 4, 190–91; Hoopes and Brinkley, *FDR and the Creation of the UN*, 205. On Germany's anti-UN propaganda campaign, see Goebbels, *Goebbels Diaries*, 292; Welch, *Third Reich*, 111.

4. Examinations of the "good war" myth include O'Neill, *Democracy at War*; Adams, *Best War Ever*; Geoffrey C. Ward, *The War: An Intimate History, 1941–1945* (New York: Knopf, 2007); Kenneth D. Rose, *Myth and the Greatest Generation*; Bodnar, *"Good War."*

5. Buhite and Levy, *FDR's Fireside Chats*, 199, 220–29, 202–3; Surveys of Intelligence Materials nos. 11 and 12, 23 February, 2 March 1942, both in Survey of Intelligence Materials (1941–42), box 11, Alphabetical Subject File, OFF Bureau of Intelligence, RG 208. For a discussion of Pearl Harbor's effect on the American mind-set, see Rosenberg, *Date Which Will Live*, 11–23.

6. Report 15a, 25 June 1942, Surveys Division Reports, box 11, Alphabetical Subject File, OFF Bureau of Intelligence, RG 208.

7. Ibid.

8. Blum, *V Was for Victory*, 230; Moser, *Twisting the Lion's Tail*, 154–55.

9. Davis quoted in Culbert, *News for Everyman*, 143–44. One critic, Representative Clare Boothe Luce, claimed that FDR's signature action was a wetted index finger raised to gauge the shifting winds of public opinion so that he could set his political compass accordingly (Cull, *Selling War*, 143). Leigh discusses the White House's use of polling data in *Mobilizing Consent*, 99. See also Marks, *Wind over Sand*, 165; Polenberg, *War and Society*, 91–92.

10. MacLeish quoted in Horten, *Radio Goes to War*, 52; Dallek, *Franklin D. Roosevelt*, 360–61, 419, 441, 505, 522; Leigh, *Mobilizing Consent*, 109, 117.

11. Buhite and Levy, *FDR's Fireside Chats*, 198–205.

12. Ibid., 206–18.

13. OFF Bureau of Intelligence, Survey no. 27, 10 June 1942, Minutes, Committee on War Information, June 1942, box 11, Subject File, Records of the Historian, RG 208.

14. Breckinridge Long to Henry L. Stimson, 13 May 1942, 811.4061 Motion Pictures/667, RG 59; OFF Bureau of Intelligence, Recommendations to Accompany Survey no. 27, 13 June 1942, Minutes, Committee on War Information, June 1942, meeting agenda, 15 June 1942, all in box 11, Subject File, Records of the Historian, RG 208.

15. OFF Bureau of Intelligence, Survey no. 27, 10 June 1942, OFF Bureau of Intelligence, Recommendations to Accompany Survey no. 27, 13 June 1942, both in box 11, Subject File, Records of the Historian, RG 208.

16. Worksheet, Propaganda file, box 213, Harry L. Hopkins Papers, FDRL; OWI, *Government Information Manual for the Motion Picture Industry*, 8 June 1942, OWI, *Government Information Manual for the Motion Picture Industry* (revised), 29 April 1943, both in Manual Material—Hollywood Office, box 1438, MR.

17. OWI, *Government Information Manual for the Motion Picture Industry*, 8 June 1942, *Government Information Manual for the Motion Picture Industry* (revised), 29 April 1943, both in Manual Material—Hollywood Office, box 1438, MR.

18. "Uncle Sucker?," *Time*, 18 August 1941, 64–66; Cantril, *Public Opinion*, 411–12; *Congressional Record*, 78th Cong., 1st sess., 1943, 89, pt. 7, p. 8863.

19. Feature review, 19 May 1943, Motion Picture Reviews and Analyses, box 3511, BMP, Overseas Operations Branch, RG 208.

20. OWI, *Government Information Manual for the Motion Picture Industry*, 8 June 1942, Manual Material—Hollywood Office, box 1438, MR; Roosevelt, annual address to Congress, in Roosevelt, *Public Papers*, 9:672; Normal Rockwell, Four Freedom posters, 1943, 208-PMP-43–46, RG 208, Still Picture Branch.

21. Mohandas Gandhi to FDR, 1 July 1942, in *FRUS 1942*, 1:678–79; Randolph quoted in Polenberg, *War and Society*, 105. See also Borgwardt, *New Deal for the World*, 8–9.

22. For the development of wartime domestic consensus against the backdrop of common enemies, see Wall, *Inventing the "American Way*,*"* 8, 105, 133.

23. William R. Weaver, "Films Fostering Hate for Axis Approved," *Motion Picture Herald*, 3 October 1942, 34; OWI, *Government Information Manual for the Motion Picture Industry*, 8 June 1942, *Government Information Manual for the Motion Picture Industry* (revised), 29 April 1943, both in Manual Material—Hollywood Office, box 1438, MR.

24. *Bugs Bunny Nips the Nips* (Warner Bros., 1944); Doherty, *Projections of War*, 137; Dower, *War without Mercy*, 81.

25. OWI, *Government Information Manual for the Motion Picture Industry* (revised), 29 April 1943, Manual Material—Hollywood Office, box 1438, MR; Dower, *War without Mercy*, 81–92, 185.

26. Pyle quoted in Dower, *War without Mercy*, 78–79; Buhite and Levy, *FDR's Fireside Chats*, 198–205; Doherty, *Projections of War*, 124; Koppes and Black, *Hollywood Goes to War*, 279–83, 298.

27. "This Is the Enemy" (poster), n.d., 44-PA-101, "Don't Let That Shadow Touch Them" (poster), 1942, 44-PA-97, Ben Shahn, "This Is Nazi Brutality" (poster), 1942, 44-PA-245, all in Office of Government Reports Records, RG 44, Still Picture Branch, NARA.

28. "Lookout Monkeys" (poster), n.d., 44-PA-378, "Warning! Our Homes Are in Danger Now!" (poster), 1942, 44-PA-2314, both in ibid.

29. David Low, untitled illustration, *London Evening Standard*, 7 July 1941, British Cartoon Archive, University of Kent, Canterbury; Frank Capra to Lowell Mellett, 1 May 1942, War Department, box 1464, Correspondence with Other Government Agencies, BMP, Domestic Operations Branch, RG 208.

30. Capra, *Name above the Title*, 330–32; Doherty, *Projections of War*, 23.

31. "United We Win" (poster), 1943, War Manpower Commission, 44-PA-370, Office of Government Reports Records, RG 44, NARA; *Guadalcanal Diary*, dir. Lewis Seiler (Twentieth Century–Fox, 1943); *Bataan*, dir. Tay Garnett (MGM, 1943); Gerstle, *American Crucible*, 204–6.

32. Another great escape tale, *Desperate Journey*, follows the members of an RAF international squadron—an American (Ronald Reagan), an Australian (Errol Flynn), and a Canadian included—as they make their way to Allied territory after being shot down over Nazi Germany (*Desperate Journey*, dir. Raoul Walsh [Warner Bros, 1942]).

33. Wallace, *Democracy Reborn*, 190; Film Information Sheet 17, December 1942, Press Notices of Documentary Films, box 1596, Non-Theatrical Division, BMP, Domestic Operations Branch, RG 208; script review, n.d., Motion Picture Reviews and Analyses, box 3524, BMP, Overseas Operations Branch, RG 208; Wall, *Inventing the "American Way,"* 112–13; Clare Boothe Luce quoted in Blum, *V Was for Victory*, 285. For more criticism of Wallace, see Arthur Krock, "In the Nation: Mr. Wallace's Vision of the Post-War World," *NYT*, 24 December 1942, 14.

34. Film Information Sheet 3, August 1942, Press Notices of Documentary Films, box 1596, Non-Theatrical Division, BMP, Domestic Operations Branch, RG 208.

35. Miguel Covarrubias, *United Nations* (drawing), 1942, Cartoon Drawings Collection, Prints and Photographs Division, LC. All other referenced posters are from the online World War II Poster Collection, Northwestern University Library, http://www.library.northwestern.edu/libraries-collections/evanston-campus/government-information/world-war-ii-poster-collection (accessed 11 November 2011).

36. Roosevelt, Flag Day Proclamation, 9 May 1942, United Nations Day poster, n.d., both in United Nations, box 24, Subject File, OFF, RG 208; memorandum for the Committee on War Information, [June 14, 1942], Minutes, Committee on War Information, June 1942, box 11, Subject File, Records of the Historian, RG 208.

37. Radio script, "Toward the Century of the Common Man," n.d., United Nations Campaign, box 12, Decimal File of the Director, 303.5-310, RG 208. The internationalist chord struck by Donne's poetry must have reverberated, as it had inspired Ernest Hemingway's 1940 novel, *For Whom the Bell Tolls*, a sympathetic account of a fictional American's service on behalf of the antifascist Republicans during the Spanish Civil War. Paramount released a 1943 movie version of Hemingway's book that starred Gary Cooper and Ingrid Bergman.

38. Radio script, "Toward the Century of the Common Man," n.d., United Nations Campaign, box 12, Decimal File of the Director, 303.5-310, RG 208.

39. FDR, radio address, 14 June 1942, in Roosevelt, *Public Papers*, 11:288-89.

40. "Entire Nation Celebrates," *LAT*, 15 June 1942, 7; *Bulletin*, 20 June 1942, 548-50; "Topics of Sermons That Will Be Heard in City Churches Tomorrow," 13 June 1942, *NYT*, 10.

41. Robert Cromie, "Chicagoans Parade 15 Hours," *Chicago Tribune*, 15 June 1942, 1, 3.

42. Ibid.

43. "Moscow Unfurls Flags of Allies; Russians See Victory in New Pacts," *NYT*, 15 June 1942, 1; "Aspirations of the United Nations Voiced by President Roosevelt and 16 Envoys," *NYT*, 15 June 1942, 4.

44. James MacDonald, "All Britain Joins Biggest War Fete," 15 June 1942, *NYT*, 1; Craig Thompson, "Midlands Put on Impressive Show," 15 June 1942, *NYT*, 6; "Aspirations of the United Nations Voiced by President Roosevelt and 16 Envoys," *NYT*, 15 June 1942, 4; Leslie Gilbert Illingworth, "United Will to Win" (illustration), *London Daily Mail*, 15 June 1942, British Cartoon Archive, University of Kent, Canterbury. *Common Cause*, a short MOI docudrama featuring two conversations—one between a Royal Navy officer and a Soviet pilot, the other between a Chinese and an American—pointed to deeper similarities among the UN's four major powers despite superficial differences. Both *United Nations* and *Common Cause* are available at the Film and Photograph Archives, Imperial War Museum, London.

45. Blum, *V Was for Victory*, 262-71.

46. Willkie, *One World*, 2, 160.

47. Ibid., 151-52, 155, 157, 174-75.

48. Robert Gale Woolbert, "Recent Books on International Relations," *Foreign Affairs*, October 1943, 160; Reinhold Niebuhr, "Mr. Willkie's Two Odysseys," *Nation*, 24 April 1943, 604-6.

49. Thomas J. Knock, "History with Lightning: The Forgotten Film *Wilson*," in *Hollywood as Historian*, edited by Rollins, 97, 107.

50. Quoted in ibid., 99, 89.

51. Review, *Time*, 7 August 1944, 84; BC, review, *NYT*, 2 August 1944, 18.

52. Review, *Time*, 7 August 1944, 84; Knock, "History with Lightning," 91.

53. Jay Robert Nash and Stanley Ralph Ross, eds., *Motion Picture Guide* (Chicago: Cinebooks, 1986), 3867; review, *Time*, 7 August 1944, 84; Knock, "History with Lightning," 101–3, 106.

54. Hazel Bruce, review, *San Francisco Chronicle*, 30 August 1944, 7; BC, reviews, *NYT*, 2 August 1944, 18, 10 September 1944; Knock, "History with Lightning," 99, 103, 105. Contemporary scholarly works on Wilson include Thomas A. Bailey, *Woodrow Wilson and the Lost Peace* (New York: Macmillan, 1944); Thomas A. Bailey, *Woodrow Wilson and the Great Betrayal* (New York: Macmillan, 1945); Herbert C. F. Bell, *Woodrow Wilson and the People* (Garden City, N.Y.: Doubleday, Doran, 1945); Gerald W. Johnson, *Woodrow Wilson: The Unforgettable Figure Who Has Returned to Haunt Us* (New York: Harper, 1944). An abridged version of the day's most authoritative biography—Ray Stannard Baker's multivolume *Woodrow Wilson: Life and Letters*, first published from 1927 to 1940—would be published in 1946.

55. Arthur Boran to Mr. Barnes, 22 August 1944, Roslyn Van Hoven to FDR, 15 August 1944, both in Zanuck file, OF 73; Costigliola, "Broken Circle," 710.

56. Paramount's *The Hitler Gang* likewise ended with a nod to what would break up the Nazi underworld: the forces of the United Nations.

57. Cantril, *Public Opinion*, 372–74.

58. Polenberg, *War and Society*, 209–10, 214.

59. Bonnet, *United Nations*, iii, 79–81, 97–100; Divine, *Second Chance*, 55–56, 78, 85–87, 124, 143, 149, 152, 166.

60. Roosevelt, *Public Papers*, 12:3. FDR also evoked the four policemen metaphor during his 1943 State of the Union address and his August talks in Ottawa with Canadian prime minister William Lyon Mackenzie King. See Roosevelt, *Public Papers*, 12:21–34, 365–69.

61. *FRUS 1943*, 299, 487, 497.

62. Minutes, Press Subcommittee meeting, 12 December 1941, untitled file, box 1, UNIO Records (S-0537), United Nations Archives, New York; agenda, 98th United Nations Information Board meeting, 24 October 1944, Editorial and Documentary file, box 2, UNIO Records. The existing scholarship naturally focuses on the postwar United Nations Organization's public diplomacy at the expense of its direct progenitor—that of the wartime UN coalition. See Mark D. Alleyne, *Global Lies?: Propaganda, the UN, and World Order* (New York: Palgrave, 2003); Seth A. Center, "The United Nations Department of Public Information: Intractable Dilemmas and Fundamental Contradictions," in *The Global Public Relations Handbook: Theory, Research, and Practice*, edited by Krishnamurthy Sriramesh and Dejan Vercic (New York: Routledge, 2009), 889–90; Seth A. Center, "Supranational Public Diplomacy: The Evolution of the UN Department of Public Information and the Rise of Third

World Advocacy," in *United States and Public Diplomacy*, edited by Osgood and Etheridge, 135–63.

63. Minutes, Press Subcommittee meeting, 12 December 1941, agenda, 52nd Inter-Allied Information Committee meeting, 14 July 1942, both in untitled file, box 1, UNIO Records; subcommittee minutes and reports, 9 September 1942, Washington Meeting file, box 2, UNIO Records; "Notes on Arrangements for the Production of the United Nations Educational Kit," [14 February 1944], Editorial and Documentary file, box 2, UNIO Records.

64. *United News*, no. 77 (OWI, 1943), RG 208; *FRUS 1943*, 641; *Bulletin*, 6 November 1943, 309; Roosevelt, *Public Papers*, 12:532–33; Buhite and Levy, *FDR's Fireside Chats*, 273–81.

65. "The Midwest and the United Nations," [February 1945], Editorial and Documentary file, box 2, UNIO Records; *United News*, no. 117 (OWI, 1944), RG 208.

66. *Bulletin*, 22 October 1944, 479, 11 February 1945, 179–81.

67. Ibid., 18 March 1945, 431–34.

68. FDR, Fourth Inaugural Address, 20 January 1945, in Roosevelt, *Public Papers*, 13:524.

Chapter 4

1. Historians have discovered many Anglo-American tensions hidden beneath the veneer of the special relationship. See Engel, *Cold War at 30,000 Feet*, 17–52; Louis, *Imperialism at Bay*; Stoler, *Allies in War*; Thorne, *Allies of a Kind*; Woods, *Changing of the Guard*.

2. Scholars have detailed either British or American wartime propaganda but not always its transatlantic character. See Brewer, *To Win the Peace*; Winkler, *Politics of Propaganda*. According to one review, even a leading work overlooks the extensive "cross-pollination of personnel and ideas that proliferated" among Anglo-American propagandists (Susan L. Carruthers, "Winning Friends and Influencing Americans," *Diplomatic History* 24 [Winter 2000]: 141).

An extensive literature ably analyzes wartime movies without always connecting them to geopolitics. See, for example, Glancy, *When Hollywood Loved Britain*; Krome, "'Weapon of War'"; Koppes and Black, *Hollywood Goes to War*; Dick, *Star-Spangled Screen*.

3. Allen quoted in Hathaway, *Great Britain and the United States*, 7.

4. Dumbrell, *Special Relationship*, 11.

5. Glancy, *When Hollywood Loved Britain*, 196.

6. *How Green Was My Valley*, dir. John Ford (Twentieth Century–Fox, 1941); *Cavalcade*, dir. Frank Lloyd (Twentieth Century–Fox, 1933); Anthony Eden to War Cabinet, "Reactions in the United States to the Beveridge Report," 10 February 1943, A 1005/34/45, FOR 371/34127.

7. Unfavorable press included Manny Farber, "War Horses," *New Republic*,

15 June 1942, 830–31; Edgar Anstey, review, 17 July 1942, box 3522, Motion Picture Reviews and Analyses, Motion Picture Division, LAO. Positive reactions included OWI feature review, 4 August 1942, Motion Picture Reviews and Analyses, Motion Picture Division, LAO; Charles A. Aaronson, review, *Motion Picture Daily*, n.d., review, *Variety*, 13 May 1942, both in *Mrs. Miniver* file, PCAC; "Hollywood Spanked for 'Sloughing' Cause of Democracy in War Films," *Variety*, 17 June 1942, 1.

8. *Random Harvest*, dir. Melvyn LeRoy (MGM, 1942); Quentin Reynolds, "In Which He Serves," *Collier's*, 2 January 1943, 22; BC, review, *NYT*, 24 December 1942, sec. 1, p. 18.

9. Glancy, *When Hollywood Loved Britain*, 131–42.

10. OFF Bureau of Intelligence, Report 15a, 25 June 1942, Surveys Division Reports, box 11, Alphabetical Subject File, RG 208; "Revival," *Time*, 31 May 1943, 21.

11. Cantril, *Public Opinion*, 1108–9; Darryl F. Zanuck to Stephen T. Early, 28 February 1942, Miscellaneous file, box 6, OF 48a (England).

12. "We're Not Perfect Ourselves," *Collier's*, 4 April 1942, 66. See also Bruce Bliven, "Britain's Problem of Leadership," *New Republic*, 6 July 1942, 7; David Low, "Was Colonel Blimp Right?," *London Evening Standard*, 14 October 1942. Colonel Blimp was a rotund, sybaritic, cartoon character created by *London Evening Standard* illustrator David Low in 1934 to satirize the British ruling class. Michael Powell and Emeric Pressburger subsequently turned Low's character into the centerpiece of a feature film, *The Life and Death of Colonel Blimp* (1943), over Churchill's objections. On the controversy surrounding the film, see Chapman, *British at War*, 192–94; Aldgate and Richards, *Best of British*, 79–91.

13. Moser, *Twisting the Lion's Tail*, 157; editorial quoted in Horten, *Radio Goes to War*, 49.

14. Meriwether, *Proudly We Can Be Africans*, 60; Von Eschen, *Race against Empire*, 1–2, 7–8; Plummer, *Rising Wind*, 71–74; Gerald Horne, "Race from Power: U.S. Foreign Policy and the General Crisis of White Supremacy," in *Window on Freedom: Race, Civil Rights, and Foreign Affairs, 1945–1988*, edited by Brenda Gayle Plummer (Chapel Hill: University of North Carolina Press, 2003), 53.

15. Cantril, *Public Opinion*, 274; "An Open Letter to the People of England," *Life*, 12 October 1942, 34; Michael Straight, "Is It a People's War?," *New Republic*, 16 November 1942, 633; Charles Clayton Morrison, "No Victory without India," *Christian Century*, 21 October 1942, 1278.

16. On Anglo-American trade and monetary disputes, see Richard N. Gardner, *Sterling-Dollar Diplomacy in Current Perspective: The Origins and the Prospects of Our International Economic Order* (New York: Columbia University Press, 1980); Thomas W. Zeiler, *Free Trade, Free World: The Advent of GATT* (Chapel Hill: University of North Carolina Press, 1999); Francine McKenzie, *Redefining the Bonds of Commonwealth, 1939–1948: The Politics of Preference* (New York: Palgrave, 2002).

17. Moser, *Twisting the Lion's Tail*, 155–58; O'Neill, *Democracy at War*, 166; Mark A.

Stoler, "The United States: The Global Strategy," in *Allies at War*, edited by David Reynolds, Kimball, and Chubarian, 67; Thorne, *Allies of a Kind*, 288.

18. Stettinius quoted in Dallek, *Franklin D. Roosevelt*, 505–6; T. North Whitehead, "British Publicity in the United States Based on a Visit in October 1941," 20 July 1942, A 6845/399/45, FOR 371/30679; Thomas Baird, "Production Plans for the U.S.A.," n.d., Spewack file, box 1446, MR; Harold Butler, "Publicity Policy in the U.S.," August 1943, A 7669/34/45, FOR 371/34129; Halifax quoted in Mikhail N. Narinsky and Lydia V. Pozdeeva, "Mutual Perceptions: Images, Ideals, and Illusions," in *Allies at War*, edited by David Reynolds, Kimball, and Chubarian, 325. See also Cole, *Roosevelt and the Isolationists*, 514, 516.

19. Stimson and Bundy, *On Active Service*, 429–30; OFF quoted in Brewer, *To Win the Peace*, 94; OWI, *Government Information Manual for the Motion Picture Industry*, 8 June 1942, OWI, *Government Information Manual for the Motion Picture Industry* (revised), 29 April 1943, both in Manual Material—Hollywood Office, box 1438, MR.

20. Harold Butler, "Publicity Policy in the U.S.," August 1943, A 7669/34/45, FOR 371/34129; T. North Whitehead, "British Publicity in the United States Based on a Visit in October 1941," 20 July 1942, A 6845/399/45, FOR 371/30679; Dumbrell, *Special Relationship*, 13, 16; David Reynolds, *Britannia Overruled*, 178.

21. Sir Gerald Campbell to Lord Radcliffe, 20 February 1942, A 1833/399/45, FOR 371/30668; T. North Whitehead, "British Publicity in the United States Based on a Visit in October 1941," 20 July 1942, A 6845/399/45, FOR 371/30679; MOI American Division, "Plan of Publicity in the U.S.A.," 21 February 1942, A 2695/399/45, FOR 371/30668. Procolonial propaganda included "British Imperialism, 1944," a special episode of *March of Time* praised by Ambassador Halifax for discussing the subject "in a friendly fashion" (Halifax to MOI, 19 August 1944, AN 3207/2113/45, FOR 371/38696).

22. MOI, "Plan of Publicity in the U.S.A.," 21 February 1942, A 2695/399/45, FOR 371/30668; Harold Butler, memorandum, [August 1943], A 7792/34/45, FOR 371/34129; Harold Butler, "Publicity Policy in the U.S.," August 1943, A 7669/34/45, FOR 371/34129; Stoler, *Allies in War*, 186.

23. OWI and MOI officials, memorandum of conversation, n.d., British Information Service file, box 1432, MR. The Joint Committee's meeting minutes are located in Policy & Procedures 3-1—Joint Committee Agenda & Minutes (1942–43), box 5, Records of the Director, 1942–45, RG 208.

24. *A Yank at Eton*, dir. Norman Taurog (MGM, 1942). The movie was maligned by the OWI, however, for perpetuating a negative stereotype of British elitism. See feature review, 1 October 1942, Reviews and Activities Reports, box 1440, MR.

25. Glancy, *When Hollywood Loved Britain*, 123–26.

26. David Hackett Fischer, *Albion's Seed: Four British Folkways in America* (New York: Oxford University Press, 1989); Burk, *Old World, New World*, 529–59; David Reynolds, *Rich Relations*, 413–28.

27. Script review, 1 March 1943, box 3529, Motion Picture Reviews and Analyses, Motion Picture Division, LAO.

28. *Journey Together*, dir. John Boulting (RAF Film Production Unit, 1945); "Britain's Best," *Time*, 20 May 1946, 89; Aldgate and Richards, *Britain Can Take It*, 280, 286–87, 294–95; David Reynolds, *Rich Relations*, 35. The army's educational efforts included U.S. Army Special Services Division, *Instructions*; *Welcome to Britain*; *Battle of Britain*.

29. Aldgate and Richards, *Britain Can Take It*, 294.

30. The U.S. title for *A Matter of Life and Death* was *Stairway to Heaven* (Chapman, *British at War*, 85).

31. Kimball, *Churchill and Roosevelt*, 2:155–56; review, *Variety*, 9 April 1943, in *Desert Victory* file, PCAC; David Lardner, "Westward Ho!," *New Yorker*, 17 April 1943, 39.

32. John G. Winant to Secretary of War, 20 March 1944, 840.6 Films, London, Department of State Post (London) Records, RG 84. For more on the movie's troubled production, see Capra, *Name above the Title*, 352; Aldgate, "Mr. Capra Goes to War," 28, 32–33.

33. Chapman, "'Yanks Are Shown,'" 542, 549.

34. Ibid., 547–48.

35. Reed quoted in Nicholas Wapshott, *The Man Between: A Biography of Carol Reed* (London: Chatto and Windus, 1990), 169. On Eisenhower's views, see Kenneth A. Osgood, "Form before Substance: Eisenhower's Commitment to Psychological Warfare and Negotiations with the Enemy," *Diplomatic History* 24 (Summer 2000): 410; Kenneth A. Osgood, *Total Cold War: Eisenhower's Secret Propaganda Battle at Home and Abroad* (Lawrence: University of Kansas Press, 2006).

36. "New Pictures," *Time*, 17 September 1945, 95–96; Philip T. Hartung, "Test of Victory," *Commonweal*, 21 September 1945, 553–55; BC, review, *NYT*, 7 September 1945, sec. 1, p. 1; Chapman, "'Yanks Are Shown,'" 545.

37. Culbert, *News for Everyman*, 111–12; Horten, *Radio Goes to War*, 76–77; poster, n.d., 44-PA-794, Office of Government Reports Records, RG 44, NARA; Frank W. Fox, *Madison Avenue Goes to War: The Strange Military Career of American Advertising, 1941–1945* (Provo, Utah: Brigham Young University Press, 1975), 52. The MOI also published pro-Allied posters. See MIR 3/322, 3/1184.

38. Sikorsky, "From British Cassandra to American Hero"; Murrow quoted in Kimball, *Forged in War*, 16.

39. Kimball, *Churchill and Roosevelt*, 1:2; Kimball, *Forged in War*, 12, 23, 33.

40. Sir John Martin, *Downing Street: The War Years—Diaries, Letters, and a Memoir* (London: Bloomsbury, 1991), entry dated 10 August 1941; Churchill, *Grand Alliance*, 431–32; Borgwardt, *New Deal for the World*, 1–4.

41. Borgwardt, *New Deal for the World*, 4.

42. *Complete Presidential Press Conferences of Franklin D. Roosevelt* (New York: Da Capo, 1972), 18:382, 392; "From the Capital," *Newsweek*, 5 January 1942, 23.

43. Clifford Berryman, "Twas the Night before Christmas," drawing, [1941], LC-USZ62-128835, Cartoon Drawings Collection, Prints and Photographs Division, LC; Winston Churchill, *The Second World War* (London: Cassell, 1948–54), 3:540; Sikorsky, "From British Cassandra to American Hero," 33. Churchill and Roosevelt symbolized the alliance in Allied and enemy cartoons alike: See, for example, Charles G. Werner, "Big Guns," drawing, *Newsweek*, 5 January 1942, 22; "Churchill im Weissen Haus" [Churchill at the White House], drawing, n.d., LC-USZ62-33490, Cartoon Drawings Collection, Prints and Photographs Division, LC; Seppla [Joseph Plank], "Axis Bombs Severing FDR and Churchill's 'Hands across the Sea,'" drawing, n.d., LC-USZ61-1565, Cartoon Drawings Collection, Prints and Photographs Division, LC.

44. Frank L. Kluckhohn, "Congress Thrilled: Prime Minister Warns of Dark Days but Holds Victory Is Certain," *NYT*, 27 December 1941, 1; "Global Strategy against Axis Shaped up in Three Capitals," *Newsweek*, 5 January 1942, 18–19, 23; *Time*, 5 January 1942, 12; "Amid Seesawing Fortunes of War, Churchill Solidifies Anglo-American Friendship in Speech before Congress," *Life*, 5 January 1942, 28; Alan Barth to R. Keith Kane, 29 December 1941, Survey of Intelligence Materials 20–28 (April–June 1942), box 11, Alphabetical Subject file, OFF Records, RG 208; Sikorsky, "From British Cassandra to American Hero," 33.

45. *FRUS 1945*, 2:80; Lord Halifax to Anthony Eden, 19 February 1945, in *Confidential Dispatches*, edited by Hachey, 237–39; Cantril, *Public Opinion*, 369–70; Dimbleby and Reynolds, *Ocean Apart*, 153; Blum, *V Was for Victory*, 275. Contemporary academics also supported a permanent Anglo-American alliance: See, for example, Yale law professor Percy Elwood Corbett, *Britain: Partner for Peace* (New York: Harcourt, Brace, 1946).

46. Fayette W. Allport to Eric Johnston, 24 September 1946, 841.4061 Motion Pictures/10-2346, RG 59; Jarvie, *Hollywood's Overseas Campaign*, 180, 182.

47. Denis W. Brogan, *The English People* (New York: Knopf, 1943), 272–73; Gallup, *Gallup International Public Opinion Polls*, 1:160–61; Mass Observation quoted in Jose Harris, "Great Britain: The People's War?," in *Allies at War*, edited by David Reynolds, Kimball, and Chubarian, 253. See also David Reynolds, *Rich Relations*, 35–42, 434.

48. *London Times* quoted in Chapman, *British at War*, 249; Lejeune quoted in "American Films Win British Critic," *Chicago Sun*, [1943], and "The Flicks as Propaganda," *New York Herald Tribune*, 10 March 1943, both in Propaganda file (reel 10), MPAA.

49. Richard R. Ford to John Begg, 21 October 1941, 841.4061 Motion Pitures/327, RG 59; Thomas Baird, "Notes on Suitability of U.S. Films for Non-Theatrical Distribution in Britain," 14 April 1942, 841.4061 Motion Pictures/383, RG 59; "British Film

Envoy Scores Our Phony War Romances, Dramas," *Hollywood Reporter*, 26 June 1942, in Russian Films file, Motion Pictures and World War II Collection, Academy of Motion Picture Arts and Sciences, Beverly Hills, California.

50. Francis S. Harmon to Fayette W. Allport, 11 May 1945, War Activities Committee file (reel 8), MPAA; John G. Winant to Archibald MacLeish, 23 May 1942, 841.4061 Motion Pictures/387, RG 59; Ferdinand Kuhn to Ulric Bell, 7 January 1943, Kuhn file, box 3509, Records of the Chief, Motion Picture Division, LAO. For more on *Objective, Burma!* (dir. Raoul Walsh, Warner Bros., 1945), see Jarvie, "Burma Campaign on Film."

51. Elmer Davis to OWI Branch Directors, Staff Order 13, 29 January 1943, Poynter file, box 16, MP; "OWI Information Program in Allied Countries," n.d., box 1716, Records of the Chief, Liaison Office, Overseas Operations Branch, RG 208; OWI London Films Division, "Survey: Non-Theatrical Distribution in the United Kingdom," September 1943, 841.4061 Motion Pictures/465, RG 59; Ferdinand Kuhn to Elmer Davis, [1945], War Activities Committee file (reel 8), MPAA; David Reynolds, *From World War to Cold War*, 3, 179-98. The program's more than three dozen documentaries included *Henry Browne, Farmer, Women in Defense, Harvest for Tomorrow*, and *Cowboys*.

52. *Parliamentary Debates*, Commons, 5th ser., vol. 406 (1944), col. 1823; George Orwell, *The Collected Essays, Journalism, and Letters of George Orwell*, vol. 2, *My Country Right or Left, 1940-1943* (New York: Harcourt, Brace and World, 1968), 278-80; Gallup, *Gallup Poll*, 1:62-63; Aldgate and Richards, *Britain Can Take It*, 287-89; Dickinson and Street, *Cinema and State*, 154-55.

53. U.K. Cinematograph Films Council, *Tendencies to Monopoly*, 6, 29, 35.

54. U.S. State Department, Division of European Affairs, memorandum, 18 June 1942, 811.4061 Motion Pictures/734, RG 59; Henry Morgenthau Jr. Diary, October 1942, 579:87-89, FDRL; Jarvie, *Hollywood's Overseas Campaign*, 370.

55. Jarvie, *Hollywood's Overseas Campaign*, 192-93, 196-97; Woods, *Changing of the Guard*, 1-2, 150.

56. *Parliamentary Debates*, Lords, 5th ser, vol. 130 (1944), col. 933; John G. Winant to Secretary of State, 24 September 1945, 841.4061 Motion Pictures/9-2445, RG 59; London embassy to Secretary of State, 6 November 1945, 841.4061 Motion Pictures/11-645, RG 59; "Choice Is Bacon or Bogart," *London Daily Herald*, 17 November 1945, in Foreign Relations—Great Britain file (reel 10), MPAA.

57. Avery F. Peterson to John G. Winant, 16 February 1944, WHH to John G. Winant, Cordell Hull, and Edward Stettinius, 18 October 1944, both in 840.6 Films, Department of State Post (London) Records, RG 84; Fayette W. Allport to Foreign Managers, 27 November 1945, Foreign Relations—Great Britain file (reel 10), MPAA. The film trade war is detailed in Trumpbour, *Selling Hollywood*, 183-99.

Chapter 5

1. William H. Standley to Secretary of State, 25 May 1943, Russia: July 1942–43 file, box 49, President's Secretary's File, FDRL. Several scholars mention *Mission to Moscow*'s Kremlin exhibition in passing. See Gaddis, *United States and the Origins*, 44–45; Taubman, *Stalin's American Policy*, 59; David Culbert, "Our Awkward Ally: *Mission to Moscow* (1943)," in *American History/American Film*, edited by O'Connor and Jackson, 136–37; David Culbert, "Introduction," in *Mission to Moscow*, edited by Culbert, 36–37.

2. Nisbet, *Roosevelt and Stalin*, 107. Other critics include Marks, *Wind over Sand*, 169; Perlmutter, *FDR and Stalin*, 215, 217. Watt also writes, though uncritically, of FDR's belief that, without other leverage, Stalin would "have to be courted, wooed, constantly chatted up" (*Succeeding John Bull*, 101).

3. See Dallek, *Franklin D. Roosevelt*, 533–34; Kimball, *Juggler*, 8, 14, 185, 198–200.

4. *FRUS 1943*, 9; Costigliola, "Broken Circle," 679.

5. Costigliola, "After Roosevelt's Death," 5.

6. A handful of historians recall wartime Soviet-American cultural diplomacy, including Parks, *Culture, Conflict, and Coexistence*, 69, 84–86, 96–97; Hixson, *Parting the Curtain*, 6.

7. For an explanation of the rationale behind the Kremlin's movie purge penned by Britain's ambassador to Moscow, Sir Stafford Cripps, see Cripps to MOI Foreign Division, 10 August 1940, F 109/52, MIR 1/611. For more on the purge and Hollywood's continuing influence on Soviet cinema, see Kenez, *Cinema and Soviet Society*, 133–34; Richard Taylor, "Red Stars, Positive Heroes, and Personality Cults," in *Stalinism and Soviet Cinema*, edited by Richard Taylor and Spring, 76–77; Maya Turovskaya, "1930s and 1940s: Cinema in Context," in *Stalinism and Soviet Cinema*, edited by Richard Taylor and Spring, 237; Youngblood, "'Americanitis,'" 151–52; Youngblood, *Movies for the Masses*, 19–20, 31–34, 51, 53, 55, 61–64, 66, 174. Other forms of American popular culture, including jazz, were also suppressed. See Starr, *Red and Hot*. On the relative liberalism of the postrevolutionary years, see Stites, *Revolutionary Dreams*, 6–7.

8. On Soviet caricatures of capitalists and of the United States, see All-Union Communist Party Central Committee, decree, 20 May 1941, f. 17, o. 125, d. 71, l. 1, RGASPI; Union of Soviet Socialist Republics, All-Union State Film Foundation, *Soviet Feature Films*, 1:487–88; Kenez, *Cinema and Soviet Society*, 157–66, 169–70, 173; Turovskaya, "1930s and 1940s," 47; Parks, *Culture, Conflict, and Coexistence*, 121–22.

9. Soviet wartime propaganda policy is detailed by Miner, *Stalin's Holy War*, 10–11; Barber and Harrison, *Soviet Home Front*, 68–79; Mikhail N. Narinsky, "The Soviet Union: The Great Patriotic War?," in *Allies at War*, edited by David Reynolds, Kimball, and Chubarian, 271, 273; Sergei Drobashenko and Peter Kenez, "Film Pro-

paganda in the Soviet Union, 1941–1945: Two Views," in *Film and Radio Propaganda*, edited by Short, 96, 111.

10. For discussions of the wartime travails of the Soviet motion picture industry, see R. N. Iurenev, "Kinoiskusstvo voennykh let [Film Art during the War Years]," in *Sovetskaia kul'tura v gody Velikoi Otechestvennoi voiny* [Soviet Culture during the Great Patriotic War], 236; Kenez, *Cinema and Soviet Society*, 105–7, 130–32, 134, 137, 140–44, 186–88, 192–93. Soviet industrialists' views of the United States are explored in Wilson, *Ideology and Economics*, 8–9.

11. Pero Atashev for Grigorii Aleksandrov, "An Evening of American and Soviet Cinematic Friendship," plan, 10 August 1942, f. 5283, o. 14, d. 122, ll. 48, 50, GARF; Alexander Dovzhenko, "Wartime Cooperation in the Allied Countries," speech, August 1942, f. 5283, o. 14, d. 122, l. 11, GARF; Ivan G. Bol'shakov, "American and English Films," speech, 21 August 1942, f. 5283, o. 14, d. 122, l. 129, GARF; "Moscow Conference on American and British Cinema," 21–22 August 1942, Vladimir I. Bazykin file, box 1432, MR.

12. William H. Standley to Cordell Hull and FDR, 23 August 1942, 861.4061 Motion Pictures/15, RG 59; William H. Standley to Secretary of State, 23 June 1942, 711.61/854, RG 59; William H. Standley Diary, 21–22 August 1942, Russian Memoranda: 1942–43 file, box 17, William H. Standley Papers, Doheny Library, University of Southern California, Los Angeles; William H. Standley Diary, n.d., Correspondence—John Young/ WHH file, box 17, Standley Papers; Standley and Ageton, *Admiral Ambassador*, 48, 244–45.

13. For discussions of FDR's thinking, see Dallek, *Franklin D. Roosevelt*, 337–44, 350–51, 360; Bennett, *Franklin D. Roosevelt*, 55; Gaddis, *Russia, the Soviet Union, and the United States*, 150; Heinrichs, *Threshold of War*, 105, 141, 145. Winston Churchill also courted Stalin. See Miner, *Between Churchill and Stalin*, 253–54.

14. Elbridge Durbrow, memorandum of conversation, 22 August 1942, in *FRUS 1942*, 3:630; Division of European Affairs, memorandum, 27 August 1942, 861.4061 Motion Pictures/15, RG 59.

15. Samuel Spewack for Robert Sherwood, 16 November 1943, Moscow Cables, box 829, Office of Policy Coordination, Director of Overseas Operations, RG 208; "The OWI and the USSR," n.d., OWI and the USSR file, box 1716, Records of the Chief, Liaison Office, Overseas Operations Branch, RG 208; William H. Standley to Cordell Hull and FDR, 23 August 1942, 861.4061 Motion Pictures/15, RG 59. Newsreels and documentaries included *United News*, nos. 3, 5 (OWI, 1942), nos. 44, 57 (OWI, 1943); *Tanks: A Defense Report on Film* (Office for Emergency Management, 1942); *Beyond the Line of Duty* (Army Air Forces/Warner Bros., 1942); *Bomber: A Defense Report on Film* (Office for Emergency Management, 1941).

16. For more on *Soiuzkinozhurnal*, see Mikhail N. Narinsky and Lydia V. Pozdeeva, "Mutual Perceptions: Images, Ideals, and Illusions," in *Allies at War*, edited by David Reynolds, Kimball, and Chubarian, 310–11; D. W. Spring, "Soviet Newsreel

and the Great Patriotic War," in *Propaganda, Politics, and Film*, edited by Pronay and Spring, 280, 284–86.

17. *FRUS 1943*, 3:644n; Standley and Ageton, *Admiral Ambassador*, 306, 315, 319–20, 326, 379; William H. Standley Diary, n.d., Correspondence—John Young/WHH file, box 17, Standley Papers; William H. Standley for Secretary of State, "Report on the Exchange of Information between the United States and the Soviet Union," 7 April 1943, 861.4061 Motion Pictures/45, RG 59.

18. Joseph E. Davies to Lowell Mellett, 31 December 1941, Davies file, box 11, MP; MacLean, "Joseph E. Davies," 73–75. John Dewey was the book's most vocal critic. See Dewey, "Russia's Position," *NYT*, 11 January 1942, E7; Westbrook, *John Dewey*, 487–88.

19. Joseph E. Davies to Stephen T. Early, 6 January 1943, Davies file, box 3, Stephen T. Early Papers, FDRL; [Marvin McIntyre], memorandum, 23 July 1942, President's Personal File 1381, FDRL; Joseph E. Davies to Jack L. Warner, 4 March 1943, Scrapbook file, *Mission to Moscow* Collection, WBA; Culbert, "Introduction," 13, 16–17, 25.

20. Joseph E. Davies Diary, 23 November 1942, in *Mission to Moscow*, edited by Culbert, 251.

21. Nelson Poynter to Robert Buckner, 3 December 1942, Poynter file, box 16, MP; "Notes re. Rushes on 'Mission to Moscow,'" 6 January 1943, *Mission to Moscow* file, box 3521, Motion Picture Reviews and Analyses, Motion Picture Division, LAO; Nelson Poynter, "Weekly Log of Activities," 26 December–2 January 1942, 1943, Weekly Log file, box 3510, Records of the Chief, LAO.

22. Script reviews, 28, 30 November 1942, Reviews and Activities Reports, box 1439, MR; feature review, 28 April 1943, *Mission to Moscow* file, box 3521, Motion Picture Reviews and Analyses, Motion Picture Division, LAO.

23. Robert Buckner to David Culbert, 1, 14 January 1978, in *Mission to Moscow*, edited by Culbert, 254; *Mission to Moscow*; advertisements, *Soviet Russia Today*, July 1943, inside front cover, *NYT*, 25 April 1943, sec. 2, p. 4; BC, "Missionary Zeal: The Ecstasies in *Mission to Moscow* Raise Doubts on Political Films," *NYT*, 9 May 1943, sec. 2, p. 3; "*Mission to Moscow*: Davies Movie Whitewashes Russia," *Life*, 10 May 1943, 39. Polina Molotov was in fact commissar of the Soviet cosmetic industry. See Zubok and Pleshakov, *Inside the Kremlin's Cold War*, 80.

24. On Davies's influence and private views, see *FRUS 1943*, 3:504–5; Culbert, "Introduction," 24.

25. Culbert, "Introduction," 21, 23–24. The movie's explanation for the Nazi-Soviet Pact echoed the one given by Moscow. See Nikolai Sivachev and Nikolai N. Yakovlev, *Russia and the United States*, translated by Olga Adler Titelbaum (Chicago: University of Chicago Press, 1979), 122–23.

26. Eugene Lyons, "Memo on Movie Reviewers," *American Mercury*, July 1943, 81. For discussions of FDR's thinking, see Bennett, *Franklin D. Roosevelt*, 88; Dal-

lek, *Franklin D. Roosevelt*, 379–82; Gaddis, *Russia, the Soviet Union, and the United States*, 153–60. On Soviet-German peace talks and their implications for American policymakers, see Mastny, *Russia's Road*, 73–80, 84–85; Warren F. Kimball, "Stalingrad: A Chance for Choices," *Journal of Military History* 60 (January 1996): 91, 103, 106; Gaddis, *United States and the Origins*, 73.

27. Joseph E. Davies, "What We Didn't Know about Russia," *Reader's Digest*, March 1942, in *American Views of Soviet Russia*, edited by Filene, 144; Bertram D. Hulen, "Washington Hails Reds' Step as Great Gain for the Allies," *NYT*, 23 May 1943, 1; Foglesong, *American Mission and the "Evil Empire,"* 84–104; Mark, "October or Thermidor?," 937–41, 944–47.

28. *United News*, no. 68 (OWI, 1943); George Taylor, "The Potentialities of Psychological Warfare," 29 March 1943, Washington Office file, box 125, Correspondence with Government Agencies, Office of Policy Coordination, Director of Overseas Operations, RG 208; FDR to Joseph Stalin, 5 May 1943, Russia: July 1942–43 file, box 49, President's Secretary's File, FDRL. FDR's views are plumbed in Forrest Davis, "Roosevelt's World Blueprint," *Saturday Evening Post*, 10 April 1943, 21; Welles, *Where Are We Heading?*, 37; Mark, "October or Thermidor?," 944, 946; Dunn, *Caught between Roosevelt and Stalin*, 3–5. For the Davies mission, see MacLean, "Joseph E. Davies," 83–86.

29. Kenez, *Cinema and Soviet Society*, 148; Zubok and Pleshakov, *Inside the Kremlin's Cold War*, 82; Volkogonov, *Stalin*, 127, 131.

30. Nelson Poynter to Joseph E. Davies, 8 May 1943, Poynter file, box 16, MP; Culbert, "Our Awkward Ally," 136–37; *Three Russian Girls*, dir. Fedor Ozep and Henry Kesler (United Artists, 1944).

31. Standley and Ageton, *Admiral Ambassador*, 380; William H. Standley to Secretary of State, 25 May 1943, Cordell Hull for FDR, memorandum, 27 May 1943, both in Russia: July 1942–43 folder, box 49, President's Secretary's File, FDRL.

32. Joseph E. Davies to Harry M. Warner, 24 May 1943, in *Mission to Moscow*, edited by Culbert, 261; *FRUS 1943*, 3:657.

33. Stefan Sharff, "Soviet Capital Sees 'Mission to Moscow,'" *NYT*, 28 July 1943, sec. 1, p. 18. Critics have argued that both Roosevelt's Soviet policy and the film fostered the Kremlin's belief that the United States would acquiesce to any action, thus encouraging the Soviet Union's postwar expansion in Eastern Europe and elsewhere. See Taubman, *Stalin's American Policy*, 39, 59; Mastny, *Russia's Road*, 84–85.

34. On Moscow's mid-1943 foreign policy, see Taubman, *Stalin's American Policy*, 38–40, 74–75; Robert C. Tucker, *Stalin in Power: The Revolution from Above, 1928–1941* (New York: Norton, 1990), 223–35; Zubok and Pleshakov, *Inside the Kremlin's Cold War*, 6, 12, 26–35; Vladimir O. Pechatnov, *The Big Three after World War II: New Documents on Soviet Thinking about Post-War Relations with the United States and Great Britain*, Cold War International History Project, Working Paper 13 (Washington, D.C.: Wilson Center, 1995), 5–6, 8–9, 16–17; Vojtech Mastny, *The Cold War and*

Soviet Insecurity: The Stalin Years (New York: Oxford University Press, 1996), 6, 21, 23; Volkogonov, *Stalin*, 484–86. Although the Kremlin abolished the Comintern in May 1943, the Party Central Committee's Department of International Information clandestinely continued to direct the worldwide communist movement. See McDermott and Agnew, *Comintern*, 204–11.

35. Stefan Sharff, "Soviet Capital Sees 'Mission to Moscow,'" *NYT*, 28 July 1943, sec. 1, p. 18.

36. The British embassy in Moscow monitored the Soviet press. See "Monthly Report on the Distribution of British Films in the USSR," July 1943, N 5651/9/38, FOR 371/36921. On official Soviet commendations, see W. Averell Harriman to Secretary of State, 22 January 1944, 861.4061 Motion Pictures/79, RG 59.

37. Andrei N. Andrievsky for Solomon A. Lozovskii, "Agreement," 29 May 1943, f. 13, o. 5, p. 14, d. 246, ll. 2–3, Secretariat of Vice Commissar for Foreign Affairs Lozovskii, Archive of the Foreign Policy of the Russian Federation, Moscow; Vassily Zarubin, "Information about the Films Exchange Agreement with the U.S. Embassy," October 4, 1943, f. 13, o. 5, p. 14, d. 246, l. 7, Archive of the Foreign Policy of the Russian Federation.

38. "Sales of American Films to Soviet Russia," June 16, 1943, WHH to John G. Bryson, 15 June 1943, both in Foreign Relations—Russia file (reel 10), MPAA; Breckenridge Long to WHH, 28 June 1943, Correspondence—John Young/WHH file, box 17, Standley Papers; "Proposal of Admiral Standley to American Motion Picture Industry through Mr. Hays, 16 June 1943, 840.6 Motion Pictures, Department of State Post (Moscow) Records, RG 84.

39. George F. Kennan, "Motion Picture Program for USSR," 18 February 1946, Department of State Post (Moscow) Records, RG 84; Aram Khachaturyan, "First Soviet Review of U.S. Film Sent to 'Daily,'" *Film Daily*, 17 November 1944, *Song of Russia* file, Production Code Files, PCAC; Vsevolod Pudovkin to Samuel Goldwyn, 26 April 1944, f. 5283, o. 14, d. 245, l. 20, GARF.

40. Zaslavsky quoted in Maxwell M. Hamilton for Secretary of State, "American Films in Soviet Union," 30 May 1944, 861.4061 Motion Pictures/124, RG 59; Maj. Gen. F. H. Osborn for Gen. George C. Marshall, memorandum, 28 February 1944, Orientation Film—*Battle of Russia* Collection, Orientation Film Production Case Files, 1942–45, Chief Signal Officer Records, RG 111, NARA; Marsha Siefert, "Allies on Film: U.S.-USSR Filmmakers and *The Battle of Russia*," in *Extending the Borders*, edited by Siefert, 387–88.

41. Brooks, *Thank You, Comrade Stalin!*, 182, 185, 193; Diane P. Koenker and Ronald D. Bachman, *Revelations from the Russian Archives: Documents in English Translation* (Washington, D.C.: Library of Congress, 1997), 647, 656.

42. Engerman, *Modernization*, 4–6, 9; Pells, *Radical Visions*, 61–69; Filene, *American Views of Soviet Russia*, ix–x; Ceplair and Englund, *Inquisition in Hollywood*, 106–9.

43. On Davies's views, see Maddux, *Years of Estrangement*, 63–68; *Kansas City Star* quoted in Maddux, "Red Fascism, Brown Bolshevism," 89; John Dewey, "The Moscow Trials," in *Later Works*, 11:328. *New York Times* Moscow correspondent Walter Duranty, a fellow traveler, informed readers that the purges expunged an insurrection directed by exiled Bolshevik Leon Trotsky. See S. J. Taylor, *Stalin's Apologist: Walter Duranty, the New York Times' Man in Moscow* (New York: Oxford University Press, 1990), 267–72.

44. "Just One Choice," *Christian Science Monitor*, 2 June 1939, 22; "Thanks, Mr. Stalin; Thanks, Mr. Hitler," *Collier's*, 18 November 1939, 74. On the intellectual currency of "totalitarianism," see Adler and Patterson, "Red Fascism," 1050; Gleason, *Totalitarianism*, 31–32, 43–44, 47–50; Maddux, "Red Fascism, Brown Bolshevism," 93, 97–100.

45. Levering, *American Opinion*, 46; Roeder, *Censored War*, 145.

46. *Congressional Record*, 77th Cong., 1st sess., 1941, 87, pt. 6, p. 6899, pt. 7, p. 7305, 2nd sess., 1942, 88, pt. 1, pp. 799–800; Norman Thomas, letter to the editors, *Nation*, 31 January 1942, 124; J. M. Gillis, "No Alliance with Atheism," *Catholic World*, 5 January 1943, 395; Foglesong, *American Mission and the "Evil Empire,"* 86; Gleason, *Totalitarianism*, 48, 54–55; Levering, *American Opinion*, 50–53, 76–77.

47. Cantril, *Public Opinion*, 370; OFF Bureau of Intelligence, Report 23, "The United Nations," 2 June 1942, Polling Division, United Nations Report, box 7, Alphabetical Subject File, RG 208; OFF Bureau of Intelligence, Survey of Intelligence Materials 27, 10 June 1942, Survey of Intelligence Materials #20–28 (April–June 1942), box 11, Alphabetical Subject File, RG 208; Levering, *American Opinion*, 72.

48. Memorandum of conversation, 11 September 1941, in *FRUS 1941*, 1:832; "Proposed List of Films to Interpret the Issues of This War," October 1942, Poynter file, box 1443, MR; Dallek, *Franklin D. Roosevelt*, 296, 379–82; Gaddis, *United States and the Origins*, 73.

49. OWI, *Government Information Manual for the Motion Picture Industry* (revised), 29 April 1943, Manual Material—Hollywood Office, box 1438, MR; "Proposed List of Films to Interpret the Issues of This War," October 1942, Poynter file, box 1443, MR.

50. OWI, *Government Information Manual for the Motion Picture Industry* (revised), 29 April 1943, Manual Material—Hollywood Office, box 1438, MR.

51. Film Information Sheet 35, "Report from Russia," May 1943, box 1596, Press Notices of Documentary Films, Records of the Non-Theatrical Division, Domestic BMP, RG 208. Examples include *The City That Stopped Hitler—Heroic Stalingrad*; *Our Russian Ally* (OWI, n.d.); *Report from Russia* (OWI, 1943); *People of Russia* (MGM, n.d.); *Russian Revels* (Universal, 1943).

52. Short reviews, 29 March 1943, 16 December 1942, Reviews and Activities Reports, box 1439, MR.

53. Kenez, *Cinema and Soviet Society*, 189–90; Peter Kenez, "Black and White: The War on Film," in *Culture and Entertainment*, edited by Stites, 162.

54. Review, *NYT*, 17 August 1942, sec. 1, p. 19; review, *Hollywood Reporter*, 24 November 1942, in *Moscow Strikes Back* file, PCAC; David E. Lilienthal, *The TVA Years, 1939–1945* (New York: Harper and Row, 1964), 583.

55. Several scholars have explored the film, including David Culbert, "'Why We Fight': Social Engineering for a Democratic Society at War," in *Film and Radio Propaganda*, edited by Short, 185–86.

56. Jennifer R. Jenkins, "'Say It with Firecrackers': Defining the War Musical of the 1940s," *American Music* 19 (Autumn 2001): 315–39; Diane Holloway, *American History in Song: Lyrics from 1900 to 1945* (San Jose: Authors Choice, 2001), 399.

57. Kazin, *New York Jew*, 85–86; reviews, *Variety*, 29 September, 6 October 1943, in *Battle of Russia* file, PCAC; BC, review, *NYT*, 15 November 1943, sec. 1, p. 23.

58. "Hollywood Spanked for 'Sloughing' Cause of Democracy in War Films," *Variety*, 17 June 1942, 1; Ceplair and Englund, *Inquisition in Hollywood*, 109, 150, 156–57.

59. David Lardner, "Repercussions Would Help," *New Yorker*, 8 May 1943, 58–59; BC, "Missionary Zeal: The Ecstasies in *Mission to Moscow* Raise Doubts on Political Films," *NYT*, 9 May 1943, sec. 2, p. 3; Dwight Whitney, "'Mission to Moscow': It May Not Be Accurate History but It Corrects Old Prejudices," *San Francisco Chronicle*, 12 June 1943, Scrapbook file, *Mission to Moscow* Collection, WBA; Koppes and Black, *Hollywood Goes to War*, 207–8.

60. Manny Farber, "Mishmash," *New Republic*, 10 May 1943, 636; "'Mission to Moscow': Davies Movie Whitewashes Russia," *Life*, 10 May 1943, 39; John Dewey and Suzanne La Follette, "Several Faults Are Found in 'Mission to Moscow' Film," *NYT*, 9 May 1943, sec. 4, p. 8; Quentin Reynolds, *Curtain Rises*, 80. Dewey and La Follette's letter initiated a brief public exchange about the movie's merits. See Arthur Upham Pope, "'Mission to Moscow' Film Viewed as Historical Realism," *NYT*, 16 May 1943, sec. 4, p. 12; John Dewey and Suzanne La Follette, "Moscow Film Again Attacked," *NYT*, 24 May 1943, 14.

61. Eugene Lyons, "The Progress of Stalin-Worship," *American Mercury*, June 1943, 693–97; "Trotskyists Protest 'Mission to Moscow' Film," press release, [1943], Scrapbook file, *Mission to Moscow* Collection, WBA; Philip T. Hartung, "Hollywood's Mission," *Commonweal*, 21 May 1943, 125; Nathan D. Shapiro, "Mission to Moscow," *Commonweal*, 4 June 1943, 168; *Congressional Record*, 78th Cong., 1st sess., 1943, 89, pt. 10, p. A2570.

62. Orville F. Grahame to Warner Bros., 10 May 1943, W. F. Flowers to Warner Bros., 21 May 1943, Alice McCarthy to Warner Bros., 8 May 1943, all in Scrapbook file, *Mission to Moscow* Collection, WBA; Culbert, "Introduction," 34.

63. Nelson Poynter for Lowell Mellett, memorandum, 12 May 1942, box 3511,

Motion Picture Reviews and Analyses, Motion Picture Division, LAO; Koppes and Black, *Hollywood Goes to War*, 119; Westbrook Pegler, "Fair Enough," *LAT*, 24 June 1943, in Story file, *Action in the North Atlantic* Collection, WBA. Other pro-Soviet features include *The Boy from Stalingrad* (Columbia, 1943), *The Girl from Leningrad* (United Artists, 1943), *Days of Glory* (Gregory Peck's first starring role), and *Counterattack.*

64. Philip K. Scheuer, "Town Called Hollywood: Russian Collective Village Is Built in Hollywood," *LAT*, 18 April 1943, C2. For more on Goldwyn's opposition to "message" pictures, see chapter 1.

65. On Ukrainian collaboration with the Germans in the war's early days, see Barber and Harrison, *Soviet Home Front*, 28–29.

66. Script review, 12 May 1943, feature review, 5 October 1943, Ulric Bell to Samuel Goldwyn, 24 September 1943, all in box 3522, Motion Picture Reviews and Analyses, Motion Picture Division, LAO; Koppes and Black, *Hollywood Goes to War*, 213–14.

67. Script review, 18 December 1942, Reviews and Activities Reports, box 1440, MR.

68. Ibid.

69. *U.S. News and World Report* quoted in Elaine Tyler May, *Homeward Bound*, 19–20; Laville, "'Our Country Endangered by Underwear,'" 625–27, 632–34.

Several scholars have explored cinema's use of gendered discourse to communicate ideas about foreign peoples and international affairs. See Rosenberg, "'Foreign Affairs'"; Landy, *Cinematic Uses*, 153, 162, 169–70, 173–74, 183–86, 188, 190; Marchetti, *Romance and the "Yellow Peril"*; Kaplan, *Looking for the Other*.

70. Strada and Troper, *Friend or Foe?*, 12. Late war American culture became more conservative regarding portrayals of women, often upholding marriage, motherhood, and housewifery in an attempt to restore gender norms. See Elaine Tyler May, *Homeward Bound*, 47, 59–63, 69–72, 75; Hartmann, *Homefront and Beyond*, 38–39; D'Emilio, *Sexual Politics*, 23–39.

71. Script review, 18 December 1942, Reviews and Activities Reports, box 1440, MR.

72. Milt Livingston, review, *Motion Picture Daily*, 29 December 1943, in *Song of Russia* file, PCAC; BC, review, *NYT*, 11 February 1944, sec. 1, p. 17; script review, 18 December 1942, Reviews and Activities Reports, box 1440, MR.

73. Denis Morrison, "Russian Characters in Yank Films Are Now Dignified and Gallant," *Variety*, 28 October 1942, 15; "Die, but Do Not Retreat," *Time*, 4 January 1943, 23–24; Horten, *Radio Goes to War*, 60. The special 29 March 1943 issue of *Life* is discussed in Levering, *American Opinion*, 114–15; Polenberg, *War and Society*, 40–41. Pro-Soviet books included Wallace Carroll, *Inside Warring Russia* (Winston-Salem, N.C.: United Press Associates, 1942); Wallace Carroll, *We're in This with Russia* (Boston: Houghton Mifflin, 1942); Walter Graebner, *Round Trip to Russia* (Philadelphia: Lippincott, 1943).

74. "Die, but Do Not Retreat," *Time*, 4 January 1943, 24; Joseph E. Davies, "What We Didn't Know about Russia," *Reader's Digest*, March 1942, in *American Views of*

Soviet Russia, edited by Filene, 145; Quentin Reynolds quoted in Levering, *American Opinion*, 74; Dunn, *Caught between Roosevelt and Stalin*, 3–5.

75. Cantril, *Public Opinion*, 370–71; Levering, *American Opinion*, 117, 119.

76. "U.S. Opinion on Russia," *Fortune*, September 1945, 233–38; Cantril, *Public Opinion*, 370–71; Levering, *American Opinion*, 106, 108, 116–17, 138.

77. Philip T. Hartung, "One Good Gripe; Three Fair Films," *Commonweal*, 5 November 1943, 72; review, *Time*, 29 November 1943, 92; "Valentine Russe," *Newsweek*, 8 November 1943, 86; "Red Serenade," *Newsweek*, 21 February 1944, 88; Koppes and Black, *Hollywood Goes to War*, 213–14.

78. Blum, *V Was for Victory*, 234, 237–38, 240, 295–99; Polenberg, *War and Society*, 171–74, 185, 194, 208.

79. *Congressional Record*, 77th Cong., 2nd sess., 1942, 88, pt. 9, p. A2953; Arthur Krock, "The Problem Anterior to Italian Peace," *NYT*, 27 July 1943, 16; Blum, *V Was for Victory*, 40. Secret Soviet correspondence declassified and released decades later confirmed that the OWI did employ several party members with ties to Moscow's agents. See Haynes and Klehr, *Venona*, 196–200.

80. Pro-Allied stories in Soviet publications included "Litvinov Broadcasts to American Farmers," *Information Bulletin of the Embassy of the USSR*, 14 January 1943, 1–2; "American Built Planes—Symbol of Soviet-American Friendship," *Information Bulletin of the Embassy of the USSR*, 19 February 1944, 6–7; Joseph E. Davies, "Our Debt to Our Soviet Ally," *Soviet Russia Today*, June 1942; "Los Angeles Salutes the USSR," *Soviet Russia Today*, January 1943, 14–15, 30.

81. Vladimir Bazykin, report, 13 October 1942, f. 17, o. 125, d. 214, ll. 6–8, RGASPI; L. Kislova, "Plan for Scenarists Conference," 22 March 1943, f. 17, o. 125, d. 214, l. 20, RGASPI; L. Kislova to Grigorii V. Aleksandrov, 13 March 1943, f. 17, o. 125, d. 214, l. 5, RGASPI.

82. Maxim Litvinov to Nicholas Napoli, 6 July 1942, Story file, *Mission to Moscow* Collection, WBA; Loy W. Henderson to Vassily Zarubin, 2 October 1942, Vassily Zarubin to Loy W. Henderson, 14 October 1942, both in 840.6 Motion Pictures, Department of State Post (Moscow) Records, RG 84; Vladimir Bazykin to Lowell Mellett, 19 January 1943, "Notes about the Scenario 'Russia,'" 9 January 1943, both in Bazykin file, box 1432, MR; Samuel Goldwyn to Lowell Mellett, 9 June 1942, Goldwyn file, box 1435, MR.

83. Benjamin Vishnevsky, "Film Director Kalatozov Coming to Hollywood," *Information Bulletin of the Embassy of the USSR*, 8 July 1943, 6; "Soviet-U.S. Film Post-War Ties," *Variety*, 11 August 1943, 1, 44; Ivan G. Bol'shakov to Anastas I. Mikoyan, 1 April 1942, f. 5446, o. 43, d. 1080, l. 264, GARF; Mikhail Kalatozov, report notes, 10 June 1944, f. 17, o. 125, d. 291, ll. 92, 84–85, RGASPI; George F. Kennan to Department of State, 24 October 1944, 861.4061 Motion Pictures/10-2444, RG 59; memorandum of conversation, 9 November 1944, 861.4061 Motion Pictures/11-944, RG 59; memorandum of conversation, 29 November 1944, 861.4061 Motion Pictures/11-2944, RG

59; W. Averell Harriman to Department of State, 21 February 1945, 861.4061 Motion Pictures/2-2145, RG 59.

84. Vsevolod Pudovkin to Mikhail Kalatozov, 26 April 1944, f. 5283, o. 14, d. 245, l. 53, GARF; Irskii, report, 10 February 1943, f. 17, o. 125, d. 214, l. 4, RGASPI; J. Edgar Hoover to Adolf A. Berle Jr., 26 April 1944, 861.4061 Motion Pictures/109, RG 59; J. Edgar Hoover to Adolf A. Berle Jr., July 24, 1944, 861.4061 Motion Pictures/7-2444, RG 59; Charles Bohlen and Vladimir Bazykin, memorandum of conversation, 8 November 1943, f. 192, o. 10, p. 71, d. 29, l. 50, Archive of the Foreign Policy of the Russian Federation, Moscow; Zubok and Pleshakov, *Inside the Kremlin's Cold War*, 85.

85. Special FBI agent, report, 11 October 1943, in *Movies and American Society*, edited by Ross, 213–17.

86. *New York Herald Tribune*, 10 October 1943, in Propaganda file (reel 8), MPAA; *Congressional Record*, 78th Cong., 2nd sess., 1944, 90, pt. 11, pp. A4094–95, 79th Cong., 1st sess., 1945, 91, pt. 12, p. A3438; Ceplair and Englund, *Inquisition in Hollywood*, 208–12.

87. Barghoorn, *Soviet Image*, 229, 242; Stefan Sharff, "Soviet Capital Sees 'Mission to Moscow,'" *NYT*, 28 July 1943, sec. 1, p. 18. On the popular deconstruction and reassembly of American culture abroad, see Rob Kroes, "Americanisation: What Are We Talking About?," in *Cultural Transmissions and Receptions*, edited by Kroes, Rydell, and Bosscher, 303; Fiske, *Understanding Popular Culture*, 5, 11, 15, 19–20, 25, 36, 44, 103–6, 126. Distinctions between popular and elite responses are made by Richard Pells, "Who's Afraid of Steven Spielberg?," *Diplomatic History* 24 (Summer 2000): 500–501.

88. *NYT*, 7 June 1940, sec. 1, p. 27; *Edison, the Man*, dir. Clarence Brown (MGM, 1940); *Charley's Aunt*, dir. Archie Mayo (Twentieth Century–Fox, 1941); *Sun Valley Serenade*, dir. H. Bruce Humberstone (Twentieth Century–Fox, 1941); *His Butler's Sister*, dir. Frank Borzage (Universal, 1943); *Appointment for Love*, dir. William A. Seiter (Universal, 1941); *The Men in Her Life*, dir. Gregory Ratoff (Columbia, 1941); *NYT*, 6 September 1941, sec. 1, p. 20; American Film Institute, *American Film Institute Catalog*, F3:564–65, F4:92–93, 403–4, 1049–50, 1527–28, 2378–79; Starr, *Red and Hot*, 193. Lillian Hellman's *The Little Foxes*, directed by William Wyler (RKO, 1941), was the lone exception to positive portrayals of American life.

89. WHH, "Service of American Motion Pictures in Developing Better Understanding between American and Soviet Peoples," 5 October 1943, Foreign Relations—Russia file (reel 10), MPAA; Standley and Ageton, *Admiral Ambassador*, 214, 244; W. Averell Harriman to Secretary of State, "American Motion Pictures in the Postwar World," 13 April 1944, 800.4061/458, RG 59; Costigliola, "'Mixed Up' and 'Contact,'" 797. For a discussion of the renewed confidence in the American Way, see chapter 1.

90. W. Averell Harriman to Secretary of State, "American Motion Pictures in the Postwar World," 13 April 1944, 800.4061/458, RG 59; W. Averell Harriman to Secretary

of State, 6 November 1945, 861.4061 Motion Pictures/11-645, RG 59; Edward Ames, "Cultural Lags in the Soviet Union," 27 October 1945, 842 Cultural Relations, Department of State Post (Moscow) Records, RG 84; Barghoorn, *Soviet Image*, 242.

91. *FRUS 1946*, 6:698, 707; Barghoorn, *Soviet Image*, xiii, 229–30; George F. Kennan, "Motion Picture Program for USSR," 18 February 1946, Department of State Post (Moscow) Records, RG 84. Kennan reiterated his views in "The Sources of Soviet Conduct" (p. 577) and in an undelivered letter to Freeman Matthews, 1945, Writings and Publications (1934–49) file, box 23, George F. Kennan Papers, Seeley G. Mudd Manuscript Library, Princeton University, Princeton, N.J.

92. Union of Soviet Socialist Republics, All-Union State Film Foundation, *Soviet Feature Films*, vol. 3 appendixes, 15–23; George F. Kennan to Secretary of State, 14 December 1945, 840.6 Motion Pictures, Department of State Post (Moscow) Records, RG 84; Drobashenko and Kenez, "Film Propaganda," 96. U.S. documentaries distributed in the Soviet Union included *Power and the Land* (Rural Electrification Administration, 1940); *Democracy in Action*; *Price of Victory*.

93. W. Averell Harriman to Secretary of State, 25 August 1944, 861.4061 Motion Pictures/8-2544, RG 59; W. Averell Harriman to Secretary of State, 11 September 1944, 861.4061 Motion Pictures/9-1144, RG 59; [John F.] Melby to Ferdinand Kuhn and Robert Riskin, 24 June 1944, Foreign Relations—Russia file (reel 10), MPAA; Parks, *Culture, Conflict, and Coexistence*, 96.

94. "All-Soviet Union Communist Party Central Committee Propaganda and Agitation Administration Meeting Regarding the Film Question," minutes, 26 April 1946, f. 17, o. 125, d. 378, ll. 82–83, RGASPI. On the postwar Soviet purification drive, see Weiner, *Making Sense of War*, 7–8, 21–22; Zubok and Pleshakov, *Inside the Kremlin's Cold War*, 123–25.

95. W. Averell Harriman to Secretary of State, 25 August 1944, 861.4061 Motion Pictures/8-2544, RG 59; W. Averell Harriman to Secretary of State, 11 September 1944, 861.4061 Motion Pictures/9-1144, RG 59; Costigliola, "'Mixed Up' and 'Contact,'" 791, 794; Costigliola, "After Roosevelt's Death," 1–2. British diplomats came to a similar conclusion. See Christopher F. A. Warner, minute, 3 February 1945, N 941/491/38, FOR 371/47912. On Harriman's interpretation of Soviet actions and its resonance in Washington, see Bennett, *Franklin D. Roosevelt and Victory*, 132–34; Isaacson and Thomas, *Wise Men*, 230–31, 238–39, 263, 265.

96. Costigliola, "After Roosevelt's Death," 2–5; Samuel Spewack, *The Busy, Busy People* (Boston: Houghton Mifflin, 1948).

Chapter 6

1. The other wartime installments in the Chan series were 1942's *Castle in the Desert*; 1944's *Black Magic* and *The Chinese Cat*; and 1945's *The Jade Mask*, *The Scarlet Clue*, and *The Shanghai Cobra*. Huang, *Charlie Chan*, traces the character's factual roots and cultural resonance.

2. Said, *Orientalism*, 1–7; Tchen, *New York before Chinatown*, xxi–xxii.

3. Black, *Hollywood Censored*, 1, 226; Leff and Simmons, *Dame in the Kimono*, 7, 288; Moy, *Marginal Sights*.

4. Review of *The Chinese Parrot*, *Variety*, 11 January 1928, in *1926–1929*, vol. 3 of *Variety Film Reviews*, n.p.; Robert G. Lee, *Orientals*, 2; Moon, *Yellowface*, 6.

5. Frank Chin, "The Sons of Chan," in *Chinaman Pacific and Frisco R.R. Co.*, 131–32; Chin, *Bulletproof Buddhists*, 95–98; Gish Jen, "Challenging the Asian Illusion," *NYT*, 11 August 1991, sec. 2, p. 1; Elaine Kim, preface to *Charlie Chan Is Dead*, edited by Hagedorn, xiii. The letters of complaint are quoted in Huang, *Charlie Chan*, 283–84.

6. Said, *Orientalism*, 21; Leong, *China Mystique*, 1–2; Yoshihara, *Embracing the East*, 6; Klein, *Cold War Orientalism*, 11–17; Thomson, Stanley, and Perry, *Sentimental Imperialists*. See also McAlister, *Epic Encounters*, 270; Little, *American Orientalism*. According to Hunt, *Ideology and U.S. Foreign Policy*, 17–18, 69–77, 139–40, hierarchical racial logic historically guided U.S. foreign policy toward Asia and the developing world.

7. Moon, *Yellowface*, 6, 8; Lhamon, *Raising Cain*, 6, 44, 117–18, 127, 139; Rogin, *Blackface, White Noise*, 12, 16, 30–31, 103, 209–50. See also Yoshihara, *Embracing the East*, 1.

8. Earl Derr Biggers, *Keeper of the Keys* (1932; Chicago: Academy Chicago, 2009), 100; Huang, *Charlie Chan*, xvi–xvii, 194, 282.

9. Chang's views are documented in Eleanor Berneis, feature review, 8 December 1943, *Charlie Chan in Secret Service* file, box 3513, Motion Picture Reviews and Analyses, Motion Picture Division, LAO; Huang, *Charlie Chan*, xviii, 136–45, 160, 250–52, 257–58.

10. See, for example, the OWI's production files on *Charlie Chan in Mexico* and *Charlie Chan in the Secret Service*, box 3513, Motion Picture Reviews and Analyses, RG 208; Gerstle, *American Crucible*, 187–88.

11. Ngai, *Impossible Subjects*, 202–4, 224.

12. Jesperson, *American Images*, xvii; Hunt, *Making of a Special Relationship*, 299.

13. Marchetti, *Romance and the "Yellow Peril*," 1, 3–5; A. T. Steele, *The American People and China* (New York: McGraw-Hill, 1966), 22.

14. Wong has been rediscovered by modern critics, who recount *The Good Earth* (dir. Sidney Franklin [MGM, 1937]) episode. See Anthony B. Chan, *Perpetually Cool: The Many Lives of Anna May Wong* (Lanham, Md.: Scarecrow, 2003), 164–65; Graham Russell Gao Hodges, *Anna May Wong: From Laundryman's Daughter to Hollywood Legend* (New York: Palgrave, 2004), 150–55; Leong, *China Mystique*, 75–77.

15. Leong, *China Mystique*, 101–2. The *Los Angeles Times* tracked Wong's extensive defense work, which also included selling U.S. war bonds and serving as a civil defense warden. See "Anna May Wong Adds Work of Air-Raid Warden to Duties," *LAT*, 8 December 1942, 13; Alma Whitaker, "Women's Activities: Sugar and Spice," *LAT*, 10 December 1942, A8.

16. OFF Bureau of Intelligence, Study 27, 10 June 1942, Minutes, Committee on War Information, box 11, Subject File, Records of the Historian, RG 208; Cantril, *Public Opinion*, 369.

17. OFF Bureau of Intelligence, Study 27, 10 June 1942, Minutes, Committee on War Information, box 11, Subject File, Records of the Historian, RG 208; OFF Bureau of Intelligence, Survey no. 23, 13 May 1942, Survey of Intelligence Materials nos. 20–28 (April–June 1942), box 11, Alphabetical Subject File, RG 208.

18. OFF Bureau of Intelligence, Recommendations to Accompany Survey no. 27, 13 June 1942, Minutes, Committee on War Information, box 11, Subject File, Records of the Historian, RG 208; OFF Bureau of Intelligence, Report no. 23, 2 June 1942, Polling Division—United Nations Report, box 7, Alphabetical Subject File, Records of the Historian, RG 208; OFF Bureau of Intelligence, Survey no. 16, 25 March 1942, Survey of Intelligence Materials nos. 2–19 (1941–1942), box 11, Records of the Historian, RG 208; Koppes and Black, *Hollywood Goes to War*, 235.

19. OFF Bureau of Intelligence, Survey no. 16, 25 March 1942, Survey of Intelligence Materials nos. 2–19 (1941–1942), box 11, Records of the Historian, RG 208; OFF Bureau of Intelligence, Recommendations to Accompany Survey no. 27, 13 June 1942, Minutes, Committee on War Information, box 11, Subject File, Records of the Historian, RG 208.

20. OWI, *Government Information Manual for the Motion Picture Industry*, 8 June 1942, OWI, *Government Information Manual for the Motion Picture Industry* (revised), 29 April 1943, both in Manual Material—Hollywood Office, box 1438, MR.

21. OWI, *Government Information Manual for the Motion Picture Industry*, 8 June 1942, OWI, *Government Information Manual for the Motion Picture Industry* (revised), 29 April 1943, both in Manual Material—Hollywood Office, box 1438, MR.

22. "How to Tell Japs from the Chinese," *Life*, 22 December 1941, 81; U.S. Army Special Service Division, *Pocket Guide*; Dower, *War without Mercy*.

23. *They Got Me Covered*, dir. David Butler (Samuel Goldwyn Productions, 1943).

24. Enthusiastic reviews included "Air Corps Epic," *Wall Street Journal*, 17 November 1944, 8; Norbert Lusk, "Eastern Critics Acclaim War Picture," *LAT*, 23 November 1944, A9; BC, "Happy Medium," *NYT*, 26 November 1944, 1.

25. Peg Fenwick, script review, 8 June 1943, Sandy Roth, feature review, 13 December 1943, both in *Gung Ho!* file, box 3517, Motion Picture Reviews and Analyses, RG 208. Opposing reviews include Nelson B. Bell, "Makin Island Attack Forms Thrilling Basis of Keith's Gung Ho!," *WP*, 9 March 1944, 10; BC, "*Gung Ho!*—A Lurid Action Film about the Makin Island Raid," *NYT*, 26 January 1944, 23. I am grateful to Evan Dawley for pointing out the roots of the American adoption of "gung ho."

26. "The Camera Overseas: 136 Million People See This Picture of Shanghai's South Station," *Life*, 4 October 1937, 102.

27. Yoshida, *Making of the "Rape of Nanking,"* 37.

28. "Lady from China," *NYT*, 19 February 1943, 18; Elizabeth Green and Craighill

Handy, "Two Great Ambassadors of the New Order: Anson Burlingame and Mei-ling Chiang," *South Atlantic Quarterly* 42 (October 1943): 399; Jesperson, *American Images*, 95, 101–2.

29. "How to Tell Japs from the Chinese," *Life*, 22 December 1941, 81; U.S. Army Special Service Division, *Pocket Guide*; Jesperson, *American Images*, 73, 79–81.

30. OFF, Poster PA-44-2097A, 1942, World War II Posters, Office of Government Reports Records, RG 44, NARA; OWI, *Government Information Manual for the Motion Picture Industry*, 8 June 1942, Manual Material—Hollywood Office, box 1438, MR.

31. M. Thorson, feature review, 23 September 1942, *Flying Tigers* file, box 3516, Motion Picture Reviews and Analyses, RG 208.

32. Nelson Poynter, report, "Trends in Hollywood Pictures," 24 May 1943, Weekly Log, box 3510, Los Angeles Office, Records of the Chief, BMP, Domestic Operations, RG 208; Koppes and Black, *Hollywood Goes to War*, 223.

33. Richard H. Davis, "Motion Pictures in Free China," 7 April 1943, 893.4061 Motion Pictures/334, RG 59; George Atcheson to Secretary of State, telegram 1181, 14 May 1943, 893.4061 Motion Pictures/335, RG 59; WHH to Francis Colt de Wolf, 23 May 1944, 800.4061 Motion Pictures/471, RG 59; Kitamura, *Screening Enlightenment*, 17–20.

34. Richard H. Davis, "Motion Pictures in Free China," 7 April 1943, 893.4061 Motion Pictures/334, RG 59.

35. Randolph Sailer to William S. Cunningham, 21 March 1944, *Keys to the Kingdom* file, box 3520, Motion Picture Review and Analyses, RG 208; Eric Johnston, "America's World Chance," *Reader's Digest*, June 1945, 5–9; Walter Gould to Carl E. Milliken, 29 March 1945, 893.4061 Motion Pictures/5-345, RG 59. See also memorandum, 7 January 1944, Materials Related to U.S. Films in China, MPAA.

36. Chungking to State, telegram 538, 30 March 1945, 893.4061 Motion Pictures/3-3045, RG 59.

37. Walter Gould to Carl E. Milliken, 29 March, 10 April 1945, 893.4061 Motion Pictures/5-345, RG 59; memorandum, 7 January 1944, Materials Related to U.S. Films in China, MPAA.

38. Patrick J. Hurley to Secretary of State, telegram 777, 14 May 1945, 893.4061 Motion Pictures/5-1445, RG 59; Chungking to State, telegram 1161, 13 July 1945, 893.4061 Motion Pictures/7-1345, RG 59.

39. Secretary of State to Chongqing, telegram 55, 29 January 1942, 811.42793/527A, RG 59. Fairbank, *America's Cultural Experiment*, provides a useful overview of the program, which continued until the Chinese Revolution.

40. Willys Peck, memorandum, 10 June 1941, 811.42793/464, RG 59; Fairbank, *America's Cultural Experiment*, 148; *Central Daily News* (Chengdu) summarized in Motion Picture Bureau, monthly report, April–May 1943, Motion Pictures (OB), box 2, Records Relating to the Overseas Branch, Records of the Historian, RG 208;

Power and the Land (Rural Electrification Administration, 1940); *Tanks: A Defense Report on Film* (Office for Emergency Management, 1942). The U.S. Department of Agriculture produced *Democracy in Action*, *The River*, and *The Heritage We Guard*.

41. BC, review, *NYT*, 21 January 1943, 27.

42. "*China Girl* Will Screen," *LAT*, 11 January 1943, 8. Marchetti, *Romance and the "Yellow Peril,"* 1, identifies seventeen other Asian-Caucasian sexual dramas produced between 1915 and 1986.

43. Thorp, *America at the Movies*, 24; "*China Girl* Will Screen," *LAT*, 11 January 1943, 8; Warren H. Pierce to Jason Joy, 25 November 1942, L. Williams, feature review, 25 November 1942, both in *Dixie Dugan* file, box 3515, Motion Picture Review and Analyses, RG 208.

44. John T. McManus, "Communiqué on *China Girl*," *PM*, 8 February 1943, 20; Ernest L. Schier, "Capitol's *China Girl* Replaces Real Drama with Tepid Romance," *WP*, 29 January 1943, 12; Lusk, "Hecht-Hathaway Combine Viewed as Disappointment," *LAT*, 27 January 1943, 12; Edith Werner, *New York Mirror*, 22 May 1943, quoted in UNIO, "An American in China," *The War and Films*, n.d., *China* file, box 3513, Motion Picture Reviews and Analyses, RG 208.

45. Barbara Berch, "The New Sylvia Sidney," *NYT*, 18 February 1945, 3; Bell, "Cagney Turns Himself Loose against Enemy," *WP*, 5 May 1945, 5; Bell, "Blood on the Sun Is Turbulent Vehicle for Pugnacious Star," *WP*, 9 August 1945, 7; "Cagney Battles Jap Spy Ring in New Feature," *LAT*, 18 June 1945, A3; "James Cagney in Spy Story Set in Japan," *Christian Science Monitor*, 21 June 1945, 4; Philip K. Scheuer, "Cagney Foils Plotting Nips Dynamically," *LAT*, 23 June 1945, A5; BC, review, *NYT*, 29 June 1945, 12.

46. T. K. Chang to Robert T. M. Vogel, 20 August 1943, *Dragon Seed* file, box 3515, Motion Picture Reviews and Analyses, RG 208.

47. Eleanor Berneis, feature review, 25 May 1944, *Dragon Seed* file, box 3515, Motion Picture Reviews and Analyses, RG 208.

48. [Lillian R. Bergquist], notes, 15 September 1942, Eleanor Berneis, script review, 11 August 1943, and Eleanor Berneis, feature review, 25 May 1944, all in *Dragon Seed* file, box 3515, Motion Picture Reviews and Analyses, RG 208; Paul P. Kennedy, "When East Meets West," *NYT*, 16 July 1944, 3; Doherty, *Projections of War*, 321. Favorable commentary included Marjorie Kelly, "A High-Powered Film Is Shown; Theater Notes," *WP*, 17 August 1944, 5; Edwin Schallert, "Story of China Hits Epic Class," *LAT*, 18 August 1944, 11.

49. Richard P. Cooke, "Film of China," *Wall Street Journal*, 21 July 1944, 8; Agee quoted in Koppes and Black, *Hollywood Goes to War*, 242.

50. T. K. Chang to Robert T. M. Vogel, 20 August 1943, *Dragon Seed* file, box 3515, Motion Picture Reviews and Analyses, RG 208; review, *NYT*, 21 July 1944, 16; BC, "Spoken Freely," *NYT*, 30 July 1944; BC, "The Long Film," *NYT*, 23 July 1944, 1; *Chicago Tribune* quoted in Koppes and Black, *Hollywood Goes to War*, 242.

51. M. Thorson, script review, 16 November 1942, *New Yorker* quoted in UNIO, "An American in China," both in *China* file, box 3513, Motion Picture Reviews and Analyses, RG 208.

52. Lillian R. Bergquist, feature review, 22 March 1943, M. Thorson, script review, 16 November 1942, both in *China* file, box 3513, Motion Picture Reviews and Analyses, RG 208.

53. Quoted in UNIO, "An American in China," *China* file, box 3513, Motion Picture Reviews and Analyses, RG 208.

54. Peg Fenwick, synopsis review, 6 January 1943, Warren H. Pierce to Eugene R. O'Neil, 8 January 1943, both in *Keys of the Kingdom* file, box 3520, Motion Picture Reviews and Analyses, RG 208. These films represented only the tip of the cinematic iceberg. At least nine more features as well as innumerable shorts and documentaries touted China in some way: MGM's *A Yank on the Burma Road* (1942); Paramount's *Night Plan from Chungking* (1943) and *The Story of Dr. Wassell* (1944); Monogram's *China's Little Devils* (1945); RKO's *China Sky* (1945); and Universal's *Destination Unknown* (1942), *Escape from Hong Kong* (1942), *Halfway to Shanghai* (1942), and *The Amazing Mrs. Holliday* (1943).

55. Peg Fenwick and Dorothy Jones, script review, 19 January 1944, *Keys of the Kingdom* file, box 3520, Motion Pictures and Analyses, RG 208.

56. Ibid.

57. Peg Fenwick, script review, 23 February 1944, William S. Cunningham to Jason Joy, 26 February 1944, both in *Keys of the Kingdom* file, box 3520, Motion Pictures and Analyses, RG 208.

58. William S. Cunningham to Randolph Sailer, 13 April 1944, *Keys of the Kingdom* file, box 3520, Motion Pictures and Analyses, RG 208; Koppes and Black, *Hollywood Goes to War*, 242–46.

59. Virginia Richardson, feature review, 11 December 1944, *Keys of the Kingdom* file, box 3520, Motion Picture Reviews and Analyses, RG 208.

60. BC, review, *NYT*, 30 December 1944, 15; Thomas M. Pryor, "Taking a Peek at Peck," *NYT*, 7 January 1945, 3; Schallert, "Keys Story Appeals in Highlights," *LAT*, 13 January 1945, 5; Bell, "*Keys of the Kingdom* Creates a New Star," *WP*, 15 February 1945, 7.

61. Cantril, *Public Opinion*, 952–53.

Conclusion

1. Photo 26-G-2343, U.S. Coast Guard Records, RG 26, Still Picture Unit, NARA. The portrait of Churchill, Roosevelt, and Stalin accompanied published reports about Yalta: "'Big 3' Peace Formula Revealed," *LAT*, 13 February 1945, 1; Lansing Warren, "Yalta Parley Ends," *NYT*, 13 February 1945, 1; *FRUS 1945*, 798, 975.

2. Mollie Panter-Downes, "Letter from London," *New Yorker*, 19 May 1945, 46;

Photo 111-SC-205398, Chief Signal Officer Records, RG 111, NARA; David Reynolds, *Rich Relations*, 409.

3. UNIO, *United Nations Conference*, 9–10, 13.

4. *FRUS 1945*, 1:486, 1046, 1541; UNIO, *United Nations Conference*, 27, 34; Schlesinger, *Act of Creation*, 251–52. The national signatories included Argentina, Australia, Belgium, Bolivia, Brazil, Byelorussian Soviet Socialist Republic, Canada, Chile, China, Columbia, Costa Rica, Cuba, Czechoslovakia, Denmark, Dominican Republic, Ecuador, Egypt, El Salvador, Ethiopia, France, Greece, Guatemala, Haiti, Honduras, India, Iran, Iraq, Lebanon, Liberia, Luxembourg, Mexico, Netherlands, New Zealand, Nicaragua, Norway, Panama, Paraguay, Peru, Philippine Commonwealth, Saudi Arabia, Syria, Turkey, Ukrainian Soviet Socialist Republic, Union of South Africa, United Kingdom, United States, USSR, Uruguay, Venezuela, and Yugoslavia.

5. Overy, *Why the Allies Won*, 22–23, 285–86, 325. Comparative studies of Allied and Axis cinematic propaganda are methodologically fraught and few and far between, but Fox gives the nod to the former in her thoughtful *Film Propaganda*, 311–12.

6. Hovland, Lumsdaine, and Sheffield, *Experiments on Mass Communication*, 32–42, 55–64, 254–55. The other volumes in the series, all by Samuel A. Stouffer et al., are *The American Soldier: Adjustment during Army Life* (Princeton: Princeton University Press, 1949); *The American Soldier: Combat and Its Aftermath* (Princeton: Princeton University Press, 1949); and *Measurement and Prediction* (Princeton: Princeton University Press, 1950).

7. Vance Packard, *The Hidden Persuaders* (1957; New York: Ig, 2007); Lizabeth Cohen, *A Consumers' Republic: The Politics of Mass Consumption in Postwar America* (New York: Knopf, 2003), 298–302; Engerman, "American Knowledge," 603–4. For more on the "magic keys," the midcentury theory that if certain codes could be inserted into a communicated message (the key) then human cognition or emotion could be modified (or turned), see Shearon A. Lowery and Melvin L. DeFleur, *Milestones in Mass Communication Research: Media Effects*, 3rd ed. (White Plains, N.Y.: Longman, 1995), 163–88.

8. MacLeish, *Popular Relations and the Peace*, 3, 10–11; Macmahon, *Memorandum*, xi–xv, 73–88. Macmahon cited Mayer, "Fact into Film."

9. Moscow Embassy to Secretary of State, 21 September 1948, 861.4061 Motion Pictures/9-2148, RG 59; Dean Acheson to Moscow Embassy, 11 April 1947, 861.4061 Motion Pictures/4-1147, RG 59. Kennan considered culture an excellent tool for not only containing Soviet expansion but also undermining the Kremlin's authority behind the Iron Curtain. See Kennan, "Sources of Soviet Conduct," 571, 577, 580–81; George F. Kennan to R. Gordon Wassen, February 4, 1947, folder 8, box 28, George F. Kennan Papers, Seeley G. Mudd Manuscript Library, Princeton University, Prince-

ton, N.J.; George F. Kennan, "Comments on the General Trend of U.S. Foreign Policy," 20 August 1948, box 23, Kennan Papers. For more on film's Cold War use by various U.S. institutions, see Cora Sol Goldstein, *Capturing the German Eye: American Visual Propaganda in Occupied Germany* (Chicago: University of Chicago Press, 2009); Kitamura, *Screening Enlightenment*; Amy C. Garrett, "Marketing America: Public Culture and Public Diplomacy in the Marshall Plan Era, 1947–1954" (Ph.D. diss., University of Pennsylvania, 2004); Cull, *Cold War and the United States Information Agency.*

10. Hovland, Lumsdaine, and Sheffield, *Experiments on Mass Communication*, 42–45, 63–65, 255, 265–75; Joseph T. Klapper, *The Effects of Mass Media: A Report to the Director of the Public Library Inquiry* (New York: Bureau of Applied Social Research, 1950); Paul F. Lazarsfeld, *The People's Choice: How the Voter Makes Up His Mind in a Presidential Campaign* (New York: Duell, Sloan, and Pearce, 1944). The "limited effects" and Lazarsfeld's "two-step flow" models, among others, are outlined in Lowery and DeFleur, *Milestones*, 91, 162–63.

11. Churchill quoted in George C. Herring, *From Colony to Superpower: U.S. Foreign Relations since 1776* (New York: Oxford University Press, 2008), 605. Journalistic accounts of the San Francisco Conference include Bob Considine, "Russia Wins Three Votes in Security Assembly," *WP*, 28 April 1945, 1; James B. Reston, "Big Three Wrestle Again over Poland," *NYT*, 3 May 1945, 1, 16; James B. Reston, "Little Nations Balking on Vote Procedure Issue," *LAT*, 22 May 1945, 2; *North by Northwest*, dir. Alfred Hitchcock (MGM, 1959); Fousek, *To Lead the Free World.*

12. Bohlen quoted in Gaddis, *Cold War*, 83; *Encounter at the Elbe* (*Vstrecha na Elbe*), dir. Grigorii Aleksandrov (Mosfilm, 1949); *The Manchurian Candidate*, dir. John Frankenheimer (United Artists, 1962). American anti-Soviet and anti-Chinese films of the era include *The Iron Curtain*, dir. William Wellman (Twentieth Century-Fox, 1948); *The Red Menace*, dir. R. G. Springsteen (Republic, 1949); *Peking Express*, dir. William Dieterle (Paramount, 1951); *Big Jim McLain*, dir. Edward Ludwig (Warner Bros., 1952); and *China Venture*, dir. Don Siegel (Columbia, 1953). See also David Reynolds, *One World Divisible*, 1–2; Shaw, *Hollywood's Cold War*; Whitfield, *Culture of the Cold War*, 127–52.

13. *FRUS 1947*, 3:340; *My Son John*, dir. Leo McCarey (Paramount, 1952); *I Was a Communist for the FBI*, dir. Gordon Douglas (Warner Bros., 1951); Costigliola, "After Roosevelt's Death," 21; Costigliola, "Nuclear Family," 163–65; Costigliola, "'Unceasing Pressure,'" 1310.

14. U.S. Congress, House, Committee on Un-American Activities, *Hearings*, 1–2; Doherty, *Projections*, 266. For a fulsome account of the hearings, see Ceplair and Englund, *Inquisition in Hollywood*, 254–98.

15. U.S. Congress, House, Committee on Un-American Activities, *Hearings*, 10, 33.

16. Ibid., 34–36, 38–39.

17. Ibid., 71–72, 75, 80–81.

18. Ibid., 83, 89, 166.

19. Ibid., 56–68, 164–71, 213–25, 280–89; *Congressional Record*, 78th Cong., 2nd sess., 1944, 90, pt. 8, pp. A1143–44; Ceplair and Englund, *Inquisition in Hollywood*, 210, 212; Gabler, *Walt Disney*, 451–53; Vaughn, *Ronald Reagan in Hollywood*, 145–48.

20. Cripps, *Hollywood's High Noon*, 206–33; Bernhard, *U.S. Television News and Cold War Propaganda*; Doherty, *Cold War, Cool Medium*.

SELECTED BIBLIOGRAPHY

Archival Sources

Academy of Motion Picture Arts and Sciences, Beverly Hills, California
    Motion Picture Association of America General Correspondence
    Motion Pictures and World War II Collection
    Production Code Administration Collection
Archive of the Foreign Policy of the Russian Federation, Moscow
    Vice-Commissar Solomon A. Lozovskii Records, Fond 13
    Washington Embassy Records, Fond 192
Franklin D. Roosevelt Presidential Library and Museum, Hyde Park, New York
    Stephen T. Early Papers
    Harry L. Hopkins Papers
    Map Room Papers
    Lowell Mellett Papers
    Henry Morgenthau Jr. Diary
    Peter Odegard Papers
    Official File
    President's Personal File
    President's Secretary's File
    Still Photographs
Imperial War Museum, London, United Kingdom
    Film and Video Archive
Library of Congress, Washington, D.C.
    Motion Picture, Broadcasting, and Recorded Sound Division
    Prints and Photographs Division
Seeley G. Mudd Manuscript Library, Princeton University, Princeton, New Jersey
    Fight for Freedom Papers
    George F. Kennan Papers
National Archives and Records Administration II, College Park, Maryland
    Chief Signal Officer Records, RG 111
    Department of State Records, RG 59
    Department of State, Foreign Service Posts Records, RG 84
    Motion Picture Films and Sound and Video Recordings
    Office of Government Reports Records, RG 44
    Office of War Information Records, RG 208
    Photographs and Graphic Works
National Archives, Kew, United Kingdom
    Foreign Office Records

Ministry of Information Records
Russian State Archive for Social and Political History, Moscow
    Central Committee of the Communist Party of the Soviet Union Records, Fond 17
State Archive of the Russian Federation, Moscow
    All-Union Society for Cultural Relations with Foreign Countries Records, Fond
        5283
    Council of People's Commissars of the USSR Records, Fond 5446
United Nations Archives, New York
    United Nations Information Organization Records
University of Kent, Canterbury
    British Cartoon Archive
University of Southern California, Los Angeles
    William H. Standley Papers, Doheny Library
    Warner Bros. Archives, School of Cinema-Television

Films

Action in the North Atlantic. Directed by Lloyd Bacon. Warner Bros., 1943.
All Quiet on the Western Front. Directed by Lewis Milestone. Universal, 1930.
America Moves Up. Directed by Ralph Elton. Crown Film Unit, 1941.
The Battle of Britain. Directed by Frank Capra. U.S. War Department, 1943.
The Battle of China. Directed by Frank Capra. U.S. War Department, 1944.
The Battle of Russia. Directed by Frank Capra and Anatole Litvak. U.S. War
    Department, 1943.
Blood on the Sun. Directed by Frank Lloyd. United Artists, 1945.
Bombs over Burma. Directed by Joseph H. Lewis. Producers Releasing, 1942.
A Canterbury Tale. Directed by Michael Powell and Emeric Pressburger. Archers,
    1944.
Casablanca. Directed by Michael Curtiz. Warner Bros., 1942.
Charlie Chan in the Secret Service. Directed by Phil Rosen. Monogram, 1944.
China. Directed by John Farrow. Paramount, 1943.
China Girl. Directed by Henry Hathaway. Twentieth Century–Fox, 1942.
The Circus [Tsirk']. Directed by Grigorii Aleksandrov. Mosfilm, 1936.
The City That Stopped Hitler—Heroic Stalingrad. Directed by Leonid Varlamov.
    Central Newsreel Studio/Paramount, 1943.
Common Cause. U.K. Ministry of Information, 1942.
Comrade X. Directed by King Vidor. MGM, 1940.
Counterattack. Directed by Zoltan Korda. Columbia, 1945.
Days of Glory. Directed by Jacques Tourneur. RKO, 1944.
Democracy in Action. U.S. Department of Agriculture, 1942.
Desert Victory. Directed by Roy Boulting and David MacDonald. British Army/U.S.
    War Department, 1943.

Dr. Ehrlich's Magic Bullet. Directed by William Dieterle. Warner Bros., 1940.

Dragon Seed. Directed by Jack Conway and Harold S. Bucquet. MGM, 1944.

Eagle Squadron. Directed by Arthur Lubin. Universal, 1942.

Flying Tigers. Directed by David Miller. Republic, 1942.

Foreign Correspondent. Directed by Alfred Hitchcock. Wanger/United Artists, 1940.

49th Parallel. Directed by Michael Powell. Ortus Films, 1941.

Gung Ho! Directed by Ray Enright. Universal, 1943.

The Hitler Gang. Directed by John Farrow. Paramount, 1944.

I Live in Grosvenor Square. Directed by Herbert Wilcox. Herbert Wilcox
    Productions, 1945.

In Which We Serve. Directed by Noel Coward. Rank/Two Cities, 1942.

The Keys of the Kingdom. Directed by John M. Stahl. Twentieth Century–Fox, 1944.

Lady from Chungking. Directed by William Nigh. Producers Releasing, 1942.

The Life and Death of Colonel Blimp. Directed by Michael Powell and Emeric
    Pressburger. Archers/Independent Producers, 1943.

The Lion Has Wings. Directed by Michael Powell. London Film Productions/
    United Artists, 1939.

Listen to Britain. Directed by Humphrey Jennings. Crown Film Unit, 1942.

London Can Take It. Directed by Harry Watt. Crown Film Unit, 1940.

A Matter of Life and Death. Directed by Michael Powell and Emeric Pressburger.
    Archers, 1946.

Mission to Moscow. Directed by Michael Curtiz. Warner Bros., 1943.

Mr. Smith Goes to Washington. Directed by Frank Capra. Columbia, 1939.

Mrs. Miniver. Directed by William Wyler. MGM, 1942.

Moscow Strikes Back. Directed by Ilya Kopalin and Leonid Varlamov. Central
    Newsreel Studios/Republic, 1942.

Ninotchka. Directed by Ernst Lubitsch. MGM, 1939.

The North Star. Directed by Lewis Milestone. RKO, 1943.

Oswego. Directed by Willard Van Dyke. U.S. Office of War Information, 1943.

Prelude to War. Directed by Frank Capra. U.S. War Department, 1942.

The Price of Victory. Pine-Thomas Studios/Paramount, 1942.

Sahara. Directed by Zoltan Korda. Columbia, 1943.

The Sea Hawk. Directed by Michael Curtiz. Warner Bros., 1940.

Sergeant York. Directed by Howard Hawks. Warner Bros., 1941.

Sherlock Holmes and the Secret Weapon. Directed by Roy William Neill. Universal,
    1943.

Song of Russia. Directed by Gregory Ratoff. MGM, 1944.

The Stilwell Road. U.S. War Department, 1945.

Target for Tonight. Directed by Harry Watt. Crown Film Unit, 1941.

That Hamilton Woman. Directed by Alexander Korda. Korda Films/United Artists,
    1941.

Thirty Seconds over Tokyo. Directed by Sam Zimbalist. MGM, 1944.

This above All. Directed by Anatole Litvak. Twentieth Century–Fox, 1942.

This Is the Army. Directed by Michael Curtiz. Warner Bros., 1943.

Thunder Birds. Directed by William A. Wellman. Twentieth Century–Fox, 1942.

The True Glory. Directed by Carol Reed. British Army/U.S. War Department, 1945.

Tunisian Victory. Directed by Frank Capra and Hugh Stewart. British Army/U.S. War Department, 1944.

Two-Way Street: Quick Facts about Lend-Lease. Monogram/Producers Releasing, 1945.

United Nations. U.K. Ministry of Information, 1942.

United News. U.S. Office of War Information, 1942–45.

Watchtower over Tomorrow. U.S. Office of War Information/U.S. Department of State, 1945.

The Way to the Stars. Directed by Anthony Asquith. Two Cities, 1945.

A Welcome to Britain. Directed by Anthony Asquith. U.K. Ministry of Information, 1943.

We Sail at Midnight. Directed by Julian Spiro. Crown Film Unit, 1943.

The White Cliffs of Dover. Directed by Clarence Brown. MGM, 1944.

Wilson. Directed by Henry King. Twentieth Century–Fox, 1944.

A Yank in the RAF. Directed by Henry King. Twentieth Century–Fox, 1941.

Government Documents

Fairbank, Wilma. *America's Cultural Experiment in China, 1942–1949.* Washington, D.C.: U.S. Government Printing Office, 1976.

MacLeish, Archibald. *Popular Relations and the Peace.* Washington, D.C.: U.S. Government Printing Office, 1945.

Macmahon, Arthur W. *Memorandum on the Postwar International Information Program of the United States.* Washington, D.C.: U.S. Government Printing Office, 1945.

U.K. Cinematograph Films Council. *Tendencies to Monopoly in the Cinematograph Film Industry: Report of a Committee Appointed by the Cinematograph Films Council.* London: His Majesty's Stationery Office, 1944.

U.K. Parliament. *Parliamentary Debates, Commons and Lords.* London: His Majesty's Stationery Office, 1939–45.

Union of Soviet Socialist Republics. Embassy. *Information Bulletin of the Embassy of the USSR.* Washington, D.C.: Embassy of the USSR, 1942–45.

Union of Soviet Socialist Republics. All-Union State Film Foundation [Vsesoiuznyi Gosudarstvennyi Fond Kinofil'mov]. *Soviet Feature Films: An Annotated Catalog* [Sovetskie Khudozhestvennye Fil'my: Annotirovannyi Katalog]. Vol. 1. Moscow: Iskusstvo, 1961.

U.S. Army Special Service Division. *Instructions for American Servicemen in Britain.* Washington, D.C.: U.S. Department of War, 1942.

———. *Pocket Guide to China.* Washington, D.C.: U.S. Government Printing Office, 1942.

U.S. Bureau of the Census. *Historical Statistics of the United States: Colonial Times to 1970.* Washington, D.C.: U.S. Government Printing Office, 1975.

U.S. Congress. *Congressional Record.* Washington, D.C.: U.S. Government Printing Office, 1939–45.

———. House. Committee on Un-American Activities. *Hearings Regarding the Communist Infiltration of the Motion Picture Industry.* 80th Cong., 1st sess., 20–24 and 27–30 October 1947. Washington, D.C.: U.S. Government Printing Office, 1947.

———. Senate. Committee on Interstate Commerce. *Propaganda in Motion Pictures: Hearings.* 77th Cong., 1st sess., 9–26 September 1941. Washington, D.C.: U.S. Government Printing Office, 1942.

U.S. Department of State. *Foreign Relations of the United States, 1939.* Vol. 2, *General: The British Commonwealth and Europe.* Washington, D.C.: U.S. Government Printing Office, 1956.

———. *Foreign Relations of the United States, 1941.* Vol. 1, *General: The Soviet Union.* Washington, D.C.: U.S. Government Printing Office, 1958.

———. *Foreign Relations of the United States, 1942.* Vol. 1, *General: The British Commonwealth, the Far East.* Washington, D.C.: U.S. Government Printing Office, 1960.

———. *Foreign Relations of the United States, 1942.* Vol. 3, *Europe.* Washington, D.C.: U.S. Government Printing Office, 1961.

———. *Foreign Relations of the United States, 1943. The Conferences at Cairo and Tehran.* Washington, D.C.: U.S. Government Printing Office, 1961.

———. *Foreign Relations of the United States, 1943.* Vol. 3, *The British Commonwealth, Eastern Europe, the Far East.* Washington, D.C.: U.S. Government Printing Office, 1963.

———. *Foreign Relations of the United States, 1945. Conferences at Malta and Yalta.* Washington, D.C.: U.S. Government Printing Office, 1955.

———. *Foreign Relations of the United States, 1945.* Vol. 1, *General: The United Nations.* Washington, D.C.: U.S. Government Printing Office, 1967.

———. *Foreign Relations of the United States, 1945.* Vol. 2, *The Conference of Berlin (The Potsdam Conference).* Washington, D.C.: U.S. Government Printing Office, 1960.

———. *Foreign Relations of the United States, 1946.* Vol. 6, *Eastern Europe, the Soviet Union.* Washington, D.C.: U.S. Government Printing Office, 1969.

———. *Foreign Relations of the United States, 1947.* Vol. 3, *The British*

Commonwealth, Europe. Washington, D.C.: U.S. Government Printing Office, 1972.

United Nations Information Organization. *United Nations Conference on International Organization: The Story of the Conference in San Francisco.* New York: United Nations Information Organization, [1945].

Periodicals

American Journal of Sociology

American Mercury

Bulletin (U.S. Department of State)

Catholic World

Chicago Sun

Chicago Tribune

Christian Century

Christian Science Monitor

Collier's

Commonweal

Film Daily

Foreign Affairs

Fortune

Harper's

Hollywood Reporter

Life

Los Angeles Times

Motion Picture Daily

Motion Picture Herald

Nation

New Republic

Newsweek

New Yorker

New York Herald Tribune

New York Mirror

New York Times

PM

Public Opinion Quarterly

Reader's Digest

San Francisco Chronicle

Saturday Evening Post

Scribner's Commentator

South Atlantic Quarterly

Soviet Russia Today

Time

The Times (London)

Variety

Vital Speeches of the Day

Wall Street Journal

Washington Post

Published Sources

Adams, Michael C. C. *The Best War Ever: America and World War II.* Baltimore: Johns Hopkins University Press, 1994.

Adler, Les K., and Thomas G. Patterson. "Red Fascism: The Merger of Nazi Germany and Soviet Russia in the American Image of Totalitarianism, 1930s–1950s." *American Historical Review* 75 (April 1970): 1046–64.

Aldgate, Anthony. "Mr. Capra Goes to War: Frank Capra, the British Army Film Unit, and Anglo-American Travails in the Production of *Tunisian Victory*." *Historical Journal of Film, Radio, and Television* 11, no. 1 (1991): 21–39.

Aldgate, Anthony, and Jeffrey Richards. *Best of British: Cinema and Society from 1930 to the Present.* Rev. ed. London: Tauris, 1999.

———. *Britain Can Take It: The British Cinema in the Second World War.* 2nd ed. Edinburgh: Edinburgh University Press, 1994.

Allen, H. C. *Great Britain and the United States: A History of Anglo-American Relations, 1783–1952*. New York: St. Martin's, 1955.

Alpers, Benjamin L. *Dictators, Democracy, and American Public Culture: Envisioning the Totalitarian Enemy, 1920s–1950s*. Chapel Hill: University of North Carolina Press, 2003.

Ambler, Charles. "Popular Films and Colonial Audiences: The Movies in Northern Rhodesia." *American Historical Review* 106 (February 2001): 81–105.

American Film Institute. *The American Film Institute Catalog of Motion Pictures Produced in the United States*. 23 vols. Berkeley: University of California Press, 1993–99.

Anderson, Benedict. *Imagined Communities: Reflections on the Origin and Spread of Nationalism*. Rev. ed. London: Verso, 2006.

Appy, Christian G., ed. *Cold War Constructions: The Political Culture of United States Imperialism, 1945–1966*. Amherst: University of Massachusetts Press, 2000.

Barber, John, and Mark Harrison. *The Soviet Home Front, 1941–1945: A Social and Economic History of the USSR in World War II*. London: Longman, 1991.

Barghoorn, Frederick C. *The Soviet Image of the United States: A Study in Distortion*. 1950; Port Washington, N.Y.: Kennikat, 1969.

Baughman, James L. *Henry R. Luce and the Rise of the American News Media*. Rev. ed. Baltimore: Johns Hopkins University Press, 2001.

Belmonte, Laura A. *Selling the American Way: U.S. Propaganda and the Cold War*. Philadelphia: University of Pennsylvania Press, 2008.

Bender, Thomas, ed. *Rethinking American History in a Global Age*. Berkeley: University of California Press, 2002.

Bennett, Edward M. *Franklin D. Roosevelt and the Search for Victory: American-Soviet Relations, 1939–1945*. Wilmington, Del.: Scholarly Resources, 1990.

Berg, A. Scott. *Lindbergh*. New York: Putnam's, 1998.

Berle, Adolf A., Jr. *Navigating the Rapids, 1918–1971*. New York: Harcourt Brace Jovanovich, 1973.

Bernays, Edward L. *Crystallizing Public Opinion*. New York: Boni and Liveright, 1923.

———. *Democratic Leadership in Total War*. Cleveland: Western Reserve University Press, 1943.

———. *Propaganda*. New York: Liveright, 1928.

———. *Speak Up for Democracy*. New York: Viking, 1940.

Bernhard, Nancy E. *U.S. Television News and Cold War Propaganda, 1947–1960*. New York: Cambridge University Press, 1999.

Birdwell, Michael E. *Celluloid Soldiers: The Warner Bros. Campaign against Nazism*. New York: New York University Press, 1999.

Black, Gregory D. *Hollywood Censored: Morality Codes, Catholics, and the Movies*. New York: Cambridge University Press, 1994.

Blum, John Morton. *V Was for Victory: Politics and American Culture during World War II*. New York: Harcourt Brace Jovanovich, 1976.

Blumer, Herbert. *Movies and Conduct*. New York: Macmillan, 1933.

Bodnar, John. *The "Good War" in American Memory*. Baltimore: Johns Hopkins University Press, 2010.

Bonnet, Henri. *The United Nations: What They Are; What They May Become*. Chicago: World Citizens Association, 1942.

Bordwell, David. *Narration in the Fiction Film*. Madison: University of Wisconsin Press, 1985.

Borgwardt, Elizabeth. *A New Deal for the World: America's Vision for Human Rights*. Cambridge: Belknap Press of Harvard University Press, 2005.

Buhite, Russell D., and David W. Levy, eds. *FDR's Fireside Chats*. Norman: University of Oklahoma Press, 1992.

Burgoyne, Robert. *Film Nation: Hollywood Looks at U.S. History*. Minneapolis: University of Minnesota Press, 1997.

Brewer, Susan A. *To Win the Peace: British Propaganda in the United States during World War II*. Ithaca: Cornell University Press, 1997.

———. *Why America Fights: Patriotism and War Propaganda from the Philippines to Iraq*. New York: Oxford University Press, 2009.

Brooks, Jeffrey. *Thank You, Comrade Stalin!: Soviet Public Culture from Revolution to Cold War*. Princeton: Princeton University Press, 2000.

Burk, Kathleen. *Old World, New World: The Story of Britain and America*. London: Little, Brown, 2007.

Calder, Angus. *The Myth of the Blitz*. London: Cape, 1991.

———. *The People's War, 1939–1945*. London: Cape, 1969.

Cantril, Hadley. *Gauging Public Opinion*. 1944; Port Washington, N.Y.: Kennikat, 1972.

———. *The Invasion from Mars: A Study in the Psychology of Panic*. 1940; New Brunswick, N.J.: Transaction, 2005.

———, ed. *Public Opinion, 1935–1946*. Princeton: Princeton University Press, 1951.

Capra, Frank. *The Name above the Title: An Autobiography*. New York: Macmillan, 1971.

Casey, Steven. *Cautious Crusade: Franklin D. Roosevelt, American Public Opinion, and the War against Nazi Germany*. New York: Oxford University Press, 2001.

Caute, David. *The Dancer Defects: The Struggle for Cultural Supremacy during the Cold War*. New York: Oxford University Press, 2003.

Cayton, Mary Kupiec. "The Making of an American Prophet: Emerson, His Audiences, and the Rise of the Culture Industry in Nineteenth-Century America." *American Historical Review* 92 (June 1987): 597–620.

Ceplair, Larry, and Steven Englund. *The Inquisition in Hollywood: Politics in the Film Community, 1930–1960*. Urbana: University of Illinois Press, 2003.

Chapman, James. *The British at War: Cinema, State, and Propaganda, 1939–1945*. London: Tauris, 1998.

———. "'The Yanks Are Shown to Such Advantage': Anglo-American Rivalry in the Production of *The True Glory*." *Historical Journal of Film, Radio, and Television* 16, no. 4 (1996): 533–54.

Charters, W. W. *Motion Pictures and Youth: A Summary*. New York: Macmillan, 1933.

Chin, Frank. *Bulletproof Buddhists and Other Essays*. Honolulu: University of Hawai'i Press, 1998.

———. *The Chinaman Pacific and Frisco R.R. Co.: Stories*. Minneapolis: Coffee House, 1988.

Churchill, Winston S. *The Grand Alliance*. Boston: Houghton Mifflin, 1950.

Cole, Wayne S. *Charles A. Lindbergh and the Battle against American Intervention in World War II*. New York: Harcourt Brace Jovanovich, 1974.

———. *Roosevelt and the Isolationists, 1932–1945*. Lincoln: University of Nebraska Press, 1983.

Costigliola, Frank. "After Roosevelt's Death: Dangerous Emotions, Divisive Discourses, and the Abandoned Alliance." *Diplomatic History* 34 (January 2010): 1–23.

———. *Awkward Dominion: American Political, Economic, and Cultural Relations with Europe, 1919–1933*. Ithaca: Cornell University Press, 1984.

———. "Broken Circle: The Isolation of Franklin D. Roosevelt in World War II." *Diplomatic History* 32 (November 2008): 677–718.

———. "'Mixed Up' and 'Contact': Culture and Emotion among the Allies in the Second World War." *International History Review* 20 (December 1998): 791–805.

———. "The Nuclear Family: Tropes of Gender and Pathology in the Western Alliance." *Diplomatic History* 21 (Spring 1997): 163–83.

———. "'Unceasing Pressure for Penetration': Gender, Pathology, and Emotion in George Kennan's Formation of the Cold War." *Journal of American History* 83 (March 1997): 1309–39.

Cripps, Thomas. *Hollywood's High Noon: Moviemaking and Society before Television*. Baltimore: Johns Hopkins University Press, 1997.

Culbert, David, ed. *Mission to Moscow*. Madison: University of Wisconsin Press, 1980.

———. *News for Everyman: Radio and Foreign Affairs in Thirties America*. Westport, Conn.: Greenwood, 1976.

Cull, Nicholas J. *The Cold War and the United States Information Agency: American Propaganda and Public Diplomacy, 1945–1989*. Cambridge: Cambridge University Press, 2008.

———. *Selling War: The British Propaganda Campaign against American "Neutrality" in World War II*. New York: Oxford University Press, 1995.

Dallek, Robert. *The American Style of Foreign Policy: Cultural Politics and Foreign Affairs*. New York: Knopf, 1983.

———. *Franklin D. Roosevelt and American Foreign Policy, 1932–1945*. New York: Oxford University Press, 1979.

Decherney, Peter. *Hollywood and the Culture Elite: How the Movies Became American*. New York: Columbia University Press, 2005.

de Grazia, Victoria. *The Culture of Consent: Mass Organization of Leisure in Fascist Italy*. Cambridge: Cambridge University Press, 1981.

———. *Irresistible Empire: America's Advance through Twentieth-Century Europe*. Cambridge: Belknap Press of Harvard University Press, 2005.

———. "Mass Culture and Sovereignty: The American Challenge to European Cinemas, 1920–1960." *Journal of Modern History* 61 (March 1989): 53–87.

D'Emilio, John. *Sexual Politics, Sexual Communities: The Making of a Homosexual Minority in the United States, 1940–1970*. 2nd ed. Chicago: University of Chicago Press, 1998.

Dewey, John. *The Later Works, 1925–1953*. 17 vols. Edited by Jo Ann Boydston. Carbondale: Southern Illinois University Press, 1981.

Dick, Bernard F. *The Star-Spangled Screen: The American World War II Film*. Lexington: University Press of Kentucky, 1987.

Dickinson, Margaret, and Sarah Street. *Cinema and State: The Film Industry and the Government, 1927–1984*. London: British Film Institute, 1985.

Dimbleby, David, and David Reynolds. *An Ocean Apart: The Relationship between Britain and America in the Twentieth Century*. New York: Random House, 1988.

Divine, Robert A. *Second Chance: The Triumph of Internationalism in America during World War II*. New York: Atheneum, 1967.

Doenecke, Justus D., ed. *In Danger Undaunted: The Anti-Interventionist Movement of 1940–1941 as Revealed in the Papers of the America First Committee*. Stanford, Calif.: Hoover Institution Press, 1990.

———. *Storm on the Horizon: The Challenge to American Intervention, 1939–1941*. Lanham, Md.: Rowman and Littlefield, 2000.

Doenecke, Justus D., and John E. Wilz. *From Isolation to War, 1931–1941*. Arlington Heights, Ill.: Harlan Davidson, 1991.

Doherty, Thomas. *Cold War, Cool Medium: Television, McCarthyism, and American Culture*. New York: Columbia University Press, 2003.

———. *Hollywood's Censor: Joseph I. Breen and the Production Code Administration*. New York: Columbia University Press, 2007.

———. *Projections of War: Hollywood, American Culture, and World War II*. New York: Columbia University Press, 1993.

Dower, John W. *War without Mercy: Race and Power in the Pacific War*. New York: Pantheon, 1986.

Dumbrell, John. *A Special Relationship: Anglo-American Relations from the Cold War to Iraq.* New York: Palgrave Macmillan, 2006.

Dunn, Dennis J. *Caught between Roosevelt and Stalin: America's Ambassadors to Moscow.* Lexington: University Press of Kentucky, 1998.

Engel, Jeffrey A. *Cold War at 30,000 Feet: The Anglo-American Fight for Aviation Supremacy.* Cambridge: Harvard University Press, 2007.

Engerman, David C. "American Knowledge and Global Power." *Diplomatic History* 31 (September 2007): 599–622.

———. *Modernization from the Other Shore: American Intellectuals and the Romance of Russian Development.* Cambridge: Harvard University Press, 2003.

Fielding, Raymond. *March of Time, 1935–1951.* New York: Oxford University Press, 1978.

Filene, Peter G., ed. *American Views of Soviet Russia, 1917–1965.* Homewood, Ill.: Dorsey, 1968.

Fiske, John. *Understanding Popular Culture.* Boston: Unwin Hyman, 1989.

Foglesong, David S. *The American Mission and the "Evil Empire": The Crusade for a Free Russia since 1881.* New York: Cambridge University Press, 2007.

Fousek, John. *To Lead the Free World: American Nationalism and the Cultural Roots of the Cold War.* Chapel Hill: University of North Carolina Press, 2000.

Fox, Jo. *Film Propaganda in Britain and Nazi Germany: World War II Cinema.* New York: Berg, 2007.

Frakes, Margaret. "Why the Movie Investigation?" *Christian Century,* 24 September 1941, 1172–74.

Freidel, Frank. *Franklin D. Roosevelt: A Rendezvous with Destiny.* Boston: Little, Brown, 1990.

Gabler, Neal. *An Empire of Their Own: How the Jews Invented Hollywood.* New York: Anchor, 1988.

———. *Life: The Movie: How Entertainment Conquered Reality.* New York: Knopf, 1998.

———. *Walt Disney: The Triumph of the American Imagination.* New York: Knopf, 2006.

Gaddis, John Lewis. *The Cold War: A New History.* New York: Penguin, 2005.

———. "The Corporatist Synthesis: A Skeptical View." *Diplomatic History* 10 (October 1986): 357–62.

———. *Russia, the Soviet Union, and the United States: An Interpretive History.* 2nd ed. New York: McGraw-Hill, 1990.

———. *The United States and the Origins of the Cold War, 1941–1947.* New York: Columbia University Press, 1972.

Gallup, George H., ed. *The Gallup International Public Opinion Polls: Great Britain, 1937–1975.* 2 vols. New York: Random House, 1976.

————, ed. *The Gallup Poll: Public Opinion: 1935–1971*. 3 vols. New York: Random House, 1972.

Gallup, George H., and Saul Forbes Rae. *The Pulse of Democracy: The Public Opinion Poll and How It Works*. New York: Simon and Schuster, 1940.

Gary, Brett. *The Nervous Liberals: Propaganda Anxieties from World War I to the Cold War*. New York: Columbia University Press, 1999.

Gerstle, Gary. *American Crucible: Race and Nation in the Twentieth Century*. Princeton: Princeton University Press, 2002.

Gienow-Hecht, Jessica C. E. "Shame on U.S.? Academics, Cultural Transfer, and the Cold War—A Critical Review." *Diplomatic History* 24 (Summer 2000): 465–94.

————. *Transmission Impossible: American Journalism as Cultural Diplomacy in Postwar Germany, 1945–1955*. Baton Rouge: Louisiana State University Press, 1999.

Glancy, H. Mark. *When Hollywood Loved Britain: The Hollywood 'British' Film, 1939–1945*. Manchester: Manchester University Press, 1999.

Gleason, Abbott. *Totalitarianism: The Inner History of the Cold War*. New York: Oxford University Press, 1995.

Goebbels, Joseph. *The Goebbels Diaries, 1942–1943*. Edited by Louis P. Lochner. New York: Doubleday, 1948.

Gould-Davies, Nigel. "Rethinking the Role of Ideology in International Politics during the Cold War." *Journal of Cold War Studies* 1 (Winter 1999): 90–109.

Guback, Thomas H. *The International Film Industry: Western Europe and America since 1945*. Bloomington: Indiana University Press, 1969.

Hachey, Thomas E., ed. *Confidential Dispatches: Analyses of America by the British Ambassador, 1939–1945*. Evanston, Ill.: New University Press, 1974.

Hagedorn, Jessica, ed. *Charlie Chan Is Dead: An Anthology of Contemporary Asian American Fiction*. New York: Penguin, 1993.

Hartmann, Susan. *The Homefront and Beyond: American Women in the 1940s*. Boston: Twayne, 1982.

Hathaway, Robert M. *Great Britain and the United States: Special Relations since World War II*. Boston: Twayne, 1990.

Haynes, John Earl, and Harvey Klehr. *Venona: Decoding Soviet Espionage in America*. New Haven: Yale University Press, 1999.

Heinrichs, Waldo. *Threshold of War: Franklin D. Roosevelt and American Entry into World War II*. New York: Oxford University Press, 1988.

Herzstein, Robert E. *Henry R. Luce: A Political Portrait of the Man Who Created the American Century*. New York: Scribner, 1994.

Hixson, Walter L. *Parting the Curtain: Propaganda, Culture, and the Cold War, 1945–1961*. New York: St. Martin's, 1997.

Hogan, Michael J. *The Marshall Plan: America, Britain, and the Reconstruction of Western Europe, 1947–1952*. Cambridge: Cambridge University Press, 1987.

Holaday, Perry W., and George D. Stoddard. *Getting Ideas from the Movies*. New York: Macmillan, 1933.

Hoopes, Townsend, and Douglas Brinkley. *FDR and the Creation of the UN*. New Haven: Yale University Press, 1997.

Horten, Gerd. *Radio Goes to War: The Cultural Politics of Propaganda during World War II*. Berkeley: University of California Press, 2002.

Hovland, Carl I., A. A. Lumsdaine, and F. D. Sheffield. *Experiments on Mass Communication*. Vol. 3 of *Studies in Social Psychology in World War II*. Princeton: Princeton University Press, 1949.

Huang, Yunte. *Charlie Chan: The Untold Story of the Honorable Detective and His Rendezvous with American History*. New York: Norton, 2010.

Hunt, Michael. *Ideology and U.S. Foreign Policy*. New Haven, Conn.: Yale University Press, 1987.

———. *The Making of a Special Relationship: The United States and China to 1914*. New York: Columbia University Press, 1983.

Ickes, Harold L. *The Secret Diary of Harold L. Ickes*. 3 vols. New York: Simon and Schuster, 1954.

Iriye, Akira. *Cultural Internationalism and World Order*. Baltimore: Johns Hopkins University Press, 1997.

Isaacson, Walter, and Evan Thomas. *The Wise Men: Six Friends and the World They Made*. New York: Simon and Schuster, 1986.

Jarvie, Ian C. "The Burma Campaign on Film: *Objective, Burma!* (1945), *The Stilwell Road* (1945), and *Burma Victory* (1945)." *Historical Journal of Film, Radio, and Television* 8, no. 1 (1988): 55–73.

———. *Hollywood's Overseas Campaign: The North Atlantic Movie Trade, 1920–1950*. Cambridge: Cambridge University Press, 1992.

Jesperson, T. Christopher. *American Images of China, 1931–1949*. Stanford, Calif.: Stanford University Press, 1996.

Kaplan, E. Ann. *Looking for the Other: Feminism, Film, and the Imperial Gaze*. New York: Routledge, 1997.

Kazin, Alfred. *New York Jew*. New York: Knopf, 1978.

Kenez, Peter. *Cinema and Soviet Society, 1917–1953*. Cambridge: Cambridge University Press, 1992.

Kennan, George F. "The Sources of Soviet Conduct." *Foreign Affairs* 25 (July 1947): 566–82.

Kennedy, David M. *Over Here: The First World War and American Society*. New York: Oxford University Press, 1980.

Kimball, Warren F., ed. *Churchill and Roosevelt: The Complete Correspondence*. 3 vols. Princeton: Princeton University Press, 1984.

———. *Forged in War: Roosevelt, Churchill, and the Second World War*. New York: Morrow, 1997.

———. "The Incredible Shrinking War: The Second World War, Not (Just) the Origins of the Cold War." *Diplomatic History* 25 (Summer 2001): 347–65.

———. *The Juggler: Franklin Roosevelt as Wartime Statesman*. Princeton: Princeton University Press, 1991.

Kitamura, Hiroshi. *Screening Enlightenment: Hollywood and the Cultural Reconstruction of Defeated Japan*. Ithaca: Cornell University Press, 2010.

Klein, Christina. *Cold War Orientalism: Asia in the Middlebrow Imagination, 1945–1961*. Berkeley: University of California Press, 2003.

Koppes, Clayton R., and Gregory D. Black. *Hollywood Goes to War: How Politics, Profits, and Propaganda Shaped World War II Movies*. New York: Free Press, 1987.

———. "What to Show the World: The Office of War Information and Hollywood, 1942–1945." *Journal of American History* 64 (June 1977): 87–105.

Korda, Michael. *Charmed Lives: A Family Romance*. New York: Random House, 1979.

Koskoff, David E. *Joseph P. Kennedy: A Life and Times*. Englewood Cliffs, N.J.: Prentice-Hall, 1974.

Kouwenhoven, John A. "The Movies Better Be Good!" *Harper's*, May 1945, 538–39.

Kroes, Rob, Robert W. Rydell, and Doeko F. J. Bosscher, eds. *Cultural Transmissions and Receptions: American Mass Culture in Europe*. Amsterdam: VU University Press, 1993.

Kuisel, Richard F. *Seducing the French: The Dilemma of Americanization*. Berkeley: University of California Press, 1993.

Landy, Marcia. *Cinematic Uses of the Past*. Minneapolis: University of Minnesota Press, 1996.

Lasswell, Harold D. *Propaganda Technique in the World War*. 1927; Cambridge: MIT Press, 1971.

Lasswell, Harold D., Ralph D. Casey, and Bruce Lannes Smith, eds. *Propaganda and Promotional Activities: An Annotated Bibliography*. 1935; Chicago: University of Chicago Press, 1969.

Laville, Helen. "'Our Country Endangered by Underwear': Fashion, Femininity, and the Seduction Narrative in *Ninotchka* and *Silk Stockings*." *Diplomatic History* 30 (September 2006): 623–44.

Lavine, Harold, and James Wechsler. *War Propaganda and the United States*. New Haven: Yale University Press, 1940.

Lee, Loyd E. "We Have Just Begun to Write." *Diplomatic History* 25 (Summer 2001): 367–81.

Lee, Robert G. *Orientals: Asian Americans in Popular Culture*. Philadelphia: Temple University Press, 1999.

Leff, Leonard J., and Jerold L. Simmons. *The Dame in the Kimono: Hollywood, Censorship, and the Production Code*. Lexington: University Press of Kentucky, 2001.

Leigh, Michael. *Mobilizing Consent: Public Opinion and American Foreign Policy, 1937-1947*. Westport, Conn.: Greenwood, 1976.

Leong, Karen J. *The China Mystique: Pearl S. Buck, Anna May Wong, Mayling Soong, and the Transformation of American Orientalism*. Berkeley: University of California Press, 2005.

Levering, Ralph B. *American Opinion and the Russian Alliance, 1939-1945*. Chapel Hill: University of North Carolina Press, 1976.

Lhamon, W. T., Jr. *Raising Cain: Blackface Performance from Jim Crow to Hip Hop*. Cambridge: Harvard University Press, 1998.

Lippmann, Walter. *The Phantom Public*. New York: Harcourt, Brace, 1925.

———. *Public Opinion*. New York: Harcourt, Brace, 1922.

Little, Douglas. *American Orientalism: The United States and the Middle East since 1945*. Chapel Hill: University of North Carolina Press, 2004.

Long, Breckinridge. *The War Diary of Breckinridge Long: Selections from the Years 1939-1944*. Edited by Fred L. Israel. Lincoln: University of Nebraska Press, 1966.

Louis, William Roger. *Imperialism at Bay, 1941-1945: The United States and the Decolonization of the British Empire*. Oxford: Clarendon, 1977.

Lowe, Herman. "Washington Discovers Hollywood." *American Mercury*, April 1945, 407-14.

Lowry, Edward G. "Trade Follows the Film." *Saturday Evening Post*, 7 November 1925, 12-13, 151, 158.

Luce, Henry R. "The American Century." *Life*, 17 February 1941, 61-65.

MacDonnell, Francis. *Insidious Foes: The Axis Fifth Column and the American Home Front*. New York: Oxford University Press, 1995.

MacLean, Elizabeth Kimball. "Joseph E. Davies and Soviet-American Relations, 1941-1943." *Diplomatic History* 4 (January 1980): 73-94.

MacLeish, Archibald. *A Time to Speak: The Selected Prose of Archibald MacLeish*. Boston: Houghton Mifflin, 1941.

MacLeish, Archibald, William S. Paley, and Edward R. Murrow. *In Honor of a Man and an Idea: Three Talks on Freedom*. New York: n.p., 1941.

Maddux, Thomas R. "Red Fascism, Brown Bolshevism: The American Image of Totalitarianism in the 1930s." *Historian* 40 (November 1977): 85-103.

———. *Years of Estrangement: American Relations with the Soviet Union, 1933-1941*. Tallahassee: University Presses of Florida, 1980.

Mahl, Thomas E. *Desperate Deception: British Covert Operations in the United States, 1939-1944*. Washington, D.C.: Brassey's, 1998.

Maier, Charles S. *Recasting Bourgeois Europe: Stabilization in France, Germany, and Italy in the Decade after World War I*. Princeton: Princeton University Press, 1975.

Marchetti, Gina. *Romance and the "Yellow Peril": Race, Sex, and Discursive Strategies in Hollywood Fiction*. Berkeley: University of California Press, 1993.

Mark, Eduard. "October or Thermidor?: Interpretations of Stalinism and the Perception of Soviet Foreign Policy in the United States, 1927–1947." *American Historical Review* 94 (October 1989): 937–62.

Marks, Frederick W., III. *Wind over Sand: The Diplomacy of Franklin Roosevelt.* Athens: University of Georgia Press, 1988.

Mastny, Vojtech. *Russia's Road to the Cold War: Diplomacy, Warfare, and the Politics of Communism, 1941–1945.* New York: Columbia University Press, 1979.

Mathews, Basil. *United We Stand: The Peoples of the United Nations.* Boston: Little, Brown, 1943.

May, Elaine Tyler. *Homeward Bound: American Families in the Cold War Era.* New York: Basic Books, 1988.

May, Lary. *The Big Tomorrow: Hollywood and the Politics of the American Way.* Chicago: University of Chicago Press, 2000.

Mayer, Arthur L. "Fact into Film." *Public Opinion Quarterly* 8 (Summer 1944): 206–25.

McAlister, Melani. *Epic Encounters: Culture, Media, and U.S. Interests in the Middle East, 1945–2000.* Berkeley: University of California Press, 2001.

McDermott, Kevin, and Jeremy Agnew. *The Comintern: A History of International Communism from Lenin to Stalin.* New York: St. Martin's, 1997.

Meriwether, James H. *Proudly We Can Be Africans: Black Americans and Africa, 1935–1961.* Chapel Hill: University of North Carolina Press, 2002.

Metz, Christian. *Film Language.* New York: Oxford University Press, 1974.

Miner, Steven Merritt. *Between Churchill and Stalin: The Soviet Union, Great Britain, and the Origins of the Grand Alliance.* Chapel Hill: University of North Carolina Press, 1988.

———. *Stalin's Holy War: Religion, Nationalism, and Alliance Politics, 1941–1945.* Chapel Hill: University of North Carolina Press, 2003.

Mock, James R., and Cedric Larson. *Words That Won the War: The Story of the Committee on Public Information, 1917–1919.* Princeton: Princeton University Press, 1939.

Moon, Krystyn R. *Yellowface: Creating the Chinese in American Popular Music and Performance, 1850s–1920s.* New Brunswick: Rutgers University Press, 2005.

Moser, John E. "Gigantic Engines of Propaganda: The 1941 Senate Investigation of Hollywood." *Historian* 63 (June 2001): 731–52.

———. *Twisting the Lion's Tail: American Anglophobia between the World Wars.* New York: New York University Press, 1999.

Moy, James S. *Marginal Sights: Staging the Chinese in America.* Iowa City: University of Iowa Press, 1993.

Murrow, Edward R. *This Is London.* New York: Simon and Schuster, 1941.

Ngai, Mae M. *Impossible Subjects: Illegal Aliens and the Making of Modern America.* Princeton: Princeton University Press, 2004.

Ninkovich, Frank A. *The Diplomacy of Ideas: U.S. Foreign Policy and Cultural Relations, 1938–1950*. Cambridge: Cambridge University Press, 1981.

———. *Global Dawn: The Cultural Foundation of American Internationalism, 1865–1890*. Cambridge: Harvard University Press, 2009.

Nisbet, Robert. *Roosevelt and Stalin: The Failed Courtship*. Washington, D.C.: Regnery Gateway, 1988.

Nye, Gerald P. "War Propaganda: Our Madness Increases as Our Emergency Shrinks." *Vital Speeches of the Day*, 15 September 1941, 720–23.

Nye, Joseph S., Jr. *Bound to Lead: The Changing Nature of American Power*. New York: Basic Books, 1990.

———. *Soft Power: The Means to Success in World Politics*. New York: Public Affairs, 2004.

O'Connor, John E., and Martin A. Jackson, eds. *American History/American Film: Interpreting the Hollywood Image*. New York: Ungar, 1979.

Olivier, Laurence. *Confessions of an Actor*. London: Weidenfeld and Nicolson, 1982.

O'Neill, William L. *A Democracy at War: America's Fight at Home and Abroad in World War II*. New York: Free Press, 1993.

Osgood, Kenneth, and Brian Etheridge, eds. *The United States and Public Diplomacy: New Directions in Cultural and International History*. Boston: Brill, 2009.

Overy, Richard. *Why the Allies Won*. New York: Norton, 1995.

Parks, J. D. *Culture, Conflict, and Coexistence: American-Soviet Cultural Relations, 1917–1958*. Jefferson, N.C.: McFarland, 1983.

Pells, Richard. *Not Like Us: How Europeans Have Loved, Hated, and Transformed American Culture since World War II*. New York: Basic Books, 1997.

———. *Radical Visions and American Dreams: Culture and Social Thought in the Depression Years*. New York: Harper and Row, 1973.

Perkins, Bradford. *The Great Rapprochement: England and the United States, 1895–1914*. New York: Atheneum, 1968.

Perlmutter, Amos. *FDR and Stalin: A Not So Grand Alliance, 1943–1945*. Columbia: University of Missouri Press, 1993.

Peterson, Ruth C., and L. L. Thurstone. *Motion Pictures and the Social Attitudes of Children*. New York: Macmillan, 1933.

Plummer, Brenda Gayle. *Rising Wind: Black Americans and U.S. Foreign Affairs, 1935–1960*. Chapel Hill: University of North Carolina Press, 1996.

Polenberg, Richard. *War and Society: The United States, 1941–1945*. Philadelphia: Lippincott, 1972.

Pronay, Nicholas, and D. W. Spring, eds. *Propaganda, Politics, and Film, 1918–1945*. London: Macmillan, 1982.

Qualter, Terence. *Opinion Control in the Democracies*. New York: St. Martin's, 1985.

Reeves, Nicholas. *The Power of Film Propaganda: Myth or Reality?* London: Cassell, 1999.

Reynolds, David. *Britannia Overruled: British Policy and World Power in the Twentieth Century*. New York: Longman, 1991.

―――. *The Creation of the Anglo-American Alliance, 1937–1941: A Study in Competitive Co-Operation*. Chapel Hill: University of North Carolina Press, 1981.

―――. *From World War to Cold War: Churchill, Roosevelt, and the International History of the 1940s*. New York: Oxford University Press, 2006.

―――. *Lord Lothian and Anglo-American Relations, 1939–1940*. Philadelphia: American Philosophical Society, 1983.

―――. *One World Divisible: A Global History since 1945*. New York: Norton, 2000.

―――. *Rich Relations: The American Occupation of Britain, 1942–1945*. London: HarperCollins, 1995.

Reynolds, David, Warren F. Kimball, and A. O. Chubarian, eds. *Allies at War: The Soviet, American, and British Experience, 1939–1945*. New York: St. Martin's, 1994.

Reynolds, Quentin. *The Curtain Rises*. New York: Random House, 1944.

Richards, Jeffrey. *Age of the Dream Palace: Cinema and Society in Britain, 1930–1939*. London: Routledge, 1990.

Roan, Jeanette. *Envisioning Asia: On Location, Travel, and the Cinematic Geography of U.S. Orientalism*. Ann Arbor: University of Michigan Press, 2010.

Roddick, Nick. *A New Deal in Entertainment: Warner Brothers in the 1930s*. London: British Film Institute, 1983.

Roeder, George H., Jr. *The Censored War: American Visual Experience during World War II*. New Haven: Yale University Press, 1993.

Rogin, Michael. *Blackface, White Noise: Jewish Immigrants in the Hollywood Melting Pot*. Berkeley: University of California Press, 1996.

Rollins, Peter C., ed. *Hollywood as Historian: American Film in a Cultural Context*. Lexington: University Press of Kentucky, 1983.

Roosevelt, Franklin D. *The Public Papers and Addresses of Franklin D. Roosevelt*. 13 vols. Edited by Samuel I. Rosenman. New York: Harper, 1950.

Rose, Kenneth D. *Myth and the Greatest Generation: A Social History of Americans in World War II*. New York: Routledge, 2008.

Rose, Sonya O. *Which People's War?: National Identity and Citizenship in Wartime Britain, 1939–1945*. New York: Oxford University Press, 2003.

Rosenberg, Emily S. *A Date Which Will Live: Pearl Harbor in American Memory*. Durham: Duke University Press, 2003.

―――. "'Foreign Affairs' after World War II: Connecting Sexual and International Politics." *Diplomatic History* 18 (Winter 1994): 59–70.

―――. *Spreading the American Dream: American Economic and Cultural Expansion, 1890–1945*. New York: Hill and Wang, 1982.

Rosenstone, Robert A. *Visions of the Past: The Challenge of Film to Our Idea of History*. Cambridge: Harvard University Press, 1999.

Ross, Steven J., ed. *Movies and American Society*. Malden, Mass.: Blackwell, 2002.

Rosten, Leo C. *Hollywood: The Movie Colony, the Movie Makers*. New York: Harcourt, Brace, 1941.

Said, Edward W. *Orientalism*. New York: Pantheon, 1978.

Schatz, Thomas. *Boom and Bust: American Cinema in the 1940s*. Berkeley: University of California Press, 1999.

Schlesinger, Stephen C. *Act of Creation: The Founding of the United Nations*. Boulder, Colo.: Westview, 2003.

Schwarz, Jordan A. *Liberal: Adolf A. Berle and the Vision of an American Era*. New York: Free Press, 1987.

Scott, Joan Wallach. *Gender and the Politics of History*. New York: Columbia University Press, 1988.

Shaw, Tony. *Hollywood's Cold War*. Amherst: University of Massachusetts Press, 2007.

Sherry, Michael S. *In the Shadow of War: The United States since the 1930s*. New Haven: Yale University Press, 1995.

Short, K. R. M., ed. *Film and Radio Propaganda in World War II*. Knoxville: University of Tennessee Press, 1983.

———. "RAF Bomber Command's *Target for Tonight* (1941)." *Historical Journal of Film, Radio, and Television* 17, no. 2 (1997): 181–218.

———. "*That Hamilton Woman* (1941): Propaganda, Feminism, and the Production Code." *Historical Journal of Film, Radio, and Television* 11, no. 1 (1991): 3–19.

Shulman, Holly Cowan. *The Voice of America: Propaganda and Democracy, 1942–1945*. Madison: University of Wisconsin Press, 1990.

Siefert, Marsha, ed. *Extending the Borders of Russian History*. Budapest: Central European University Press, 2003.

Sikorsky, Jonathan. "From British Cassandra to American Hero: The Churchill Legend in the World War II American Media." *Finest Hour* 108 (Autumn 2000): 30–35.

Silber, Nina. *The Romance of Reunion: Northerners and the South, 1865–1900*. Chapel Hill: University of North Carolina Press, 1993.

Sklar, Robert. *Movie-Made America: A Cultural History of American Movies*. Rev. ed. New York: Vintage, 1994.

Smith, Tony. *America's Mission: The United States and the Worldwide Struggle for Democracy in the Twentieth Century*. Princeton: Princeton University Press, 1994.

Sovetskaia kul'tura v gody Velikoi Otechestvennoi voiny [Soviet Culture during the Great Patriotic War]. Moscow: Nauka, 1976.

Sproule, J. Michael. *Propaganda and Democracy: The American Experience of Media and Mass Persuasion*. Cambridge: Cambridge University Press, 1997.

Staiger, Janet. *Interpreting Films: Studies in the Historical Reception of American Cinema*. Princeton: Princeton University Press, 1992.

———. *Perverse Spectators: The Practices of Film Reception*. New York: New York University Press, 2000.

Standley, William H., and Arthur A. Ageton. *Admiral Ambassador to Russia*. Chicago: Regnery, 1955.

Starr, S. Frederick. *Red and Hot: The Fate of Jazz in the Soviet Union, 1917–1980*. New York: Oxford University Press, 1983.

Steele, Richard W. *Propaganda in an Open Society: The Roosevelt Administration and the Media, 1933–1941*. Westport, Conn.: Greenwood, 1985.

Stimson, Henry L., and McGeorge Bundy. *On Active Service in Peace and War*. New York: Harper, 1947.

Stites, Richard, ed. *Culture and Entertainment in Wartime Russia*. Bloomington: Indiana University Press, 1995.

———. *Revolutionary Dreams: Utopian Vision and Experimental Life in the Russian Revolution*. New York: Oxford University Press, 1989.

Stoler, Mark A. *Allies and Adversaries: The Joint Chefs of Staff, the Grand Alliance, and U.S. Strategy in World War II*. Chapel Hill: University of North Carolina Press, 2000.

———. *Allies in War: Britain and America against the Axis Powers, 1940–1945*. New York: Hodder Arnold, 2005.

———. *The Politics of the Second Front: American Military Planning and Diplomacy in Coalition Warfare, 1941–1943*. Westport, Conn.: Greenwood, 1977.

Strada, Michael J., and Harold R. Troper. *Friend or Foe?: Russians in American Film and Foreign Policy, 1933–1991*. Lanham, Md.: Scarecrow, 1997.

Susman, Warren, ed. *Culture and Commitment, 1939–1945*. New York: Braziller, 1973.

Sweeney, Michael S. *The Secrets of Victory: The Office of Censorship and the American Press and Radio in World War II*. Chapel Hill: University of North Carolina Press, 2001.

Taubman, William. *Stalin's American Policy: From Entente to Détente to Cold War*. New York: Norton, 1982.

Taylor, Philip M., ed. *Britain and the Cinema in the Second World War*. New York: St. Martin's, 1988.

———. *British Propaganda in the Twentieth Century*. Edinburgh: Edinburgh University Press, 2001.

Taylor, Richard, and Derek Spring, eds. *Stalinism and Soviet Cinema*. London: Routledge, 1993.

Tchen, John Kuo Wei. *New York before Chinatown: Orientalism and the Shaping of American Culture, 1776–1882*. Baltimore: Johns Hopkins University Press, 1999.

Thompson, Kristin. *Exporting Entertainment: America in the World Film Market, 1907–1934*. London: British Film Institute, 1985.

Thomson, James C., Jr., Peter W. Stanley, and John Curtis Perry. *Sentimental

Imperialists: The American Experience in East Asia. New York: Harper and Row, 1981.

Thorne, Christopher. *Allies of a Kind: The United States, Britain, and the War against Japan, 1941–1945.* New York: Oxford University Press, 1978.

Thorp, Margaret. *America at the Movies.* London: Faber and Faber, 1946.

Toplin, Robert Brent. *History by Hollywood: The Use and Abuse of the American Past.* Urbana: University of Illinois Press, 1996.

———. *Reel History: In Defense of Hollywood.* Lawrence: University Press of Kansas, 2002.

Trachtenberg, Alan. *Reading American Photographs: Images as History, Mathew Brady to Walker Evans.* New York: Hill and Wang, 1989.

Trumpbour, John. *Selling Hollywood to the World: U.S. and European Struggles for Mastery of the Global Film Industry, 1920–1950.* Cambridge: Cambridge University Press, 2002.

Tye, Larry. *The Father of Spin: Edward L. Bernays and the Birth of Public Relations.* New York: Crown, 1988.

Variety Film Reviews. 24 vols. to date. New York: Garland, 1983.

Vasey, Ruth. *The World According to Hollywood, 1918–1939.* Madison: University of Wisconsin Press, 1997.

Vaughn, Steven. *Holding Fast the Inner Lines: Democracy, Nationalism, and the Committee on Public Information.* Chapel Hill: University of North Carolina Press, 1980.

———. *Ronald Reagan in Hollywood: Movies and Politics.* New York: Cambridge University Press, 1994.

Volkogonov, Dmitri. *Stalin: Triumph and Tragedy.* Translated by Harold Shukman. New York: Grove Weidenfeld, 1991.

Von Eschen, Penny M. *Race against Empire: Black Americans and Anticolonialism, 1937–1957.* Ithaca: Cornell University Press, 1997.

Wagnleitner, Reinhold. *Coca-Colonization and the Cold War: The Cultural Mission of the United States in Austria after the Second World War.* Translated by Diana M. Wolf. Chapel Hill: University of North Carolina Press, 1994.

Wall, Wendy. *Inventing the "American Way": The Politics of Consensus from the New Deal to the Civil Rights Movement.* New York: Oxford University Press, 2008.

Wallace, Henry A. *Democracy Reborn.* Edited by Russell Lord. New York: Reynal and Hitchcock, 1944.

Wanger, Walter. "120,000 American Ambassadors." *Foreign Affairs* 18 (October 1939): 45–59.

———. "The Role of Movies in Morale." *American Journal of Sociology* 47 (November 1941): 378–83.

Waples, Douglas, ed. *Print, Radio, and Film in a Democracy.* Chicago: University of Chicago Press, 1942.

Warner, Harry M. "Hollywood Obligations in a Producer's Eyes." *Christian Science Monitor*, 16 March 1939, 3.

Watt, Donald Cameron. *Succeeding John Bull: America in Britain's Place, 1900–1975*. Cambridge: Cambridge University Press, 1984.

Weiner, Amir. *Making Sense of War: The Second World War and the Fate of the Bolshevik Revolution*. Princeton: Princeton University Press, 2001.

Welch, David. *The Third Reich: Politics and Propaganda*. London: Routledge, 1993.

Welles, Sumner. *Where Are We Heading?* New York: Harpers, 1946.

Westbrook, Robert B. *John Dewey and American Democracy*. Ithaca: Cornell University Press, 1991.

Whitfield, Stephen J. *The Culture of the Cold War*. 2nd ed. Baltimore: Johns Hopkins University Press, 1996.

Willkie, Wendell L. *One World*. New York: Pocket Books, 1943.

Wilson, Joan Hoff. *Ideology and Economics: U.S. Relations with the Soviet Union, 1918–1933*. Columbia: University of Missouri Press, 1974.

Winkler, Allan M. *The Politics of Propaganda: The Office of War Information, 1942–1945*. New Haven: Yale University Press, 1978.

Woods, Randall Bennett. *A Changing of the Guard: Anglo-American Relations, 1941–1946*. Chapel Hill: University of North Carolina Press, 1990.

Yoshida, Takashi. *The Making of the "Rape of Nanking": History and Memory in Japan, China, and the United States*. New York: Oxford University Press, 2006.

Yoshihara, Mari. *Embracing the East: White Women and American Orientalism*. New York: Oxford University Press, 2003.

Youngblood, Denise J. "'Americanitis': The *Amerikanshchina* in Soviet Cinema." *Journal of Popular Film and Television* 19 (Winter 1992): 148–56.

———. *Movies for the Masses: Popular Cinema and Soviet Society*. Cambridge: Cambridge University Press, 1992.

———. *Russian War Films: On the Cinema Front, 1914–2005*. Lawrence: University Press of Kansas, 2007.

Zaretsky, Natasha. *No Direction Home: The American Family and the Fear of National Decline, 1968–1980*. Chapel Hill: University of North Carolina Press, 2007.

Zubok, Vladislav, and Constantine Pleshakov. *Inside the Kremlin's Cold War: From Stalin to Khrushchev*. Cambridge: Harvard University Press, 1996.

Unpublished Source

Krome, Frederic James. "'A Weapon of War Second to None': Anglo-American Film Propaganda during World War II." Ph.D. diss., University of Cincinnati, 1992.

INDEX

Italic page numbers refer to illustrations.

Abbott, Bud, 81

Academy Awards, 35, 41, 56, 76, 139; documentaries, 105, 156, 159; *Dragon Seed*, 247; *The Good Earth*, 226; *The Keys of the Kingdom*, 253; *Mrs. Miniver*, 20, 136, 138, 141; *Sahara*, 109; *Wilson*, 124–25

Action in the North Atlantic (movie, 1943), 99, 198, 209, 271

Adventures of Robin Hood, The (movie, 1938), 56, 71

African Americans, 5, 57, 100–101, 106, 144, 222, 223

Agee, James, 247

Ahn, Philip, 249

Aleksandrov, Grigorii, 208, 268

Allen, Devere, 71

Allen, H. C., 137

Allport, Fayette W., 167

Allport, Gordon, 35

All Quiet on the Western Front (movie, 1930), 34, 56

America at the Movies (Thorp), 34

America First Committee, 27, 82, 85, 87

America Moves Up (newsreel, 1941), 77

American Association for the United Nations, 128

"American Century," 15, 18, 46, 111, 224, 240, 267

American Declaration of Independence, 90

American Federation of Labor, 118

American Film Center, 28, 33

American Journal of Sociology, 39

American Mercury, 27

American Revolution, 95, 98

American Volunteer Group, 234–35, 240

Ames, Edward, 212–13

Anderson, Benedict, 5

Anderson, Marian, 106

Andrews, Dana, 199

Andrievsky, Andrei N., 184, 214

Anglo-American partnership, 5, 136–37, 279 (n. 34), 295 (n. 1); criticism of, 143–48; documentaries promoting, 157–59; U.S. Department of State and, 164, 165; after World War II, 163, 299 (n. 45). *See also* Churchill, Winston S.; Great Britain; Movies: Anglo-American partnership and; Roosevelt, Franklin D.

Anglophobia, 5, 19, 56–57, 62, 80, 145–47, 168

Anstey, Edgar, 65, 66

Anti-Nazi movies: *Casablanca*, 107, 108–9; *Charlie Chan in the Secret Service*, 217–18, *218*; *Confessions of a Nazi Spy*, 40, 61; documentaries, 77–78, 105–7, 157–58, 191–93; *Foreign Correspondent*, 69–71; *The Hitler Gang*, 103, 294 (n. 56); *The Sea Hawk*, 71–74; *That Hamilton Woman* (movie, 1941), 74–77, 82; *This above All*, 142; U.S. isolationism and, 53–55, 82–88. See also *Mrs. Miniver*

Anti-Semitism, 20, 40, 54, 87

Appointment for Love (movie, 1941), 212

Armstrong, Louis, 212

Arnold, Edward, 44

Asquith, Anthony, 153–54

Atlantic Charter, 147, 161

Atlantic Monthly, 36

Atomic bomb, 103

Atrocity Propaganda (Read), 57

Attenborough, Richard, 153

Baird, Thomas, 164

Baker, Ray Stannard, 123, 124, 125, 294 (n. 54)

Balfour, John, 64

Barghoorn, Frederick C., 211, 213

Barrett, Edward, 97

Barrymore, Diana, 149

Bataan (movie, 1943), 107

Battle Fleets of England (newsreel, 1939), 66

Battle of Britain, The (documentary, 1943), 193, 264, 266

Battle of China, The (documentary, 1944), 231–32, 233–34

Battle of Russia, The (documentary, 1943), 170, 185–86, 193–95, 206

Baxter, Anne, 199

Bazykin, Vladimir, 208

Beddington, Jack, 74

Behavioral psychology, 28–29, 281 (n. 9)

Behind the Rising Sun (movie, 1943), 102, 226

Bell, Ulric, 42, 52, 85, 86, 200

Bendix, William, 248

Benét, Stephen Vincent, 116

Bennett, Bruce, 109

Bennett, Marion T., 197

Benny, Jack, 211

Berch, Barbara, 244

Bergman, Ingrid, 108, 293 (n. 37)

Berle, Adolf A., Jr., 49, 50–51, 132, 209

Berlin, Irving, 126

Bernays, Edward L., 30–31, 36

Bernstein, Sidney, 61, 66, 139, 164

Berryman, Clifford, 162

Beveridge Report, 140

Biddle, Francis, 32

Biggers, Earl Derr, 217, 222

Big House (movie, 1930), 34

Blackface minstrelsy, 220, 222

Black Fury (movie, 1935), 38

Blockade (movie, 1938), 39

Blood on the Sun (movie, 1945), 12, 226, 241, 243, 245

Blum, John Morton, 22

Blumer, Harold, 33–34

Bogart, Humphrey, 80, 99, 167, 196, 198, 264; *Casablanca* and, 8, 19, 108–9, 134, 248; *Sahara* and, 19, 109–11, *110*

Bohlen, Charles E., 267–68

Bol'shakov, Ivan G., 172, 173, 175, 184

Bombardier (movie, 1943), 230

Bombs over Burma (movie, 1942), 227

Bone, Homer T., 83

Boothby, Robert J., 167

Borah, William E., 57

Boyer, Charles, 212

Bracken, Brendan, 147

Breen, Joseph I., 37, 250, 252

Brewer, Roy, 210

Bridges, Styles, 145

Britain on Guard (newsreel, 1940), 66

Britain's RAF (newsreel, 1940), 66

British Air Ministry, 79

British Broadcasting Corporation (BBC), 60, 67, 119, 148, 159

British Information Services, 64, 117–18, 146, 147, 148, 164

British Library of Information, 60, 164

British Ministry of Information (MOI): American Division, 58, 64, 148; Anglo-American partnership and, 146, 147–48, 159; British-made propaganda for U.S. market and, 8, 59–60, 65, 66, 77, 99–100, 119, 153; documentaries and, 8, 65, 66, 99–100, 140, 155–59, 293 (n. 44); Hollywood movie industry and, 61, 64, 65; Hollywood movies and, 71, 72, 74, 79, 139, 140, 155, 164, 165, 166; Hollywood newsreels and, 65–67, 146; posters and, 113, 298 (n. 37); radio propaganda and, 60, 67, 148, 159

British Press Service, 60

British Propaganda at Home and in the United States (Squires), 57

British Security Co-Ordination, 75

Brogan, Denis W., 163

Brooklyn Eagle, 250

Brooks, C. Wayland, 83

Brooks, Jeffrey, 186

Brown, Clarence, 210

Bruce, Hazel, 125

Bryce, Lord James, 57

Bryce Report. See *Report of the Committee on Alleged German Outrages*

Buck, Pearl S., 7, 221, 226, 245, 247

Buckner, Robert, 176, 177

Buck Privates (movie, 1941), 81

Bugs Bunny Nips the Nips (cartoon, 1944), 102

Bukharin, Nikolai, 178

Butler, Harold, 146, 147, 148

Byrnes, James F., 44–45

Cabin in the Sky (movie, 1943), 212

Cagney, James, 196, 241, 243, 245

Cagney, William, 241, 245

Cairo Conference, 1, 129, 234

Campbell, Gerald, 64, 117–18, 121, 147

Canterbury Tale, A (movie, 1944), 154–55

Cantril, Hadley, 29, 35

Capra, Frank, 7–8, 15, 16, 19, 20, 42, 221, 233, 241, 266; *Mr. Smith Goes to Washington* and, 44, 45; pro-Soviet movies and, 170, 185–86, 193–94; *Why We Fight* film series and, 10, 104–7, 134, 157, 170, 193–94, 231–32, 264

Captain Blood (movie, 1935), 71

Carlson, Evans, 231

Carnegie, Dale, 18, 279 (n. 32)

Carnegie Foundation, 264

Carroll, Gordon, 27

Carroll, John, 235

Cartoons, 90, 102, 104, 119, 161–62, 188, 296 (n. 12)

Casablanca (movie, 1942), 8, 19, 71, 103, 107–9, 134, 248

Casablanca Conference, 181

Catholic Church, 37, 197, 250, 252

Catholic World, 188

Caught in the Draft (movie, 1941), 81

Cavalcade (movie, 1933), 139

Celler, Emanuel, 28

Century Group, 60, 63, 65

Chamberlain, Neville, 58, 159–60

Chamberlin, William Henry, 26, 27, 32

Chandler, A. B. "Happy," 145

Chang, T. K., 223, 245, 247–48, 252

Chang Apana, 217

Chaplin, Charlie, 44, 81, 172

Charge of the Light Brigade, The (movie, 1936), 56

Charley's Aunt (movie, 1941), 211

Charlie Chan, 21, 217–18, 219, 220, 222–23, 253, 255, 311 (n. 1)

Charlie Chan Carries On (movie, 1931), 219

Charlie Chan in the Secret Service (movie, 1944), 217–18, *218*, 223

Charlie Chan Is Dead (Kim), 220

Chaucer, Geoffrey, 154

Chekhov, Anton, 192, 194

Chennault, Claire, 234

Cherrington, Ben M., 43

Chiang Kai-Shek. *See* Jiang Jieshi

Chicago, 70–71, 93, 118, 128

Chicago Daily News, 226

Chicago Tribune, 85, 87, 118, 143, 145, 188, 248

Childs, Stephen, 58

Chin, Frank, 220, 223

China: Communism and, 221, 254, 268; documentaries about U.S. for, 239–40; documentaries promoting, 231–32, 233–34, 316 (n. 54); Hollywood movie industry and, 236–39; Japan and, 232, 233, 236, 240–41, 245–46, 248–50; print media promoting, 232–33, 234; religion and, 233, 250, 253; United Nations and, 4–5, 221, 227–28, 245, 247, 251, *262*; U.S. foreign relations and, 217, 221–22, 312 (n. 6); U.S. public opinion and, 11, 92, 220–21, 224–25, 227–28, 229, 254–55; U.S. racism and, 4–5, 12–13, 224, 229. *See also* Movies

China (movie, 1943), 21, 224, 232, 248–50, 253, 255

China Defense Supplies, 252

China Girl (movie, 1942), 12, 15, 226, 232, 240–41, 242, 243–44, 248, 253, 315 (n. 41)

Chinese exclusion acts, 4–5, 224

Ching Wah Lee, 230

Christian Century, 27, 33, 70–71, 83, 85, 144

Christian Science Monitor, 26, 38, 45, 187, 245

Churchill, Jennie, 150, 162

Churchill, Randolph, 150

Churchill, Winston S., 2, 58, 143, 228, 234; Anglo-American partnership and, 11, 15, 20, 137, 147, 156, 157, 159–63, 168, 267; British Empire and, 144–45; British propaganda and, 55, 77, 156; Hollywood movies and, 74, 75, 296 (n. 12); Soviet Union and, 181, 302 (n. 13); at Tehran summit, 1–2, 130, 205, 256; United Nations and, 89, 90, 113, 119, 129; V for Victory and, 160–61, 162

Cinematograph Film Acts of 1927 and 1938 (British), 61–62

Cinematograph Films Council (British), 166

Circus, The (*Tsirk'*, movie, 1936), 171

City of Courage (documentary, 1942), 191

Clark, D. Worth, 83, 86, 87, 88

Clark, Joel Bennett "Champ," 83, 84, 86

Coca-Cola, 159

Cold War, 23, 170, 171, 203, 207, 216; movies and, 266, 268–69, 317–18 (n. 9), 318 (n. 12)

Collier's Weekly, 67, 143–44, 187, 205

Collins, Richard, 200, 209, 270

Colonel Blimp, 143, 146, 160, 296 (n. 12)

Columbia Broadcasting System (CBS), 36, 67, 77, 94

Columbia Studios, 9, 45, 109, 110

Comics, 159, 217, 229

Committee for Cultural Freedom, 26, 27

Committee of One Million, 188

Committee on Public Information (CPI), 15, 25, 281 (n. 15)

Committee on War Information, 97

Commonweal, 59, 74, 82, 159, 197, 206

Communications Group, 29

Communism: anticommunist movies and, 195, 268–69, 318 (n. 12); China and, 221, 254, 268; Hollywood movie industry and, 22, 187, 196, 197, 207–8, 209–10, 216, 269–72; Soviet Union and, 23, 180, 183, 304–5 (n. 34); U.S. anticommunism and, 186, 188, 190, 197, 206–7, 210, 216, 269–72, 309 (n. 79)

Communist Party of the United States of America (CPUSA), 187, 196, 198, 200, 207, 209, 271

Comrade X (movie, 1940), 195, 203

Confessions of a Nazi Spy (movie, 1939), 40, 54, 61, 81, 84, 193

Connally, Tom, 180

Convoy (movie, 1940), 84

Cooper, Alfred Duff, 59

Cooper, Gary, 8, 142, 210, 271, 293 (n. 37)

Copland, Aaron, 199

Costello, Lou, 81

Costigliola, Frank, 170, 268

Council for Democracy, 65

Covarrubias, Miguel, 113

Coward, Noel, 66, 139, 141

Cowell, F. R., 59

Cranes Are Flying, The (movie, 1958), 208

Creel, George, 15, 25

Criminal Code, The (movie, 1931), 34

Cronin, A. J., 250, 252

Crossman, Melville. *See* Zanuck, Daryl F.

Crowther, Bosley, 68, 70, 74, 123, 125, 195, 196, 248

Cruikshank, Robin, 148

Culbert, David, 182

Curtiz, Michael, 20, 71, 108, 176

Daily Mail, 119

Daily Telegraph, 167

Daily Worker, 196

Dale, Edgar, 30

Daniels, Josephus, 125

Davies, Joseph E., 187, 205; *Mission to Moscow* and, 169, 177–80, 181–84, 232; *Mission to Moscow* book and, 175–76, 196, 303 (n. 18)

Davis, Bette, 56

Davis, Elmer, 36, 94, 97, 207

Davis, Richard H., 237

Day, Laraine, 69

Day, Stephen A., 127

Days of Glory (movie, 1944), 253, 307–8 (n. 63)

Declaration of the United Nations, 3, 89–90, 117, 121, 128, 134, 147, 162, 258, 276–77 (n. 6)

Democracy in Action (documentary, 1942), 111–12, 240

"Democratic propaganda," 29–31, 32, 51–52

De Rochemont, Louis, 65

Desert Victory (documentary, 1943), 155–56

Destination Tokyo (movie, 1943), 230

Devil's Island (movie, 1939), 43

Devotions upon Emergent Occasions (poem, Donne), 116

Dewey, John, 22, 27, 187, 196, 303 (n. 18), 307 (n. 60)

Dewey, Thomas E., 127, 163

Dies, Martin J., 188, 196, 198, 210, 269

Dirty Dozen, The (movie, 1967), 231

Disney, Walt, 210, 271

Ditter, John, 207

Dr. Ehrlich's Magic Bullet (movie, 1940), 24

Documentary News Letter, 159

Doherty, Thomas, 269

Donne, John, 116, 293 (n. 37)

Doolittle, James H., 230

Doolittle Raid, 230

Douglas, Melvyn, 196

Dragon Seed (Buck), 7, 245

Dragon Seed (movie, 1944), 7, 8, 21, 232, 245–48, 253

Drake, Francis, 158

Drums (movie, 1938), 74

Dubinsky, David, 188

Duck Soup (movie, 1933), 43

Dumbarton Oaks proposals, 132

Dunne, Irene, 153

Durbin, Deanna, 212

Durbrow, Elbridge, 174, 215

Eagle Squadron (movie, 1942), 13, 149–50, 154, 235, 236

Eagle Squadrons, 78, 79, 149

Early, Stephen T., 86, 143, 176

Edison, the Man (movie, 1940), 211

Edward VIII (king of England), 150

Ehrenburg, Ilya, 186

Ehrlich, Paul, 24

Eisenhower, Dwight D., 158, 264, 267

Eisenstein, Sergei, 173

Ellington, Duke, 212

Encounter at the Elbe (movie, 1949), 268

Engerman, David, 14

England. *See* Great Britain

Epstein, Julius, 108

Epstein, Philip, 108

Fairbank, John K., 240

Fairbank, Wilma, 240

Fairbanks, Douglas, 219

Farber, Manny, 196

Farrow, John, 249

Federal Bureau of Investigation (FBI), 22, 209, 230

Ferguson, Otis, 75, 76

Fight for Freedom Committee, 60, 85, 141

Films Exchange Agreement, 62, 63

Finland, 177, 179

Fire over England (movie, 1937), 72, 76

Fish, Hamilton, 93, 127

Flag Day, 113

Flight Command (movie, 1940), 81, 84

Flowers, W. F., 197–98

Flying Tigers (movie, 1942), 21, 224, 232, 234–36, 249, 253, 255

Flynn, Errol, 20, 56, 71, 72, 292 (n. 32)

Flynn, John T., 27, 82–83, 84, 86

Fonda, Henry, 39

Fong, Benson, *218*, 219, 230, 253

Fontaine, Joan, 142

Ford, John, 234

Ford, Richard R., 164

Foreign Affairs, 39, 122

Foreign Agents Registration Act of 1938, 28, 209

Foreign Correspondent (movie, 1940), 20, 68–71, 81, 88, 149

Fortune (magazine), 95, 97, 206

49th Parallel (movie, 1940), 59–60

Foster, Preston, 151

Four Feathers, The (movie, 1939), 74

Four Freedoms, 11, 111; China and, 21, 221, 234, 250; Great Britain and, 144, 161; Roosevelt and, 45–46, 100, 117, 147, 189; Soviet Union and, 189, 190, 192; United Nations and, 100, 113, 117, 122

Fox, William, 40

Frakes, Margaret, 83, 85

Frankenheimer, John, 268

Freedom of information as fifth freedom, 49

Free World Association, 111

Freud, Sigmund, 30

Fu Manchu, 218, 223, 225–26

Gable, Clark, 7, 35, 43, 195

Gallup, George, 30

Gallup Poll, 81

Gandhi, Mohandas, 5, 100

Garbo, Greta, 35, 195, 203

Garson, Greer, *138*, 139, 141, 264

General Foods, 176

General Motors, 104

George VI (king of England), 119, 162

Germany. *See* Nazi Germany

Gershwin, Ira, 199

Goebbels, Joseph, 10, 26, 27, 32, 65, 70

Goldwyn, Samuel, 37, 48, 61, 87, 198, 200

Gone with the Wind (movie, 1939), 76, 124

Goodbye Mr. Chips (movie, 1939), 81, 210

Good Earth, The (Buck), 221, 226

Good Earth, The (movie, 1937), 221, 226, 245, 312 (n. 14)

Gould, Walter, 238

Government Information Manual for the Motion Picture Industry (OWI), 36, 98–99, 146, 228–29

Grable, Betty, 79, 80

Grahame, Orville F., 197

Granger, Lester, 144

Grant, Cary, 243, 267

Grauman's Chinese Theatre, 35, 243

Great Britain: American GIs and, 13, 150, *151*, *152*, 153, 257, *260*, 298 (n. 28); British Empire, 5, 56, 57, 74, 84, 94, 100, 143–47; British propaganda for U.S market and, 25, 57–60; class system, 66, 139–40, 141, 143, 296 (n. 12); Hollywood movie industry and, 8, 20–21, 61–65, 163, 166–68; Hollywood movies played in, 163–66; Lend-Lease and, 63, 66, 71, 76–77, 81, 143, 145, 146, 156; Soviet Union and, 181, 302 (n. 13), 305 (n. 36), 311 (n. 95); United Nations Day and, 119, *120*; U.S. Anglophobia and, 5, 19, 145–47, 168; U.S. public opinion and, 58, 80–81, 85, 92–93, 150, 206, 227–28; World War II, before U.S. involvement and, 29, 55–56, 58–59. *See also* Anglo-American partnership; British Ministry of Information; Movies

Great Depression, 25, 44, 62, 186

Great Dictator, The (movie, 1940), 81, 84, 172

Great Terror, 187, 199. *See also* Stalin, Joseph

Grew, Joseph, 102, 133, 145

Grierson, John, 65

Groupthink, 29

Guadalcanal Diary (movie, 1943), 107

Gunga Din (movie, 1939), 56
"Gung ho," 231, 313 (n. 25)
Gung Ho! (movie, 1943), 107, 230–31, 236

Halifax, Lord, 63, 64, 119, 146, 163
Harding, Ann, 178
Harding, Warren G., 16
Hardwicke, Cedric, 123
Harlow, Jean, 35
Harper's, 51
Harriman, W. Averell, 23, 186, 212, 214–15, 268
Harrison, Pete, 45
Harrison, Rex, 154
Harrison's Reports, 45
Hathaway, Henry, 244
Hays, Will H., 16, 38, 41, 45, 51; China and, 237, 238; export of Hollywood movies and, 17–18, 47–48; Hollywood movie industry and U.K. and, 62, 63–64, 65, 167; movie censorship and, 39–40; pro-British films and, 82, 85; Soviet Union and, 185, 212
Hearst, William Randolph, 143, 196
Hecht, Ben, 240, 244
Hellman, Lillian, 198, 206–7, 208, 209, 310 (n. 88)
Hell's Angels (movie, 1930), 35
Henie, Sonja, 211
Henreid, Paul, 108
Hepburn, Katharine, 21, 221, 222, 246, 247, 248, 255
Heritage We Guard, The (documentary, 1940), 240
Herron, Frederick L., 62
Hidden Persuaders, The (Packard), 265
His Butler's Sister (movie, 1943), 212
Hitchcock, Alfred, 8, 20, 55, 68–69, 70, 71, 88, 267
Hitler, Adolf, 26, 29, 38, 87, 94, 159, 179, 180, 187
Hitler Gang, The (movie, 1944), 103, 294 (n. 56)
Hitler's Children (movie, 1943), 103

Hollywood Anti-Nazi League, 38, 60, 187
Hollywood movies. *See* Movies
Hollywood Reporter, 164, 192
Hollywood Ten, 230, 271, 272
Holmes, Julius Cecil, 132–33
Holway, C. P., 46
Hook, Sidney, 26
Hoover, Herbert, 9
Hoover, J. Edgar, 22, 209
Hope, Bob, 81, 118, 230
Hopkins, Harry, 41, 198
Hopper, Hedda, 210
Horne, Lena, 212
House Un-American Activities Committee (HUAC), 22, 188, 196, 198, 210, 269–72
Hovland, Carl I., 264, 266
How Green Was My Valley (movie, 1941), 139
Hughes, Howard, 35
Hull, Cordell, 50, 90, 145, 167, 173; movie industry and, 20–21, 45, 47–48, 63–65
Hunter, Kim, 155, *156*
Hurley, Patrick J., 239
Huston, John, 157
Huston, Walter, 177, *179*, 184, 199, 245, 246, 247, 248

I Am a Fugitive from a Chain Gang (movie, 1932), 38
Idiot's Delight (movie, 1939), 43
I Live in Grosvenor Square (movie, 1945), 13, 154, 235, 241
India, 144
Information Bulletin, 208, 309 (n. 80)
Ingram, Rex, 109, *110*
Inter-Allied Information Committee, 129
International Squadron (movie, 1941), 78, 79–80
Interstate Commerce Committee, 83
In Which We Serve (movie, 1942), 66, 141
Iron Curtain, The (movie, 1948), 268

Italy, 26, 108, 207
It Happened One Night (movie, 1934), 7–8, 35
It's a Wonderful Life (movie, 1946), 251
I Was a Communist for the FBI (movie, 1951), 268

Jagger, Dean, 154, 235
Japan, 4, 5, 92, 95, 127; China and, 232, 233, 236, 240–41, 245–46, 248–50; U.S. propaganda against, 31, 101, 102–3, 105, 106, 118, 229, 230, 241–43
Jarratt, A. W., 61
Jarrico, Paul, 200, 209, 270
Jen, Gish, 220, 223
Jennings, Humphrey, 140
Jesperson, T. Christopher, 224
Jiang, Madame, 13, 129, 233
Jiang Jieshi, 4, 183; United Nations and, 90, 113, 129; U.S. alliance and, 160, 217, 221, 233, 234, 238, 253, 254; U.S. public opinion and, 15, 228, 254
John, Rosamund, 153
Johnny in the Clouds. See Way to the Stars, The
Johnson, Nunnally, 250
Johnson, Van, 230
Johnston, Eric, 238, 271
Joint Declaration of the United Nations. *See* Declaration of the United Nations
Jonassen, Christen T., 257
Journal American, 27
Journey's End (movie, 1930), 34, 74
Journey Together (movie, 1945), 153
Judd, Walter, 234
J. Walter Thompson Agency, 29

Kalatozov, Mikhail, 208, 209
Kaltenborn, H. V., 130
Kansas City Star, 187
Kazan, Elia, 222
Kazin, Alfred, 194–95
Keeper of the Keys (Biggers), 222
Kemenov, Vladimir S., 172, 173, 175

Kenez, Peter, 181
Kennan, George F., 23, 213, 266, 268, 311 (n. 91), 317–18 (n. 9)
Kennedy, Joseph P., 16, 45, 62
Keys of the Kingdom, The (movie, 1944), 15, 21, 224–25, 232, 250–53, *254*, 255
Kim, Elaine, 220
Kimball, Warren F., 160
King, Henry, 124
Kippen, Manart, 178, *179*
Klapper, Joseph, 266
Klein, Christina, 221
Knox, Alexander, 122, 123, 124
Knox, Frank, 117
Koch, Howard, 71, 74, 108, 270
Komitet po Delam Kinematografii (Committee on Cinematography Affairs, KDK), 172, 174, 185, 190–91, 213
Korda, Alexander, 20, 54, 59, 72, 74–77, 82
Korngold, Erich Wolfgang, 72
Krock, Arthur, 207
Kuhn, Frederick, 164–65
Kupper, Charles, 85
Kuwa, George, 219

Ladd, Alan, 21, 224, 248, 249–50
Lady from Chungking (movie, 1942), 227
Lady Hamilton. See That Hamilton Woman
Laemmle, Carl, 40
La Follette, Suzanne, 196, 307 (n. 60)
Lamarr, Hedy, 203
Lang, Fritz, 81
Lasswell, Harold D., 28, 29, 30, 33
Lavine, Harold, 57
Lawson, John Howard, 109, 198, 209, 271
Lazarsfeld, Paul, 266
League of Nations, 3, 6, 19, 94, 122–24, 125, 126, 178, 184
Lean, David, 141
Leigh, Vivien, 20, 76
Lejeune, C. A., 154, 164
Lend-Lease Act of 1941, 100, 111–12; criticism of, 82, 99; Great Britain and,

63, 66, 71, 76–77, 81, 143, 145, 146, 156;
Soviet Union and, 174, 189, 192, 198
Leong, Karen, 221
Lhamon, W. T., Jr., 222
Life (magazine), 65, 87, 144, 162, 196,
229, 234; "American Century" edi-
torial, 15, 46; pro-British films and,
70, 77; pro-Soviet films and, 178, 191,
200, 204
Lilienthal, David E., 192
Lincoln, Abraham, 106–7
Lindbergh, Charles, 83, 87
Lion Has Wings, The (movie, 1939), 59,
74–75, 76
Listen to Britain (documentary, 1942),
140
Literatura i Iskusstvo (Literature and
Art), 186
"Little Albert," 29, 281 (n. 9)
Little Caesar (movie, 1930), 38
Little Foxes, The (play, Hellman), 198
Litvak, Anatole, 193, 194
Litvinov, Maxim, 89, 119, 169, 178, 184,
208, 211
Litvinov, Tania, 211
Lives of a Bengal Lancer, The (movie,
1935), 56
Lloyd, Frank, 34
Lodge, Henry Cabot, 123
Loew, Arthur L., 51
Loew's, 40, 51, 86
Loft, Arthur, *218*
London Can Take It (newsreel, 1940), 7,
8, 66–68, 81, 121, 191
London Evening Standard, 90, 296
(n. 12)
London Times, 163
Long, Breckinridge, 45, 49, 63, 64, 96
Loo, Richard, 249
"Lookout Monkeys" (poster), 104
Lorentz, Pare, 240
Los Angeles Times, 48, 198, 241, 243, 244,
245
Lothian, Lord, 58, 62–63
Low, David, 90, 104, 296 (n. 12)

Lowe, Herman, 52
Lozovskii, Solomon A., 175, 185
Lubitsch, Ernst, 195
Luce, Clare Boothe, 111, 134, 290 (n. 9)
Luce, Henry R., 10, 65, 125, 196; "Ameri-
can Century" and, 15, 18, 46, 111, 224,
240; China and, 46, 221, 224, 233, 253
Luke, Keye, 219
Lynd, Robert S., 29
Lyons, Eugene, 70, 197

MacArthur, Douglas, 193
MacLeish, Archibald, 32, 36, 38, 67, 94,
97, 164, 265
MacMahon, Alice, 247
Macmahon, Arthur W., 265, 266
Macmillan, Harold, 148
MacMurray, Fred, 78
Madame Butterfly (movie, 1932), 243
Maisky, Ivan M., 119
Maltese Falcon, The (movie, 1941), 80
Maltz, Albert, 271
Manchurian Candidate, The (movie,
1962), 268
Man Hunt (movie, 1941), 81
Mankiewicz, Joseph L., 251
Mannheim, Carl, 179
Man Who Knew Too Much, The (movie,
1934), 69
Man Who Knew Too Much, The (movie,
1956), 69
Mao Zedong, 4, 221, 233, 254, 268
Marchetti, Gina, 225
March of Time, 65, 66, 191
March on Washington Movement, 101,
144
Marshall, George C., 193
Marshall, John, 28
Marvin, Lee, 231
Marx Brothers, 43, 44
Massey, Raymond, 155
Mass Observation, 163
Mathews, Basil, 13, 256
Matter of Life and Death, A (movie,
1946), 154, 155, *156*, 165, 298 (n. 30)

May, Mark A., 34

Mayer, Louis B., 9, 40, 61, 270–71

McCaleb, Kenneth, 74

McCarran, Pat, 188

McCarthy, Alice, 198

McCloy, John J., 97

McCormick, Anne O'Hare, 206

McCormick, Robert, 143

McCrea, Joel, 69

McFarland, Ernest, 83, 86

McManus, Jack, 196

Meet John Doe (movie, 1941), 42, 44

Mellett, Lowell, 37, 41, 85, 97

Meredith, Burgess, 157

Metro-Goldwyn-Mayer (MGM), 9, 40, 43, 86, 211, 230; pro-British films and, 13, 61, 78, 81, 136, 138, 139, 153; pro-China films and, 7, 221, 226, 232, 245, 246, 247–48, 316 (n. 54); pro-Soviet films and, 12, 22, 170, 182, 185, 191, 200, 204, 207, 245

Midsummer's Night's Dream, A (movie, 1935), 56

Mikoyan, Anastas, 169

Miles, Bernard, 157

Milestone, Lewis, 199

Miller, Alice Duer, 153

Miller, Glenn, 212

Miller, Seton I., 71, 72, 74

Milliken, Carl E., 238

Mills, John, 153

Miscegenation, 12, 225, 226, 241, 243, 244, 255, 315 (n. 42)

Mrs. Miniver (movie, 1942), 13, 15, 137–41, *138*, 142, 143, 148, 150; Academy Awards and, 20, 136, 138, 141; reviews of, 141, 295–96 (n. 7)

Mission to Moscow (Davies), 175–76, 196, 303 (n. 18)

Mission to Moscow (movie, 1943), 175, *179*, 206, 216, 245, 264, 303 (n. 25), 304 (n. 33); Chinese content and, 232; investigation of as pro-communist, 269–70; production of, 176–79; screenplay of, 71; Soviet footage and,

8, 208; Soviet public opinion and, 211; Stalin and, 7, 15, 22, 169–70, 177, 178, *179*, 181–85, 199, 205; U.S. public opinion and, 196–98, 247, 307 (n. 60)

Mr. Deeds Goes to Town (movie, 1936), 42, 44

Mr. Smith Goes to Washington (movie, 1939), 44–45

Mitchell, Thomas, 251

Mitchum, Robert, 231

Modern Times (movie, 1936), 44

Molotov, Polina, 178, 303 (n. 23)

Molotov, Vyacheslav, 129, 169, 174, 175, 181, 182, 183, 184, 185, 208

Monogram studio, 218, 224, 316 (n. 54)

Montgomery, Douglass, 153

Montgomery, George, 240, *242*

Moon, Krystyn R., 222

Moon Is Down, The (movie, 1943), 103

Moreland, Mantan, *218*, 223

Morris, Lee, 125

Mortal Storm (movie, 1940), 81

Moscow Declaration, 130

Moscow Strikes Back (documentary, 1942), 191–92, 193, 271

Motion Picture Alliance for the Preservation of American Ideals, 22, 210, 271

Motion Picture Association of America, 271

Motion Picture Daily, 70, 77, 141, 204

Motion Picture Herald, 70, 200

Motion Picture Producers and Distributors of America (MPPDA), 16, 51, 85; British restrictions on Hollywood movies and, 20–21, 62–65, 167; China and, 237, 238–39; export of Hollywood movies and, 17–18, 47–48, 212; movie censorship and, 38, 39–40; Soviet Union and, 185, 212; World War II in Europe and, 60–61, 62

Movies: American movie-goers and, 1940s, 7–8, 78, 263; Anglo-American partnership and, 13, 19–20, 136–43, 148–59, 163–68, 295 (n. 2); anticommunist, 195, 268–69, 318 (n. 12); anti-Japanese, 102, 241, 243; antitrust litigation and, 18–19, 40–41, 61, 272, 282–83 (n. 35); British-made, for U.S market, 59–60, 77–78, 140; censorship and, 37–38, 41–42, 51; Charlie Chan movies before World War II, 219, 220; Charlie Chan movies during World War II, 217–18, *218*, 220–21, 223, 224, 253, 311 (n. 1); Chinese American leads and, 219, 227; Chinese American supporting actors and, 21, 219, 226, 230, 249, 253, 255; Chinese leads played by white people and, 12, 21, *218*, 218, 219–27, 241–45, *242*, 246, 247, 249, 253, 255; Chinese stories and, 43, 218, 224–25; Cold War propaganda and, 266, 268–69, 317–18 (n. 9), 318 (n. 12); corporatism and, 16, 17, 42–43, 51, 279 (n. 29); House investigation into pro-British interventionist motives in, 55, 83–88; Jews and, 10, 40, 60, 87, 209; piracy and, 237, 238, 239; postwar federal policy and, 47, 49–52, 284–85 (n. 55); pro-British Hollywood, after U.S. entered War, 20, 136–43, *138*, 146, 148–59, *156*; pro-British Hollywood, before U.S. entered War, 53–55, 56, 61, 68–83, 142, 149; pro-China, 7, 8, 12–13, 15, 21, 221–22, 224–26, 227, 228–36, 240–55, 316 (n. 54); pro-Soviet, 7, 8, 12, 15, 21, 169–71, 176–85, *179*, 190–205, *201*, 211, 245, 307–8 (n. 63); promoting trade, 17–18, 41, 47, 239; pro–United Nations, 8, 19, 98–100, 107–11, 122–26, 152–53, 155, 198, 263–64, 292 (n. 32), 293 (nn. 37, 44), 294 (n. 56); rise of Nazism and, 38–41, 53–54, 55, 60–61, 86, 282 (n. 28); social effects of, 33–36, 39; "soft power" and, 18, 46–47, 48, 164, 212–13; Soviet, 171, 172, 181, 213, 237, 268; for Soviet Union, 22–23, 211–14, 215, 216, 310 (n. 88); U.S. foreign relations and, 9–10, 16, 18, 37, 43–45,

48–49, 53–54, 168; World War II propaganda and, 15–23, 24–25, 32–33, 36–37, 47–48, 52, 98, 99–111, 266–67, 272–73, 279 (n. 30), 292 (n. 32). *See also* Academy Awards; Anti-Nazi movies; Motion Picture Producers and Distributors of America; Office of War Information; Production Code Administration

Movie theaters, 7, 35
Movietone News, 65, 191
Muhammad, Elijah, 144
Mumford, Lewis, 35
Muni, Paul, 226
Murray, Wallace, 49
Murrow, Edward R., 7, 67, 68, 69, 121, 160
Mussolini, Benito, 26, 105, 108
My Son John (movie, 1952), 268

Naish, J. Carrol, 109
Nanking Massacre, 232, 249
Nation, 46, 87
National Asian American Telecommunications Association, 220
National Association for the Advancement of Colored People (NAACP), 57, 144
National Broadcasting Company (NBC), 116–17
National Committee for the Study of Social Values in Motion Pictures, 33
National Opinion Research Center, 127
National Urban League, 144
Navy Blues (movie, 1941), 81
Nazi Germany: extermination camps, 157–58; Great Britain and, 25, 66, 74–75, 143, 146–47; Hollywood movie industry and, 38–41, 53–54, 55, 60–61, 86, 282 (n. 28); propaganda by, 10, 25–26, 27, 32, 42, 65, 143; Soviet Union and, 180, 183, 186–88, 190, 191–92; U.S. propaganda against, 77–78, 101–2, 103–4, 118, 146. *See also* Anti-Nazi movies; Movies: rise of Nazism and

Nazi-Soviet Pact (1939), 4, 174, 177, 179, 183, 187, 303 (n. 25)
Neagle, Anna, 154
Neutrality Acts, 56
New Republic, 82, 87, 125, 144, 196
News Chronicle, 154
News of the Day, 191
Newsreels, 65–68, 77–78, 130, 132, 162, 259; *London Can Take It*, 7, 8, 66–68, 81, 121, 191; *Soiuzkinozhurnal*, 175, 186, 191, 213
Newsweek, 74, 80, 162, 206, 207
New York Daily Mirror, 206-7
New York Daily News, 143
New Yorker, 156, 196, 248
New York Herald Tribune, 27, 75
New York Mirror, 74, 244
New York Post, 125
New York Times, 38, 95, 97, 103, 123, 189, 206, 207; pro-British films and, 68, 70, 77, 80, 159, 164–65; pro-China films and, 233, 241, 244, 248, 253; pro-Soviet films and, 178, 183, 192, 195, 196, 204, 211
New York Times Magazine, 176
New York World's Fair (1939), 272
Niebuhr, Reinhold, 122
Ninotchka (movie, 1939), 195, 203
Niven, David, 155, *156*
North by Northwest (movie, 1959), 69, 267
North Star (movie, 1943), 22, 182, 185, 198–200, 206, 208, 209, 245
Nugent, Frank, 38
Numbered Men (movie, 1930), 34
Nye, Gerald P., 53–54, 55, 56, 82, 83–84, 86, 87, 127, 143

Oberon, Merle, 59
Objective, Burma! (movie, 1945), 165, 167
Observer, The, 154, 164
Odegard, Peter, 31
Office of Facts and Figures (OFF), 31, 32; Bureau of Intelligence, 96, 97, 98; China and, 227-28, 234; Great Britain and, 146, 159; posters, 113, *114*, 116, 159, 234; United Nations and, 96, 97, 98, 113, *114*, 116; U.S. public opinion and, 92, 94
Office of Government Reports (OGR), 31, 37
Office of Strategic Services, 180
Office of War Information (OWI): Bureau of Motion Pictures (BMP), 32–33, 36–37, 42, 85, 103, 176, 195, 200; China and, 21, 221, 238, 239–40; Communism and, 207, 309 (n. 79); complaints to movie industry, 103, 153, 164–65, 195, 297 (n. 24); documentary commissions, 99–100, 111, 112, 132, 134, 239–40, 300 (n. 51); establishment of, 9, 32, 97–98; movie industry and, 9, 10, 16, 32–33, 36–37, 41–42, 46–47, 141, 189–90, 223–24, 228–29, 236; posters and, 32, 99, 113, *115*; pro-China films and, 231, 235–36, 243–44, 245–46, 247, 248, 250–52; pro-China, 223–24, 228–29, 234; pro-British, 146, 148, 160, 165, 236; pro–United Nations, 9, 101-2, 113; propaganda orchestration and, 97–100; pro-Soviet Hollywood movies and, 9, 22, 176–77, 182, 189–90, 195, 199–200, 201, 203, 204, 208; pro-Soviet propaganda and, 181, 191, 207; pro–United Nations films and, 19, 102, 107, 110, 111, 112, 126, 130, 132, 134; pro–United Nations poster, *115*; Soviet Union and, 22, 172–73, 174, 189, 213, 214, 215; World War II ending and, 265–66
O'Hara, Albert, 252
Ohio State University, 30, 33
Oland, Warner, 219, 220, 223
Olivier, Laurence, 20, 75, 76, 82
One Night in Lisbon (movie, 1941), 78, 88
One World (Willkie), 10, 19, 91, 121–22, 128, 263
Ong Wen-hao, 229
Organization of Chinese Americans, 220

Orientalism (Said), 218
Orlova, Liubov', 171, 268
Orwell, George, 166
Oscars. *See* Academy Awards
Oswego (documentary, 1943), 19, 112–13, 134, 240
Overy, Richard, 262

Packard, Vance, 265
Palache, Albert, 166
Palache Committee, 166
Panter-Downes, Mollie, 257
Paramount, 9, 37, 62, 103, 268, 272; pro-British films, 78, 88; pro-China movies, 21, 232, 249, 250, 255, 316 (n. 54); pro–United Nations films, 111, 293 (n. 37), 294 (n. 56)
Paramount News, 65, 191
Park, E. L., 219
Pathé News, 65, 191
Patterson, Joseph M., 143
Pavlov, Ivan, 28
Payne Fund studies, 33–34, 266
Peck, Gregory, 21, 221, 224–25, 252, 253, *254*, 307–8 (n. 63)
Pegler, Westbrook, 198
People's Republic of China, 255
Peters, Susan, 200, *201*, 203
Peterson, Horace C., 57
Peterson, Ruth C., 34
Philadelphia Inquirer, 52
Philadelphia Record, 125
Pidgeon, Walter, *138*, 139
Pinky (movie, 1949), 222
Pittman, Key, 45
PM, 125, 196, 244, 250
Pocket Guide to China (U.S. Army), 229
Post, Marjorie Merriweather, 176, 178
Posters, 32, 99, 103–4, 107, 159, 186, 234, 298 (n. 37); pro–United Nations, 11, 111, 113, *114–15*, 116, 130, *131*
Potsdam Conference, 15, 162
Powell, Michael, 59, 154, 155, 156, 296 (n. 12)
Power, Tyrone, 8, 79, 142, 240

Power and the Land (documentary, 1940), 240
Poynter, Nelson, 36–37, 41, 52, 101, 141, 176, 195, 198, 236, 240
Pravda, 184, 186
Prelude to War (documentary, 1942), 10, 19, 104–7, 193, 231, 264
Pressburger, Emeric, 59, 154, 155, 156, 296 (n. 12)
Price, Dennis, 155
Price, Vincent, 251
Price of Victory, The (documentary, 1942), 19, 111
Pride and Prejudice (movie, 1940), 81
Prince and the Pauper, The (movie, 1936), 71
Princeton University, 29, 31
Private Life of Henry VIII, The (movie 1933), 56
Private Lives of Elizabeth and Essex, The (movie, 1939), 56, 71
Producers Releasing Corporation, 227
Production Code Administration (PCA): antimiscegenation rule, 12, 219, 226, 241, 243, 244, 255; Catholic Church and, 250, 252; censorship and, 37, 39, 40, 61; crime and adultery censorship, 43–44, 76; establishment of, 33
Propaganda and Promotional Activities (Lasswell), 28
Propaganda for War (Peterson), 57
Public Opinion Quarterly, 265
Pudovkin, Vsevolod, 173, 185, 209
Pulse of Democracy, The (Gallup), 30
Purple Heart (movie, 1944), 230
Pyle, Ernie, 103

Quigley, Martin, 200
Quon, Marianne, *218*, 219, 249

Racism, 4–5, 12–13, 21, 102, 219, 224, 229, 255. *See also* "Yellowface"
Radek, Karl, 178
Radio: British propaganda for United

States and, 148, 159; internationalism, 67; Murrow's London broadcasts, 7, 67, 68, 69, 121, 160; pro-Soviet, 116–17, 204; pro–United Nations, 116–17, 258–59; *War of the Worlds* broadcast, 29

Radio-Keith-Orpheum (RKO), 9, 62, 102, 103, 208, 226; pro-China films and, 230, 316 (n. 54); pro-Soviet films and, 182, 185, 198–99

Rainer, Luise, 226

Rains, Claude, 44, 72

Rand, Ayn, 271

Randolph, A. Philip, 100–101, 144

Random Harvest (movie, 1942), 141, 164

Rankin, John E., 210

Rathbone, Basil, 141

Read, James M., 57

Reader's Digest, 205

Reagan, Ronald, 79–80, 126, 234, 271, 292 (n. 32)

Rebecca (movie, 1940), 68

Red Menace, The (movie, 1949), 268

Reed, Carol, 20, 157, 159

Remarque, Erich Maria, 56

Report of the Committee on Alleged German Outrages, 57

Republic of China (ROC). *See* China

Republic Studio, 232, 235, 236, 255

Reston, James "Scotty," 189

Reyhner, Alice C., 85

Reynolds, David, 153, 165

Reynolds, Quentin, 67, 68, 196–97, 205

Reynolds, Robert R., 210

Richardson, Ralph, 59

Riefenstahl, Leni, 105

Riskin, Robert, 16, 42

River, The (documentary, 1938), 240

Robeson, Paul, 194

Robinson, Edward G., 24, 38, 153, 191, 192

Robson, Flora, 72, 73

Rockefeller, Nelson, 16, 31, 97

Rockefeller Foundation, 28, 29, 265

Rockwell, Norman, 100, 107, 112

Rogers, Will, 44

Rogin, Michael, 222

Rommel, Erwin, 155

Rooney, Mickey, 149

Roosevelt, Franklin D., 6, 29, 290 (n. 9); Anglo-American partnership and, 20, 137, 143, 156, 157, 159–63; China and, 217, 224, 234, 255; death, 215; Fireside Chats, 82, 94–96, 97, 121, 132, 289 (n. 57); Four Freedoms, 45–46, 100, 117, 147, 189; Hollywood movie industry and, 20–21, 37, 38, 41, 45, 49, 61, 63, 85–86, 210, 272; presidential election, 1940, 81, 121; presidential election, 1944, 124, 127, 207; Soviet Union and, 94, 169–70, 173–74, 176, 179–82, 183, 189, 214, 304 (n. 33); Stalin and, 22, 170, 175, 180–82, 183, 215, 301 (n. 2); Tehran summit, 1–2, 2, 129, 130, 132, 205, 256, 268; United Nations and, 89–90, 94, 95–96, 97, 100, 113–17, 119, 128–29, 132, 133–34, 267, 294 (n. 60); World War II in Europe and, 10, 81, 82, 85, 87; World War II propaganda, after United States' entry into War, 10–11, 18, 27–28, 31–32, 103, 113–17, 119, 121, 125–26, 234, 280 (n. 7); World War II propaganda, before United States' entry into War, 9, 26–27, 41, 45–46, 54–55, 58, 61, 63, 64–65, 285 (n. 5); World War II propaganda for Soviet Union and, 176, 179, 183, 185, 189, 207, 210, 215, 270, 304 (n. 33); World War II U.S. involvement and, 92, 93–96, 97, 100. *See also* Office of War Information

Royal Air Force (RAF), 59, 77, 151, 155, 159; Americans serving in, 78–80, 149, 153, 292 (n. 32)

Royal Navy, 57, 75, 141

Sabatini, Rafael, 71

Sahara (movie, 1943), 11, 19, 109–11, *110*, 134

Said, Edward, 4, 218, 221

Sanders, George, 69

Sanders of the River (movie, 1935), 74

San Francisco Chronicle, 125, 196
San Francisco Examiner, 145
San Francisco Press Club, 245
Saturday Evening Post, 17, 100
Schenck, Nicholas, 40, 86, 87
Scott, Randolph, 231
Scribner's Commentator, 83
Sea Hawk, The (movie, 1940), 20, 71–74,
    75, 81
Second Red Scare, 210, 216, 268
Selznick, David O., 68, 76, 124, 250
Sergeant York (movie, 1941), 8, 81, 84, 142
Shahn, Ben, 104
Sharff, Stefan, 211
Shaw, George Bernard, 20
Shaw, G. Howland, 49
Sherlock Holmes and the Secret Weapon
    (movie, 1943), 141
Sherman Antitrust Act, 18–19, 40–41, 272
Sherriff, R. C., 74
Sherwood, Robert, 32, 43, 97
Short, William H., 33
Shostakovich, Dmitri, 194
Showmen's Trade Review, 247
Shuttleworth, Frank K., 34
Sidney, Sylvia, 12, 226, 243, 244–45
Sim, Sheila, 155
Skouras, Spyres P., 48
Slesinger, Donald, 28, 33
Smith, Gerald L. K., 188
Smith, Kate, 126
"Social engineering," 264–65, 266, 317
    (nn. 6–7)
Soiuzintorgkino, 184, 185, 208, 213–14
Soiuzkinozhurnal (All-Union News-
    reel), 175, 186, 191, 213
Sojin Kamiyama, 219
Somervell, Rupert G., 166
Song of Russia (movie, 1944), 22, 182,
    201, 207, 208, 209, 214, 215, 270–71; as
    Hollywood romance, 12, 15, 170, 185,
    200–204, 241
Son of the Gods (movie, 1930), 34
Soong, Mayling. See Jiang, Madame
Soong, T. V., 89

So Proudly We Hail (movie, 1943), 37
South Atlantic Quarterly, 233
Soviet Central Newsreel Studio, 191
Soviet Information Bureau (Sovinform-
    buro), 174, 175, 185
Soviet Russia Today, 208
Soviet Union: Communism and, 23,
    180, 183, 304–5 (n. 34); documentaries
    about U.S. for, 213, 311 (n. 92); docu-
    mentaries promoting, 170–71, 185–86,
    190–95; Great Britain and, 181, 302
    (n. 13), 305 (n. 36), 311 (n. 95); Holly-
    wood movie industry and, 172–73,
    184–87, 208–10, 212, 213–14; Holly-
    wood movies and, 22–23, 211–14, 215,
    216, 310 (n. 88); Hollywood movies
    promoting, 7, 8, 12, 15, 21, 169–71, 176–
    85, 179, 190–205, 201, 211, 245, 307–8
    (n. 63); Hollywood movies purged
    from, 22, 23, 171, 172, 214–15, 301 (n. 7);
    religion and, 101, 180, 188, 193, 197;
    Soviet-made documentaries, 191–92;
    Soviet movies, 171, 172, 181, 213, 237,
    268; Soviet propaganda, 26, 172, 175,
    208–9; Stalin's purges and, 4, 187, 306
    (n. 43); United Nations and, 4, 100,
    116–17, 119, 169, 170, 172, 173–74, 180,
    182, 194; U.S. foreign relations and, 4,
    171, 267–68, 301 (nn. 2, 7); U.S. pro-
    paganda during World War II and,
    11, 116–17, 174–80, 204–5, 256–57, 258,
    259; U.S. public opinion and, 92, 94,
    143, 180, 187, 188–89, 202–3, 205–7,
    215–16, 227–28, 254–55; U.S. rela-
    tions during World War II and, 49–50,
    169–70, 172, 173–74, 179–82, 189–90,
    210–11, 214–15, 304 (n. 33), 304–5
    (n. 34); women and, 12, 202–3. See
    also Nazi-Soviet Pact; Office of War
    Information; Roosevelt, Franklin D.;
    Stalin, Joseph
Spanish Civil War, 39, 108, 293 (n. 37)
Speak Up for Democracy (Bernays), 30
Spewack, Samuel, 215
Squires, James Duane, 57

Stack, Robert, 149, 235

Stagecoach (movie, 1939), 234

Stalin, Joseph: Hollywood movies and, 181, 185, 186; purges of, 4, 177, 178, 181, 187, 199, 215, 306 (n. 43); Tehran summit, 1–2, 2, 130, 205, 256, 268; United Nations and, 90, 100, 113, 129; U.S. public opinion and, 196, 206, 228; U.S. relations during World War II and, 4, 93–94, 160, 169–70, 174–75, 180–87; World War II propaganda and, 11, 15, 22, 177, 178, 205, 215. See also *Mission to Moscow* (movie, 1943): Stalin and; Roosevelt, Franklin D.; Soviet Union

Standley, William H., 169, 173, 174, 175, 182–83, 186, 212

Stanley, Oliver H., 62

Stassen, Harold E., 128

Stephenson, William, 75

Stettinius, Edward R., Jr., 50, 145, 146, 167, 192

Stewart, Hugh, 156–57

Stewart, James, 44

Steyne, Alan N., 63

Stilwell Road, The (documentary, 1945), 234

Stimson, Henry L., 96, 146, 157, 193

Stinebower, Leroy, 50

Stone, Harlan F., 162

Stone, I. F., 25

Strada, Michael J., 203

Stradner, Rosa, 251

Straight, Michael, 87, 144

Stripling, Robert, 269–70

Sun Valley Serenade (movie, 1941), 211–12

Sutton, John, 151

Sweet, John, 155

Taber, John, 207

Taft, Robert A., 207

Tamiroff, Akim, 248

Tanaka Giichi, Baron, 241

Tanaka Memorial, 241, 243

Tanks (documentary, 1942), 240

Target for Tonight (documentary, 1941), 77–78

Taylor, Robert, 200, *201*, 210, 271

Tchaikovsky, Pyotr, 192, 194

Tchen, John Kuo Wei, 218

Tehran summit, 1–2, 2, 3, 129, 130, 132, 134, 170, 183, 186, 205, 256, 268

Telegraphic Agency of the Soviet Union, 174

Television, 272

Tenney, Jack, 196, 210

Thalberg, Irving, 226

That Hamilton Woman (movie, 1941), 20, 54, 74, 75–77, 81, 82, 84

They Got Me Covered (movie, 1943), 230

Thief of Baghdad, The (movie, 1924), 219

Third Man, The (movie, 1949), 59, 157

Thirteen, The (screenplay, 1937), 109

39 Steps, The (movie, 1935), 69

Thirty Seconds over Tokyo (movie, 1944), 230, 233, 236, 253, 271

This above All (movie, 1942), 142–43

"This Is Nazi Brutality" (poster, Shahn), 104

This Is the Army (movie, 1943), 126

Thomas, J. Parnell, 269–70

Thomas, Lowell, 130

Thomas, Norman, 188

Thompson, Dorothy, 27

Thorp, Margaret, 34, 35, 49, 243

Three Russian Girls (movie, 1944), 182

Thunder Birds (movie, 1942), 150–53, 154, 226, 234

Thurstone, L. L., 34

Tierney, Gene, 12, 151, 152, 222, 226, 241, *242*, 244, 255

Time (magazine), 99, 191, 204–5, 228; Churchill and, 160, 162; pro-British films and, 59, 65, 74, 80, 154, 159; pro–United Nations films and, 123, 125

Tobey, Charles W., 83, 84

Tojo, Hideki, 104, 229

Toler, Sidney, 21, 218, *218*, 220, 221, 222, 223, 224, 255

Tolstoy, Leo, 192, 194
Totalitarianism, 25–28, 280 (n. 3)
Tracy, Spencer, 230
Treasury Star Parade, 204
Treaty of Versailles, 6, 25, 108, 122–23
Triumph of the Will (documentary, 1935), 105
Troper, Harold R., 203
Trotsky, Leon, 178, 306 (n. 43)
Trotti, Lamar, 123, 125
Trout, Bob, 77
True Glory, The (documentary, 1945), 11, 20, 157–59, 257, 264
Truman, Harry S, 15, 162, 188, 215, 265, 267
Trumbo, Dalton, 230, 271
Tukhachevskii, M., 178
Tunisian Victory (documentary, 1944), 20, 156–57
Twentieth Century-Fox, 9, 10, 40, 48, 65, 103, 122, 191, 230; *China Girl* and, 226, 232, 240–44; *The Keys of the Kingdom* and, 15, 21, 232, 250–54, 255; pro-British films and, 78, 141
Two-Way Street, The (documentary, 1945), 99–100

Uncle Sam—The Non-Belligerent (newsreel, 1940), 66
United Artists, 9, 12, 39, 76, 182, 226, 238
United China Relief, 227, 233, 234
United Kingdom. *See* Great Britain
United Nations (UN): China and, 4–5, 221, 227–28, 245, 247, 251, 262; compared to family, 11–12, 13, 23, 100, 128–29, 132, 134, 256, 258; documentaries promoting, 106–7, 111–13, 157, 158–59, 192, 293 (n. 44); initial members, 89, 259, 276–77 (n. 6), 317 (n. 4); movies promoting, 8, 19, 98–100, 107–11, 122–26, 152–53, 155, 198, 263–64, 292 (n. 32), 293 (nn. 37, 44), 294 (n. 56); postwar development, 3, 23, 267–68, 294–95 (n. 62); postwar expectations, 100, 122, 128–30, 158–59, 257–58, 261–

63, 294 (n. 60); propaganda and, 5–6, 9, 10–11, 88, 98–99, 100–102, 111–21, *114–15*, 130–34, *131*, 256; public opinion and, 1–3, 92–93, 94–97, 125–26, 127–28, 143–46; San Francisco Conference and, 128, 245, 258–59, 261, *262*, 267; Soviet Union and, 4, 100, 116–17, 119, 169, 170, 172, 173–74, 180, 182, 194; UNO Charter and, 261, *262*, 317 (n. 4). *See also* Declaration of the United Nations
United Nations (poster), 113
"United Nations (Victory Song), The," 194
United Nations Conference on International Organization, 257–59, 261, 267
United Nations Day, 113, 116–19, *120*, 130, 134, 186
United Nations Food and Agriculture Organization, 130
United Nations Information Office (UNIO), 14, 129–30
United Nations Information Organization (UNIO), 130, *131*, 132, 134, 258, 267
United Nations Organization (UNO), 11, 132, 134, 245, 263, 267; founding of, 14, 128, 259, 261
United Nations Organization Charter, 132, 261, *262*, 317 (n. 4)
United Nations Relief and Rehabilitation Administration, 130
United Nations Week, 112, 130
United News, 174, 175, 181
United Newsreel, 130, 132
U.S. Army, 150, 256–57; propaganda and, 102, 104–5, 229, 264, 266, 298 (n. 28)
U.S. Army Air Force, 153
U.S. Chamber of Commerce, 238, 271
U.S. Department of Agriculture, 111–12
U.S. Department of Justice, 18, 28, 40, 209, 272
U.S. Department of State: Anglo-American partnership and, 164,

165; China and, 237, 238–39; Division of Cultural Relations, 15, 42–44; film propaganda after World War II, 265, 266, 317–18 (n. 9); movie industry and, 18, 19, 20–21, 42–44, 45, 46, 47–49, 50–51, 63, 64–65, 284–85 (n. 55); Soviet Union and, 22–23, 174, 208, 209, 213, 311 (n. 91); Telecommunications Division, 237, 284–85 (n. 35); United Nations and, 16, 90, 132–33

U.S. Department of the Treasury, 31, 100, 204

U.S. Information Agency, 266

U.S. isolationism, 30, 75, 122, 163, 248; Anglophobia and, 5, 56–57, 168; outbreak in Europe of World War II and, 27, 55–57, 64, 168; after Pearl Harbor, 88, 93, 94, 127, 143; reaction to Hollywood British propaganda and, 20, 53–55, 70–71, 80, 82–88, 121; after World War I, 3–4, 25, 53, 56, 123, 125

U.S. Marine Corps, 231

U.S. Navy, 145

U.S. News and World Report, 203

U.S. Office of Censorship, 9, 41–42, 252. *See also* Office of War Information

U.S. Office of Education, 130

U.S. Supreme Court, 26, 272, 282–83 (n. 35)

United States v. Paramount Pictures, Inc., et al., 272

U.S. War Department, 10, 264

Universal News, 65, 191

Universal Pictures, 9, 40, 56, 85, 316 (n. 54)

University of Chicago, 28, 33, 34

Upravlenie Propagandy i Agitatsii (Propaganda and Agitation Administration), 172, 208, 214

USSR. *See* Soviet Union

Van Dyke, Wilbur, 112

Van Hoven, Roslyn, 125

Vansittart, Robert, 75

Variety, 9, 37, 51, 59, 70, 141, 156, 195, 197, 204, 219

Vasiliev, Georgii, 186

Veidt, Conrad, 103

V for Victory, 107, 160–61, 162, 194, 198

Vidor, King, 195, 210

Vietnam War, 14

Voice of America, 31–32, 174, 207, 213

Vsesoiuznoe Obshchestvo Kul'turnykh Sviazei s Zagranitsei (All-Union Society for Cultural Relations with Foreign Countries, VOKS), 172, 174, 185, 186, 208, 209

Waldorf Statement, 271, 272

Wallace, Henry A., 15, 111, 116, 122, 261

Wall Street Journal, 247

Walt Disney Studios, 106

Wanger, Walter, 10, 39, 60, 85; *Eagle Squadron* and, 13, 149, 236; *Foreign Correspondent* and, 68, 70, 71; *Gung Ho!* and, 230–31

War Activities Committee, 19, 112

War Manpower Commission, 107

Warner, Albert, 38

Warner, Harry M., 10, 87, 198; anti-Nazism and, 38, 40, 41, 60, 61, 74, 86; pro-Soviet films and, 176, 178, 183

Warner, Jack L., 10, 87, 198; anti-Nazism and, 38, 40, 41, 60, 61; pro-Soviet films and, 176, 178, 269–70

Warner Bros., 9, 24, 38, 43, 81, 102, 165, 230; anti-Nazi movies, 40, 54, 107; pro-British films, 65, 66, 71, 73–74, 78, 79, 80; pro-Soviet films and, 7, 176, 177–79, 196, 197–98, 208, 232; pro-United Nations films, 99, 107, 126. *See also Mission to Moscow*

War of the Worlds (H.G. Wells), 29

War of the Worlds (Orson Welles), 29, 71

War Propaganda and the United States (Lavine and Wechsler), 57

Washington, George, 91, 95, 234

Washington Evening Star, 161–62

Washington Post, 87–88, 244

Washington Star, 45

Watch on the Rhine (play, Hellman), 198

Watchtower over Tomorrow (documentary, 1945), 19, 132

Waterloo Bridge (movie, 1940), 81

Watson, John B., 29, 281 (n. 9)

Watt, Harry, 65, 77

Wayne, John, 21, 210, 224, 234, 235, 264

Way to the Stars, The (movie, 1945), 153–54, 165, 226

Wechsler, James, 57

Wee Willie Winkie (movie, 1937), 56

Welles, Orson, 29, 71

Welles, Sumner, 49, 63, 117, 125

Wells, H. G., 29

We Sail at Midnight (docudrama, 1943), 99

West of Shanghai (movie, 1937), 43

We Won't Forget (newsreel, 1941), 77

Wheeler, Burton K., 54, 66, 82, 83, 85, 93, 127, 145

White, Walter, 57, 144

White Cliffs of Dover, The (movie, 1944), 153

Whitehead, T. North, 147–48

Whitney, Dwight, 196

Whitty, May, 140, 141

Whyte, Frederick, 64, 65

Why We Fight (film series), 10, 104, 134, 157, 170, 193, 231, 264

Wilcox, Herbert, 154

Williams, Roscoe, 77

Willkie, Wendell L., 10, 19, 86, 87, 91, 121–22, 125, 128, 133, 186, 252, 263

Wilson (movie, 1944), 19, 122–26

Wilson, Horace, 63

Wilson, Woodrow, 6, 19, 25, 94, 122–26, 294 (n. 54)

Winant, John G., 119, 157, 167

Winnington, Richard, 154

Winters, Roland, 220

Wong, Anna May, 219, 226–27, 241, 243, 255, 312 (nn. 14–15)

Wong, H. S., 232

Wood, John S., 271

Wood, Kingsley, 64

Wood, Sam, 210, 271

World Citizens Association, 128

World War I, 53, 56, 90, 91; Anglophobia and, 57, 80; movies about, 34, 81, 126; propaganda and, 5, 15, 25, 57; U.S. isolationism after, 3–4, 25, 53, 56, 123, 125

World War II: American worldview and, 14–15, 19, 88, 90–91, 119–22, 126–27, 133, 134–35, 145, 168, 278 (n. 26); the Blitz, 66–68, 69–70, 121, 142, 160, 191; D-Day, 157–58, 213, 257; ending, 256–57, *258*, *259*, *260*, 268; Germany, before U.S. involvement, 26, 29, 40, 58, 73–74, 81; Germany's invasion of Russia, 80, 171, 188, 191–92, 193, 199; as "good war," 6, 14, 91, 277 (n. 12); multimedia coverage of, 1–2, 6–7, 90–91, 256–57, 262–65, 277 (nn. 11–12); Nanking Massacre, 232, 249; nationalism and, 13–14, 15, 278 (nn. 25, 28); in North Africa, 107–11, 155–57; in the Pacific, 91–92, 103, 230–32, 234, 236; "Pacific First" movement, 5, 145, 146, 147; Pearl Harbor, 3, 31, 88, 89–90, 91, 95, 127, 137; Stalingrad, 180, 186, 190, 193, 205; women and, 11–12, 203, 308 (nn. 69–70). *See also* Anglo-American partnership; Great Britain; Nazi Germany; Office of War Information; Roosevelt, Franklin D.; Soviet Union; Stalin, Joseph

Wuthering Heights (movie, 1938), 56

Wyler, William, 141

Yale University, 34

Yalta, 205, 256, 268, 316–17 (n. 1)

Yank (magazine), 102

Yank at Eton, A (movie, 1942), 149, 164, 297 (n. 24)

Yank at Oxford, A (movie, 1938), 78

Yank in London, A. See *I Live in Grosvenor Square*

Yank in the RAF, A (movie, 1941), 8,

78–79, 80, 81, 83, 88, 149, 150, 234, 236, 240

"Yellowface," 12, 21, 218, *218*, 219–27, 241–45, *242*, 246, 247, 249, 253, 255

Yoshihara, Mari, 221

Young, Loretta, 249

Young Dr. Malone (radio soap opera), 159

Yung, Victor Sen, 219, 249

Zanuck, Daryl F., 10, 40, 48, 55, 60, 61, 86, 143; pro-British films and, 78–79, 80, 85, 88, 141–42, 149, 150, 236; pro-China films and, 12, 234, 240, 241, 242, 243, 244, 248; pro–United Nations films, 19, 122, 123, 124, 125

Zarubin, Vassily, 175, 208

Zaslavsky, D., 186

Zhdanov, Andrei A., 23, 214